LIBRARY IN A BOOK

SEXUAL HARASSMENT

Constance Jones

Facts On File, Inc.

AN INFOBASE HOLDINGS COMPANY

LIBRARY IN A BOOK: SEXUAL HARASSMENT

Facts On File, Inc.
11 Penn Plaza
New York NY 10001

Library of Congress Cataloging-in-Publication Data

Jones, Constance.
Sexual harassment / by Constance Jones.
    p. cm. — (Library in a book)
Includes bibliographical references and index.
ISBN 0-8160-3273-4 (alk. paper)
    1. Sexual harassment—United States. I. Title. II. Series.
HQ1237.5.U6J66 1996
305.42—dc20   96-18508

Text design by Ron Monteleone

This book is printed on acid-free paper.

Printed in the United States of America

MP FOF 10 9 8 7 6 5 4 3 2 1

CONTENTS

Acknowledgments   vi

PART I
OVERVIEW OF THE TOPIC   1

Chapter 1
Introduction to Sexual Harassment   2

Chapter 2
The Law of Sexual Harassment   35

Chapter 3
Chronology   56

Chapter 4
Biographical Listings   64

PART II
GUIDE TO FURTHER RESEARCH   69

Chapter 5
How to Research Sexual Harassment   70

Chapter 6
Annotated Bibliography   73

Chapter 7
Organizations and Agencies   179

APPENDICES   197

Appendix A   Title VII of the 1964
Civil Rights Act   198

Appendix B   EEOC Guidelines on Sexual
Harassment, from the 1990 Guidelines on
Discrimination Because of Sex   199

Appendix C   Title IX of the 1972
Education Amendments   201

Appendix D   42 U.S.C. § 1983   202

Appendix E   18 U.S.C. § 241 and 242   203

Appendix F   U.S. Supreme Court Ruling:
Franklin v. Gwinnett County Public Schools   204

Appendix G   U.S. Supreme Court Ruling:
Harris v. Forklift Systems, Inc.   217

Appendix H   U.S. District Court for the
District of Minnesota: *Jenson v.
Eveleth Taconite Company*   223

Appendix I   Supreme Court of New Jersey Ruling: *Lehmann v. Toys
'R' Us, Inc.*   233

Appendix J   U.S. Supreme Court Ruling:
Meritor Savings Bank v. Vinson   260

Index   274

ACKNOWLEDGMENTS

The author would like to thank Val Clark for her expert and tireless research assistance, Nicole Bowen for her editorial faith and forebearance, Carolyn DeLuca for her generous attention at the Georgetown University Library Reference Desk, Louise Quayle for unwittingly turning the tide of this project, and Heather Lewis, as always, for her steadfast support.

PART I

OVERVIEW OF THE TOPIC

CHAPTER 1

INTRODUCTION TO SEXUAL HARASSMENT

Today, nearly every American has heard of sexual harassment, either through personal experience at work or school, through secondhand stories from friends or peers, or through media reports of current events. Professor Anita Hill's charges against Associate Justice Clarence Thomas, the Tailhook scandal, accusations from Senator Bob Packwood's female colleagues, and Paula Jones's allegations of misconduct by President Bill Clinton: These and other highly publicized incidents have heightened individual, corporate, and governmental awareness of the existence, nature, and impact of sexual harassment. Schools, universities, and businesses have established programs for the prevention and punishment of sexual harassment; federal, state, and local governments have passed legislation; courts at all levels have ruled on lawsuits. Yet the debate continues as to just what sexual harassment is, how widespread the problem might be, and how it is best dealt with.

DEFINING SEXUAL HARASSMENT

Like other forms of sexual misconduct and sexual crime, sexual harassment is first about power and second about sex. It is, at its core, the coercive, exploitative, and improper use of power for sexual gratification. According to psychologists, the perpetrator gains sexual pleasure by intimidating a target who does not have the power to retaliate or resist. Because harassers select victims who have less social or economic power, the vast majority of harassment is perpetrated by bosses against subordinates, by men against women, by teachers against students, and in other such relationships. Harassers are most often older, more respected, and more financially secure than their victims. Even when harassment does not seem to fit this mold, as when a woman harasses a man or when one co-worker harasses another, a second look generally confirms the pattern: The woman may be the man's employer; the offending co-worker may be a male and his target a female.

Feminists view sexual harassment in terms of male dominion over society as a whole. It is but one example of women's economic and social oppression by men, the argument goes, and helps to perpetuate male domination. Harassment strips the victim (presumably female) of all identity and value except as a sexual object, placing her in a sex role instead of a work role. The official definition of sexual harassment written by the National Advisory Council on Women's Educational Programs reflects this notion, describing harassment as "the use of authority to emphasize the sexuality or sexual identity of a student in a manner which prevents or impairs the student's full enjoyment of educational benefits, climate or opportunity."

The ongoing confusion and disagreement over the definition and significance of sexual harassment arises in large part from the mistaken focus on its sexual component. When defined as a sexual issue, sexual harassment is a private, personal matter of no concern to school, business, or government officials. But this denies the fundamental role that power imbalances and sexual inequality play in harassment, and this perspective plays on myths about male and female sexuality. Such myths include the notions that women "ask for it," that they send mixed signals to men, and that when they say no they mean yes. Likewise, the beliefs that men "can't help it" and that certain male behavior is only natural, harmless "mischief" muddy the waters. They recast sexual harassment as a minor problem of misperception, misunderstanding, or miscommunication between men and women.

Some critics complain that those who seek official remedies for sexual harassment want special treatment and protection, when all they need is to learn how to stick up for themselves. If they are harassed, they should just ignore it and it will go away. Others assert that true harassment is quite rare and that most charges are false, stemming from the accuser's hypersensitivity or even from some malevolence against the accused. A favorite countercharge against those who make accusations of sexual harassment is that they merely seek retaliation for a "love affair gone sour." In direct contradiction, other skeptics claim that behavior perceived as harassment is in fact a normal reflection of social reality, inevitable wherever men and women have contact. In this view, charges of harassment unfairly hurt the reputation of the accused, and regulations and laws can only make normal human interaction unnecessarily difficult.

Where, then—if anywhere—does "normal human interaction" or "natural" male behavior cross the line to become offensive or abusive? Is there a single, absolute standard of sexual harassment that applies to all people and all situations? Can this line be drawn by law, or is it a subjective boundary that can be defined only by individuals for themselves? If society defines sexual harassment too broadly, women may begin to feel victimized where they didn't before and men may distance themselves from women, broadening the gender gap at work and school. If it is too narrowly defined, perpetrators will have license to continue truly harmful behavior. As employers, educators, legislators, and judges try to find the right balance, they must contend with the basic reality that different people have different sexual boundaries.

What some people see as sexually offensive, others find flattering or enticing. Depending on their cultural, religious, and socioeconomic background, two people of the same gender may have very different attitudes toward sexuality, and may make very different distinctions between harassment and benign expression. Even two people of similar backgrounds may react differently to the same situation: Surveys have shown, for instance, that a person who has had a mutual, enjoyable sexual experience with a co-worker is less likely to be offended by sexual behavior in the workplace. But the single most important factor in sexual attitudes is gender.

Psychologists have determined that men and women have markedly different reactions to a wide range of behavior, such as complimentary or insulting comments, looks and gestures, non-sexual and sexual touching, and socializing or dating in the workplace. In general, women define harassment more broadly than men do and are more likely to be offended by activity they define as sexual. Where men may see sexual opportunity, women may often sense a threat. Men who receive sexual overtures at work are less likely to be offended by them and more likely to see the experience as enjoyable. Women, by contrast, describe few sexual encounters at work as desirable and most as inappropriate or unpleasant. When describing their sexual experiences at work, women are likely to refer to the men involved as "jerks," while men are likely to refer to their female counterparts as "loose."

This divergence in perception causes misunderstandings between the sexes and contributes to the problem of sexual harassment. It stems in part from the different ways in which boys and girls have historically been taught about sexuality. Boys are taught actively to seek out sexual opportunity, while girls are taught to wait for male approaches. In the course of social events, men typically make the sexual advances and women respond to them. Men know that some of their overtures will be rebuffed, and women know that they will receive some unwanted overtures. This arrangement requires women to set limits, and men to respect those limits. To some extent, modern society has broken away from these traditional gender roles, but they remain a powerful force in the attitudes and behavior of men and women alike.

Sexual harassment occurs when a perpetrator ignores a target's limits. Most definitions of harassment describe it as behavior that is not only unwelcome and one-sided but is carried out intentionally and/or repeatedly. The American Psychological Association defines sexual harassment as "deliberate or repeated comments, gestures or physical contacts of a sexual nature that are unwanted by the recipient." With regard to its own employees, the federal government of the United States adds an additional qualification, defining harassment as "deliberate or repeated *unsolicited* verbal comments, gestures or physical contact of a sexual nature that is considered to be unwelcome by the recipient." Harassment acquires its "sexual nature" either from the character of the behavior itself (the victim is harassed by sexual means) or from its motivation (the victim is harassed because of his or her sex).

Much of the confusion over what sexual harassment is or is not can be cleared up for most perpetrators by applying three criteria to the behavior in question. Words and/or deeds constitute sexual harassment if:

1.   The perpetrator would not say or do them in the presence of a spouse or lover;
2.   The perpetrator would not feel comfortable having them reported in the local paper or news broadcast; or
3.   They are not necessary to the business at hand, whether it's closing a deal or riding the bus.

Of course, there are some perpetrators who do not care how their actions are viewed, but for most a wide variety of verbal, nonverbal, and physical behavior meets these criteria at least some of the time. Depending on the situation, actions as subtle as joking, innuendo, and suggestive remarks or looks, or obvious behavior such as staring or visual appraisal, flirting, non-sexual touching, and asking for dates may fall into the category of sexual harassment. Although acceptable to some people, these activities can offend others. This type of behavior does not necessarily represent harassment, but it can signal potential trouble of a more serious nature. If the perpetrator repeats his or her deeds often enough, even mild behavior can turn into abuse.

How can such seemingly innocent behavior be construed as harassment? Certain types of comments about a co-worker's appearance, for example, are a kind of put-down, trivializing the victim's intelligence, competence, or professionalism, especially if the remarks are made frequently. Social touching that one individual deems acceptable may embarrass or anger another: Psychologists have found that men feel it is permissible in most situations to touch an acquaintance anywhere above the waist, while women feel comfortable with social touching only of the head, shoulders and arms—and then only under certain circumstances. Men and women alike perceive social touching as a prelude to sexual touching, but where men view the connection positively women more often view it negatively. And in any case, most business, educational, and social situations do not call for touching of any kind. Likewise, when management permits employees to display pornographic magazines and pictures or when companies devise titillating mottos or advertisements, they send a message of disrespect for their female staff. Organizational attitudes may in turn foster individual harassment by suggesting that sexually oriented speech and behavior is permissible and appropriate in the workplace.

Several factors influence when milder forms of behavior become harassment. The apparent intent of the perpetrator—to frighten or shock the victim, to impress or amuse others—must be taken into account, as well as his or her awareness that such actions might offend the target. The general environment (e.g., rowdy or conservative), the male/female ratio, and whether the incident takes place in public or private also come into play. Individuals may be more easily intimidated if, for instance, they are greatly outnumbered in the classroom or office by members of the opposite sex. Similarly, the relationship of the perpetrator and victim has an impact: Harassment by one's direct supervisor is more threatening than harassment by a visiting client.

A second category of behavior is clearly unacceptable on the street, in school, and at the workplace and constitutes harassment even when it happens only once. Inappropriate touch, such as standing too close, brushing up against another's body or "accidentally" grazing the hand against a woman's breasts, underarms, buttocks, sides, waist, hips, or knees, fits into this category. Perpetrators may disguise their groping by pretending to remove lint from the victim's clothing, fastening buttons, or smoothing a coat, or they may more brazenly tuck in a victim's blouse, trace the outline of her bra, or "playfully" snap her bra straps. These activities often lead to worse abuse, such as unwanted hugging, grabbing, kissing, nuzzling, and fondling. Physical harassment may be accompanied by verbal abuse such aggressive sexual propositions, come-ons, obscene remarks, and explicit conversation. At their worst, harassers in this category may engage in exhibitionism or masturbation in the presence of their victim.

Finally, the most severe forms of sexual harassment include crimes such as sexual assault and rape. Perpetrators may threaten their victims with physical or professional harm if they do not submit to sex. When their approach succeeds, it is coercion and constitutes rape. Harassers use psychological force more often than physical force to obtain sex, but some do violently attack their victims.

THE HISTORY OF SEXUAL HARASSMENT

Sexual harassment has a long history that has touched not only all fields of work but also schools and universities, government and military agencies, churches and nonprofit organizations, and nearly every public setting and facet of daily life. In the last half of the 20th century, harassment has seemed to mushroom as women have increasingly ventured out of their traditional, family-based roles and into the workplace, the higher echelons of education, and politics and the professions. Perceived by many men as a threat to male economic and social dominance, women have encountered ongoing discrimination. Sexual harassment, a form of discrimination meant to keep women "in their place," mirrors society's timeless patterns of violence against women.

Violence and discrimination against women, including sexual harassment, are both a product and a prop of sexual inequality. This inequality encompasses the notion that the workplace and, indeed, all public space is male territory. Historically, this belief supported claims that work outside the home is unnatural for women and harms their physical, mental, and spiritual health. It has been used to rationalize the concentration of women in low-paying jobs and the payment of lower wages to women who do the same work as men. When a man wants or needs a job held by a woman, the same belief has been used to justify the loss of her job in his favor. And, finally, the assumption that women have less value as people and as workers has long been used as an excuse for sexual harassment.

History includes many accounts of the sexual harassment of female slaves, serfs, and servants by their male masters and employers. In cultures from Ancient Egypt to the United States before the Civil War, slave-owning men had almost complete license to subject enslaved women to their sexual appetites. One example comes from the court records of Callaway County, Missouri, where a slave named Celia was hanged in December 1855 after murdering the master who had raped her repeatedly. The feudal lords of medieval Europe enjoyed the same prerogative with female serfs, as until recently did the male heads of households that employed female servants, although to a lesser extent. In a story entitled "How I Went Out to Service" and in a novel entitled *Work*, Louisa May Alcott, the author of *Little Women*, described her ordeal as a 16-year-old live-in nurse for a family in Dedham, Massachussets, in 1855. Carrie Davies, an 18-year-old Toronto housemaid, shot her lecherous employer in 1915 and was acquitted.

Outside the domestic sphere, women have been equally harassed. Women have always worked outside the home—as peddlers, laundresses, farmhands, artisans, and the like—but those who dared venture into better-paying occupations met swift retaliation, often in the form of sexual harassment. In 1835, for instance, printers in Boston launched a campaign of intimidation to force women typesetters out of their traditionally male jobs.

During the Industrial Revolution of the 19th century, an entire class of young women left home en masse to go to work. The phenomenon was most widespread in England and the United States, particularly in the textile and garment industries. Most so-called factory girls were unmarried and between 15 and 30 years old; starting in the 1860s young immigrant women flooded into American factories as well. Their youth, their lack of a husband's protection, and their linguistic and cultural differences made factory girls especially vulnerable to mistreatment by male supervisors. Poorly paid for long hours, forced to work at a feverish pitch in dangerous surroundings, they frequently encountered sexual harassment. Many bosses offered workday perks in exchange for sexual favors, firing those who refused to comply. Knowing their bosses had complete freedom to dismiss them, many factory girls submitted to leers, gropes, remarks, and sexual assault in order to keep their jobs.

Thousands of women went to work in the textile mills of New England, starting in the 1830s. An Exeter, New Hampshire, periodical called *The Factory Girls' Album* printed an article in October 1846, warning women workers that many who "abandon their virtue to obtain favors" lose their jobs anyway. The same year, New Hampshire's *Nashua Gazette* published an anonymous letter from "A Factory Girl in the Nashua Corporation," who told of the dangers facing factory girls. Their supervisors, the letter read, "can do with them as any passion may dictate or any caprice suggest, with perfect impunity of the law." And from Lowell, Massachusetts, labor leader Sarah Bagley wrote in the May 15, 1846, issue of the *Voice of Industry* that factory girls should "shrink as from the abyss of infamy, from the steady gaze or stealthy touch of the *fiend* in human form."

Even as they contended with harassment on the job, women faced similar obstacles as they became more visible on the street. A Wisconsin woman filed assault and battery charges against one harasser in 1875 and won $1,000 in damages. Testifying in the case, *Croaker v. Chicago and Northwestern Railway Company*, she described how a train conductor had put his hand in her muff and kissed her several times. After "being wronged" in this manner, she asserted, she experienced great mental suffering.

Toward the end of the 19th century, the number of retail sales jobs in cities skyrocketed. Once again, large numbers of young women entered a new field, and once again, they encountered long hours, low pay, and sexual harassment. Along with their bosses, the male public at large viewed the new breed of saleswoman as promiscuous and immoral, fair game for sexual pranks and propositions. Men of the prosperous classes seemed especially prone to abuse shop girls. Working women in Victorian London complained of frequent harassment by "well-drest men"; one noted that "Gentlemen is much greater blackguards than what blackguards is."

Although a problem throughout the 20th century, sexual harassment until recently received little political or legal attention. Indeed, the term *sexual harassment* was not widely heard before the 1960s, when feminists began to draw attention to economic and social discrimination against women. During that decade, American culture—and women's place in it—underwent some profound changes. The advent of the sexual revolution, the introduction of the birth-control pill, and popular culture's focus on sexuality brought sex out of the shadows. Large numbers of women entered the workforce around the world as the modern women's movement took off. Conditioned to expect the sexual and social docility as well as the economic dependence of women, many men resented the changes or attempted to exploit them. In this atmosphere sexual harassment flourished.

Amidst the general social foment, Congress passed and President Lyndon Johnson signed the 1964 Civil Rights Act. The law articulated the federal government's commitment to protecting the civil rights of racial, ethnic, and religious minorities, as well as of women. Certain that they could prevent passage of the bill, its opponents had at the last minute added sex to the list of protected categories, but their scheme backfired. Women's rights were now protected by law. Among other things, the act created the Equal Employment Opportunity Commission (EEOC) and included an article known as Title VII, which prohibited employment discrimination on the basis of race, color, religion, national origin, and sex. However, it would be a decade before the courts accepted sexual harassment as a form of discrimination.

Meanwhile, the federal government continued to advance its civil rights agenda. In 1969, the Department of Defense drafted its Human Goals Charter, which established a policy of equal respect for all servicemen and service-women, for civilian employees of the military, and for members of military families. The directive served as the basis of equal opportunity programs in the armed forces and eventually produced the military's commitment to maintaining an "environment free from sexual harassment." In 1972, hoping to strengthen the Civil Rights Act of 1964, Congress passed the Equal Employment Opportunity Act, which gave the EEOC the power to enforce Title VII (the justice department had previously had that responsibility). President Richard Nixon also signed the Education Amendments of 1972, whose Title IX prohibits sex bias in educational institutions that receive federal funding. Administered by the Department of Education, the law applies to almost all American schools and universities.

Federal courts heard the first sexual harassment cases in the mid-1970s. The plaintiffs in these cases claimed that sexual harassment is a form of sex discrimination and is therefore illegal under Title VII. The earliest efforts to equate harassment with discrimination failed. The judge who ruled on one of these cases, *Corne v. Bausch & Lomb*, dismissed harassment as a "personal peculiarity" that has no legal implications. In *Miller v. Bank of America*, the court found that sexual harassment represents "isolated misconduct" for which employers bear no responsibility. Nor did courts accept harassment as sex discrimination in *Barnes v. Train* or *Tomkins v. Public Service Electric & Gas* Co.

The tide began to turn in 1976, when a lower court in Washington, D.C., recognized narrowly defined instances of sexual harassment as discrimination.

In that case, *Williams v. Saxbe,* a Department of Justice information officer named Diane Williams had been fired nine days after she refused to have sex with her supervisor. The court ruled that quid pro quo ("this for that") harassment is discrimination; that is, when the victim's job status or benefits depend on whether she submits to or resists the harasser's advances. The court awarded Williams $16,000 in back pay, but its decision was reversed on appeal.

At the same time, studies were beginning to support feminist claims about the prevalence and dangers of sexual harassment. *Redbook* magazine conducted a groundbreaking survey of its mostly female readership and found that 88% of the respondents had been sexually harassed at least once, and 50% had either been fired or knew of someone who had been fired from a job for resisting harassment. A 1975 survey of United Nations employees found that 32 of the 144 women working there—22%—had been harassed, while 50% of the women and 31% of male employees had either experienced or witnessed sexual harassment by superiors.

Filed in 1977, *Alexander v. Yale University* was the first sexual harassment complaint to be made in the courts under Title IX. The plaintiff was an undergraduate who claimed a professor had lowered her grade on a paper in his course because she refused to sleep with him. Alexander lost her case in Connecticut District Court and the United States Court of Appeals dismissed it in 1980, but the district court's ruling stated that "academic advancement conditioned upon submission to sexual demands constitutes sex discrimination in education, just as questions of job retention or promotion tied to sexual demands from supervisors have become increasingly recognized as potential violations of Title VII's ban against sex discrimination in employment."

That recognition included the 1977 reversal of the *Barnes v. Train* decision in a case now called *Barnes v. Castle.* The U.S. Court of Appeals for the District of Columbia accepted harassment as quid pro quo discrimination, ruling that "But for her womanhood, the woman wouldn't have lost her job." The following year, President Jimmy Carter signed the Civil Service Reform Act barring sex discrimination in federal employment. Scholarly studies of sexual harassment began to appear, and the first major book on the topic, *Sexual Shakedown: The Sexual Harassment of Women at Work* by Lin Farley, was published. Magazines and newspapers printed a flurry of articles, including Margaret Mead's "A Proposal: We Need Taboos on Sex at Work," which appeared in *Redbook.*

As the 1970s drew to a close, the fight against sexual harassment picked up momentum. In 1979 the Ninth Circuit Court reversed the *Miller v. Bank of America* ruling. After a series of hearings aired allegations of harassment within the federal government, the White House Office of Personnel issued a directive to all government offices defining harassment and stating that such behavior would not be tolerated. Noted law professor Catherine A. MacKinnon published her seminal book on the legal issues surrounding sexual harassment. The volume, entitled *Sexual Harassment of Working Women: A Case of Discrimination*, argues that sexual harassment is a form of sex discrimination because almost all of its victims are women. On the international front, the United Nations adopted its Convention on the Elimination of All Forms of Discrimination Against Women, which advises member nations that women have the right to equal employment and safe, healthy working conditions.

The year 1980 proved a banner year for victims of sexual harassment. In January, Illinois became the first state to outlaw the sexual harassment of state employees and to publish anti-harassment guidelines and requirements for its state agencies to follow. The move came on the heels of a survey conducted by the Illinois Task Force on Sexual Harassment, which reported that 63% of the 1,495 female state employees who answered the survey considered harassment to be a big problem on the job. Among the survey respondents, 52% had been subject to sexual remarks or teasing, 25% to touching or grabbing, 20% to direct sexual propositions, and 2% to coercive sex (rape).

The federal government also took action against sexual harassment in 1980. Under the leadership of chairwoman Eleanor Holmes Norton, the EEOC drafted its "Guidelines on Discrimination Because of Sex." The guidelines broadened the definition of illegal harassment beyond "unwanted sexual overtures" and quid pro quo abuses to include the workplace climate as a whole. If the general atmosphere of a workplace antagonizes women on the basis of their sex, they are the victims of harassment just as surely as if one or more individuals harassed them directly. Citing the new guidelines, a federal appeals court ruling in the case of *Brown v. City of Guthrie* established a legal precedent for claims of so-called hostile work environment harassment. The following year, in its ruling on *Bundy v. Jackson*, another federal appeals court supported the EEOC guidelines on hostile work environment. Other courts, however, initially refused to accept the broadened definition of sexual harassment.

A flood of sexual harassment studies and surveys appeared in 1981. *Redbook* published its second reader survey on the issue, which found that 85% of the respondents had experienced harassment. The United States Merit Systems Protection Board, which protects government employees under the 1978 Civil Service Reform Act, published its survey of federal employees. The report found that in the period from May 1978 to May 1980, 42% of female and 15% of male civil service workers had been harassed, at an estimated cost to the government of $189 million in lost productivity, health expenses, and employee turnover.

Sexual Harassment

Also in 1981, another government agency, the Bureau of National Affairs, published the results of its study of employer attitudes and practices concerning harassment. Among the personnel executives who participated, 53% felt that the EEOC's guidelines concerning employer liability were excessive, 42% said their companies had written a harassment policy, and 27% claimed to be developing one. Only 6% of companies provided sexual harassment awareness training to all their employees; 25% trained supervisors only. The executives characterized most harassment complaints as minor and noted that 84% of the complaints were made by low-level employees such as laborers, clerical workers, and secretaries. Forty-six percent of the complaints involved the worker's immediate supervisor; only 42% resulted in formal warnings and 11% in the discharge of the offender.

A survey of corporate managers published in the *Harvard Business Review* further illuminated management's attitude toward sexual harassment. Although managers agreed that harassment becomes a more serious offense when perpetrated by more senior personnel, the men and women in the study disagreed on the prevalence of harassment in the workplace. Half the women surveyed believed that the extent of harassment had not been exaggerated, while two-thirds of the men believed it had. In general, managers believed that women should be able to handle sexual tensions on their own; the apparent lack of corporate concern prompted the majority of women to fear reprisal if they were to report an incident of sexual harassment.

In the public sector, Congress passed a 1983 law—commonly referred to as Section 1983—that forbids states to engage in any conduct that deprives individuals of their rights. Under this law, state officials can be held liable in sexual harassment cases. The early 1980s also saw several important lawsuits. A Wisconsin court ruled in favor of a male social services worker who had been harassed by a female supervisor (*Huebschen v. Department of Health and Social Services*). In two separate cases, *Henson v. City of Dundee* and *Katz v. Dole*, two U.S. circuit courts of appeal established the legal definitions of quid pro quo and hostile work environment harassment. The District Court for the District of Delaware ruled in *Toscano v. Nimmo* that an employee can claim sexual harassment if a co-worker receives special treatment from a supervisor because of a sexual relationship. And in *Shellhammer v. Lewallen*, a federal court found that sexual harassment by landlords or building supervisors violates the Fair Housing Act.

Around the world, studies showed that sexual harassment respects no borders: 84% of Spanish women, 58% of Dutch women, and 31% of Austrian women reported they had been the victims of serious harassment. International organizations spoke out against sexual harassment. In 1984, the Council of Ministers of the European Community declared that member states have an obligation to improve respect for women at work. A 1986 resolution adopted by the European Community Parliament condemned sexual violence, including sexual harassment. The U.N. adopted the Nairobi Forward-Looking Strategies for the Advancement of Women, which addressed working conditions and sexual harassment. And the International Labour Organisation's Equal Opportunities and Equal Treatment for Men and Women in Employment guidelines included suggestions for preventing sexual harassment.

Experts continued to study the problem of sexual harassment. A 1985 study of working women by Barbara Gutek showed that, although nearly half of those surveyed had been harassed, none had taken legal action against their harasser. The Association of American Colleges released a 1986 study showing that 32% of tenured and 49% of untenured faculty women at Harvard University had suffered sexual harassment. The following year, the U.S. Department of Labor reported that 37% of the women working in the department had been harassed. In its 1988 report on the problem, the U.S. Merit Systems Protection Board estimated that sexual harassment of federal employees cost the government $267 million between 1985 and 1987 and predicted the cost in 1988 alone would reach $189 million. Overseas, a Swedish survey found that, of the 17% of workers who experienced harassment, fully a third were so badly treated that they had to leave their job. A British study showed that 73% of that nation's workers had been harassed, while a survey of Norwegian women revealed that, for 21% of harassment victims, the abuse had taken the form of rape or attempted rape.

Despite mounting evidence on the widespread and harmful effects of sexual harassment, courts remained skeptical that a hostile work environment constitutes harassment. In 1986, a Missouri court rejected a hostile work environment complaint made by a saleswoman against a hospital that showed the pornographic film *Deep Throat* at a meeting. An administrative assistant whose co-workers displayed obscene posters and whose supervisor badgered her with sexual comments filed suit in *Rabidue v. Osceola Refining Company*, but a federal appeals court in Cincinnati rejected her hostile work environment claims. An attorney employed by the federal Securities and Exchange Commission lost her 1988 case, *Broderick v. Ruder*, in which she complained of a hostile work environment where favors were granted to female employees who complied with the sexual demands of their male superiors. However, Broderick later won her case on appeal.

Although the courts widely accepted quid pro quo harassment as sex discrimination by the mid-1980s, the hostile work environment concept still met with much resistance. But in its first ruling on sexual harassment, on June 19, 1986, the United States Supreme Court not only accepted EEOC guidelines that equated sexual harassment with sex discrimination but also endorsed the hostile work environment argument. Argued in part by Catherine A. MacKinnon, *Meritor Savings Bank v. Vinson* (see appendix J) involved a bank employee whose supervisor fondled her in front of other employees, followed her into the women's rest room, exposed himself to her, and forced her to have intercourse. A district court had rejected Vinson's arguments in 1980 (the case was then called *Vinson v. Taylor*), but the Supreme Court reversed that decision. Writing for the court, Justice Thurgood Marshall noted that "Title VII affords employees the right to work in an environment free from discriminatory intimidation, ridicule and insult." The decision represented a major advance in attempts to combat sexual harassment.

The business community began to take the issue of sexual harassment more seriously. *Forbes* magazine calculated that only 0.0091% of the female workforce filed charges with the EEOC in 1988, but blamed women's fear of reprisal for the low number. A 1988 *Working Woman* survey of Fortune 500 companies placed the percentage at 1.4 complaints for every 1,000 women employees. Nevertheless, that survey showed that 90% of the companies had received harassment complaints in the past and more than a third had been sued over the issue. Other research revealed that sexual harassment was not limited to lower-level workers. In 1990, more than half the professional women surveyed by a newsletter called *Working Smart* said they had been harassed; a 1989 study by the *National Law Journal* showed a 60% harassment rate for the 3,000 women lawyers surveyed at the country's top 250 law firms.

The military continued to report problems with sexual harassment. In 1988, male students at the U.S. Naval Academy in Annapolis made national news when, during a hazing ritual, they chained female midshipman Gwen Marie Dreyer to a urinal to taunt and photograph her. Two years later, the Department of Defense published a survey that showed 64% of its female employees and 17% of its male employees had been harassed. Likewise, a 1991 survey by the U.S. Navy showed that 75% of navy women and 50% of navy men believed sexual harassment takes place within their commands. In an effort to combat the problem, the Pentagon directed all military service branches and academies to initiate programs to eliminate harassment, outlining seven minimum requirements to be met by the programs.

Also in the news, in 1990 neurosurgeon and professor Frances K. Conley resigned from her post at Stanford University after 25 years of employment because male surgeons continually harassed her and her female students. She agreed in 1991 to return to work when the school's dean promised to find a new department head, but only one of the harassers was disciplined, with a demotion in 1992. In 1990 the EEOC updated its 1980 guidelines on sexual harassment, adding regulations on how to define and prevent it. At the same time, the Council of Ministers of the European Community issued a definition of sexual harassment to the community's member states. The definition encompassed both quid pro quo and hostile work environment offenses.

Introduction to Sexual Harassment

By then, sexual harassment lawsuits had become commonplace in the United States. In 1991, the Sixth U.S. Circuit Court of Appeals ruled in *Robinson v. Jacksonville Shipyards* that obscene pinups posted in the workplace create a hostile work environment and thus constitute harassment. The Ninth U.S. Circuit Court of Appeals heard *Ellison v. Brady*, the case of a San Mateo, California, woman subject to persistent pressure for dates and two frightening notes from an infatuated colleague at the Internal Revenue Service. Ruling in her favor, the court concluded that sexual harassment should be evaluated from the standpoint of the "reasonable woman" instead of the standpoint of the male-biased "reasonable person" traditionally used as a legal standard. *Boston Herald* sportswriter Lisa Olson won $500,000 in compensation from the New England Patriots football team. She claimed that team members had exposed themselves and made obscene remarks when she attempted to conduct locker-room interviews after a game in September 1990.

The biggest sexual harassment story of 1991—and, perhaps, the most notorious case in American history—broke on October 5, 1991. That day, National Public Radio revealed that Clarence Thomas, whom President George Bush had nominated to the Supreme Court, had been accused of sexual harassment. His accuser was Anita F. Hill, a law professor at the University of Oklahoma who had worked for Thomas at the Department of Education and at the EEOC in the early 1980s. Both were attorneys, both were African-Americans, but Thomas was staunchly conservative and Hill a liberal. After the news was leaked, Hill came forward in the press two days before the Senate Judiciary Committee was scheduled to vote on Thomas' nomination. When she made her charges public, the committee was forced to postpone its vote to October 15 and schedule a special hearing.

At the behest of Senate aides, Hill had submitted a confidential affidavit to the committee on September 10, charging that Thomas had sexually harassed her from 1981 to 1983. The FBI did not investigate her allegations until two weeks later and turned up nothing to warrant voting down the nomination. In an October 7 news conference, Hill explained why she had come forward, denied she had any political motivation for making the charges, and criticized the Judiciary Committee for its failure to investigate fully. She then flew to Washington to testify before the committee.

Chaired by Senator Joseph R. Biden Jr. (D-Delaware), the 14 white, male members of the Senate Judiciary Committee heard testimony from Hill, Thomas, and other witnesses. In response to questions from the committee Hill stated that Thomas has sexually harassed her in a variety of ways when she worked for him: He told her in explicit detail the plots of pornographic movies he had seen and boasted of his sexual attributes and prowess. Thomas flatly denied Hill's charges as "lies," "sleaze," "dirt," and "gossip," calling the hearings a "high-tech lynching for uppity blacks." Over several days, the committee called on witnesses who praised Thomas's character and who attempted to discredit Hill. A number of women who had worked for Thomas testified that he had not harassed them; Hill's detractors variously labeled her a psychotic, a lesbian, and a nymphomaniac. In the end, the committee approved Thomas's nomination to the Supreme Court and the Senate confirmed him in a 52–48 vote.

Carried live on television, the Hill-Thomas hearings mesmerized the nation. Across the country, men and women debated the merits of the case. A poll by *The New York Times* showed that 58% of Americans believed Thomas and 24% believed Hill, while 45% favored Thomas's confirmation and 20% opposed it. *The New York Times* also found that four out of 10 women surveyed said they had been sexually harassed and five out of 10 men said they had done something that could be construed as harassment. Thrusting the issue into the national consciousness, the Hill-Thomas episode helped redefine sexual harassment as an organizational rather than a personal problem. Corporations, institutions, and governments recognized the necessity of formulating and enforcing sexual harassment policy.

Organizations took these steps not only to protect their employees and members but also to protect themselves, for public pressure had forced President Bush to reevaluate his earlier veto of the 1991 Civil Rights Act. The bill originally passed by Congress sanctioned the use of jury trials in sexual discrimination cases and allowed the award of compensatory and punitive damages for pain and suffering that resulted from intentional sexual discrimination. In the wake of the Hill-Thomas hearings, Bush had no choice but to sign a compromise version that put a cap on the size of the awards.

As a consequence both of the enormous publicity given sexual harassment and of the more favorable law, increasing numbers of victims filed lawsuits. The *Wall Street Journal* reported a jump in the number of harassment cases involving businesses, while the EEOC reported a 62% increase in the number of harassment complaints it received between 1991 and 1992. One such case, *Jenson v. Eveleth Taconite*, set the precedent that made sexual harassment a recognized basis for class-action lawsuits. In it, a group of women mine workers in Duluth, Minnesota, complained of widespread sexual harassment at their workplace and argued that all women working at the site were subject to a hostile work environment. A federal court judge agreed that harassment can be so pervasive and severe it affects an entire group. The women thus won the right to file the first-ever class-action harassment suit.

In 1992, even before the dust had settled on the Hill-Thomas hearings, another sexual harassment scandal rocked the nation. That April, the Naval Investigative Service (NIS) and the U.S. Navy's inspector general released reports on sexual harassment at the September 1991 convention of the Tail-hook Association, a private organization of navy and Marine Corps fliers, in Las Vegas. The two reports revealed that 26 women, 14 of whom were junior officers, were abused at the convention and that many of the senior officers in attendance knew of the assaults but did nothing to stop them or punish the offenders. At the Las Vegas Hilton, where the convention took place, porno-graphic films and exotic dancers had entertained aviators in "hospitality suites." Alcohol flowed freely, and throughout the hotel, women were subjected to obscene remarks and widespread groping. Women who walked down one third-floor corridor, referred to as "the gauntlet," had to defend themselves against dozens of junior officers who grabbed at and attempted to fondle them. However, citing a lack of cooperation by the officers questioned, the reports named only two perpetrators and stated that no formal charges would be filed.

Secretary of the Navy H. Lawrence Garrett III had ordered the investiga-tions in response to complaints by a female pilot, Lieutenant Paula Coughlin, and several other women in October 1991. By April 1992, the only officer to be disciplined was Coughlin's commander, Rear Admiral John W. Snyder Jr., who was demoted for his failure to act on Coughlin's complaint. Con-gress—and the American public—suspected a cover-up; after all, 5,000 aviators had attended Tailhook. To counter growing criticism, the NIS conducted a second investigation and released another report on June 17. That report described the abuse of many more women by drunken pilots who engaged in Tailhook traditions such as streaking, mooning, exposing their genitals, strip-ping women, and shaving women's legs. Noting that 55 pages had been omitted from the first NIS report, the follow-up revealed that investigators had inten-tionally failed to mention that Garrett had visited some of the hospitality suites and witnessed some of the misconduct.

On June 18, Garrett ordered the navy and the Marine Corps to begin disciplinary proceedings against 70 unnamed officers and asked the Defense Department to take over the investigation. After Secretary of Defense Richard B. Cheney briefed him on the controversy, President Bush invited Lt. Coughlin to the White House for a talk on June 26. The same day, Garrett resigned, reportedly at Cheney's request. While the Defense Department investigation continued, Acting Secretary of the Navy Sean C. O'Keefe ordered the imple-mentation of harassment prevention initiatives. In July, Assistant Chief of Naval Operations Vice Admiral Richard M. Dunleavy retired at a reduced rank when it was discovered he had seen the gauntlet in action and took no steps against the men involved.

Released in September 1992, the first part of the Pentagon's Tailhook report sharply criticized the navy's investigations of the incident. It denounced naval investigators for their unwillingness to implicate senior officials in the scandal, for their sexist attitudes and assumptions, for their failure to question Tailhook attendees above the rank of lieutenant commander and for their rushed approach to the investigation. When these findings were made public, O'Keefe asked two of the admirals responsible for the botched investigations for their resignation and reassigned a third to lesser duties. Navy efforts to discipline Tailhook offenders continued after the Pentagon released its final report on the Tailhook scandal, in April 1993. The report directly implicated a total of 117 officers in the sexual abuse of 83 women and seven men and cited 51 others for lying to investigators. According to the report, hundreds more knew of the misconduct but did nothing to stop or report it. John H. Dalton, the new secretary of the navy appointed by President Bill Clinton, appointed a Marine Corps lieutenant general and a navy vice admiral to take disciplinary action against the perpetrators. But only seven officers were disciplined before the statute of limitations on their violations ran out in September 1993.

While the Tailhook scandal unraveled, the battle against sexual harassment continued elsewhere. In 1992, the army launched an investigation of approximately 100 harassment claims made by women at the Army Aviation and Troop Command and the Army Reserve Personnel Center in St. Louis. The Stroh Brewery in Minnesota killed a sexually suggestive advertising campaign after five women employees complained it contributed to a sexually hostile work environment for female plant workers. In *Meek v. Michigan Bell Telephone*, a Michigan appeals court decided that a Jewish woman who was sexually and religiously harassed could file suit against her former employer even though she had already been fired. And the Supreme Court heard arguments in *Franklin v. Gwinnett County Public Schools* (formerly *Franklin v. Hill*) (see appendix F), in which a high school student charged her teacher with sexual harassment. Ruling in favor of the plaintiff, the court found that students can sue their teachers and schools for monetary damages under Title IX of the Education Amendments of 1972.

Outside the federal courts, New York state decided to address sexual harassment within its own boundaries. In mid-1992, Governor Mario Cuomo established the Governor's Task Force on Sexual Harassment to investigate the prevalence of sexual harassment in the state, to make policy recommendations, to design standards for evaluating cases of harassment, to foster public awareness of the problem, to develop training programs for use by businesses, and to suggest ways to eliminate workplace harassment. In December, the task force reported that sexual harassment was a serious problem in the state, with significant implications for the economy. The report made 34 recommendations on preventing and stopping harassment, including the revision of state law, the establishment of public education efforts, and the formulation of strong anti-harassment policies to be followed by state agencies.

Introduction to Sexual Harassment

Next door, the New Jersey Supreme Court issued a landmark ruling in *Lehmann v. Toys 'R' Us, Inc.* (see appendix I). Theresa Lehmann had sued her employer for sexual harassment by her supervisor from 1985 to 1987. Despite repeated complaints to management, nothing was done to discipline her supervisor. Lehmann refused a transfer and quit, immediately filing a civil suit. Rejecting her claims of hostile work environment harassment, the New Jersey Superior Court dismissed her case but awarded her $5,000 for one incident of battery by her supervisor. Lehmann appealed; when the case reached the state supreme court it was decided in her favor. Based on precedents set in several previous federal cases, the ruling recognized the difference between male and female perspectives and established the reasonable woman standard for measuring sexual harassment. The decision represented a landmark because it was the first reasonable woman ruling to lay out a clear and detailed definition of that standard.

Meanwhile, Senator Brock Adams (D-Washington) terminated a bid for reelection amidst allegations of sexual harassment, although he denied the charges against him. At least nine women claimed the senator had harassed them, one describing an incident in which he drugged her at his home. Senator Daniel K. Inouye (D-Hawaii) and Senator Dave Durenberger (R-Minnesota) also faced accusations of harassment, but their cases were overshadowed by that of Senator Bob Packwood (R-Oregon). On November 22, 1992, 10 women who had worked with Packwood between 1969 and 1980 made charges of sexual harassment against the senator. The charges were particularly startling in light of his prominence as an advocate of women's rights. Packwood at first denied their claims, then attempted to discredit his accusers, then issued an ambiguous statement that admitted no wrongdoing but expressed regret for any misunderstanding his behavior may have caused. As more women told of harassment at the senator's hands, Packwood blamed his misconduct on a drinking problem and entered treatment for alcoholism. The Senate Rules Committee declined a petition by Oregon voters to oust Packwood from office, but the Senate Ethics Committee launched an investigation. Finally admitting some degree of guilt, Packwood pledged to cooperate with the probe. But when the committee subpoenaed his diaries in October 1993, Packwood refused to turn them over. Concerned that the senator was altering them, a federal district court judge seized the diaries in December. The investigation broadened to include charges that Packwood tampered with evidence and also that he abused his position to get his wife a job. Finally, in September 1995, the Ethics Committee ruled against Packwood, and he resigned.

While Congress grappled with sexual harassment in its own ranks, the Supreme Court once again addressed the problem of sexual harassment in the private sector. The court's unanimous November 9, 1993, ruling in *Harris v. Forklift Systems Inc.* broadened the definition of sexual harassment. In the case,

Teresa Harris, a manager at the Nashville firm, charged her employer, Charles Hardy, with harassment in the form of dirty jokes, lewd comments, and sexual innuendo between April 1985 and October 1987. His behavior finally left her no alternative but to quit. The Supreme Court rejected the position of several lower courts that Harris could not claim harassment because she was able to continue working and did not suffer psychological harm. Writing for the nation's highest court, Justice Sandra Day O'Connor noted that Title VII takes many factors into account and protects victims of harassment "before the harassing conduct leads to a nervous breakdown."

SEXUAL HARASSMENT IN THE UNITED STATES TODAY

The social, economic, and political impact of the 1991 Hill-Thomas hearings continues to be felt in the United States today. The shift in attitudes concerning sexual harassment has increased the ranks of those who believe Hill's claims, but many people remain confused and uncomfortable about appropriate workplace behavior. While greater numbers of women are willing to come forward when harassed, many companies and institutions continue to follow the poor example of the Senate Judiciary Committee in responding to those complaints.

Recent studies show that at any given point in time at least 15% of working women have been harassed within the past year; 40% to 60% of American women suffer harassment at some point in their career. Yet a *Working Woman* survey shows that only 21% of women feel justice is done in harassment cases. Sixty percent report that such charges are either ignored or the harassers are not sufficiently punished—and 55% say most harassers get off scot-free. A 1993 *Washington Post* poll of women working on Capitol Hill found that half the respondents had either been harassed or knew of someone who had, and that a third of the harassment cases involved wrongdoing on the part of a congressman or senator.

In September 1994, illustrating the persistence of sexual harassment as a problem in the workplace, a San Francisco jury awarded nearly $7 million in punitive damages to Rena Weeks, a legal secretary who was harassed while working at the firm of Baker & McKenzie. Weeks alleged that Martin Greenstein, a senior partner at the international firm, repeatedly grabbed her and made sexual remarks to her in 1991. In her suit, Weeks claimed the firm had failed to discipline Greenstein even though numerous women had complained about him as early as 1987. He had been transferred from Chicago to Palo Alto, California, after one reprimand, then was sent to sensitivity training in response to Weeks' charges. Weeks, however, was transferred after complaining and quit two months later. The jury agreed that Baker & McKenzie had not fulfilled its obligations toward its female employees. It ordered the firm to pay Weeks $50,000 for her emotional distress and $6.9 million in punitive damages, twice what she had asked for. In addition, Greenstein was ordered to pay Weeks $225,000. At press time, Baker & McKenzie was planning its appeal.

At school, the situation is no better for girls. In a 1993 *Seventeen* magazine poll, 89% of 4,200 girls aged 9 to 19 reported harassment such as pinching or grabbing, with 39% of the respondents experiencing at-school harassment on a daily basis. The *Seventeen* survey indicated that the problem peaks between ages 13 and 16, while a survey commissioned by the American Association of University Women showed that most at-school harassment occurs in the 6th through 9th grades, peaking in 7th grade. That survey, the 1993 "Hostile Hallways" poll of 8th- to 11th-graders by Lou Harris and Associates, also found that 85% of girls and 76% of boys report experiencing harassment at school. Most harassment comes at the hands of fellow students, but 25% of girls said they had been harassed by a teacher or other school employee. Sexual harassment of girls by boys includes everything from obscene graffiti, jokes, and taunts to bra-snapping or skirt-flipping "days," and from groping and pinching to assembling lists of "sluts" or "dogs." Although aware of much of this harassment, many teachers and administrators consider it normal behavior for boys and do little to stop it. At a result, many girls feel helpless and fearful: 33% of girls responding to the Harris poll said they did not want to come to school after being harassed and 39% reported feeling afraid in school.

In 1993, seven-year-old Cheltzie Hentz of Eden Prairie, Minnesota, got tired of feeling afraid of the boys who had been taunting and teasing her on the school bus. She filed and won a Title IX lawsuit against her school district for failing to protect her against discrimination. But harassment of girls by boys continues. Recent news broadcasts have included reports of the rape of a 13-year-old girl on a crowded school bus in Fort Worth, the sexual assault of numerous girls aged 10 to 16 by competing members of a Los Angeles gang called the Spur Posse, the abuse of a retarded 17-year-old girl in Glen Ridge, New Jersey, by 12 boys armed with bats and brooms, and attacks against girls at public pools in New York City, where boys formed "whirlpools" to surround and molest girls.

At college, young women also experience sexual harassment. Numerous studies by management consultant Freada Klein have found that 40% of undergraduate women and 28% of female graduate students have been harassed. Other recent surveys place the figure for undergraduates at 30% to 89% and for graduate students at 35% to 60%. Meanwhile, 11% of all (male and female) university staff and 14% of all faculty say they have been harassed by their peers or superiors. Perhaps more interestingly, 26% of male faculty members say they have had voluntary sexual contact with students, while 48% of female faculty say they have been harassed by students. As in other settings, most victims of campus harassment do not report it. Some try to ignore or avoid the harasser, others change their major or choose different courses as the result of harassment. Even if they confront their harasser privately, as surveys show 70% do, both student and faculty victims of campus harassment may suffer permanent damage to their academic career. A rebuffed harasser may retaliate; in the case of a student harassed by a teacher such retaliation can be especially harmful, both psychologically and academically.

Long a male bastion, military academies such as West Point and Annapolis offer an even more hostile work environment to the female student. A 1992 Air Force Academy study showed that 78% of female cadets and 52% of male cadets hear sexist and demeaning comments about women on a daily basis. The following year, a study of all the academies showed that 80% of female cadets had either experienced or heard about sexist comments within the past year. In February 1994, the U.S. General Accounting Office (GAO) released a statement on harassment at the military academies. Although few cases of harassment are formally reported, the GAO survey showed that nearly all women and virtually no men experience harassment—especially verbal—and subsequent stress at the academies. According to the report, fully one-half to three-quarters of all academy women encounter one or more of the following forms of harassment at least once a month: comments, jokes, or name-calling; suggestive posters, graffiti, or pictures; obscene gestures or catcalls; sexually explicit letters or messages; exclusion by male cadets; sexual horseplay or hijinks; pressure for dates; or unwanted sexual advances. Although all the academies have instituted prevention and investigation procedures, most female cadets are afraid to go through the formal grievance channels and choose to deal with harassment informally. The GAO noted that none of the academies systematically evaluated or tracked the results of their sexual harassment policies in order to seek improvement.

Chastened by the Tailhook scandal and pressured by Congress, the Pentagon has recognized the need to correct the persistent problem of sexual harassment in the military. The U.S. House Armed Services Committee has called for action by the top leaders of the various service branches to end sex discrimination in much the same way the military reined in racial discrimination after World War II. In particular, the navy has established a stricter harassment policy that encompasses a more extensive training program and holds officers wholly accountable for their actions and those of their subordinates. The navy's efforts at prevention and correction include a toll-free Sexual Harassment Advice and Counseling Hotline and a "green-light, yellow-light, red-light" poster that defines acceptable, questionable, and objectionable behavior. Nevertheless, the navy continues to have problems with sexual harassment. For example, in 1993 naval aviators based in San Diego targeted Representative Pat Schroeder (D-Colorado), an outspoken critic of harassment in the military, with obscene T-shirts and banners.

Women working for other government agencies have had some success combating sexual harassment. In one case, the Central Intelligence Agency (CIA) settled a sex discrimination case brought by Janine M. Brookner, its former station chief in Jamaica. One of the first women to reach the upper echelons of the agency, Brookner had worked there for 24 years as an officer in the prestigious covert operations directorate. While heading up the CIA's Jamaica office, she disciplined some of her subordinates for misconduct and reported one agent to her superiors for repeatedly beating his wife unconscious. In 1992, these same agents accused her of drinking heavily, dressing suggestively, and sexually harassing them. The CIA inspector general conducted an investigation without interviewing Brookner or her allies, then issued a report that called Brookner a promiscuous alcoholic. On his recommendation, Brookner was denied a promotion to the post of Prague station chief and was assigned a desk job at CIA headquarters in Langley, Virginia.

Brookner filed a discrimination suit in July 1994, asserting that the covert operations directorate had "a pervasive atmosphere of machismo and sexual discrimination receptive to accepting malicious and sexist allegations against women." Scores of women agents within the directorate concurred and threatened to file a class-action sex discrimination lawsuit. During the pre-trial investigation of the Brookner case, several high-ranking government officials testified to her good character and impeccable professionalism. Concluding that the accusations against Brookner were highly dubious, the CIA decided to settle her suit out of court. Without admitting any wrongdoing, the agency paid her $410,000 and opened settlement negotiations with the agents who had threatened to make the class-action claim. Those negotiations were still in progress at press time.

Outside the classroom and the workplace, Americans have become more aware of sexual harassment in its other forms. A March 1993 article in the *Harvard Law Review* described the problem of "street harassment"—catcalls and teasing by strangers in public—suggesting it should be made illegal. A 1987 article in the *Wisconsin Law Review* broached the issue of "housing harassment," in which landlords, building supervisors, and others harass female tenants. Most often targeted at poor and minority women, housing harassment encompasses abusive remarks, uninvited sexual behavior, requests for sex in place of rent, forced sexual activity, and retaliation against those who resist.

SEXUAL HARASSMENT AND THE INDIVIDUAL

Who are the victims of sexual harassment? As many as a half of all working women are sexually harassed during their career, about 20% badly enough that they quit at least one job as a result. A study by the National Association of Working Women estimates that 90% of all sexual harassment involves a male offender and a female victim, while a Northwestern University/Medill School of Journalism survey places that figure at 65%. These and numerous other studies have shown that the single characteristic most often shared by victims of sexual harassment is their gender: Far more than any other consideration, being female greatly increases one's chances of being sexually harassed. Other contributing factors include age (a 1992 Working Woman survey showed that most harassment victims are under 34 years old and most perpetrators over 35 years old) and marital status (many perpetrators view single and divorced women as "fair game"). By contrast, an individual's appearance, style of dress, personality, and behavior have not been shown to affect the likelihood of being harassed. The victim's educational background also has little correlation to the rate of harassment; the slightly higher figures for more educated women probably result from their greater willingness to report harassment. Nor do female executives, managers, and professionals enjoy any special immunity to harassment, although they are less likely to quit their jobs when harassed.

Who are the harassers? The 1992 Working Woman survey showed that 83% of harassers are in a position of power over their victims (e.g., bosses over employees, teachers over students). The greater the power gap between harasser and victim, the more severe the harassment is likely to be. In a culture traditionally dominated by men, men are the most likely harassers and women the most likely victims. Most men do not harass, but men of all ages, classes, races, and marital status may harass the women around them. Harassers target those they perceive as socially or economically vulnerable, including young women, divorced, separated, or widowed women who have no male "protectors," single mothers, lesbians and gay men, men and women of color, new or temporary employees, and women in traditionally male jobs. Many sexual harassers also engage in racial, ethnic, or other types of harassment and may behave in a generally abusive manner toward one and all. They share a need to dominate and impress others, a desire to bully and humiliate, and an insensitivity to women's feelings and concerns. Harassers tend to define women in purely sexual terms, seeing them as women solely rather than as professionals, students,

24

or employees. When a harasser asserts his power over a woman by intimidating or denigrating her, his predatory behavior makes him feel powerful and delivers a sexual thrill.

Inversely, victims of harassment experience embarrassment, disgust, and anger when they are harassed. Afterward, their feelings may include shame, humiliation, anxiety, fear, stress, irritability, rage, depression, loss of trust, self-doubt, denial, and self-blame. Loss of self-esteem is an especially common problem for school-age girls who are harassed. Many victims also develop physical afflictions such as headaches, fatigue, nausea, sleep and appetite disturbances, uncontrolled crying, frequent colds, urinary tract infections, and stomach problems. As a general rule of thumb, the more severe the harassment the more serious its impact on the victim. Victims' emotional and physical distress can lead to absenteeism, reduced performance or productivity, and difficulty with relationships. Compounding the damage done by the harassment itself, victims are frequently denied grades, raises, promotions, and bonuses by their harasser or his defenders. Victims may be given an undesirable transfer, forced to resign, or fired outright, sometimes with long-term consequences for their career.

In part because they fear this and other kinds of reprisal, few victims of sexual harassment report harassers to the authorities. Those who choose not to report harassment are more likely to blame themselves for what happened, and surveys show that many harassment victims prefer to ignore the behavior and avoid the harasser, or else to confront the harasser privately. Not only do they worry about the personal risks of filing a formal complaint; many victims also do not want to hurt the perpetrator even though they hold him responsible for his actions. Other reasons victims hesitate to make formal charges include ignorance of the law, confusion over what constitutes harassment, denial that the incident was significant, embarrassment, reluctance to sacrifice personal privacy, belief that nothing will be done about their complaint, fear of being disbelieved, humiliated or ostracized, and anxiety that they will be perceived as crazy, vengeful, or disruptive. Frequently faced with the anger, fear, or denial of their co-workers, many victims of harassment see transferring or quitting as the easiest alternatives.

However, victims and potential victims of sexual harassment can minimize its damaging effects by taking steps to prevent and deal with the problem on a personal level. Those who have a clear notion of acceptable conduct, who remain alert to boundary violations, who understand their legal and corporate rights, and who pay attention to their feelings and instincts are less likely to be harassed. Those who are harassed are more likely to put a stop to it and preserve their self-esteem if they actively respond to the situation rather than ignoring it. Experts advise victims of harassment to detail each incident in a dated journal, to save any evidence (such as notes or phone messages) of the harassment, and to make all complaints and reports in writing. Before taking formal action, many victims find they can stop harassment simply by talking to the offender or sending a note. (An informal approach is not appropriate if the harassment involves physical abuse or threats.) If that doesn't work, enlisting the informal aid of the perpetrator's friends, colleagues, or superiors can have the desired results. When informal efforts fail, victims are advised to identify any rules and laws the harasser has violated, to find witnesses who can corroborate the complaint, and to follow the grievance procedure of their school, company, or organization. If the institution has no grievance procedure, or if the harassment takes place outside the context of an organization, victims may file a complaint with the local office of the EEOC. They may also choose to do so if internal grievance procedures fail to have the desired results.

SEXUAL HARASSMENT AND THE LAW

In the United States, federal civil rights law recognizes sexual harassment as a form of illegal sex discrimination. Since 1980, 75% of the sex discrimination claims filed with the EEOC—more than 35,000 complaints—have had their basis in charges of sexual harassment. According to legal precedent and current EEOC guidelines, sexual behavior constitutes harassment if it affects the terms or conditions of the victim's employment, that is, if the victim must submit to it in order to gain or keep a job or to advance academically, if submission to or rejection of it shapes employment or academic decisions concerning the victim, or if the conduct unreasonably interferes with the victim's work or academic performance or creates a hostile, intimidating or offensive work environment. By law, most employers and all federally funded educational institutions are legally obligated to prevent harassment of their staff and students and to punish harassers.

Title VII of the 1964 Civil Rights Act prohibits employment discrimination on the basis of sex by employers with more than 15 employees. Similarly, Title IX of the Education Amendments of 1972 bars sex bias in education. The first sexual harassment cases to come before federal judges were filed as sex discrimination cases under Title VII. Brought in the mid-1970s, cases such as *Corne v. Bausch & Lomb*, *Barnes v. Train*, and *Miller v. Bank of America* failed to convince the courts that harassment is discrimination. The first Title IX sexual harassment suit heard in the federal courts, *Alexander v. Yale University*, likewise met with defeat in 1977.

Starting with rulings such as those in *Williams v. Saxbe*, *Barnes v. Costle* (the appeal of *Barnes v. Train*), *Tomkins v. Public Service Electric & Gas Co.*, and

Garber v. Saxon Business Products Inc., the federal courts began to accept harassment as a form of Title VII sex discrimination. In each of these cases, the harassment resulted in a loss of tangible job benefits such as a raise or promotion. The courts recognized this sort of quid pro quo harassment as discrimination because the plaintiffs clearly would not have lost those benefits had they not been women. The rulings also indicated that a company or other organization can be held liable for sexual harassment by an employee, although the victim must prove the employer's direct or indirect responsibility for the harassment.

In the late 1970s, plaintiffs won sexual harassment cases such as *Heelan v. Johns-Manville Corp.*, *Evans v. Sheraton Park Hotel*, and *Kyriazi v. Western Electric Co.* Questions raised by these and other cases prompted the EEOC to refine its definition of sexual harassment. Released in November 1980, the EEOC's "Guidelines on Discrimination Because of Sex" broadened the concept of illegal harassment beyond a strict quid pro quo interpretation to encompass harassment that creates an atmosphere in which women feel denigrated or fearful. While some courts rejected the hostile work environment concept, others upheld it in cases such as *Brown v. City of Guthrie*, *EEOC v. Sage Realty Corp.*, and *Bundy v. Jackson*. Two cases in particular—*Henson v. City of Dundee* and *Katz v. Dole*—clarified the meanings of quid pro quo and hostile work environment harassment, while *Broderick v. Ruder* and *Robinson v. Jacksonville Shipyards* further strengthened the hostile work environment precedent. In 1986, the Supreme Court heard its first sexual harassment case, *Meritor Savings Bank v. Vinson*. The court ruled that sexual harassment, including hostile work environment harassment, is illegal discrimination comparable to racial harassment and discrimination.

During the late 1980s and early 1990s, the courts continued to explore the boundaries of illegal sexual harassment. The Ninth Circuit Court's ruling in *Ellison v. Brady* introduced the reasonable woman standard for judging sexual harassment, suggesting that sexual harassment should be considered from the victim's perspective. In *Radtke v. Everett*, a Michigan appeals court concurred with the reasonable woman concept and ruled that a single incident of harassment could create a hostile work environment. The 1991 Civil Rights Act opened new options for victims of sexual harassment, allowing their cases to be heard before juries and permitting the award of compensatory and punitive damages for pain and suffering caused by intentional sexual discrimination. *Lehmann v. Toys 'R' Us, Inc.* formalized the reasonable woman principle in 1993. And the Supreme Court's 1993 decision in *Harris v. Forklift Systems* reversed a lower court requirement that victims of sexual harassment prove they suffered psychological harm in order to make a claim of Title VII sex discrimination.

Several other federal laws cover certain aspects of sexual harassment. Executive Order 11246 prohibits sex discrimination by companies that have contracts with the federal government. The Worker Compensation Act can be applied to severely distressed harassment victims who miss work or need psychotherapy. And workers who claim they have been physically or emotionally harmed by sexual harassment in the workplace can file a claim with the federal Occupational Safety and Health Administration (OSHA).

Assisted by state agencies such as fair employment practices (FEP) commissions or departments of human rights, the EEOC enforces Title VII, while the Office for Civil Rights of the federal Department of Education enforces Title IX. In addition, at least 41 states and scores of cities have their own laws against sex discrimination in employment, many of which are interpreted to cover sexual harassment or do so specifically. Some states require employers to institute harassment policies and provide sensitivity training to their employees; Minnesota and California require school systems to adopt sexual harassment policies. As of 1994, the states of Alabama, Georgia, Louisiana, Mississippi, North Carolina, North Dakota, Texas, Tennessee, and Virginia had no state laws covering sex discrimination or sexual harassment.

In some states, sexual harassment victims can bring civil suits against their harassers or employers under contract law. Alternately, individuals may sue for damages in civil court, claiming their harassment represents a tort, an "intentional and outrageous action resulting in harm." Potentially relevant torts covered by state law include interference with an employee's contract, invasion of privacy, assault and battery, intentional infliction of emotional distress, negligence, false imprisonment, and breach of contract. In a few cases, criminal charges such as rape, assault and battery, or extortion may be brought by the authorities.

Around the world, other countries with sexual harassment laws have used U.S. law as a model. Most industrialized nations have equal employment opportunity laws that prohibit sex discrimination. Some, such as Australia, New Zealand, Canada, Denmark, Sweden, Ireland, and England, specifically identify sexual harassment as a form of sex discrimination. Some countries apply general labor laws to cases of harassment. These laws, which cover employment conditions and contracts, sometimes include specific mention of sexual harassment, as in Spain, New Zealand, and Switzerland. Elsewhere, cases of sexual harassment have been handled under tort laws that cover harmful acts or negligence. Japan, Switzerland, and England are among the nations that have applied tort law to sexual harassment. In most nations, criminal law can be applied to severe cases; France has specifically made sexual harassment a criminal offense.

WORKPLACE PRACTICES AND POLICIES

The EEOC's "Guidelines on Discrimination Because of Sex" (see appendix B) provide employers with specific information on what constitutes sexual harassment and what responsibilities companies have to prevent and punish sexual harassment in the workplace. Without exception, companies are "strictly liable"—they can be sued—for harassment by members of their management staff; they are also liable for harassment among co-workers if they are aware or should be aware of it yet take no action to stop it or punish the harasser. Companies may also be held liable for the harassment of their employees by customers, suppliers, subcontractors, or others who do business with them. And if one employee gains special workplace favors through sexual activity, other employees can make a claim of sexual harassment.

In order to avoid legal liability for sexual harassment of or by their employees, businesses generally design their harassment policies to mirror the EEOC guidelines as closely as possible. Those guidelines require employers of 15 or more workers to enact anti-harassment policies and to make every effort to prevent harassment by informing employees of company policy and by providing them with anti-harassment training. The EEOC also requires businesses to establish grievance procedures and to respond formally to all rumors and complaints of sexual harassment that come to their attention. It is illegal for employers to expect their employees to handle such situations informally. Following their internal grievance procedures, employers must examine each case individually, considering all evidence in context and judging it qualitatively as well as quantitatively.

As of 1992, about 80% of Fortune 500 companies and 75% of the American Management Association's (AMA) 524 members had instituted sexual harassment policies, although fewer than half conducted training on the topic. The same year, a poll of New York City-area executives by the law firm of Jackson, Lewis, Schnitzler & Krupman showed that, between 1991 and 1992, sexual harassment jumped from 14th to 3rd in the ranking of employment issues considered critical by executives. The AMA poll showed that 52% of its member companies had dealt internally with harassment allegations in the preceding five years. Another 1992 study, conducted by *Business & Legal Reports*, showed that large companies are more likely to hear complaints of sexual harassment: 56% of companies with more than 500 employees had handled such claims, compared with only 21% of companies with fewer than 100 employees.

The AMA survey showed that about half the sexual harassment cases resulted in formal complaints and half were addressed informally. In 60% of the cases the companies punished the harasser with dismissal, reprimand, suspension, probation, or transfer, while 23% of the cases were resolved through other means and 17% were thrown out. Most managers concluded that their companies were handling harassment well; their outlook was corroborated by executives responding to a 1992 *Working Woman* survey, 80% of whom believed harassers in their companies were disciplined appropriately. However, only 21% of employees felt companies gave harassers their due, perhaps accounting for the steadily growing number of complaints filed with the EEOC. In fact, *Treasury Magazine* estimated in 1994 that American corporations would spend $1 billion over the next five years to settle sexual harassment suits. The insurance industry has taken note of the trend and now offers "employment practice liability" coverage to protect businesses against the costs of race, age, and sex discrimination suits brought by employees.

The legal costs of sexual harassment are, however, dwarfed by the expense of lost productivity. Sexual harassment not only distracts perpetrators and victims from their work, its fallout can also severely impair victims' subsequent job performance. Harassers are often poor managers whose failure to deal effectively with their subordinates can lower morale and productivity. Their staff, as well as their victims, may have higher rates of absenteeism and turnover. The cost of hiring and training new employees to replace the sexual harassment victims who quit or who are fired is potentially unending: If the perpetrator keeps his job, replacement employees are likely to experience the same kind of harassment with the same results. In 1988, a *Working Woman* survey estimated that a typical Fortune 500 company with 23,750 employees loses $6.7 million annually because of sexual harassment.

Some companies are especially vulnerable to the damage sexual harassment can do. Harassment is more prevalent where the sex ratio of workers is highly unbalanced, especially where a few women work with many men. Smaller work groups, where supervisors have a great deal of power over their subordinates, tend to see a greater incidence of harassment. An atmosphere of general sexual permissiveness boosts the rate of harassment: If management permits or encourages heavy drinking after work or at company functions, swearing on the job, sexual activity on business trips, or even certain kinds of dating behavior, men are more likely to see their female colleagues as sexual objects and targets of sexual harassment. Other corporate attitudes can also foster harassment. If management ignores or avoids the issue, writes it off as the victim's hypersensitivity, claims there is no such thing, believes that "boys will be boys," or asserts it is harmless, employees will feel greater freedom to sexually harass their co-workers.

By contrast, a different management approach can greatly reduce the incidence and cost of sexual harassment. Bans on certain activity generally fail, but in a professional work environment where employees are valued as skilled individuals, sex and work are naturally separated. A policy of equal pay and promotion opportunity for women and minorities heightens respect among all employees. And a genuine intolerance on the part of top management toward sexual harassment, coupled with a sincere commitment to eliminating it, sets the tone for the rest of the organization. Supervisors who show real concern about harassment can foster the same attitude among their subordinates, for it becomes obvious to employees that company policy is not just a tool for avoiding lawsuits or polishing the corporate image.

An effective anti-harassment policy, put in writing and made available to all employees, incorporates several elements. It provides a clear definition, based closely on EEOC guidelines, of sexual harassment and specifies which types of behavior are appropriate and inappropriate. Clearly stating the company's intolerance of harassment, the policy warns potential harassers of the consequences they face. It details an internal grievance procedure and tells employees what to do if they witness harassment or are harassed themselves. In addition to establishing complaint procedures and options for employees, the soundest harassment policies designate officers to resolve problems before litigation becomes inevitable; employees are given the names and phone numbers of these ombudsmen. Grievance procedures should be designed to bypass the complainant's immediate supervisor and ensure a prompt, fair, thorough, and confidential investigation. Follow-up after an investigation can help avert retaliation against the accuser, while frequent reminders of management's commitment to its anti-harassment measures can help maintain their effectiveness. In large companies, individual divisions may develop their own anti-harassment programs to supplement the corporate effort.

Backed up with consistent and substantive enforcement, a strong anti-harassment policy also encompasses training for every employee on company time, as well as periodic refresher sessions. Some businesses hire sexual harassment consultants or buy pre-packaged video and print training programs. Training can sensitize workers to the different ways men and women perceive sex and sexuality. Through role-playing, lectures, and other means, the most effective sexual harassment training focuses on changing behavior, for attitudes may be less tractable. Separate sessions may be designed for rank-and-file workers, for new or recently promoted employees, for senior executives and for line supervisors. Management may include harassment sensitivity in employee evaluations and reward employees who actively promote company policy.

Employers who receive complaints of sexual harassment can limit their liability by taking each charge seriously and investigating it promptly and thoroughly. While an investigation is under way, the accuser and the accused should be separated if either requests it. A team of one man and one woman, neither of whom knows the parties personally, should speak with both parties as well as any relevant witnesses. The team also gathers documentary evidence and presents its findings to management. Evaluating the charges on the basis of all information gathered, management decides on a course of action. If the charges are substantiated, the offender must be disciplined according to the severity and frequency of his conduct. Discipline might take the form of a verbal or written warning, a note in the offender's personnel file, additional sensitivity training, denial of a raise, bonus or promotion, suspension, demotion, transfer, or outright discharge. On the other hand, if the charges are dismissed, the reasons for doing so should be explainded to the complainant.

Employees who are dissatisfied with their employer's response to charges of sexual harassment can take their case outside the company. Anyone can file a complaint with the EEOC, and union members may be able to file a grievance with their local or national union. Union representatives can negotiate with a company on the part of employees or bring in an outside arbitrator to help resolve the situation. On an ongoing basis, unions can review employer policies and keep track of the incidence of and response to sexual harassment at different companies. Unions may also provide awareness training to their members and incorporate anti-harassment measures in their contracts with employers.

Perhaps more than any other employer, the armed forces have come face-to-face with sexual harassment in recent years. Each of the branches of the military has adopted its own anti-harassment policy and procedures; even the Department of Veteran Affairs offers group therapy to female veterans who suffered sexual harassment while serving. The navy's approach is typical. Its strategy to eliminate harassment is based on four principles: top leadership commitment to ending harassment; education and training of all recruits and personnel, especially those in leadership roles; accountability of all personnel for their behavior and that of their subordinates; a systematic approach to dealing with sexual harassment problems. Among the other steps it has taken, the navy has set up a Standing Committee on Military and Civilian Women in the Department of the Navy, established a system for tracking the incidence and outcome of complaints, and instituted periodic checks of naval commands. Because many victims hesitate to report harassment out of fear for their career, the navy has implemented an informal system for complaint resolution and set up a toll-free number to provide confidential counseling and advice. The navy has also tried to write clear and simple rules governing all behavior, but its efforts to expand opportunities for women are more likely to reduce harassment in the long run.

Schools and universities face unique challenges in coping with sexual harassment. In response to Title IX and pressure from students and faculty, some school districts and universities have adopted anti-harassment policies, grievance procedures, and educational programs. Meant to give students, parents, teachers, and staff the tools to combat harassment, these programs combine time-honored educational techniques with methods developed in the corporate world. Specialists have developed sexual harassment curricula for use with students of different ages. These programs, often in video format, may include case studies, student activities, teacher guidelines, and sample policies and grievance procedures. On the university level, student orientation programs, and training for faculty and staff attempt to address the ambiguity of relationships between professors and their students. The sexually charged atmosphere of college campuses makes harassment a particularly pressing issue for university policymakers. Sexual harassment is difficult to detect and prevent in a setting where the autonomy of faculty members, their power over students, the peculiar intimacy of campus life, the odd hours kept by students and faculty, and the acceptance of eccentric behavior are traditional. Among faculty, collegiality and in-group loyalty clash with intellectual and professional competition, creating an environment where victims of harassment often fear to speak out. Faculty seeking to avoid all risk of harassment charges may distance themselves from female students and colleagues, compromising women's educational or professional potential.

FUTURE TRENDS

Sexual harassment promises to remain a thorny issue for years to come. Ever since the Hill-Thomas hearings of 1991 raised the world's consciousness of sexual harassment, most people have had a heightened awareness of sexuality's place in public life. Experts have struggled to understand and quantify sexual harassment, governments have felt pressured to do something about it, organizations have worked to prevent it and to limit their own liability, and men and women have argued about it. Growing numbers of sexual harassment lawsuits are filed each year, with plaintiffs winning more and more often.

In this atmosphere, several trends have emerged. Juries have begun to grant large damage awards of a million dollars or more, encouraging organizations to cut their losses by agreeing to hefty out-of-court settlements. Attorneys on both sides of the cases that do go to court now have a wide variety of sexual harassment specialists to call upon for expert testimony. Class-action suits have become a feasible option for victims of company-wide harassment. Meanwhile, the legal definition of sexual harassment has broadened: The Supreme Court has accepted the reasonable person standard for measuring harassment, and lower federal courts have started recognizing the more sensitive reasonable woman standard. Recent lawsuits have explored the frontiers of sexual harassment. Harassment of employees by outsiders, harassment of superiors by subordinates, harassment of males by females, and harassment among members of the same sex have been recognized by the courts. Elsewhere, whistle-blowers who are fired for backing up their co-workers' charges of harassment have successfully claimed that harassment law applies to them.

Just as the law is becoming more sophisticated, sexual harassment continues to take on new contours. Most recently, growing numbers of women report harassment via e-mail in the form of explicit graphics, obscene notes, and threats sent to their computers. An April 1995 article in *The New Republic* described the phenomenon, noting that "Harassment of women is so common that women often pretend to be men to avoid sexually suggestive e-mail." Communication via electronic bulletin boards, on-line services, and the Internet fosters the exchange of ideas and information; but the anonymity of participants also gives them free reign to engage in abusive or sexually explicit dialogue. Like obscene phone callers, on-line harassers target women, particularly young girls; one reporter posing as a 15-year-old cheerleader received a flood of sexually oriented e-mail. In February 1995, a male student at the University of Michigan was arrested for going on-line with graphic descriptions of raping, torturing, and murdering a female classmate. And a Long Island woman was electronically stalked by her estranged husband, whose knowledge of cyberspace thwarted police efforts to pinpoint his location and arrest him.

CHAPTER 2

———■———

THE LAW OF SEXUAL HARASSMENT

Sexual harassment was first recognized by the U.S. courts as an illegal form of sex discrimination in 1976. Since then, rulings in hundreds of lawsuits have broadened and refined the legal definition of sexual harassment, while social forces have made it one of the most talked about workplace issues of the late 20th century. Federal civil rights legislation, government policy, state law, and corporate practice have evolved alongside public awareness of sexual harassment. Title VII of the 1964 Civil Rights Act and Title IX of the 1972 Education Amendments are now understood to prohibit sexual harassment at work and school, while detailed guidelines drafted by the Equal Employment Opportunity Commission (EEOC) define harassment and describe employers' legal obligation to prevent and stop it. In accord with the EEOC guidelines, the courts recognize two main types of sexual harassment—*quid pro quo* and *hostile work environment* harassment—as actionable forms of sex discrimination. The courts have also begun to use a new standard when evaluating the nature and severity of sexual harassment—the *reasonable woman* standard—instead of the "reasonable person" standard, which courts have traditionally interpreted from a male perspective. In some cases, criminal or tort laws apply to harassment, and some victims have sought relief through workers' compensation and unemployment insurance regulations. Most states and many cities now have their own laws covering sex discrimination, with provisions governing its prevention and legal consequences.

LEGISLATION AND ENFORCEMENT

In the legislatures and courtrooms of the United States today, sexual harassment is dealt with as a civil rights offense. Whatever the other legal features of sexual harassment—whether it involves a criminal act of violence, say, or the violation of an employee's contract—by legal definition it encroaches on the victim's constitutionally guaranteed rights. Other laws may be brought to bear upon individual cases, but civil rights law applies in every instance.

The first such law under which the courts recognized sexual harassment as a violation of the victim's rights is the Civil Rights Act of 1964, signed by President Lyndon Johnson. Designed to prohibit discrimination on the basis of race, color, religion, national origin, and sex, the act covers employment as well as public accommodations and facilities and federally assisted programs and education. When Congress was debating passage of the act, opponents of the measure added sex to the list of protected classes, certain that the predominantly male legislators would not outlaw discrimination against women. They were wrong, though: Not only did the law pass, it also protected a group that was not originally covered. Title VII of the act bars employers with more than 15 employees, employers that hold federal contracts, unions, and employment agencies from discriminating against protected individuals or groups. By banning sex discrimination in employment, the courts have since ruled, Title VII bans sexual harassment in the workplace.

Title VII also created the EEOC to enforce, administer, and interpret its provisions. Composed of five members, the EEOC by law must not include more than three members of the same political party. The members are appointed by the president, with the advice and consent of the Senate, for a term of five years. The commission is empowered to prevent any person from engaging in any unlawful employment practice as outlined in sections 703 and 704 of Title VII. Originally, enforcement power resided with the Department of Justice, but in 1972, Congress passed the Equal Employment Opportunity Act, which among other things transferred that authority to the EEOC.

In 1980, the EEOC drafted its "Guidelines on Discrimination Because of Sex," which it updated in 1990. The guidelines define sexual harassment and outline employer liability for preventing it, stopping it once it occurs, and disciplining harassers. Broadening the concept of harassment beyond "unwanted sexual overtures," the guidelines describe quid pro quo ("this for that") and hostile work environment harassment. According to the guidelines, harassment includes any unwanted or unwelcome sexual be-havior that has a negative impact on the victim's job or work environment. Employers are obligated to make every effort to eliminate this form of illegal sex discrimination, they are fully accountable for the behavior of their employees, and they are at fault if they know or should know about harassment of their employees yet fail to take steps to remedy the situation. In addition, the guidelines require employers to establish an anti-harass-ment policy that includes a training program and grievance procedures. For employees of the federal government the 1978 Civil Service Reform

Act augments Title VII, barring discrimination in federal employment. And under Executive Order 11246, employees of companies that hold contracts with the federal government can file sexual harassment complaints with the Federal Contract Compliance Commission, which may ban violators from signing any future contracts with the government.

Within 180 days of a violation, any victim of sexual harassment in the workplace can file a written complaint with a local branch of the EEOC, which most states refer to as a human rights commission. Once they file with the EEOC, the law protects complainants from retaliation by their harasser, employer, or co-workers. If the EEOC determines that harassment probably occurred, officers conduct an investigation, gathering information from the victim, the harasser, the employer, and any relevant witnesses. The agency will try to avoid litigation by negotiating a "no-fault settlement" between the employer and the employee, in which the employer compensates the employee but does not admit any guilt. If those efforts fail and if the case has the potential to set a new legal precedent, the EEOC may file a civil suit against the employer in federal court. Otherwise, the victim can request a "right to sue" letter from the agency that gives him or her the right to pursue the case privately.

The same year he signed the Equal Employment Opportunity Act, President Richard Nixon also signed the Education Amendments of 1972. Title IX of that act forbids sex discrimination in education, reading in part, "No person in the U.S. shall, on the basis of sex, be excluded from participation in, be denied the benefits of, or be subjected to discrimination under any educational program or activity receiving federal financial assistance." Since the vast majority of American educational institutions, from public elementary schools to vocational training programs to private universities, receive federal funding, the law covers almost every school. The Department of Education enforces Title IX, and school districts are required to appoint a Title IX coordinator to enforce the law and oversee grievance procedures. If an agency or institution fails to comply with the department's guidelines on sex discrimination, it may be denied further federal assistance, at least to the program or activity where the violation occurred. As with Title VII, the courts have interpreted Title IX to cover sexual harassment.

Another federal law that has been applied to cases of sexual harassment is 42 U.S.C. § 1983, commonly referred to as Section 1983. Passed in 1983 and signed by President Ronald Reagan, the measure specifically prohibits governments and government officials from engaging in conduct that deprives an individual or group of the rights guaranteed them by the constitution or by federal law. Victims of sexual harassment at the hands of government officials have cited Section 1983 to hold their harassers liable, and courts have accepted that interpretation of the law. For example, in the 1983 case *Annis v. County of*

Westchester the plaintiffs stated that they experienced such an intense level of harassment that they were forced out of the workplace. They claimed that their employer, the county of Westchester, thereby denied them the equal protection under the law guaranteed by the Fourteenth Amendment to the constitution. The court agreed, holding that this type of harassment represents sex discrimination.

Section 1983, a civil law, has two criminal counterparts in federal law: 18 U.S.C. § 241 (Section 241) makes "conspiracy against rights" a crime, while 18 U.S.C. § 242 (Section 242) does the same for "deprivation of rights under the color of law." The first of these involves the conspiracy of two or more people "to injure, oppress, threaten, or intimidate any inhabitant of any State, Territory, or District in the free exercise or enjoyment of any right or privilege secured to him by the Constitution or laws of the United States." The second law punishes "Whoever, under color of any law, statute, ordinance, regulation, or custom, willfully subjects any inhabitant or any State, Territory, or District to the deprivation of any rights or privileges . . . protected by the Constitution or laws of the United States." As a form of sex discrimination, sexual harassment deprives its victims of their rights and may thus be punishable in certain instances under these two laws.

More recently, Congress passed and President George Bush signed the 1991 Civil Rights Act, which allows for jury trials in sexual harassment cases. The law permits juries to award compensatory and punitive damages to sexual harassment victims for pain and suffering due to intentional sexual discrimination, but puts a cap on the size of those awards. Other federal laws that have been applied in cases of sexual harassment include the Workers' Compensation Act, administered by the Workers' Compensation Administration. Severely distressed harassment victims who miss work as the result of physical or emotional illness brought on by the harassment can file a claim for worker's compensation. If they can prove that their emotional or physical problems are the direct result of sexual harassment, they may be entitled to wage benefits during their disability, medical benefits paid by their employer's insurer, rehabilitation and retraining, or even permanent disability payments. Victims who claim they have been physically or emotionally harmed by workplace harassment may also file a claim with the Occupational Safety and Health Administration (OSHA), which is required by law to investigate every claim. OSHA regulations consider stress—such as that caused by sexual harassment—as a violation of the employer's obligation to provide a "safe and healthful workplace."

On the state level, victims of sexual harassment have several laws and agencies at their disposal. As of 1994, at least 40 states (excluding Alabama,

The Law of Sexual Harassment

Georgia, Louisiana, Mississippi, North Carolina, North Dakota, Texas, Tennessee, and Virginia) had laws against sex discrimination in employment. Many of these have been interpreted either to include harassment or to outlaw it explicitly. Some states require employers to institute anti-harassment policies and provide anti-harassment training to their employees. Others, such as Minnesota and California, require school systems to adopt sexual harassment policies. The state agencies known as fair employment practices (FEP) offices handle all kinds of employment discrimination cases, including those involving sexual harassment. Employees of small firms (fewer than 15 employees) that hold no government contracts are not covered by federal law, but they can file complaints with their state FEP office. In some cases, FEP and EEOC officers cooperate in harassment investigations and lawsuits. Workers who quit or are fired as the result of sexual harassment, and who otherwise meet the standard qualifications, may file a claim for unemployment insurance with their state employment compensation insurance office. Many states still view such claims warily, so harassment victims must prove that their loss of a job stems directly or even exclusively from sexual harassment. Some states require victims to notify their employers of the harassment before quitting and to give them time to remedy the situation. At press time, only six states and the District of Columbia explicitly cover workers who "voluntarily" leave their jobs because of sexual harassment.

In a very new area of the law, state tort statutes may apply to certain cases of sexual harassment. A tort is defined as an "intentional and outrageous action resulting in harm," such as interference with an employee's contract, invasion of privacy, assault and battery, intentional infliction of emotional distress, negligence, false imprisonment, or breach of contract. Any of these might be cited in a sexual harassment case, but the most frequently claimed are intentional infliction of emotional distress, battery (harmful or offensive touching), and intentional harm. Although such cases are as yet rare, victims of such torts can sue their sexual harassers for damages in civil court. If the victim can prove his or her case, a jury may require the harasser or employer to pay actual damages for the victim's loss of pay, reduction of income in a new job, cost of a job switch, lost benefits, cost of illness, and other hardships, as well as punitive damages meant to penalize the offending party.

Finally, perpetrators of severe harassment, such as rape, extortion (blackmail), and assault, may be prosecuted under state criminal laws. In these cases, victims alert authorities to the criminal activity and may testify against their harassers, but it is the law enforcement authorities who decide whether or not to file charges. Criminal prosecution of sexual harassers remains rare.

MAJOR COURT CASES

It took a decade after the passage of the 1964 Civil Rights Act for the first Title VII sexual harassment cases to reach the courts, and the first few that did failed to convince judges that harassment is a form of discrimination. Finally, in 1976, a Washington, D.C., court accepted harassment as discrimination in *Williams v. Saxbe*. But the ruling equates harassment with discrimination only in quid pro quo cases. In *Williams v. Saxbe*, the plaintiff was fired nine days after she refused to have sex with her supervisor, a clear case of sex discrimination in the form of quid pro quo harassment. After the *Williams* decision, other courts around the country slowly began to recognize quid pro quo harassment as sex discrimination, but the legal battle against sexual harassment advanced slowly. While the courts were skeptical about sexual harassment as a civil rights issue, the EEOC under Eleanor Holmes Norton boldly expanded its definition of discriminatory harassment. The agency's 1980 "Guidelines on Discrimination Because of Sex" added hostile work environment harassment to the category of prohibited sex discrimination. This form of harassment consists of sexual speech or behavior that creates an intimidating or antagonistic workplace atmosphere where targeted employees cannot enjoy the same rights and benefits as their colleagues. Even before the final guidelines were issued, a federal appeals court in Oklahoma accepted hostile work environment harassment as a Title VII violation in the case of *Brown v. City of Guthrie*, in which a woman quit her job as the result of sexually offensive working conditions. In 1981, the U.S. Court of Appeals for the District of Columbia affirmed the official EEOC guidelines in its ruling in *Bundy v. Jackson*. That decision held that sexual harassment is illegal in and of itself, whether or not it has any economic impact on the victim. Many other courts, however, remained hesitant to recognize the discriminatory nature of hostile work environment sexual harassment.

The case that finally laid out the legal parameters of quid pro quo and hostile work environment harassment was *Henson v. City of Dundee*, decided in 1982 by the Court of Appeals for the Eleventh Circuit. Defining sexual harassment as "unwelcome conduct . . . in the sense that the employee did not solicit or incite it, and in the sense that the employee regarded the conduct as undesirable or offensive," the ruling enumerated the legal elements of its two basic forms. For sexual harassment to qualify as quid pro quo discrimination, it must meet four criteria:

(1) The plaintiff belongs to a protected group (i.e., is male or female) under Title VII of the 1964 Civil Rights Act.

(2) The plaintiff is subject to unwanted sexual conduct.

(3) The harassment is based on the sex of the plaintiff.

(4)   The plaintiff is deprived of compensation or suffers other tangible harm to the terms, conditions, or privileges of employment.

Hostile work environment harassment, meanwhile, must meet five criteria to be considered sex discrimination:

(1)   The plaintiff belongs to a protected group under Title VII of the 1964 Civil Rights Act.

(2)   The plaintiff is subject to unwanted sexual conduct.

(3)   The harassment is based on the sex of the plaintiff.

(4)   The harassment has a negative impact on the terms, conditions, or privileges of employment.

(5)   The employer knows or should have known of the harassment and does not take remedial action.

These criteria remain the basis for Title VII sexual harassment cases today.

The five cases described below represent important milestones in the legal battle against sexual harassment. They either broke new ground in the legal status of sexual harassment or, in the case of Supreme Court rulings, established once and for all the judicial framework to be followed by lower courts hearing such cases. All fairly recent, these cases illustrate some of the main trends that sexual harassment litigation is likely to follow into the 21st century.

MERITOR SAVINGS BANK V. VINSON, 477 U.S. 57 (1986)

In its first ruling on sexual harassment, the Supreme Court cited *Henson* as a precedent. Handed down on June 19, 1986, the court's decision in *Meritor Savings Bank v. Vinson* recognized sexual harassment as sex discrimination under Title VII of the 1964 Civil Rights Act, even if the victim suffers no tangible or economic loss—that is, even in hostile work environment incidents. The case was argued before the court by several attorneys, including law professor Catherine A. MacKinnon, arguing on behalf of the plaintiff. In 1979, MacKinnon had published one of the first books about the topic, entitled *Sexual Harassment of Working Women: A Case of Discrimination*. The volume, still considered authoritative, contends that sexual harassment is a form of sex discrimination because it targets the members of one sex (female) almost exclusively.

Background

Sidney Taylor, a vice president of Meritor Savings Bank in Washington, D.C., hired Mechelle Vinson as a bank teller trainee in 1974. Under Taylor's supervision, Vinson was promoted first to teller, then to head teller, and finally to assistant branch manager. In the four years she worked at the bank, she established herself as a stellar employee whose advancement within the bank was based on merit alone. However, Taylor repeatedly harassed Vinson during this time, placing her under tremendous stress. As a result of the stress caused by her boss' behavior, Vinson took several sick leaves. In September 1978, she notified Taylor that she was taking sick leave for an indefinite period; two months later, while she was on leave, the bank fired her for her excessive use of that leave.

Vinson immediately brought suit against Taylor and the bank, claiming that during her four years of employment at Meritor she had "constantly been subjected to sexual harassment" by Taylor. Her complaint, *Vinson v. Taylor*, alleged that Taylor's sexual advances were unwelcome and constituted sexual harassment in violation of Title VII of the 1964 Civil Rights Act. At the 11-day bench trial before the United States District Court for the District of Columbia, Vinson testified that during her probationary period as a trainee, Taylor treated her as a father might and made no sexual advances. After her promotion, she said, he invited her to dinner; while they dined, he suggested they go to a motel to have sex. Vinson stated that at first she refused, but finally, out of fear of losing her job, she agreed to have sex with Taylor. She estimated that over the course of her employment, her boss repeatedly demanded sexual favors and that she had sexual relations with him on 40 or 50 separate occasions.

Vinson's testimony also included allegations that Taylor fondled her in the presence of other employees, followed her to the ladies' room, exposed himself to her, and forcibly raped her on several occasions. She explained that she never reported the harassment because she was afraid of Taylor. When she tried to present evidence that Taylor had harassed other women at the bank the court did not allow her to do so. For his part, Taylor denied all of Vinson's charges. The bank also denied them, stating that it had been unaware of any sexual harassment that might have occurred.

Without determining who was telling the truth, the District Court entered judgment in favor of Taylor and Meritor. Its ruling read in part:

> If [Vinson] and Taylor did engage in an intimate or sexual relationship during the time of [Vinson's] employment with [the bank], that relationship was a voluntary one having nothing to do with her continued employment at [the bank] or her advancement or promotion at that institution.

Although it did not accept Vinson's claims of harassment and discrimination, the court noted that "the bank was without notice and cannot be held liable for the alleged actions of Taylor."

Vinson appealed, and the Court of Appeals for the District of Columbia reversed the District Court's decision. Drawing support from the EEOC's "Guidelines on Discrimination Because of Sex," the court ruled that even though Vinson suffered no tangible loss due to Taylor's behavior, she was clearly subject to hostile work environment harassment. The court also noted that the "voluntary nature of Vinson's submission to Taylor's demands had to be considered in light of the unequal power relationship between the two." That is, because Taylor had the power to threaten Vinson's position at work, she did not have the option of rejecting his demands if she wished to keep her job or advance in her career with the bank. Further, the appeals court held the bank absolutely liable for the actions of its "agent" Taylor. It denied Meritor a rehearing and remanded the case to the Supreme Court for a decision on the relevance of Title VII.

Legal Issues

Vinson v. Taylor came before the Supreme Court as *Meritor Savings Bank v. Vinson*, in which Meritor was now the petitioner and Vinson the respondent. The legal issue facing the court in this case was whether a claim of hostile work environment sexual harassment is a form of sex discrimination that is actionable under Title VII. Lawyers for Meritor contended that the language of Title VII was limited to economic or tangible forms of discrimination and that Congress, by using the phrase "terms, conditions, or privileges of employment" in the statute intended to confine legal coverage to these forms of discrimination only. Lawyers for Vinson argued that unwelcome sexual advances that create an offensive or hostile work environment violate Title VII. The court had to decide if sexual harassment is a form of sex discrimination even if it causes the victim no economic or tangible loss.

In forming its opinion in *Meritor*, the court also had to take into account a number of other legal issues: whether sexual harassment of any kind is a form of sex discrimination under Title VII; whether employers are, without exception, liable for sexual harassment by their employees; whether an employer's ignorance of harassment by its employees automatically relieves it of liability; whether the existence of an employer's sexual harassment grievance procedure exempts the employer from liability, even if that procedure is not used; whether the apparent consent of the victim to the harassment eliminates liability on the part of the harasser and the employer; and whether the victim's behavior, speech, or attire has any legal relevance.

Decision

Affirming the holding of the Court of Appeals, the Supreme Court found in favor of Vinson and recognized sexual harassment as illegal sex discrimination. More specifically, the ruling holds that any sexual harassment severe or pervasive enough to create a hostile work environment is actionable as sex discrimination, even if no economic or tangible loss results. Asserting that Title VII of the 1964 Civil Rights Act is intended to "strike at the entire spectrum of disparate treatment of men and women," the court compared sex discrimination to race discrimination and sexual harassment to racial harassment. The decision quoted the Eleventh Circuit Court's ruling in *Henson v. City of Dundee*, which states:

> Sexual harassment which creates a hostile or offensive environment for members of one sex is every bit the arbitrary barrier to sexual equality at the workplace that racial harassment is to racial equality. Surely, a requirement that a man or woman run a gauntlet of sexual abuse in return for the privilege of being allowed to work and make a living can be as demeaning and disconcerting as the harshest of racial epithets.

Associate Justice William Rehnquist delivered the opinion of the court, which addressed six points:

1) Hostile work environment sexual harassment is a form of sex discrimination actionable under the Title VII employment discrimination statute.

2) An employee's allegations are sufficient to establish a claim of hostile work environment sexual harassment.

3) Sexual harassment can be claimed even in the absence of any economic impact on the employee.

4) A correct evaluation of a claim of sexual harassment should consider whether the sexual advances were unwelcome, rather than whether the employee's subsequent participation in them was voluntary.

5) Evidence of an employee's sexually provocative speech or dress is not necessarily inadmissible in sexual harassment cases.

6) The mere existence of an employer's grievance procedure and a policy against discrimination, combined with an employee's failure to invoke that procedure, does not necessarily insulate the employer from liability, although employers are not absolutely liable for the actions of employees under every circumstance.

In his concurring opinion, Associate Justice Thurgood Marshall held that, while he fully agreed with the court's conclusion that workplace sexual harassment is illegal and violates Title VII, the court's opinion fails to specify the circumstances in which an employer is responsible for such conduct under Title VII. Marshall closed that gap, writing that an employer is responsible for acts of sexual harassment in the workplace where it knows or should have known of the conduct, unless it can show that it took immediate and appropriate corrective action.

Impact

The Supreme Court's ruling in *Meritor Savings Bank v. Vinson* firmly established the working definition of sexual harassment and identified the kind of conduct that is proscribed by the provisions set forth in Title VII. In doing so, the decision refers to the EEOC guidelines, which detail the kinds of workplace conduct that may be actionable under Title VII. These include "unwelcome sexual advances, requests for sexual favors, and other verbal or physical conduct of a sexual nature." *Meritor* also reaffirmed previous rulings by other courts that there are two types of sexual harassment—hostile work environment and quid pro quo. One of the subtler points made by the Court is that an employee's apparent consent to sexual activity does not necessarily negate a claim of sexual harassment. If the harasser has the power to fire, demote, or blackball an employee, or to deny raises, bonuses, or promotions, the employee's submission to his demands cannot be considered truly voluntary.

Meritor provides a valuable Supreme Court precedent for sexual harassment cases involving hostile work environment claims. Where many courts were reluctant to recognize this type of harassment, their rulings must now reflect the Supreme Court's recognition of hostile work environment harassment.

FRANKLIN V. GWINNETT COUNTY PUBLIC SCHOOLS, 112 S.CT. 1028 (1992)

The Supreme Court's first decision on Title IX sexual harassment affirmed the right of sexual harassment victims to sue their schools or other educational institutions for monetary damages. Title IX, which outlaws sex discrimination in education, makes no provision for the award of monetary damages to victims of sex discrimination. In *Franklin v. Gwinnett County Public Schools*, a high school student nevertheless sought damages for intentional sex discrimination arising from her sexual harassment and abuse by a coach/teacher at her school. As the case made its way to the Supreme Court, the lower courts dismissed the plaintiff's complaint, but the Supreme Court ultimately decided in favor of the student.

Background

From September 1985 to August 1989, Christine Franklin was a student at North Gwinnett High School, a public school in Gwinnett County, Georgia. Andrew Hill, a sports coach and teacher employed by the school district, started harassing Franklin at the beginning of her sophomore year (September 1986) and continued harassing her constantly until the spring of her junior year (April

1988). He engaged her in conversations about her sexual experiences with her boyfriend and asked her if she ever considered having sex with an older man. On one occasion, Hill forcibly kissed Franklin on the mouth in the school parking lot. Three times, he interrupted her classes and asked her teachers to excuse her, then took her to a private office where he subjected her to coercive sexual intercourse (rape). Although teachers and administrators at the school knew about Hill's harassment of Franklin and other female students, they did nothing to stop it and discouraged Franklin from pressing charges against Hill. Hill resigned from Gwinnett High School on April 14, 1988, on the condition that the school drop the matter. The school then closed its investigation.

Franklin filed a complaint with the Office of Civil Rights (OCR) of the United States Department of Education in August 1988. Because it receives federal funding, the school system is subject to Title IX prohibitions on sex discrimination in education, which are enforced by the education department. The OCR's investigation established that Hill's sexual harassment and the school's handling of it had violated Franklin's rights. Because Hill had resigned, however, the OCR determined that the district had come into compliance with Title IX, and it ended its investigation. On December 29, 1988, Franklin sued Gwinnett County School District, filing a complaint with the United States District Court for the Northern District of Georgia. The District Court dismissed Franklin's complaint on the ground that Title IX does not authorize the award of damages in cases of intentional sex discrimination. Franklin appealed, but the Court of Appeals for the Eleventh Circuit affirmed the District Court's decision. Both courts based their judgments on legal precedents that questioned the power of courts to award monetary damages in civil rights cases where the law does not explicitly permit such awards. Franklin then appealed to the Supreme Court.

Legal Issues

The question presented before the court was whether monetary damages can be awarded in cases brought to enforce Title IX. Franklin's counsel argued that the courts should permit the award of money damages to victims of Title IX sex discrimination because as a general practice they "presume the availability of all appropriate remedies unless Congress has expressly indicated otherwise." That is, unless Congress specifically prohibits the award of damages when it writes a law, the court assumes that the victims of those who break that law have the right to compensation, including monetary damages. There is no apparent reason for the courts to abandon this principle in the case of Title IX.

Attorneys for the Gwinnett County School District argued against the traditional practice of the courts, claiming that the award of such damages violates the constitutional separation of the federal government's legislative, executive, and judicial powers. If Congress did not provide for damages awards when it drafted Title IX, the courts do not have the power to expand the law by granting such awards. The school district also argued that the courts' traditional practice of awarding appropriate remedies should not apply to Title IX cases because the law was enacted under Congress' constitutional "spending clause" powers, by which "relief may frequently be limited to that which is equitable in nature, with the recipient of federal funds thus retaining the option of terminating such receipt in order to rid itself of an injunction." In other words, because the law passed by Congress gives schools in violation of Title IX several possible ways to make restitution, the courts cannot mandate that violators pay money damages.

Decision

Associate Justice Byron White delivered the opinion of the Supreme Court on February 26, 1992. The court rejected the Gwinnett County School District's arguments and reversed the decision of the Court of Appeals. First, it dismissed the separation of powers argument because accepting it would require the court to render judgments for which no remedy is available. The court reasoned that abdicating its authority to grant damages would do more harm to the separation of powers than would continuing its customary practice. Citing *Bell v. Hood*, the court also held that "Where legal rights have been invaded and a federal statute provides for a general right to sue for such invasion, federal courts may use any available remedy to make good the wrong done." In addition, the court found that the spending clause argument did not apply to *Franklin v. Gwinnett County Public Schools*. There was no limitation on the relief available to Franklin because the school district was fully aware both of the sexual harassment and of the possibility that it would have to pay damages.

In a concurring opinion, Associate Justice Antonin Scalia added that the right at issue in this case was one that Congress did not expressly (explicitly) create, but that the Supreme Court has previously found to be implied. Unless Congress expressly legislates limitations on the remedies available under a given law, it implies that it intends the full range of remedies to be applied. In sum, monetary damages are available in Title IX sexual harassment cases.

Impact

Franklin v. Gwinnett County Public Schools broke important new ground in the law of sexual harassment, confirming the right of plaintiffs to sue for monetary damages under Title IX. Following the logic established by earlier decisions in other types of cases, both by lower courts and itself, the Supreme Court affirmed the implied right of sexual harassment victims to be compensated for the violation of their Title IX rights.

JENSON V. EVELETH TACONITE CO., 842 F. SUPP. 847 (1993)

The first class-action Title VII sexual harassment case reached federal court late in 1992. Brought by a group of women mine workers in Duluth, Minnesota, the complaint argued that sexual harassment can be so pervasive, systematic, and severe that it discriminates against an entire group or class. The plaintiffs stated a claim of sex discrimination on the basis of hostile work environment sexual harassment and sought injunctive relief that would compel their employer to correct its discriminatory practices in hiring, job assignment, promotion, compensation, discipline, and training.

Background

Lois Jenson, Kathleen O'Brien Anderson, and Patricia Kosmach, the plaintiffs in *Jenson v. Eveleth Taconite Co.*, worked in the taconite ore mines of northern Minnesota. At Eveleth Mines, the workplace was filled with pornographic graffiti, photographs, cartoons, and other material that depicted women as sexual objects, often in an extremely degrading manner. Male employees felt free to display all kinds of sexual material wherever they chose and to make sexually derogatory comments whenever they chose. Although women miners also used "generally coarse" language at Eveleth, many of the men exceeded the bounds of acceptable vulgarity in their speech. They spoke of their female co-workers—and women as a group—in terms of their body parts, commented on the sex lives of the women, constantly boasted of sexual exploits, and frequently propositioned the women. Encompassing all women at Eveleth and beyond, the attitudes and speech of the male miners created a sexualized, male-oriented, and anti-female environment. Management also engaged in sex discrimination in hiring, job assignment, promotion, compensation, discipline, and training. Women composed only 3% to 5% of the mine's hourly workforce.

Lois Jenson, an employee of Eveleth Taconite since 1975 (the first year women were hired), filed a charge of sex discrimination with the EEOC and with the Minnesota Department of Human Rights in October 1984. In 1985, the Minnesota agency found that her charges probably warranted legal action, and in 1988 the EEOC granted her the right to file a sex discrimination suit against her employer. Also in 1988, Patricia Kosmach and Kathleen O'Brien Anderson filed claims with the EEOC and received right-to-sue notices. Seeking strength in numbers, Jenson and Kosmach joined forces and filed a class action complaint in 1988, then were joined by Anderson in 1989. After class certification hearings in May and June of 1991, the United States District Court of the District of Minnesota established the plaintiff class (recognized multiple plaintiffs as a single legal entity) in December 1991. Jenson, Kosmach, and Anderson were the first sexual harassment victims to gain the right to file a class action Title VII suit.

The three plaintiffs proceeded on behalf of their class, which included all women who had applied for hourly employment or had been employed in hourly jobs at Eveleth Mines since December 30, 1983, and who had been the victims of sex discrimination. Their case went to trial on December 21, 1992.

Legal Issues

Class-action suits had been used successfully in other discrimination cases, but never in a Title VII case involving sexual harassment. For the plaintiffs in *Jenson v. Eveleth Taconite Co.* to prove their case, they had to show that their employer engaged in a "pattern or practice of unlawful discrimination in various company policies." These practices must be shown to represent "disparate treatment" of women employees or to have a "disparate impact" on them; i.e., conditions and activities in the workplace must clearly be different for men and women. If they proved their case in this so-called liability phase of the trial, they would then move to the "recovery phrase," in which individual women established their right to compensation as members of the class.

Jenson et al. described the persistent discriminatory employment practices and pervasive sexual harassment that confronted women at Eveleth Mines. They argued that the sexual behavior at the mines represented a hostile work environment under the requirements laid out in *Henson v. City of Dundee*, asserting that management knew of the problem but had done nothing to correct it.

The defendants, meanwhile, attempted to show that the plaintiffs' "proof is either inaccurate or insignificant." They claimed that hiring practices at Eveleth Mines, as well as the terms and conditions of employment, were non-discriminatory. Eveleth Taconite further alleged that it immediately and consistently investigated and corrected sexual harassment whenever it knew or reasonably should have known of its existence.

Decision

Satisfied that the plaintiff class had proven a "pattern or practice" of sex discrimination at Eveleth Mines, the court ruled in favor of Jenson et al. It further found that the atmosphere described by the plaintiffs represented hostile work environment sexual harassment sufficient to constitute a Title VII violation. Evaluating the claim according to the *Henson* requirements, the court determined that it met each criterion. First, the court acknowledged that the women were members of a group protected by Title VII. Second, the court considered the welcome or unwelcome nature of the sexual activity, finding that it was unsolicited, unwelcome, and could be regarded as undesirable or offensive. Third, the court agreed that the harassment was based upon sex. Fourth, the court held that a reasonable woman would find the terms, conditions, or privileges of her employment adversely affected. Fifth, the court concluded that Eveleth was aware of the sexual harassment.

Impact

As the first sexual harassment class-action case to reach federal court, *Jenson* represents an important step toward eradicating workplace sexual harassment under Title VII. The court's decision integrated legal standards applicable to individual claims of sexual harassment with legal standards applicable to class-action claims of sex discrimination, producing a new legal standard applicable to class-action suits involving sexual harassment. It thus provided a positive expansion of sexual harassment law, in that individual plaintiffs may now join forces to bring their claims before the court.

LEHMANN V. TOYS 'R' US, INC., 132 N.J. 587 (1993)

For courts and legislatures, one of the thorniest questions of sexual harassment is determining when it has occurred. When does sexual behavior cross the line from acceptable to unacceptable, from ambiguous to offensive? Judges and lawmakers have found it impossible to list a single set of absolutely impermissible words and actions, for a behavior that seems perfectly legitimate in one context can seem completely improper in another. Sexual harassment is not the only realm where the law grapples with this conundrum. As they have dealt with various murky areas, the courts have developed the so-called reasonable person standard to evaluate all manner of potentially illegal activity. They attempt to assess legally ambiguous behavior according to the perceptions of average, "reasonable" people. When Title VII sexual harassment lawsuits began coming to trial, judges once again turned to that standard as a measure of right or wrong. But by its very nature, the reasonable person standard proved insufficient in cases that overwhelmingly involved female plaintiffs, because of the general tendency to view the male perspective as objective or normative.

On January 23, 1991, the Court of Appeals for the Ninth Circuit took an important first step toward resolving the reasonable person problem. Ruling in *Ellison v. Brady*, the court noted that cases charging sexual harassment should be judged from the standpoint of the "reasonable woman" rather than the reasonable person. That is, the courts should evaluate potential instances of sexual harassment in light of victims' feelings and a woman's perspective. The first court to suggest that sexual harassment judgments should weigh the different attitudes of men and women, the Ninth Circuit Court noted that the reasonable woman standard should by definition exclude the idiosyncratic or atypical opinions of the "unreasonable woman," just as the same holds true for the reasonable person standard. The ruling broadened the legal view of sexual harassment; offensive behavior or a hostile work environment can fall into the category of illegal sexual harassment even if harasser or employer does not think harassment occurred. Indeed, depending on the situation, the mere presence of a known harasser might create a hostile work environment, as it did in *Ellison*.

A Michigan appeals court also recommended the use of the reasonable woman standard, when it ruled in *Radtke v. Everett* in July 1991. That decision suggested that, in certain circumstances, a reasonable woman might find her work environment hostile as the result of even a single incident of sexual harassment. But it was not until the New Jersey Supreme Court handed down its decision in *Lehmann v. Toys 'R' Us, Inc.* that the legal definition of the reasonable woman standard was laid out in detail.

Background

Joining Toys 'R' Us in Bergen County, N.J., as a file clerk in August 1981, Theresa Lehmann received several promotions until she reached the position of purchase order management supervisor. Along with about 30 other employees, she came under the supervision of Don Baylous in November 1985, when the company hired him as director of purchasing administration. Baylous and Lehmann worked together closely, and Lehmann received favorable job evaluations and promotions until she became systems analyst for the purchasing department in September 1986. Shortly thereafter, she noticed Baylous's repeated touching and groping of other female employees. He first harassed Lehmann in January 1987, telling her to show a male employee her breasts in order to encourage him to do some work. He subsequently directed her to display her breasts to his new boss and commented on her figure in a vulgar manner.

Later that month, Baylous lifted Lehmann's shirt in front of his office window, suggesting she give the employees outside "a show." Lehmann fled the office in tears. On January 22, she complained to Bill Frankfort, Baylous's direct supervisor. Frankfort told Lehmann to handle the problem herself and not to report it to Howard Moore, the executive vice president in charge of purchasing. When Lehmann delivered a letter of complaint to Frankfort, he did not open it. On January 26, Eric Jonas, manager of employee relations, called Lehmann and another female employee into his office to discuss their complaints against Baylous. Lehmann detailed her complaints and listed other women who had been harassed by Baylous, then asked Jonas to stop her boss' behavior. Jonas assured her that management would speak with Baylous, but Baylous continued to sexually harass Lehmann.

The pattern of harassment, complaints, and management neglect continued until April 6, when Lehmann took her complaints to Moore. During this time Lehmann was twice offered and twice refused a transfer; when she gave Baylous two weeks' notice of her resignation on April 7, she again refused another offer of a transfer. When she confronted Baylous with her complaints, he was initially apologetic but then became angry. Lehmann left Toys 'R' Us without working her final two weeks. The company terminated its investigation, concluding that Baylous did not harass Lehmann.

In the Bergen County Law Division of New Jersey Superior Court, Lehmann brought a civil suit against Toys 'R' Us, Baylous, and the company's personnel director. She alleged hostile work environment sexual harassment in violation of New Jersey's Law Against Discrimination (LAD), along with a variety of torts. Following a six-day bench trial, the court dismissed all her claims except for a single charge of battery, for which it awarded Lehmann $5,000 in compensatory damages. Lehmann took her case to the Appellate Division, which reversed the ruling and remanded the case to the Supreme Court of New Jersey.

Legal Issues

In reversing the Law Division's decision, the Appellate Division could not agree on the legal standards that should be applied to determine whether hostile work environment sexual harassment had occurred, and if so, what standards should be used to determine the extent of Toys 'R' Us liability for Baylous' harassment. The two questions that thus faced the New Jersey Supreme Court were: 1) What are the standards for stating an actionable claim of hostile work environment sex discrimination? and 2) What is the scope of an employer's liability for a supervisor's conduct of hostile work environment sexual harassment?

Toys 'R' Us argued that it had conducted a thorough investigation of Lehmann's charges and had been unable to find any evidence that they were true. Lehmann disputed this, contending that the company failed to fulfill the obligations of its own sexual harassment policy and grievance procedure.

Decision

The court found in favor of Lehmann, noting that Toys 'R' Us had failed to adequately investigate or otherwise address Lehmann's complaints, whether or not they were true. Without resolving the dispute as to the facts of the case, the court went on to rule on the two legal issues before it. In answer to the first question, concerning the standards used to define hostile work environment sexual harassment, the court wrote that "we cannot deny legal redress to the victims of harassment and discrimination merely because the perpetrators may be unaware of the illegality of their conduct." Recognizing that the hostile work environment theory was still evolving, the court asserted the need for "a clear and intelligible legal standard." The decision went on to "announce a new test in the hope of creating a standard that both employees and employers will be able to understand and one that employers can realistically enforce." That standard reads as follows:

> To state a claim for hostile work environment sexual harassment, a female plaintiff must allege conduct that occurred because of her sex and that a reasonable woman would consider sufficiently severe or pervasive to alter the conditions of employment and create an intimidating, hostile, or offensive working environment.

When establishing the reasonable woman standard, the court noted that, in cases of the harassment of a male, the case should be considered from the perspective of a reasonable man. The court referred to the two standards as a type of "objective standard" appropriate in hostile work environment sexual harassment cases for a number of reasons. Such a standard focuses attention on the nature of the behavior rather than its outcome and provides flexibility in dealing with a still-developing legal concept. The reasonable woman standard, the court reasoned, also fosters the elimination of real discrimination and harassment because it filters out irrelevant claims based on personal idiosyncrasy. Asserting the necessity of considering gender differences in sexual harassment cases, the court wrote that "The reasonable person standard glosses over that difference . . . and it also has a tendency to be male-biased."

The second part of the *Lehmann* ruling addressed the question of employer liability. The court held that when an employee raises a hostile work environment discrimination claim against a supervisor, the employer is strictly liable in all cases for equitable damages, that is, for repayment of the victim's economic losses. However, employers are not automatically liable to pay additional compensatory relief. An employer's liability for these damages depends on the facts of the case, and in most cases a strong argument can be made for employer liability. Employers may be liable because the authority given supervisors by employers helps those inclined to sexual harassment to carry out their crimes, and because the existence of a hostile work environment suggests employer negligence. Finally, an employer is liable for punitive damages if the plaintiff can prove that its actions directly exacerbated hostile work environment sexual harassment.

Sexual Harassment

Impact

The Supreme Court of New Jersey took a bold stride forward in the battle against sexual harassment when it adopted a gender-specific test for hostile work environment harassment. The court recognized the inherent differences in male and female perspectives on the issue of sexual harassment in the workplace, and established a precedent of respect for those differences.

HARRIS V. FORKLIFT SYSTEMS, INC., 114 S.CT. 367 (1993)

On November 9, 1993, the United States Supreme Court handed down its decision in *Harris v. Forklift Systems, Inc.*, a hostile work environment sexual harassment case. The decision broadened the legal definition of sexual harassment by establishing that harassment may be actionable even if it does not cause serious psychological harm or other injury to the victim.

Background

Teresa Harris was employed by Forklift Systems in Nashville, Tennessee, as a rental manager from April 22, 1985, until October 1, 1987. During the course of her employment, she experienced constant sexual harassment by Charles Hardy, the president of the company. Hardy continually mocked and ridiculed Harris with dirty jokes, lewd comments, and sexual innuendo. He frequently humiliated and insulted her in the presence of clients and other employees, most of whom were male, referring to women—and Harris in particular—as stupid. He suggested they negotiate her raise in a motel room and asked Harris and other female employees to reach into his front pants pockets for coins. Hardy also liked to throw objects on the ground and ask female employees to pick them up, and he frequently made comments about their clothing.

The constant harassment made Harris's job stressful and unpleasant. Anxious and emotionally upset, she cried frequently. She began to drink heavily, and her relationship with her children became strained. When Harris complained to Hardy in August 1987, he expressed surprise that she was offended by his "jokes" and promised to stop. These assurances convinced Harris to stay on the job, but the harassment resumed in September. Hardy continued to humiliate Harris in front of her co-workers, even suggesting that she had secured one account by promising sexual favors to a customer. Shortly after that incident, on October 1, Harris picked up her paycheck and quit Forklift Systems.

Harris filed a Title VII action against her former employer, claiming that Hardy's behavior produced an "abusive work environment" for her because she was a woman. The United States District Court for the Middle District of Tennessee dismissed her suit, finding that, while questionable, Hardy's conduct did not represent sexual harassment. Admitting that Hardy was a crude man who indisputably demeaned his female employees, the court agreed that a reasonable woman would find his actions offensive. However, the judge wrote, "Although Hardy may at times have genuinely offended [Harris], I do not believe that he created a working environment so poisoned as to be intimidating or abusive to [Harris]." Harris appealed, but the Court of Appeals for the Sixth Circuit affirmed the District Court's ruling. The case then went to the Supreme Court.

Legal Issues

In reviewing *Harris*, the Supreme Court sought to resolve a conflict among the lower courts as to whether hostile work environment harassment is actionable under Title VII only if it "seriously affect[s] an employee's psychological well-being or lead[s] the plaintiff to suffer injury." While the Sixth Circuit followed precedents set in such cases as *Rabidue v. Osceola Refining Co.*, other circuits followed *Ellison v. Brady* and other precedents in holding that serious psychological harm is not required to prove Title VII cases. In *Meritor Savings Bank v. Vinson*, the Supreme Court itself required only that hostile work environment sexual harassment be "sufficiently severe or pervasive to alter the conditions of the victim's employment and create an abusive working environment." It did not require that an "abusive working environment" cause emotional or other injury to the victim.

Decision

Standing by *Meritor*, the Supreme Court reversed the Sixth Circuit's ruling in *Harris*. The court expanded on its earlier decision, defining the "sufficiently severe or pervasive" hostile work environment harassment covered by Title VII to include "discriminatory intimidation, ridicule and insult." Title VII does not require proof of extreme emotional distress; it applies even before harassment becomes so bad that it causes the victim to suffer a nervous breakdown. Writing for the court, Justice Sandra Day O'Connor held that even an abusive work environment that does not seriously affect employees' psychological well-being can and often will detract from employees' job performance, discourage employees from remaining on the job, or keep them from advancing in their careers. Harassment that falls into this category violates Title VII.

Impact

The *Harris* decision made it easier for victims of hostile work environment sexual harassment to prove Title VII sex discrimination. Under its wider definition of sexual harassment, victims need not wait for their situation to deteriorate to an extreme degree before they can file a winnable Title VII claim. As a result, the ruling has the potential to reduce the damage done by sexual harassment by stopping it at an earlier or milder stage.

CHAPTER 3

CHRONOLOGY

1830s

- As the Industrial Revolution gains momentum, greatly increased numbers of women start working outside the home, particularly in the textile mills of New England.

1835

- Printers in Boston conduct a campaign of intimidation to force women typesetters out of their jobs.

1846

- Periodicals such as *The Factory Girls' Album*, the *Nashua Gazette*, and the *Voice of Industry* document the problem of sexual harassment of "factory girls."

1855

- In Callaway County, Missouri, a slave named Celia is hanged after murdering the master who repeatedly raped her.

1873

- Louisa May Alcott publishes a novel entitled *Work*, which, like her story "How I Went Out to Service," describes harassment by her employers when working as a domestic servant.

1875

- In *Croaker v. Chicago and Northwestern Railway Company*, a Wisconsin woman wins $1,000 in damages after being sexually harassed by a train conductor.

1890s

- Large numbers of women start working in the rapidly expanding retail sales industry.

Sexual Harassment

1914–18
- More than 12,000 American women enlist in the armed services during World War I.

1915
- Eighteen-year-old Carrie Davies, a Toronto housemaid, is acquitted after shooting her sexually abusive employer.

1918
- Figures released by the U.S. Bureau of Labor Statistics show that nearly 1.5 million women have joined the work force since 1911.

1919
- Passage of the 19th Amendment to the U.S. Constitution grants all American women the right to vote. The National Federation of Business and Professional Women's Clubs forms.

1935
- Trans World Airlines (TWA) hires the first "air hostesses," opening an entirely new field of "women's work."

1940
- According to U.S. Department of Labor statistics, less that 17% of married American women work outside the home. The work force includes a total of 12 million women.

1941– 45
- During World War II, hundreds of thousands of American women serve in the Women's Army Corps, Women Marines, Women's Army Air Corps, Navy WAVES and Cost Guard SPARS. By 1945, 19 million are employed in civilian jobs, many in traditionally male fields. When the war ends, millions of American women are laid off to open jobs for returning servicemen.

1960s
- Feminists introduce the term *sexual harassment* into the popular lexicon.
- The modern women's movement draws large numbers of women into the workforce.
- The sexual revolution makes sexuality an open part of daily life.

1964
- Congress passes the 1964 Civil Rights Act, signed by President Lyndon Johnson. The law includes Title VII, which prohibits employment discrimination on the basis of race, color, religion, national origin, and sex.

Chronology

- The Equal Employment Opportunity Commission (EEOC) is created.

1969
- The Department of Defense drafts its Human Goals Charter, which establishes a policy of equal respect for both sexes.

1972
- Congress passes the Equal Employment Opportunity Act, giving the EEOC the power the enforce Title VII.
- President Richard Nixon signs the Education Amendments of 1972, whose Title IX prohibits sex bias in educational institutions that receive federal funding.

1975
- Rulings in *Corne v. Bausch & Lomb, Miller v. Bank of America* and *Barnes v. Train* reject sexual harassment as a form of sex discrimination.

1976
- A lower court in Washington, D.C., recognizes quid pro quo sexual harassment as discrimination in its ruling in *Williams v. Saxbe.*
- *Redbook* magazine publishes the results of its pioneering survey, which found that 88% of its almost exclusively female readership have been sexually harassed.

1977
- In *Tomkins v. Public Service Electric & Gas Co.*, a New Jersey court refuses to recognize sexual harassment as sex discrimination.
- In *Alexander v. Yale University*, the first sexual harassment complaint to be filed under Title IX, a Connecticut Court rejects the plaintiff's case but rules that quid pro quo sexual harassment constitutes sex discrimination in education.
- The Washington, D.C., Circuit Court reverses a lower court ruling in *Barnes v. Costle* (formerly *Barnes v. Train*), accepting quid pro quo sexual harassment as sex discrimination.

1978
- President Jimmy Carter signs the Civil Service Reform Act, barring sex discrimination in federal employment.
- Lin Farley publishes *Sexual Shakedown: The Sexual Harassment of Women at Work.*
- Margaret Mead's "A Proposal: We Need Taboos on Sex at Work" appears in *Redbook.*

Sexual Harassment

1979

- The Ninth Circuit Court reverses *Miller v. Bank of America.*
- Hearings are held to investigate sexual harassment in the federal government. The White House Office of Personnel issues a directive prohibiting sexual harassment.
- Law professor Catherine A. MacKinnon publishes *Sexual Harassment of Working Women: A Case of Discrimination.*
- The United Nations adopts its Convention on the Elimination of All Forms of Discrimination Against Women.

1980

- Illinois becomes the first state to outlaw the sexual harassment of state employees.
- Under the leadership of chairwoman Eleanor Holmes Norton, the EEOC drafts its "Guidelines on Discrimination Because of Sex."
- *Brown v. City of Guthrie* cites the EEOC guidelines and establishes a legal precedent for claims of hostile work environment harassment.

1981

- *Bundy v. Jackson* concurs with EEOC guidelines on hostile work environment harassment.
- *Redbook* publishes its second reader survey, which finds that 85% of respondents have experienced harassment.
- The United States Merit Systems Protection Board and the Bureau of National Affairs publish the results of government studies of harassment.

1982

- The court's decision in *Henson v. City of Dundee* clarifies the legal definitions of quid pro quo and hostile work environment harassment.

1983

- *Katz v. Dole* further clarifies the concepts of quid pro quo and hostile work environment harassment.
- In *Toscano v. Nimmo*, Delaware District Court accepts a claim of discriminatory sexual harassment by an employee who did not receive the same consideration as a co-worker who participated in a sexual relationship with a supervisor.
- *Shellhammer v. Lewallen* establishes that sexual harassment by landlords or building supervisors violates the Fair Housing Act.
- Congress passes 42 U.S.C. § 1983, making it illegal for states to engage in any conduct that deprives individuals of their rights.

Chronology

1984

- The Council of Ministers of European Communities mandates that member states work to improve respect for women in the workplace.

1985

- The U.N. adopts the Nairobi Forward-Looking Strategies for the Advancement of Women.
The International Labour Organisation publishes its Equal Opportunities and Equal Treatment for Men and Women in Employment guidelines.

1986

- The European Communities Parliament adopts a resolution condemning sexual violence.
- Ruling in *Rabidue v. Osceola Refining Company*, a federal appeals court in Cincinnati rejects the notion of hostile work environment harassment.
- On June 19, the United States Supreme Court makes its first ruling on sexual harassment, equating it with sex discrimination and endorsing the hostile work environment principle in *Meritor Savings Bank v. Vinson*.

1988

- In *Broderick v. Ruder*, the court rejects a claim of discriminatory sexual harassment by an employee who did not receive the same consideration as a co-worker who participated in a sexual relationship with a supervisor.
- *Working Woman* publishes its sexual harassment survey of executives at Fortune 500 companies.
- Male students at the U.S. Naval Academy in Annapolis chain female midshipman Gwen Marie Dreyer to a urinal to taunt and photograph her.

1990

- Frances K. Conley, a professor of neurosurgery, resigns from her post at Stanford University in response to continual harassment of herself and her female students. She returns to work several weeks later, after the administration promises change.
- The EEOC updates its "Guidelines on Discrimination Because of Sex," adding regulations on how to define and prevent it.
- The Council of Ministers of the European Community issues a definition of sexual harassment to the community's member states.

1991

- The Department of Defense and the navy publish surveys on sexual harassment of servicemen and women. The Department of Defense directs all military service branches and academies to launch efforts to eliminate harassment.

- The Sixth U.S. Circuit Court of Appeals rules in *Robinson v. Jacksonville Shipyards* that obscene pinups posted in the workplace create a hostile work environment and thus constitute harassment.
- The Ninth U.S. Circuit Court of Appeals rules in *Ellison v. Brady* that sexual harassment must be evaluated from the standpoint of the reasonable woman.
- *Boston Herald* sportswriter Lisa Olson wins $500,000 from the New England Patriots football team for locker-room harassment by team members.
- President George Bush signs a compromise version of the 1991 Civil Rights Act, which he had previously vetoed.
- In *Jenson v. Eveleth Taconite*, the court decides the first class-action suit based on sexual harassment in favor of the plaintiffs.

September 10: Anita F. Hill, a law professor at the University of Oklahoma, submits a confidential affidavit to the Senate Judiciary Committee, charging that Supreme Court nominee Clarence Thomas sexually harassed her from 1981 to 1983, when he was her supervisor at the Department of Education and at the EEOC.

October 5: National Public Radio publicly reveals Hill's charges of sexual harassment against Thomas. The Senate Judiciary Committee is forced to postpone its vote on Thomas's nomination.

October 7: Hill holds a news conference, criticizing the Senate Judiciary Committee for failing to investigate her charges fully.

October 11–13: The Senate Judiciary Committee holds a special hearing to compile testimony from Hill, Thomas, and other witnesses. Thomas denies Hill's charges. Witnesses praise Thomas's character and attempt to discredit Hill. The American public is riveted to television coverage of the hearings.

October 15: The Senate Judiciary Committee approves Thomas's nomination. The Senate confirms him, 52-48.

1992

- The EEOC reports a 62% increase in the number of harassment complaints it received between 1991 and 1992.
- Stroh Brewery of Minnesota suspends a sexually suggestive advertising campaign after five women employees complain it contributes to a sexually hostile work environment.
- On February 26, the Supreme Court rules on *Franklin v. Gwinnett County Public Schools*, finding that victims of sexual harassment can sue their schools for monetary damages under Title IX of the Education Amendments of 1972.

Chronology

April: The Naval Investigative Service (NIS) and the navy's inspector general release reports on sexual harassment at the September 1991 convention of the Tailhook Association. The two reports reveal that 26 women, 14 of whom were junior officers, were abused at the convention. Claiming that officers refused to cooperate with their investigation, the reports name only two perpetrators and conclude that no formal charges should be filed.

June: On the 17th, the NIS releases the results of a follow-up investigation into Tailhook. The report states that 55 pages were deleted from the first report and expands original estimates of the number of women abused. Secretary of the Navy H. Lawrence Garrett is implicated as a witness to some of the misconduct. On the 18th, Garrett orders the navy and the Marine Corps to begin disciplinary proceedings against 70 unnamed officers and asks the Defense Department to take over the Tailhook investigation. On the 26th, President Bush meets with Lt. Paula Coughlin, the first woman to come forward with complaints about Tailhook. Garrett resigns, reportedly at the request of Secretary of Defense Richard B. Cheney.

July: Assistant Chief of Naval Operations Vice Admiral Richard M. Dunleavy retires at a reduced rank when it is discovered he witnessed abuse at Tailhook and did nothing to stop it.

September: The first part of the Pentagon's Tailhook report sharply criticizes the navy's investigations of the incident. Acting secretary of the navy Sean O'Keefe asks two of the admirals responsible for the investigations for their resignations and reassigns a third to lesser duties. The army launches an investigation into approximately 100 harassment claims made by women at the Army Aviation and Troop Command and the Army Reserve Personnel Center in St. Louis.

October: Senator Brock Adams (D-WA) terminates a bid for re-election amidst allegations of sexual harassment. Senator Daniel K. Inouye (D-HI) and Senator Dave Durenberger (R-MN) are also accused of harassment.

November: Ten women charge Senator Bob Packwood (R-OR) with sexual harassment between 1969 and 1980. The Senate Ethics Committee launches an investigation.

1993

- In April, the Pentagon releases its final report on the Tailhook scandal, directly implicating a total of 117 officers in the sexual abuse of 83 women and seven men, and citing 51 others for lying to investigators. Secretary of the Navy John H. Dalton appoints a Marine Corps lieutenant general and a navy vice admiral to take disciplinary action against the perpetrators. Only seven officers are disciplined before the statute of limitations on their violations runs out in September.

- Naval aviators in San Diego distribute obscene T-shirts targeting Representative Pat Schroeder (D-CO), a critic of sexual harassment in the military.

July: The New Jersey Supreme Court issues a landmark ruling in *Lehmann v. Toys 'R' Us, Inc.*, finding that courts should use the reasonable woman standard when evaluating sexual harassment suits.

October: The Senate Ethics Committee subpoenas Packwood's diaries. The senator refuses to turn them over.

November: The Supreme Court issues a unanimous ruling in *Harris v. Forklift Systems Inc.* broadening the definition of sexual harassment by asserting victims need not prove severe psychological harm in order to be covered by Title VII.

December: Concerned that Packwood is editing them, a federal district court judge seizes his diaries.

1994

- In an attempt to define acceptable and unacceptable behavior, the navy issues its "green-light, yellow-light, red-light" directive on sexual harassment.

February: The United States General Accounting Office issues a report on the prevalence of sexual harassment at military academies.

September: A San Francisco jury awards nearly $7 million in damages to Rena Weeks, a secretary who was harassed while working at the law firm of Baker & McKenzie.

December: To avoid a courtroom trial, the CIA agrees to pay $410,000 to Janine M. Brookner, a former Jamaica station chief, for sex discrimination. The agency prevented Brookner's career advancement after accepting charges of sexual harassment from subordinates whom she had disciplined.

1995

- In February, a male student at the University of Michigan is arrested after posting sexually violent e-mail messages concerning a female classmate.
- Packwood resigns from the Senate after the Ethics Committee finds him guilty of sexual harassment.

CHAPTER 4

BIOGRAPHICAL LISTINGS

The people profiled below have featured in the struggle against sexual harassment as victims, perpetrators, government officials or commentators. Because the list of those who have been publicly involved with the issue is so long, only selected persons could be included here.

Brock Adams, senator (D-WA). A long-time advocate of feminist causes, Adams was instrumental in passing women's health legislation. After the Hill-Thomas hearings, at least nine women charged him with sexual harassment dating back to 1988. He decided to cut short his 1992 reelection campaign as a result.

Louisa May Alcott, author. The author of *Little Women* also wrote two works that described her own experiences of sexual harassment when working as a live-in nurse: a story entitled "How I Went Out to Service" and a novel entitled *Work*.

Sarah Bagley, labor activist. During the 1840s, Bagley agitated on behalf of the thousands of young women who worked in the textile mills of Lowell, Massachusetts. She described the problem of sexual harassment in the May 15, 1846 issue of the *Voice of Industry*.

Joseph R. Biden, Jr., senator (D-DE). During the 1991 Hill-Thomas hearings, Biden chaired the Senate Judiciary Committee, which approved Thomas's nomination to the Supreme Court despite Hill's charges of sexual harassment.

Janine M. Brookner, CIA agent. One of the first women to reach the top levels of the CIA, Brookner sued the agency for sex discrimination in 1994. The case arose from harassment accusations made against her while serving as station chief in Jamaica. Although respected as a 24-year veteran of the covert operations directorate, Brookner lost a promotion as a result of the allegations. When she sued, investigators concluded the charges had no basis; the CIA settled her suit out of court, paying her $410,000.

Biographical Listings

George Bush, president of the United States. A Republican, Bush nominated the conservative Clarence Thomas to the Supreme Court. After national uproar about Thomas' alleged sexual harassment of Anita Hill, Bush signed the 1991 Civil Rights Act. The bill allowed sex discrimination cases to be tried before a jury, but put a cap on the size of the awards juries can make.

Jimmy Carter, president of the United States. In 1978, Carter, a Democrat, signed the Civil Service Reform Act, which barred sex discrimination in federal employment.

Celia, slave. In Callaway County, Missouri, Celia was hanged in December 1855 for murdering her sexually abusive master.

Richard B. Cheney, secretary of defense. Cheney oversaw the Pentagon during its probe of the Tailhook scandal. He reportedly forced Secretary of the Navy H. Lawrence Garrett III to resign when Garrett's role in the episode was uncovered.

Bill Clinton, President of the United States. In 1993, Paula Corbin Jones accused the president of sexually harassing her in a Little Rock hotel room in 1991. At that time, she was an Arkansas state employee and he was governor of Arkansas. In 1995 a federal court allowed Clinton to postpone any lawsuits related to Jones's claim until after he leaves office.

Frances K. Conley, professor of neurosurgery. After 25 years as a professor at Stanford Medical School, Conley resigned in 1990 in response to sexual harassment of herself and her students. She came to Stanford as an intern and chaired the faculty senate when she resigned. Conley said she had endured harassment during her entire Stanford career but did not report it out of fear for her job. She resumed her post after one of the harassers was removed as chairman of the department of neurosurgery.

Lieutenant Paula Coughlin, naval aviator. One of the women who was harassed at the Tailhook convention in 1991, Coughlin was the first to come forward publicly with charges against male aviators attending the event. Investigations of the scandal resulted in major changes to the navy's top command.

Mario Cuomo, governor of New York. In 1992, Cuomo established the Governor's Task Force on Sexual Harassment to address the problem of sexual harassment in the state. The task force was the first of its kind in the United States. Cuomo also proposed adding the "Sexual Harassment Prevention Act of 1993" to the state's human rights law.

Carrie Davies, housekeeper. In 1915, at the age of 18, Davies was acquitted of the murder of her sexually aggressive Toronto employer.

Dave Durenberger, senator (R-MN). In 1992, Durenberger was accused of sexual harassment. The case was resolved informally.

Lin Farley, author. In 1978, Farley published the first major book on sexual harassment, *Sexual Shakedown: The Sexual Harassment of Women at Work*.

Christine Franklin, high school student. In 1988 Franklin sued the Gwinnett County, GA, school district for damages after she was sexually harassed by Andrew Hill, her ninth-grade economics teacher. The case went to the Supreme Court, which ruled in 1992 that Title IX allows students to sue their schools for monetary damages if they can prove sex discrimination.

H. Lawrence Garret III, secretary of the navy. An attendee of the 1991 Tailhook convention, Garrett resigned as secretary of the navy after investigations revealed he witnessed sexual harassment at that event and failed to take disciplinary action.

Teresa Harris, forklift rental manager. Harris quit her job at the Nashville firm of Forklift Systems Inc. in 1987 and filed a Title VII sexual harassment suit against her former employer. The case ultimately went before the Supreme Court, which on November 9, 1993, unanimously ruled that victims of hostile work environment sexual harassment do not have to prove they have been severely psychologically harmed in order to be covered by Title VII. In February 1995, Forklift Systems agreed to set up a harassment policy and to pay Harris $151,435 plus interest, attorney's fees and costs.

Anita Hill, law professor, University of Oklahoma. When President George Bush nominated Clarence Thomas for the Supreme Court, Hill came forward with charges that Thomas had harassed her in the early 1980s, when she worked for him at the Department of Education and at the EEOC. She testified before the Senate Judiciary Committee in October 1991. Thomas denied Hill's charges and the committee approved his nomination. The hearings exposed sexual harassment as a major issue in public life.

Daniel K. Inouye, senator (D-HI). In the wake of the Hill-Thomas hearings, Inouye was one of several senators charged in separate incidents of sexual harassment.

Lois Jenson, mine worker. Suing her employer for hostile work environment sexual harassment, Jenson won the right to file a class-action suit on behalf of all women working at the site. The United States District Court in Minnesota decided that suit, *Jenson v. Eveleth Taconite Co.*, in favor of the class in 1993.

Lyndon B. Johnson, president of the United States. Johnson signed the Civil Rights Act of 1964, which included the measure known as Title VII. Title VII prohibits employment discrimination on the basis of race, color, national origin, religion, or sex. The courts have recognized sexual harassment as a form of Title VII sex discrimination.

Paula Corbin Jones, Arkansas state employee. In 1993, Jones made public her charges that President Bill Clinton sexually harassed her in 1991. At the time the alleged harassment took place, Clinton was the governor of

Arkansas. Jones claims that, while she was working at a state event in Little Rock, Clinton propositioned her in his hotel room. In 1995, a federal court prohibited her from taking Clinton to court until after he left office.

Theresa Lehmann, manager, Toys 'R' Us, Inc. After quitting her job as the result of continual sexual harassment by her supervisor, Lehmann filed suit against Toys 'R' Us. The case made its way to the Supreme Court of New Jersey, which, ruling in her favor in 1993, established the reasonable woman standard.

Catherine A. MacKinnon, law professor, University of Michigan. In 1979, MacKinnon published *Sexual Harassment of Working Women: A Case of Discrimination,* which is still considered one of the foremost books on the topic. She was one of the attorneys who argued *Meritor Savings Bank v. Vinson* before the Supreme Court in 1986.

Thurgood Marshall, Supreme Court associate justice. Marshall wrote a concurring opinion in *Meritor Savings Bank v. Vinson,* in which he asserted that employers are liable for sexual harassment in the workplace if they know or should know about it.

Margaret Mead, anthropologist. Mead published one of the earliest articles denouncing sexual harassment for a popular audience. "A Proposal: We Need Taboos on Sex at Work" appeared in the April 1978 issue of *Redbook.*

Richard M. Nixon, president of the United States. As president, Nixon signed the Education Amendments of 1972. The amendments included a provision called Title IX, which prohibits sex discrimination in education.

Eleanor Holmes Norton, EEOC chairman. Norton was instrumental in the formulation of the EEOC's 1980 "Guidelines on Discrimination Because of Sex." Updated in 1990, the guidelines are a vital tool for courts that handle Title VII sexual harassment cases.

Sandra Day O'Connor, Supreme Court associate justice. O'Connor wrote the decision in *Harris v. Forklift Systems Inc.,* announced by the Supreme Court on November 9, 1993. The decision defined sexual harassment, asserting that it exists whenever a "reasonable person" would be offended, even if its victims do not experience "severe psychological injury."

Sean C. O'Keefe, acting secretary of the navy. Under O'Keefe, the full extent of the 1991 Tailhook scandal was brought to light. A number of the navy's top officers resigned as a result of the investigation.

Lisa Olson, journalist. As a sports reporter for the *Boston Herald,* Olson attempted to interview members of the New England Patriots in their locker room after a 1990 football game. In 1991 she filed suit against the team, alleging that the players sexually harassed her. The team agreed to pay her $500,000 in damages.

Bob Packwood, senator (R-OR). In the wake of the Hill-Thomas hearings, more than 20 women who had worked with him from 1969 to 1980 charged

Packwood with sexual harassment. A well-known proponent of women's rights, he made several responses that admitted varying degrees of guilt but fell short of accepting responsibility. The Senate initially declined to remove Packwood from office but launched an investigation. Packwood resigned in 1995 when the results of the investigation were made public.

Ronald Reagan, president of the United States. While in office, Reagan signed the law identified as 42 U.S.C. § 1983. Section 1983 prohibits states and state officials from engaging in conduct that deprives any individual or group of its constitutional rights.

William Rehnquist, Supreme Court chief justice. In 1986, Rehnquist wrote the Supreme Court's decision in *Meritor Savings Bank v. Vinson*, in which the court ruled that hostile work environment sexual harassment is a form of Title VII sex discrimination.

Patricia Schroeder, congressional representative (D-CO). A senior member of the House Armed Services Committee, Schroeder has spoken out against sexual harassment in the military. She condemned navy commanders for failures of leadership during the Tailhook scandal and became the object of sexual ridicule by a number of junior officers and other sailors.

Clarence Thomas, Supreme Court associate justice. Nominated to the Supreme Court by President Bush, Thomas was accused of sexual harassment during his confirmation hearings before the Senate Judiciary Committee in 1991. The charges were made by law professor Anita F. Hill, who worked for Thomas in the early 1980s at the Department of Education and at the EEOC. Thomas denied the charges and the Senate confirmed him. The case sparked wide interest among the American public in the topic of sexual harassment.

Rena Weeks, legal secretary. In September 1994, a San Francisco jury awarded Weeks nearly $7 million in punitive damages as a result of her harassment by attorney Martin Greenstein while she was employed at the law firm of Baker & McKenzie.

Byron White, Supreme Court associate justice. In 1992, White wrote the court's decision in *Franklin v. Gwinnett County Public Schools*, in which a high school student sued her school over sexual harassment by her ninth-grade economics teacher. The court found that, under Title IX, students can sue for damages stemming from sex discrimination, including sexual harassment.

PART II

GUIDE TO FURTHER RESEARCH

CHAPTER 5

HOW TO RESEARCH SEXUAL HARASSMENT

A huge amount of information on sexual harassment has become available since the Hill-Thomas hearings of 1991. Researchers and students interested in learning about the topic have a wide range of resources at their disposal, including books and journals, magazine and television archives, law libraries, audiovisual material computer databases, and material published by government agencies, private organizations, and professional consultants.

For general research on the topic of sexual harassment, the card catalogs at school, university, and public libraries are the obvious place to start. In addition to listings under "sexual harassment," subject headings such as women's rights, labor law, psychology, or sexuality can turn up relevant publications of all descriptions. In turn, these can point the way to other valuable resources. Books and articles may contain lists of organizations and agencies that deal with sexual harassment issues; they may also contain extensive bibliographies of other publications on the topic. Newspapers and magazines preserved on microfilm or microfiche offer first-hand information on events as they occurred. They can be located through reader's indexes that list articles by topic. On-line, researchers can access many university libraries and other electronic databases for bibliographic information, abstracts of essays, and even complete articles.

Government agencies are also an excellent source of information. Many of these publish booklets, newsletters, or even whole books covering the many aspects of sexual harassment. The U.S. Government Printing Office offers a monthly catalog of documents published by all the federal government's departments; copies may be ordered from the GPO. Many libraries keep an archive of government documents on hand. The officers or employees of government agencies such as the EEOC or state human rights commissions may also be available for interviews, or may be able to refer researchers and students to other people or organizations that may be of assistance.

Private and professional organizations can provide up-to-the minute research and information on sexual harassment. Some of these organizations are structured simply to conduct research into the topic, others assist victims of sexual harassment in their efforts to stop harassment or file lawsuits. Again, the officers or members of such organizations may consent to face-to-face or telephone interviews that can provide a glimpse of the front lines in the fight against sexual harassment. Professional sexual harassment consultants may be able to provide similar assistance; many produce their own training programs or use other standardized training packages that are sometimes highly informative.

LEGAL RESEARCH

For the uninitiated, legal research can be frustrating and confusing. However, since much of the history of sexual harassment is legal history, research in law books, journals, and databases can turn up a tremendous amount of extremely useful information. Several good guides to legal research for the layperson are available, including a book called *Legal Research: How to Find and Understand the Law*, by Steve Elias, and a 2½-hour video entitled *Legal Research Made Easy*, both published by Nolo Press in Berkeley, California. Most large public libraries contain a set of local, state, and federal statute books, while county law libraries (maintained by many U.S. counties) offer free access to volumes containing case rulings. Law school libraries are the most complete resource for legal research, but many do not allow individual researchers who are not attorneys to use them.

Researchers and students can find information on sexual harassment law in law reviews—generally published by law schools—legal treatises, digests, and other such secondary sources. Law review articles are an excellent source of information. They provide analyses of the cases and of the current trends in the law. In addition, review articles provide illuminating commentary and pose critical questions; articles frequently offer greater insight into a particular case than the actual text of the case does. Secondary sources can also provide a researcher with the statute number of a law or the citation number of a case, an invaluable piece of information in legal research.

Equipped with a statute number or citation number, researchers can access primary sources of legal information, the volumes in which laws and court decisions are officially recorded. Those in search of federal or state statutes can refer to the United States Code or to the relevant state code volume. The statute number or citation number indicates where the law or case can be found.

Federal statute numbers indicate which "title" (volume) and which "section" contain the law—the Civil Rights Act, 42 U.S.C. 2000, can be found in section 2000 of title 42 of the United States Code. States use several similar systems. Likewise, the text of federal court rulings is published in several volumes, depending on jurisdiction: the United States Reports, the Supreme Court Reporter, the Federal Reporter (Second Series), or the Federal Supplement. Most states publish their own reporters, containing decisions made in the state courts. Each federal or state case is assigned a citation number that indicates which volume contains the ruling, which court heard the case, and on what page of the volume the listing begins. For instance, 111 S.Ct. 367, the citation for *Harris v. Forklift Systems,* indicates that the case is listed in volume 111 of the Supreme Court Reporter (S.Ct.), starting on page 367.

Computerized research tools can greatly facilitate a search for legal information on sexual harassment. One news service, All News, continually searches for articles on a designated topic and notifies the researcher each time a relevant article is found. Two other services, Westlaw and Lexis, dominate computerized legal research. Researchers enter queries for information using key words such as "sexual harassment" and are guided to the appropriate listings in the vast directories. From there, they can retrieve the most recent cases, articles, statutes, and other legal information on developments in the law and legal issues facing the courts.

CHAPTER 6

_____

ANNOTATED BIBLIOGRAPHY

BIBLIOGRAPHIES

"Appendix G: Survey of Literature" and "Appendix H: Annotated Bibliography," in *Sexual Harassment in the Federal Workplace: Is It Problem?* Washington, DC: U.S. Office of Merit Systems Review and Studies, 1981. These two bibliographies offer extensive information and sources concerning sexual harassment in the federal government and in general; 125 abstracts are presented, covering a multitude of published and non-published works.

Cook, Earleen H. and Joseph Lee Cook. *Sexual Harassment on the Job.* Monticello, IL: Vance Bibliographies, 1980. A bibliographical guide listing pre-1980 sources on sexual harassment of women and sex discrimination in the workplace.

Crocker, Phyllis. "Annotated Bibliography on Sexual Harassment in Education." *Women's Rights Reporter*, vol. 7, p. 91. A 15-page bibliography with citations on sexual relationships between students and teachers in universities and colleges. Also lists sources on sexual harassment in high school and the workplace.

Jacobs, Daniel J. "Sexual Harassment and Related Issues: A Selective Bibliography," in *Record of the Association of the Bar of the City of New York*, December 1991, vol. 15, p. 930. Cites pre-1990 sources on sexual harassment and related topics.

McCaghy, Dawn M. "Sexual Harassment: A Guide to the Literature," in *Reference Services Review*, Spring 1983, vol. 11, p. 59. Written for reference librarians; a citation of 28 sources on sexual harassment in the workplace and academia.

———. *Sexual Harassment: A Guide to Resources.* Boston: G.K. Hall, 1985. A major annotated bibliography of approximately 300 pre-1985 sources of information on the topic of sexual harassment, with author, title and subject indices.

Miller, Alan V. *Sexual Harassment of Women in the Workplace: A Bibliography with Emphasis on Canadian Publications*, Public Administration Series, Bibliography P-801. Monticello, IL: Vance Bibliographies, 1981. Extensive bibliography on sexual harassment in the workplace, with a special focus on the problem as it appears in the Canadian workplace.

Ross, Lynn C. *Career Advancement for Women in the Federal Service: An Annotated Bibliography and Resource Book*. New York: Garland Reference Library of Social Science, 1993. A monograph dealing with sexual harassment, pay equity, affirmative action, and other issues affecting women in the workplace.

Schneider, Ann. "Sexual Harassment Brief Bank and Bibliography." *Women's Rights Law Reporter*, Fall 1985, vol. 8, p. 267. An 18-page bibliography with citations addressing sexual harassment before 1985.

Siegel, Deborah L. *Sexual Harassment Research and Resources: A Report*. New York: National Council for Research on Women, 1992. Lists pre-1992 sources on sexual harassment and sex discrimination in the workplace.

Stanton, Beth Lynn. "Sexual Harassment: A Bibliography." *Capital University Law Review*, 1981, vol. 10: 3, p. 697. A listing of more than 200 citations spanning 1874 to 1980, including historical documents and contemporary articles from scholarly journals and law reviews.

Storrie, Kathleen and Pearl Dykstra. "Bibliography on Sexual Harassment." *Resource for Feminist Research*, December 1981/January 1982, vol. 10, p. 25. Consists of approximately 250 newspaper, magazine, and scholarly journal citations as well as books, articles, book reviews, and court rulings pre-1981.

Wallentine, Kenneth R. "Sex for Success: A Pathfinder for Sexual Harassment Actions," appears in *Legal Reference Services Quarterly*, 1990, vol. 10, p. 67. A pre-1990 bibliography of legal resources regarding sexual harassment.

BOOKS

EDUCATION—GENERAL INFORMATION

American Association of University Women Educational Foundation and Harris/Scholastic Research. *Hostile Hallways: The AAUW Survey on Sexual Harassment in America's Schools*. Washington, DC: The Foundation, 1994. Addresses the occurrence of sexual harassment in education; derived from studies and surveys in the field.

Annotated Bibliography

Cole, Elsa Kircher, ed. *Sexual Harassment on Campus: A Legal Compendium.* Washington, DC: National Association of College and University Attorneys, 1990. A study of the occurrence of sexual harassment on college and university campuses.

DeSole, Gloria and Leonore Hoffman, eds. *Rocking the Boat, Academic Women and Academic Processes.* New York: Modern Language Association of America, 1981. A slender volume that presents the stories of eight women who challenged university administrations on such unfair treatment as sexual harassment.

Douglas, Joel M., ed. *The Faculty Life-Cycle, A Legal Perspective: Proceedings, Fifteenth Annual Conference, May 1987.* New York: Baruch College National Center for the Study of Collective Bargaining in Higher Education and the Professions, 1987. A discussion of laws, including sexual harassment laws, pertaining to faculty members in higher education.

Dziech, Billie Wright and Linda Weiner. *The Lecherous Professor: Sexual Harassment on Campus.* Boston: Beacon Press, 1984; Urbana: University of Illinois Press, 1990 (2nd edition). An investigation of the sexual harassment of female college students by male faculty members, with prescriptions for change.

Ehrhart, Julie K. and Bernice R. Sandler. *Campus Gang Rape: Party Games?* Washington, DC: Project on the Status and Education of Women, Association of American Colleges, 1985. Focuses on the violence and abuse suffered by women students at the university level.

Larkin, June. *Sexual Harassment: High School Girls Speak Out.* Toronto: Second Story Press, 1994. Accounts of sexual harassment from female students at the high school level.

Lewis, John F., Susan C. Hastings and Anne C. Morgan. *Sexual Harassment in Education.* Topeka, KS: National Organization on Legal Problems of Education (NOLPE), 1992. Discusses sexual harassment in education, with a focus on the legalities.

Paludi, Michele Antoinette, ed. *Ivory Power: Sexual Harassment on Campus.* Albany: State University of New York Press, 1990. A comprehensive and informative collection of scholarly articles and firsthand accounts addressing the many complex issues of sexual harassment, its definition, prevention, perpetrators, victims, and impact.

Peer Harassment: Hassles for Women on Campus. Washington, DC: Project on the Status and Education of Women, Association of American Colleges, 1988. Discusses college and university sexual harassment of female students by their male classmates.

Riggs, Robert Owen, Patricia H. Murrel, JoAnn C. Cutting and the U.S. Office of Educational Research and Improvement, et al. *Sexual Harassment in Higher Education: From Conflict to Community.* Washington, DC: George

Washington University, School of Education and Human Development, 1993. Covers the various aspects of sexual harassment in academe.

Roiphe, Katie. *The Morning After: Sex, Fear, and Feminism on Campus*. Boston: Little, Brown, 1993. A skeptical look at the furor over sexual coercion on college campuses, including a chapter on sexual harassment.

Stein, Nan, Nancy Marshall and Linda R. Tropp. *Secrets in Public: Sexual Harassment in Our Schools*. Wellesley, MA: Wellesley College Center for Research on Women, 1993. Results of a study by *Seventeen* magazine for the Center for Research on Women in conjunction with the NOW Legal Defense and Education Fund.

Till, Frank J. *Sexual Harassment: A Report on the Sexual Harassment of Students*. Washington, DC: National Advisory Council on Women's Educational Programs, 1980. Case studies of sexually harassed college students.

Whitbread, Anne, Dale Spender and Elizabeth Sarah, eds. *Learning to Lose: Sexism and Education*. London: Women's Press, 1980. Includes "Female Teachers are Women First: Sexual Harassment at Work," an essay by Elizabeth Sarah on the sexual harassent of female teachers.

EDUCATION—HANDBOOKS AND MANUALS

Adams, Aileen and Gail Abarbanel. *Sexual Harassment on Campus: What Colleges Can Do*. Santa Monica, CA: Santa Monica Hospital Medical Center, 1988. A guide to administration techniques for preventing recurrent sexual harassment on college campuses.

Gittins, Naomi, ed. *Sexual Harassment in the Schoools: Preventing & Defending Against Claims*. Alexandria, VA: National School Boards Association, 1993. Outlines the kinds of sexual harassment claims made against schools and advises educators and administrators on how to avoid sexual harassment lawsuits.

Hughes, Jean and Bernice R. Sandler. *In Case of Sexual Harassment: A Guide for Women Students. We Hope It Doesn't Happen to You, But If It Does*. Washington, DC: Project on the Status and Education of Women, Association of American Colleges, April 1986, 9 pp. A "how-to" guide for women, providing comprehendsive information on the definition of sexual harassment. Incorporates prevention strategies and guidelines for taking action against perpetrators.

Shoop, Robert J. and Debra L. Edwards. *How to Stop Sexual Harassment in Our Schools: A Handbook and Curriculum Guide for Administrators and Teachers*. Boston: Allyn & Bacon, 1994. A guidebook advising teachers and administrators on what they can do to stop sexual harassment.

Stein, Nan D. and Lisa Sjostrom. *Flirting or Hurting: A Teachers' Guide on Student-to-Student Sexual Harassment in Schools (Grades 6–12)*. Washington,

DC: National Education Association, 1994. A teacher's guide developed by the National Education Association on how to address and prevent the sexual harassment of one student by another.

ESSAY COLLECTIONS

Bingham, Shereen G., ed. *Conceptualizing Sexual Harassment as Discursive Practice*. Westport, CT: Praeger, 1994. A collection of essays on the sexual harassment of women, from women's personal reactions to the Hill-Thomas hearings to sexual harassment as a theme in performance art.

Bose, Christine and Glenna Spitze, eds. *Ingredients for Women's Employment Policy*. Albany: State University of New York Press, 1987. Papers presented at a 1985 conference held at the State University of New York at Albany.

Brant, Clare and Yun Lee Too, eds. *Rethinking Sexual Harassment*. Boulder, CO: Pluto Press, 1994. A collection of essays discussing feminist theories of sexual harassment.

Buchwald, Emilie, Pamela R. Fletcher and Martha Roth, eds. *Transforming a Rape Culture*. Minneapolis: Milkweed Editions, 1993. A collection of essays featuring the viewpoints of such feminists as Andrea Dworkin, Gloria Steinem, and others.

Grauerholz, Elizabeth and Mary A. Koralewski, eds. *Sexual Coercion: A Sourcebook on Its Nature, Causes, and Prevention*. Lexington, MA: Lexington Books, D. C. Heath, 1991. Articles exploring the complexities of sexual harassment, rape, child molestation, prostitution, and other sex crimes.

Morrison, Toni, ed. *Re-Racing Justice, En-Gendering Power*. New York: Pantheon Books, 1992. Essays on the Hill-Thomas hearings, with an introduction by the Nobel prize–winning novelist.

Wall, Edmund, ed. *Sexual Harassment: Confrontations and Decisions*. Buffalo, NY: Prometheus Books, 1992. An anthology of scholarly essays on the definitions, causes, policies, and legal responses to sexual harassment in the university and in the workplace.

Wekesser, Carol, Karin L. Swisher and Christina Pierce. *Sexual Harassment*. San Diego, Greenhaven Press, 1992. Targeted at teenage readers, a collection of excerpts from books, newspapers and magazine articles that reflect different viewpoints on the controversial issue of sexual harassment.

FICTION

Conford, Ellen. *To All My Fans, With Love* (young adult). Boston: Little, Brown, 1982. Fifteen-year-old Sylvia runs away because of her foster father's advances.

Creamer, Elizabeth. "Sexual Harassment and Confessional Poets." *Kenyon Review*, Fall 1994, vol 16: 4, p. 139. A short story that portrays sexual harassment in the university setting.

Crichton, Michael. *Disclosure*. New York: Alfred A. Knopf, 1994. A best-selling novel about sexual harassment of a promising young male executive by his female boss, who accuses him of sexual harassment when he refuses her advances. The story was also made into a movie of the same name.

Cruise, Beth. *Kelly's Hero* (young adult). Toronto: Maxwell Macmillan Canada, 1993. The victim of sexual harassment by her boss, a young woman decides whether to ask for help from her boyfriend.

Hall, Lynn. *The Boy in the Off-White Hat* (young adult). New York: Scribner, 1984. A 13-year-old girl is plagued by the advances of an overly-friendly businessman during her summer job at a horse ranch.

Jacoby, Alice. *My Mother's Boyfriend and Me* (young adult). New York: Dial Books, 1987. A teenage girl is confused and upset because of advances made by her mother's 26-year-old boyfriend.

Mamet, David. *Oleanna*. New York: Random House, 1993. A play depicting the sexual relationship between a college professor and his female student. The work was also made into a movie of the same name.

Mazer, Norma Fox. *Out of Control* (young adult). New York: Morrow Junior Books, 1993. A boy joins his two best friends in attacking a female classmate and finds that his life will never be the same again.

O'Hanlon, Jacklyn. *Fair Game* (young adult). New York: Dial Press, 1977. A 15-year-old girl is terrified when she learns that her new stepfather, who is an alcoholic, has sexually threatened young girls.

Pfeffer, Susan Beth. *The Ring of Truth* (young adult). New York: Bantam Books, 1993. A 16-year-old girl lives a protected life with her grandmother until an elected official makes drunken advances that lead to a public scandal.

Thesman, Jean. *Summerspell* (young adult). New York: Simon & Schuster Books for Young Readers, 1995. The story of a 15-year-old girl who has trouble with her brother-in-law and runs away to her family's summer cabin.

GENERAL INFORMATION

Adelson, Melissa. *Shifting Identifications and Antediluvian Politics in Anita Hill's "15 Minutes."* Amherst, MA (s.n.), 1992. A detailed examination of the Hill-Thomas hearings, with a concentration on Hill's role and impact.

Black, Beryl. *Coping with Sexual Harassment*. New York: Rosen Publishing Group, 1992. A study of incidents of sexual harassment experienced by young people and suggestions for dealing with these situations.

Annotated Bibliography

Brent, Harriet Jacobs and Linda Brent, eds. *Incidents in the Life of a Slave Girl, Written by Herself.* Cambridge, MA: Harvard University Press, 1990. The autobiography of a slave woman from 1818 to 1845, covering sexual abuse by her master and subsequent escape and flight to freedom.

Brock, David. *The Real Anita Hill: The Untold Story.* New York: Free Press, 1993. An indictment of Anita Hill and her motives for charging Clarence Thomas with sexual harassment, from the perspective that Thomas is innocent.

Brownell, Arlene. "Re-Visions of Psychology: Feminism as a Paradigm of Scientific Inquiry." Paper presented at the 94th annual convention of the American Psychological Association, Washington, DC, August 22–26, 1986, 9pp. The author addresses the critical need for psychologists to understand gender-specific concerns of women clients within a larger social context of sex discrimination.

Chrisman, Robert and Robert L. Allen, eds. *Court of Appeal: The Black Community Speaks Out on the Racial and Sexual Politics of Clarence Thomas vs Anita Hill.* New York: Ballantine Books, 1992. A look at African-American opinions on the racial and sexual implications of the Hill-Thomas hearings and the impact the hearings have had on the community.

Danforth, John C. *Resurrection: The Confirmation of Clarence Thomas.* New York: Viking, 1994. The Republican senator from Missouri offers a pro-Thomas view of the Supreme Court nominee and of the Senate Judiciary Committee's investigation into the Hill-Thomas affair.

Deaux, K. *The Behavior of Women and Men.* Monterey, CA: Brooks/Cole Publishing, 1976. A study of the similarities and differences between the sexes, how these traits present themselves and the issues that arise from them.

Eisaguirre, Lynne. *Sexual Harassment* (Contemporary World Issues Series). Santa Barbara, CA: ABC-Clio, 1993. A comprehensive reference on the topic, including citations and discussions of sexual harassment lawsuits, facts, statistics, accounts, a short but handy annotated bibliography, and a list of pertinent organizations.

Gay, Kathlyn. *Right and Respect: What You Need to Know about Gender Bias and Sexual Harassment.* Brookfield, CT: Millbrook Press, 1995. This study discusses sexual harassment in school and in the workplace and examines the differences between harassment and sex discrimination.

Gilligan, C. *In a Different Voice.* Cambridge: Harvard University Press, 1982. The seminal work on traditional psychology's misperceptions of women's development and perspective, including female attitudes toward sexuality and sexual behavior.

Gochros, Harvey L., Jean S. Gochros and Joel Fischer, eds. *Helping the Sexually Oppressed.* Englewood Cliffs, NJ: Prentice-Hall, 1986. Focuses on relif for those who have been sexually harassed and oppressed.

Gooche, Terry, Jr. *What Is Sexual Harassment?* Nashville, TN: Winston-Derek Publishers, 1993. A general overview of the topic.

Hanmer, Jalna and Mary Maynard, eds. *Women, Violence and Social Control.* Highlands, NJ: Humanities Press International, 1987. How women are victimized in and by society and what can be done to amend it.

Italia, Bob. *Anita Hill: Speaking Out Against Harassment.* Edina, MN: Abdo & Daughters, 1993. A study of the life of Anita Hill and her role in bringing the issue of sexual harassment into public view. Includes a point-by-point summary of the arguments presented at the Senate Judiciary Committee's hearings on Hill's charges against Supreme Court nominee Clarence Thomas.

Kelly, Liz. *Surviving Sexual Violence.* Minneapolis: University of Minnesota Press, 1988. Explores the psychological impact of sexual harassment in addition to rape and sex crimes.

Kreps, Gary L., ed. *Sexual Harassment: Communication Implications.* Cresskill, NJ: Hampton Press, 1993. Analyzes the shades and hues of the language of sexual harassment; discusses how it occurs in different settings such as universities and offices, and offers suggestions and advice about how to identify and prevent it.

Landau, Elaine. *Sexual Harassment.* New York: Walker and Company, 1993. Discusses sexual harassment in a variety of forms, in school and at work, and offers suggestions on identifying and coping with it. Written primarily for a grade 8 through 12 readership.

Langelan, Martha J. *Back Off! How to Confront and Stop Sexual Harassment and Harassers.* New York: Fireside, 1993. An examination of the nature of harassment in various settings, using anecdotes of victims' responses.

Lightle, Juliana and Elizabeth H. Doucet. *Sexual Harassment.* Menlo Park, CA: Crisp Publications, 1992. A general introduction to and overview of the subject.

Macooby, E. *The Psychology of Sex Differences.* Stanford, CA: Stanford University Press, 1974. Explores sex differences from a psychological point of view.

Mayer, Jane and Jill Abramson. *Strange Justice: The Selling of Clarence Thomas.* Boston: Houghton-Mifflin, 1994. Two *Wall Street Journal* reporters investigate the facts and origins of the Hill-Thomas hears.

Minson, Jeffrey. *Questions of Conduct: Sexual Harassment, Citizenship, Government.* London: Macmillan, 1993. Delves into the many questions surrounding sexual harassment, including those of political ethics, social justice, liberalism and socialism.

Morewitz, Stephen John. *Sexual Harassment and Social Change in American Society*. San Francisco: Austin & Winfield, 1994. Provides an historical backdrop for sexual harassment in the United States and addresses changes in attitude and in law and legislation.

Morris, Celia. *Bearing Witness: Sexual Harassment and Beyond—Everywoman's Story*. Boston: Little, Brown, 1994. Interviews with women from diverse backgrounds on their personal experiences with sexual harassment and their growing awareness and indignation in the wake of the Hill-Thomas hearings.

Pattinson, Terry. *Sexual Harassment*. London: Futura, 1991. A general introduction to the topic.

Phelps, Timothy M. and Helen Winternitz. *Capitol Games: Clarence Thomas, Anita Hill, and the Story of a Supreme Court Nomination*. New York: Hyperion, 1992. Reviews the politics of the Hill-Thomas hearings.

Ribaudo, Linda and Darlyne Walker. *Sexual Harassment*. Syracuse, NY: New Readers Press, 1994. A general introduction to and overview of the topic.

Sexual Harassment Policy Survey of Fifty States and the District of Columbia. Upland, PA: Diane Publishing, 1991. The results of a survey on sexual harassment that covered all 50 states.

Sexual Harassment—Issues and Answers: A Guide for Education, Business, Industry. Washington, DC: College and University Personnel Association, 1986. Questions raised about and solutions suggested for sexual harassment as it emerges in education and in business.

Stanko, Elizabeth A. *Intimate Intrusions: Women's Experiences of Male Violence*. London: Routledge and Kegan Paul, 1985. Examines the sexual harassment and victimization of women in society and discusses the ways in which the police and others in positions of authority deal with complaints from women.

Star, Kelly Gillmore. *The Effects of Sexual Harassment on Performance*. Los Angeles: California School of Professional Psychology, 1984. Ph.D. Thesis that studies the impact of sexual harassment on job performance.

Sumrall, Amber Coverdale and Dena Taylor, eds. *Sexual Harassment: Women Speak Out*. Freedom, CA: Crossing Press, 1992. Women tell their stories of sexual harassment.

Swisher, Karin, ed. *At Issue: What Is Sexual Harassment?* San Diego, CA: Greenhaven Press, 1995. An introduction to and overview of the subject.

Trager, Oliver ed. *Sexual Politics in America*. New York: Facts On File, 1994. A compilation of recent newspaper and magazine articles on a variety of gender-related topics including sexual harassment, specifically the Hill-Thomas hearings, charges against Senator Bob Packwood, the Tailhook Scandal, the Supreme Court's ruling on *Harris v. Forklift Systems Inc.*, and the harassment of reporter Lisa Olson in a New England Patriots locker room.

University of Kentucky Behavioral Research Aspects of Safety and Health Working Group. *Answers and Feedback for Trouble in the Training Room Exercise.* Lexington, KY: University of Kentucky Institute for Mining and Minerals Research, 1988. Discusses results of a study of the impact of sexual harassment on worker safety and health.

Weil, Marie, Michelle Hughes and Nancy R. Hooyman. *Sexual Harassment and Schools of Social Work: Issues, Costs and Strategic Responses.* Alexandria, VA: Council on Social Work Education, 1994. Varying opinions about and approaches to coping with sexual harassment.

Wekesser, Carol, Karin L. Swisher and Christina Pierce, eds. *Sexual Harassment.* San Diego, CA: Greenhaven Press, 1992. A reference source on the subject, consisting of a collection of essay excerpts expressing contrasting viewpoints.

Wise, Sue and Liz Stanley. *Georgie Porgie: Harassment in Everyday Life.* London: Pandora, 1987. Discusses women's experiences of sexual harassment in day-to-day living.

Wiseman, J., ed. *The Sociology of Sex.* New York: Harper & Row, 1976. Includes an article by J. Rosenbauer discussing ways to objectively identify sexual harassment.

Wolfe, Leslie R. *Women, Work and School: Occupational Segregation and the Role of Education.* Boulder, CO: Westview Press, 1991. Reviews presentations given at a 1988 seminar of the Center for Women and Policy Studies.

GENERAL HANDBOOKS AND MANUALS

Bouchard, Elizabeth. *Everything You Need to Know About Sexual Harassment.* New York: Rosen Publishing Group, 1994. How to recognize sexual harassment and how to find help.

Conway, Jim and Sally Conway. *Sexual Harassment No More.* Downers Grove, IL: InterVarsity Press, 1993. Discusses how to stop the sexual harassment of women.

Deane, Nancy H., ed. *Sexual Harassment—Issues & Answers: A Guide for Education, Business and Industry.* Washington, DC: College and University Personnel Association, 1986. Discusses the various aspects of sexual harassment that arise within the specific contexts of business and education and offers tools for problem solving.

Friedman, Joel, et al. *Sexual Harassment.* Deerfield Beach, FL: Health Communications, 1992. A handbook describing what sexual harassment is and isn't, what its effects are, and what readers can do about it.

Annotated Bibliography

Gomez-Preston, Cheryl and Randi Reisfeld. *When No Means No: A Guide to Sexual Harassment.* Secaucus, NJ: Carol Publishing Group, 1993. A clear-cut, no-nonsense look at sexual harassment; where and when to draw the line.

Hodgson, Harriet W. *Power Plays: How Teens Can Pull the Plug on Sexual Harassment.* Minneapolis: Deaconess Press, 1993. A guide for teenagers on the avoidance of sexual harassment.

Katz, Montana and Veronica Vieland. *Get Smart! What You Should Know (But Won't Learn in Class) About Sexual Harassment and Sexual Discrimination.* New York: Feminist Press, 1993. A guide to sexual harassment, describing what it is, how and when it occurs, and what can be done about it.

Largen, Mary Ann. *What to Do If You're Sexually Harassed.* Arlington, VA: New Responses, 1980. Advice for those who have been sexually harassed. Outlines what actions can be taken to fight back and not be victimized.

Largen, Mary Ann and A. McAdem. *The Sexually-Harassed Woman: A Counselor's Guide.* Arlington, VA: New Responses, 1980. Advice for therapists and other professionals helping victims to cope with the emotional fallout of sexual harassment.

Maltz, Wendy (with illustrations by Carol Arian). *The Sexual Healing Journey: A Guide for Survivors of Sexual Abuse.* New York: HarperCollins, 1991. A supportive, empowering, and informative book for victims of sexual abuse. Includes stories, anecdotes, and data on the varying forms sexual abuse can take, including sexual harassment.

Mari, with Judy Hanlon, ed. *Into the Silence: Healing the Wounds of Abuse.* Victor, NY: White Oak Publications, 1992. How to overcome the physical, emotional, and psychological repercussions of sexual abuse. Sexual harassment is addressed in addition to other topics.

Meyer, Mary Coeli. *Sexual Harassment.* Princeton, NJ: Petrocelli Books, 1981. A definition of the problem of sexual harassment and a description of personal and legal tools with which to respond.

Miramontes, David J. *How to Deal with Sexual Harassment.* San Diego, CA: Network Communications, 1983. A handbook on how to cope with sexual harassment.

Nitschke, Martha. *How to Fight Sexual Harassment and Win: A Woman's Guide to Survival in a Man's World.* Wilmington, NC: Enterpress, 1993. A handbook for women who seek to empower themselves against the threat of sexual harassment.

Norman, John C., Jr., Elizabeth R. Norman and Price Vedder with Kaufman & Kammholz (legal editor). *Practical Steps to Help Prevent Sexual Harassment.* Louisville, KY: Personnel Policy Services, 1992. What to do to prevent sexual harassment from occurring in the workplace.

Okonkwo, Vincent. *Sexual Harassment and What You Must Know*. Apapa, Lagos, Nigeria: OVC International, 1985. A guide providing practical information about sexual harassment.

Paludi, Michele Antoinette and Richard B. Barickman. *Academic and Workplace Sexual Harassment: A Resource Manual*. Albany: State University of New York Press, 1991. A manual on the sexual harassment of women in general, at the workplace and in academe.

Powell, Elizabeth. *Talking Back to Sexual Pressure: What to Say . . . To Resist Persuasion . . . To Avoid Disease . . . To Stop Harassment . . . To Avoid Acquaintance Rape*. Minneapolis: CompCare Publishers, 1991. Advice on how to assert and protect individual sexual rights.

Quina, Kathryn and Nancy L. Carlson. *Rape, Incest and Sexual Harassment: A Guide for Helping Survivors*. New York: Praeger, 1989. Describes the crippling effect of sexual abuse and offers information on how to counsel victims.

Reed, Robert D. and Danek S. Kaus. *Sexual Harassment: How and Where to Find Facts and Get Help*. San Jose, CA: R & E Publishers, 1993. How to deal with sexual harassment when experiencing it. Who and where to turn to for advice and support.

Reischl, Dennis K. and Ralph R. Smith. *Federal Manager's Guide to Preventing Sexual Harassment*, 2nd ed. Huntsville, AL: FPMI Communications, 1992. A handbook on what supervisors can do to stop harassment of federal government employees.

———. *Sexual Harassment and the Federal Employee*, 2nd ed. Huntsville, AL: FPMI Communications, 1992. Handbook on preventative measures federal government employees can take to deter sexual harassment.

Sanford, Wendy, ed. *Fighting Sexual Harassment: An Advocacy Handbook*. Boston: Alyson Publications and the Alliance Against Sexual Coercion, 1981. Practical information on personal, organizational, and legal responses to sexual harassment.

Strauss, Susan and Pamela Espeland. *Sexual Harassment and Teens: A Program for Positive Change—Case Studies, Activities, Questionnaires, Laws, Guidelines, Policies, Procedures, Resources, and More*. Minneapolis: Free Spirit Publications, 1992. Addresses sexual harassment of teenagers.

Stuart, Matthew B. *Sexual Harassment and Training Guide*. Santa Ana, CA: Pacific Services, 1991. Provides a description of sexual harassment and outlines methods for its prevention.

HELPING PROFESSIONS

Fortune, Marie M. *Is Nothing Sacred? When Sex Invades the Pastoral Relationship*. New York: Harper & Row, 1989. A minister discusses a case of sexual

Annotated Bibliography

harassment of six female parishoners by their pastor, in which the victims pressed charges. Includes a general examination of sexual harassment by clergymen and its impact on parishioners.

Callan, Susan Rose. *Sexual Exploitation in the Treatment Setting: A Study of Female Survivors—A Project Based Upon an Independent Investigation.* Northampton, MA: Master's thesis in typescript for Smith College School of Social Work, 1987. A scholarly study of sexual harassment of patients by psychotherapists.

INTERNATIONAL

Center for Women's Global Leadership. *Gender Violence and Women's Human Rights in African.* New Brunswick, NJ: Center, 1994. Focuses on the status of women in Africa, examining how they are sexually victimized.

Davidson, Marilyn J. and Jill Earnshaw, eds. *Vulnerable Workers: Psychosocial and Legal Issues.* New York: John Wiley and Sons, 1991. Part of a series on occupational stress, this volume addresses discrimination in the British workplace against the handicapped, people with AIDS, women, and people of color. Labor laws and legislation are noted and sexual harassment is addressed.

Global Feminist Workshop to Organize Against Traffic in Women, with Kathleen Barry, Charlotte Bunch and Shirley Castley. *International Feminism Networking Against Female Sexual Slavery: Report of the Global Feminist Workshop to Organize Against Traffic in Women, Rotterdam, the Netherlands, April 6–15, 1983.* New York: Distributed by the International Women's Tribune Centre, 1984. Notes and reports from a workshop on the prevention of sexual abuse and sex discrimination.

Hadley, Ernest C. and George M. Chuzi. *Sexual Harassment: Federal Law.* Arlington, VA: Dewey Publications, 1994. Focuses on workplace and other sexual harassment of women in Great Britain and describes the state of sexual harassment law there.

Herbert, Carrie M. H. *Talking of Silence: The Sexual Harassment of Schoolgirls.* London: Palmer Press, 1989. Case studies of sexual harassment in Great Britain, along with case studies of child molestation and other sex crimes.

Miles, Rosalind (with illustrations by Christine Roche). *Danger! Men at Work.* London: Futura, 1983. Discusses and illustrates sex discrimination against British women in the workplace and in education, and the varying kinds of sexual harassment that take place.

Walby, Sylvia, ed. *Gender Segregation at Work.* Milton Keynes, England: Open University Press, 1988. Reveals the disparity in men's and women's pay in Great Britain and discusses sex discrimination and sexual harassment.

Sexual Harassment

Webb, Susan L. *Shockwaves: The Global Impact of Sexual Harassment.* New York: MasterMedia, 1994. An international historical overview of sexual harassment, with statistical data and background on legal activity in various nations. Abundant information on the United States.

LEGAL—GENERAL INFORMATION

Anderson, Stephen F. and James W. Mercer. *Intent vs. Impact.* Washington, DC: Bureau of National Affairs, 1989. A legal perspective on the definition of sexual harassment.

Greenbaum, Marcia L. "Sexual Harassment and Arbitration," an article in *Proceedings of New York University 35th Annual National Conference on Labor, June 9–11, 1982.* New York: New York University Press, 1983, p. 379. Arbitration methods for handling sexual harassment cases.

Kirk-Westerman, Connie et al. *Sexual Harassment Policy Initiatives in Large American Cities.* Norman: University of Oklahoma Government Resources, 1988. Overview of state policies intended to prevent sexual harassment.

Lindemann, Barbara and David Kadue. *Sexual Harassment in Employment Law.* Washington, DC: Bureau of National Affairs, 1992. A summary of the application of employment law in cases of sexual harassment in the workplace.

MacKinnon, Catharine A. *Sexual Harassment of Working Women: A Case of Sex Discrimination.* New Haven: Yale University Press, 1979. An exploration of the discriminatory nature of sexual harassment, based on interviews with victims and observers. The seminal book in the field argues that harassment represents discrimination because of its basis in gender differences and inequality.

Maschke, Karen J. *Litigation, Courts, and Women Workers.* New York: Praeger Publications, 1989. Focuses on the degree to which the legal and civil rights of women in the workplace are upheld in the court system.

Mezey, Susan Gluck. *In Pursuit of Equality: Women, Public Policy, and the Federal Courts.* New York: St. Martin's Press, 1992. Discusses women's rights from the standpoint of public policy and the law, including the right to protection against sexual harassment.

Pellicciotti, Joseph M. *Title Seven Liability for Sexual Harassment in the Workplace,* Public Employee Relations Library No. 69. Washington, DC: Journal of the International Personnel Management Association, 1988. Notes on employee rights in the workplace, and what legal protection and coverage employees have. Details corporate liability in sexual harassment suits.

86

Rafter, Nicole Hahn and Elizabeth Anne Stanko, eds. *Judge, Lawyer, Victim, Thief: Women, Gender Roles, and Criminal Justice*. Boston: Northeastern University Press, 1982. A collection of 16 papers written by law professors and professionals, grouped according to topics such as women as defendants and prisoners, women as professionals, women as victims, and women as offenders. The essays suggest that prevalent attitudes about men and women continue to have a damaging impact on how women are perceived by experts in many fields, including criminology, victimology, and law.

Sexual Harassment Litigation 1993, Litigation and Administrative Practice Course Handbook. Series: Vol. 463. New York: Practising Law Institute, 1993. A summary of sexual harassment cases heard by the courts in 1993.

Tong, Rosemarie. *Women, Sex, and the Law*. Totowa, NJ: Rowman and Allanheld, 1984. From a feminist perspective, the author examines the origins of unequal treatment of women in Anglo-American law, with reference to topics such as pornography, domestic abuse, rape, prostitution, and sexual harassment.

Ver Ploeg, Christine. *Labor Arbitration of a Sexual Harassment Case*. Minneapolis: National Practice Institute, 1986. Legal aspects of labor arbitration in cases of sexual harassment.

LEGAL—HANDBOOKS AND MANUALS

Aggarwal, Arjun Prakash. *Sexual Harassment in the Workplace*. Toronto: Butterworth Legal Publications, 1987. Addresses common occurrences of sexual harassment in the workplace.

Atwood, Hollye Stolz and National Business Institute. *Preventing and Defending Sexual Harassment Claims in Missouri*. Eau Claire, WI: National Business Institute, 1992. A study of cases of sexual harassment brought against Missouri businesses, and the implications of their outcomes.

Chan, Anja Angelica. *Women and Sexual Harassment: A Practical Guide to the Legal Protections of Title VII and the Hostile Environment Claim*. New York: Haworth Press, 1994. Informs women of their legal rights regarding sexual harassment, including recent developments in law and legislation that further protect them.

Eskenazi, Martin and David Gallen. *Sexual Harassment: Know Your Rights!* New York: Carroll & Graf, 1992. Legal questions, answers, and resources for victims of sexual harassment.

Friedman, Scott E. *Sex Law: A Legal Sourcebook on Critical Sexual Issues for the Non-Lawyer*. Jefferson, NC: McFarland and Company, 1990. An explanation in lay terms of the laws surrounding sexual issues such as harassment.

Hauck, Vern E., Ph.D. *Arbitrating Sexual Harassment Cases*. Washington, DC: Bureau of National Affairs, 1995. Information for attorneys and businesses on the arbitration of sexual harassment cases.

Lawyers Cooperative Publishing Staff. *Handling Sexual Harassment Cases: Practice Guide*. Rochester, NY: Lawyers Cooperative Publishing Co., 1993. Instructions to attorneys on how to handle sexual harassment cases.

Schlei, Barbara L. and David D. Kadue. *Sexual Harassment in Employment Law*. Washington, DC: Bureau of National Affairs, 1992. An overview of employment laws covering sexual harassment, whom they protect and to what degree.

Shilling, Dana. *Redress for Success: Using the Law to Enforce Your Rights as a Woman*. Toronto: Viking Penguin Canada, 1985. Informs women of their legal and civil rights and explains how to use the law to protect those rights.

Zack, Arnold M. *Grievance Arbitration: Issues on the Merits in Discipline, Discharge, and Contract Interpretation*. New York: Macmillan, 1989. A reference for lawyers, with information on the arbitration of sexual harassment cases.

WORKPLACE—GENERAL INFORMATION

Aggarwal, Arjun Prakash. *Sexual Harassment: A Guide for Understanding and Prevention*. Salem, NH: Butterworth U.S., Legal Publishers, 1992. Defines workplace sexual harassment, provides legal information and discusses how to prevent it.

Alder, Jonathan L. *Sexual Harassment Discrimination & Other Claims*. Salem NH: Butterworth, U.S., Legal Publishers, 1991. Focuses on the legalities of sexual harassment.

Backhouse, Constance and Leah Cohen. *The Secret Oppression: Sexual Harassment of Working Women*. Toronto: Macmillan of Canada, 1978. Examines the dynamics and issues of sexual harassment as it is experienced by women in the workplace.

———. *Sexual Harassment on the Job*. Englewood Cliffs, NJ: Prentice-Hall, 1981. A study of sexual harassment in the United States and Canada.

Baxter, Ralph H., Jr. and Lynn C. Hermle. *Sexual Harassment in the Workplace*, 3rd Edition. New York: Executive Enterprises Publications, 1989. An overview of sexual harassment in the workplace.

Berger, Gilda. *Women, Work, and Wages*. New York: Franklin Watts, 1986. A study of sexual harassment of women professionals in the United States workforce.

Betz, Nancy E. and Louise F. Fitzgerald. *The Career Psychology of Women*. San Diego, CA: Academic Press, 1987. Includes information on the attitudes of working women toward sexuality and sexual harassment in the workplace.

Annotated Bibliography

Bose, Christine. *Hidden Aspects of Women's Work*. New York: Praeger, 1987. An investigation of the subtle, unspoken issues faced by women in the workplace, including sexual harassment.

Boxer, Barbara and Nicole Boxer. *Strangers in the Senate: Politics and the New Revolution of Women in America*. Washington, DC: National Press Books, 1994. Examines the political impact of women's emergence in Congress and in other areas of politics, with information on sex discrimination and sexual harassment.

Conte, Alba. *Sexual Harassment in the Workplace: Law & Practice*. New York John Wiley and Sons Law Publications, 1994. The legalities of on-the-job sexual harassment.

Crull, Peggy. *The Impact of Sexual Harassment on the Job: A Profile of the Experiences of 92 Women*. New York: Working Women's Institute, 1979. Results of a study of 325 women who reported sexual harassment on the job to the Working Women's Institute.

Farley, Lin. *Sexual Shakedown: The Sexual Harassment of Women on the Job*. New York: McGraw Hill, 1978. The first major book published on the topic. Includes interviews, case studies, and in-depth research on sexual harassment of women in traditional and non-traditional work settings.

Gutek, Barbara A. *Sex and the Workplace*. San Francisco: Jossey Bass Publishers, 1985. This overview of sexual issues in the workplace includes extensive background material on sexual harassment.

Hadjifotiou, Nathalie. *Women and Harassment at Work*. London: Pluto Press, 1983. Details the sexual harassment of women in the workplace.

Holcombe, Barbara Jean and Charmaine Wellington. *Search for Justice: A Woman's Path to Renewed Self-Esteem from the Fear, Shame, and Anger of Sexual Harassment and Employment Discrimination*. Walpole, NH: Stillpoint Publishing, 1992. An account of the author's experience of sexual harassment as a female oil worker, with advice to readers in similar positions.

Jacobson, Aileen. *Women in Charge: Dilemmas of Women in Authority*. Toronto: Van Nostrand Macmillan, 1985. A survey of the problems, including sexual harassment, faced by women in management positions.

Kanter, Rosabeth Moss. *Men and Women of the Corporation*. New York: Basic Books, 1977. This general overview of the relationship between the sexes in the corporation includes coverage of sexual harassment.

Kearney, Katherine Grace and Thomas I. White. *Men and Women at Work*. Hawthorne, NJ: Career Press, 1994. Among other issues of workplace sexuality, addresses the problem of sexual harassment.

Matthaei, Julie A. *An Economic History of Women in America: Women's Work, the Sexual Division of Labor, and the Development of Capitalism*. New York: Schocken Books, 1982. A history of women's roles in the American workplace from colonial times to the 1980s and the evolution of attitudes toward working women.

McCann, Nancy Dodd and Thomas A. McGinn. *Harassed: 100 Women Define Inappropriate Behavior in the Workplace.* Homewood, IL: Business One Irwin, 1992. Women recount stories of their sexual harassment. Also includes general background on federal and state measures to combat it.

Neugarten, Dail Ann and Jay M. Shafritz, eds. *Sexuality in Organizations.* Oak Park, IL: Moore Publishing, 1980. This collection of scholarly essays includes several articles on the problem of and responses to sexual harassment in the workplace.

Nieva, V. F. and B. A. Gutek. *Women and Work: A Psychological Perspective.* New York: Praeger, 1981. Approaches the subject of sexual harassment and other women's workplace issues from a psychological perspective.

Northwestern National Life Employee Benefits Division. *Fear and Violence in the Workplace: A Survey Documenting the Experience of American Workers.* Minneapolis: Northwestern National Life, 1993. A report on the findings of a survey of employees on their fears. The conditions that create violence, stress, and harassment in the workplace are discussed.

Pringle, Rosemary. *Secretaries Talk: Sexuality, Power, and Work.* London: Verso, 1989. Women working as secretaries give first-person accounts of the sexual harassment they have experienced at work.

Read, Sue. *Sexual Harassment at Work.* Faltham, Middlesex, England: Aanglu Paperbacks, 1982. Sexual harassment is explored in 30 verbatim accounts of sexual harassment on the job. The evidence cited is from both Britain and the United States.

Rifking, Lawrence and Loretta F. Harper. *Sexual Harassment in the Workplace: Men and Women in Labor.* Dubuque, IA: Kendall-Hunt Publishing Co., 1991. Discusses the roles of men and women in workplace sexual harassment.

Russell, Diana E. H. *Sexual Exploitation: Rape, Sexual Child Abuse, and Workplace Harassment.* Beverly Hills, CA: Sage Publications, 1984. An investigation of sex crime in the state of California.

Sedley, Ann and Melissa Benn. *Sexual Harassment at Work.* New York: St.Martin's, 1988. A summary of the issues arising from sexual harassment on the job.

Segrave, Kerry. *The Sexual Harassment of Women in the Workplace, 1600 to 1993.* jefferson, NC: McFarland, 1994. An encompassing guide to the history of sexual harassment, from the 17th century to the present.

Stellman Ann J. *Women's Work, Women's Health.* New York: Vintage Books, 1977. Deals with the health aspects of sexual harassment and other workplace concerns.

Annotated Bibliography

Stolz, Barbara Ann. *Still Struggling: America's Low-Income Working Women Confronting the 1980s.* Lexington, MA: Lexington Books, 1985. Case studies of sexual discrimination against low-income working women in the United States.

Vroman, Georgine M., Dorothy Burnham and Susan G. Gordon, eds. *Women at Work: Socialization Toward Inequality.* New York: Gordian Press, 1988. The cultural roots of sexual inequity in the workplace. Includes a report on the 1985 Genes and Gender V Conference at Hunter College in New York City.

Walby, Sylvia, ed. *Gender Segregation at Work.* Milton Keynes, England: Open University Press, 1988. Reveals pay disparity between men and women in Great Britain, along with sexual discrimination and harassment.

Williamson, Jane. *Equality in Librarianship: A Guide to Sex Discrimination Issues.* Chicago: American Library Association, 1981. Report on the sexual harassment of women librarians.

Working Women United Institute. *Sexual Harassment on the Job: Questions and Answers.* New York: Working Women United Institute, 1975.

WORKPLACE—HANDBOOKS AND MANUALS

Aaron, Titus E. with Judith A. Isaksen. *Sexual Harassment in the Workplace: A Guide to the Law and a Research Overview for Employers and Employees.* Jefferson, NC: McFarland, 1993. A reference source on the legal aspects of sexual harassment, for both employers and employees.

Agonito, Rosemary. *No More "Nice Girl": Power, Sexuality and Success in the Workplace.* Holbrook, MA: Bob Adams, 1993. Advises women on what they can do to protect and defend themselves against sexual harassment in the workplace while at the same time achieving success in their careers. Also covers sex roles and sex discrimination laws and policies.

Baridon, Andrea P. and David R. Eyler. *Working Together: The New Rules and Realities for Managing Men and Women at Work.* New York: McGraw-Hill, 1994. How to manage personnel in light of personal relations between the sexes, sex differences, and sexual harassment.

Bravo, Ellen and Ellen Cassedy. *The 9 to 5 Guide to Combating Sexual Harassment: Candid Advice from 9 to 5, the National Association of Working Women.* New York: John Wiley and Sons, 1992. Practical advice from 9 to 5, also known as the National Association of Working Women, an organization dedicated to fighting sexual harassment.

Colatosti, Camille and Elissa Karg, introduction by Diana Kilmury. *Stopping Sexual Harassment: A Handbook.* Detroit: Labor Notes, 1992. Preventative measures to take against sexual harassment in the workplace.

91

Collier, Rohan. *Combating Sexual Harassment in the Workplace.* Bristol, PA: Open University, 1995. What to do to eliminate sexual harassment in the workplace.

Cooper, Ken. *Stop It Now.* St. Louis: Ken Cooper Communications, 1985. An overview for employees and managers of the causes, indicators, results, and prevention of sexual harassment in the workplace.

Diamond, Robin, L. Feller and N.F. Russo. *Sexual Harassment Action Kit.* Washington, DC: Federation of Organizations for Professional Women, 1981. A pamphlet containing prevention steps, an employee action checklist, and a list of options for the victim. Includes an annotated list of publications and organizations that deal with sexual harassment.

Freedman, Warren. *The Employment Contract: Rights and Duties of Employers and Employees.* Westport, CT: Quorum Books (Greenwood Publishing Group), 1989. Includes information on the legal obligations of employers and employees concerning sexual harassment.

Fried, Elizabeth N. *Sex, Laws & Stereotypes: Authentic Workplace Anecdotes and Practical Tips for Dealing with ADA, Sexual Harassment, Workplace Violence and Beyond.* Dublin, DH: Intermediaries Press, 1994. Covers all aspects and areas of sexual harassment of women and advises them of their rights and what they can do to combat harassment in the workplace.

Hashey, Kelley M. *The Maine Workplace Resource Guide to Discrimination and Harassment.* Bangor, ME: KH International, 1993. A resource for working women, particularly for those who are residents of Maine.

Herbert, Carrie M. H. *Eliminating Sexual Harassment at Work.* London: Fulton, 1994. Discusses sexual harassment in the workplace and various steps toward its eradication.

Lindemann, Barbara and David D. Kadue. *Preventing Sexual Harassment: A Fact Sheet for Employees.* Washington, DC: Bureau of National Affairs, 1992. Facts about sexual harassment; what to do to stop it.

———. *Primer on Sexual Harassment.* Washington, DC: Bureau of National Affairs, 1992. Discusses what sexual harassment is, where and how it occurs, and the law and legislation.

Lloyd, Kenneth L. *Sexual Harassment: How to Keep Your Company Out of Court.* New York: Panel Publishers, 1992. A guide for managers, CEO's, and entrepreneurs on how to prevent sexual harassment suits from being brought against their companies.

Ludwig, Dorene. *But It Was Just a Joke . . . ! Theater Scenes & Monologues for Eliminating Sexual Harassment: A Performance Manual & Workshop Guide.* Los Angeles: University of California, 1991. Role-playing scenes and monologues illustrate how sexual harassment takes place and how women react to and cope with it.

Annotated Bibliography

McQueen, Iris. *Sexual Harassment in the Workplace: The Management View.* Citrus Heights, CA: McQueen and Son Publishing Co., 1983. An overview of sexual harassment in the workplace from management's perspective.

McWhirter, Darien A. *Your Rights at Work.* New York: John Wiley and Sons, 1993. This summary of employees' legal rights includes information on sex discrimination and sexual harassment.

NiCarthy, Ginny, Naomi Gottlieb and Sandra Coffman. *You Don't Have to Take It!: A Woman's Guide to Confronting Emotional Abuse at Work.* Seattle, WA: Seal Press, 1993. Concrete advice for women in the workplace; how to recognize, address, and combat sexual harassment.

Omilian, Susan M. *What Every Employer Should Be Doing About Sexual Harassment.* Madison, CT: Business and Legal Reports, 1986. A guide for employers on how to identify sexual harassment and what to do to prevent it from occurring within their businesses.

Orlando, Jeanette. *Sexual Harassment in the Workplace: A Practical Guide to What It Is and What to Do About It.* Los Angeles: Women's Legal Clinic Center Against Sexual Harassment, 1981. A comprehensive handbook offering step-by-step guidance for people who wish to end sexual harassment in the workplace.

Petrocelli, William and Barbara Kate Repa. *Sexual Harassment on the Job.* Berkeley: Nolo Press, 1992. A legal guide for victims of sexual harassment. Written by two attorneys, this book gives detailed, step-by-step advice on what to do when confronted with the threat of sexual harassment: how to recognize it and how to stop it.

Pfeiffer & Co. Staff. *Addressing Sexual Harassment in the Workplace—Trainer's Package.* San Diego: Pfeiffer & Co., 1992. A training kit for personnel managers, addressing what to do about and how to handle sexual harassment in the workplace.

Sexual Harassment Manual for Managers and Supervisors. Chicago: Commerce Clearing House, 1991. A guidebook for managers of personnel.

Tamminen, Julie M. *Sexual Harassment in the Workplace: Managing Corporate Policy.* New York: Wiley, 1994. How to enact and successfully incorporate corporate policies against sexual harassment amongst employees.

Thorne, Joan Vail. *The Silent Contract: Sexual Harassment in the Workplace, with a Discussion Guide and Suggested Discussion Questions.* New York: Plays for Living, 1993. Role-playing and other exercises provide insight into sexual harassment in the workplace.

Vanhyning, Memory L. *Crossed Signals: How to Say No to Sexual Harassment.* Los Angeles: Infotrends, 1993. Defending oneself against sexual harassment on the job.

Wagner, Ellen J. *Sexual Harassment in the Workplace: How to Prevent, Investigate, and Rescue Problems in Your Organization.* New York: American Management

Association, 1992. What to do from a managerial point of view when confronted with instances of sexual harassment in the workplace and how to conduct a proper investigation.

Webb, Susan L. *Step Forward: Sexual Harassment in the Workplace: What You Need to Know.* New York: Mastermedia, 1992. How women can cope with and try to stop workplace sexual harassment.

――――. *What You Need to Know about Sexual Harassment in the Workplace.* Englewood Cliffs, NJ: Maxwell Macmillan, 1991. A general guidebook.

――――. *Sexual Harassment . . . Shades of Grey: Guidelines for Managers, Supervisors, and Employees.* Seattle, WA: Premiere, 1991. Teaches preventative measures for dealing with sexual harassment in the workplace.

BOOK REVIEWS

Alsdurf, James M. *Christ Today,* July 16, 1990, vol. 34, p. 53. Review of Marie M. Fortune's book, *Is Nothing Sacred? When Sex Invades the Pastoral Relationship.* The reviewer credits the author for tackling a disturbing and often unacknowledged problem but remarks that the book should have included a discussion of morality and ethics in the church and in the Bible itself.

Benn, Melissa. *New Statesman,* March 8, 1985, vol. 109, p. 26. Review of Elizbeth Anne Stanko's book, *Intimate Intrusions: Women's Experience of Male Violence.* Commends the author's presentation of women's victimization, both by men and by themselves.

Booklist, April 1, 1986, vol. 82, p. 1129. Review of Dawn M. McCaghy's annotated bibliography, *Sexual Harassment: A Guide to Resources.* Praises the work as an important and useful reference on an increasingly controversial subject.

Booklist, July 1933, vol. 89, p. 2004. A thumbnail review and summary of Barbara Lindemann and David D. Kadue's book, *Primer on Sexual Harassment.*

Bostick, Sharon. *Library Journal,* September 15, 1993, vol. 118, p. 94. Review of Katherine Roiphe's book, *The Morning After: Sex, Fear and Feminism on Campus.*

Burton, Melody. "Book Reviews: Reference." *Library Journal,* November 15, 1993, vol. 118: 19, p. 68. Review of Lynn Eisaguirre's book, *Sexual Harassment: A Reference Handbook.*

Childress, Valerie. *School Library Journal,* May 1993, vol. 39, p. 135. Review of *Sexual Harassment,* edited by Carol Wekesser, Karin L. Swisher, and Christina Pierce.

Annotated Bibliography

Cohen, Jacob. *National Review*, July 5, 1993, vol. 45, p. 47. Review of the controversial book by David Brock, *The Real Anita Hill: The Untold Story*.

Cotter, Kathleen. "Book Review: Junior High Up." *School Library Journal*, July 1994, vol. 40: 7, p. 122. Review of Lynn Eisaguirre's book, *Sexual Harassment: A Reference Handbook*.

Crull, Peggy. *Indiana Labor Relations Review*, April 1987, vol. 40, p. 447. Review of Barbara A. Gutek's book, *Sex and the Workplace*.

Dwyer, Virginia. *Booklist*, March 1, 1994, vol. 90, p. 1168. Review of the anthology *Bearing Witness: Sexual Harassment and Beyond—Everywoman's Story*, edited by Celia Morris.

Eastland, Terry. *Commentary*, August 1993, vol. 96, p. 39. Review of David Brock's *The Real Anita Hill: The Untold Story*.

The Economist, January 22, 1994, vol. 330, p. 95. A critique of Katherine Roiphe's book, *The Morning After: Sex, Fear and Feminism on Campus*.

Elshtain, Jean Bethke. *New Republic*, September 6, 1993, vol. 209, p. 32. Review of David Brock's book, *The Real Anita Hill: The Untold Story*.

Emery, Margaret. *Time*, September 20, 1993, vol. 142, p. 88. Review of Katherine Roiphe's *The Morning After: Sex, Fear and Feminism on Campus*.

Friedrichs, D.O. *Choice*, July/August 1985. Review of *Intimate Intrusions: Women's Experience of Male Violence*, by Elizabeth Anne Stanko.

Gutmann, Stephanie. *National Review*, October 18, 1993, vol. 45, p. 66. Review of Katherine Roiphe's book, *The Morning After: Sex, Fear and Feminism on Campus*.

Harriford, D. *Choice*, June 1986, vol. 23, p. 1570. Review of Barbara A. Gutek's book, *Sex and the Workplace*, noting that it will serve as an excellent guidebook for managers in the workplace.

Havris, Kathryn. *School Library Journal*, August 1993, vol. 39, p. 198. Review of *Sexual Harassment*, by Elaine Landau.

Iannone, Carol. *Commentary*, September 1993, vol. 96, p. 51. Review of Katherine Roiphe's first book, *The Morning After: Sex, Fear and Feminism on Campus*.

Kaminer, Wendy. *The New York Times Book Review*, September 19, 1993. Review of *The Morning After: Sex, Fear and Feminism on Campus*, by Katherine Roiphe.

Klatte, M. *Choice*, June 1994, vol. 31, p. 1662. Review of *Bearing Witness: Sexual Harassment and Beyond—Everywoman's Story*, an anthology of women's accounts of sexual harassment edited by Celia Morris.

Lacayo, Richard. *Time*, June 28, 1993, vol. 141, p. 70. Review of David Brock's *The Real Anita Hill: The Untold Story*.

MacRitchie, Dorothy J. "Reviews: Social Studies" *Book Report*, January/February 1994, vol. 12: 4, p. 62. Review of Elaine Ladau's book, *Sexual Harassment*.

Mayer, Jane and Jill Abramson. *New Yorker*, May 24, 1993, vol. 69, p. 90. Review of David Brock's *The Real Anita Hill: The Untold Story*, criticizing it for basing its argument on numerous pieces of erroneous information.

Miller, Beverly. *Library Journal*, February 15, 1994, vol. 119, p. 176. Review of *Bearing Witness: Sexual Harassment and Beyond—Everywoman's Story*, edited by Celia Morris.

O'Rourke, Joseph C. *Readings*, March 1992, vol. 7, p. 26. Review of Wendy Maltz's book, *The Sexual Healing Journey: A Guide for Survivors of Sexual Abuse*.

Peelle, J.E. *Choice*, July/August, 1985, vol. 22, p. 1618. Review of Dawn M. McCaghy's annotated bibliography, *Sexual Harassment: A Guide to Resources*.

Pollitt, Katha. *New Yorker*, October 4, 1993, vol. 69, p. 220. Review of Katherine Roiphe's book, *The Morning After: Sex, Fear and Feminism on Campus*.

Rochman, Hazel. *Booklist*, December 1, 1993, vol. 90, p. 687. Review of Bob Italia's book, *Anita Hill: Speaking Out Against Harassment*.

Segal, Troy. "Sexual Harassment: The Age of Anxiety." *Business Week*, July 6, 1992, issue 3273, p. 16. Reviews three books by Susan L. Webb: *Sexual Harassment on the Job*, *Sexual Harassment in the Workplace* and *Step Forward*.

Stark, Kio. *Nation*, January 31, 1994, vol. 258, p. 137. Review of Katherine Roiphe's book, *The Morning After: Sex, Fear and Feminism on Campus*.

Stevenson, Deborah. Untitled article in *Bull Cent Child Books*, September 1993, vol. 47, p. 15. Review of Elaine Landau's book, *Sexual Harassment*.

Sullivan, Kathleen M. *New York Review of Books*, August 12, 1993, vol. 40, p. 12. Lengthy review of David Brock's book, *The Real Anita Hill: The Untold Story*.

Thernstrom, Abigail. *Times Literary Supplement*, July 23, 1993, no. 4712, p. 26. Review of David Brock's *The Real Anita Hill: The Untold Story*.

Thom, Mary. *Ms.*, March/April 1994, vol. 4, p. 76. Review of *Bearing Witness: Sexual Harassment and Beyond—Everywoman's Story*, edited by Celia Morris.

Tierno, Michael. *Library Journal*, July 1991, vol. 116, p. 117. Review of *The Sexual Healing Journey: A Guide for Survivors of Sexual Abuse*, by Wendy Maltz.

Toth, Luann. *School Library Journal*, January 1994, vol. 40, p. 122. Review of Bob Italia's book, *Anita Hill: Speaking Out Against Harassment*.

White, Pamela Cooper. *Christ Century*, February 7–14, 1990, vol. 107, p. 156. Review of Marie M. Fortune's book, *Is Nothing Sacred? When Sex Invades the Pastoral Relationship*.

Wilkinson, Signe. *The New York Times Book Review*, May 23, 1993, p. 11. Review of David Brock's *The Real Anita Hill: The Untold Story*, praising its successful refutation of Anita Hill's charges of sexual harassment by Supreme Court nominee Clarence Thomas.

Winter, E. *Choice*, March 1994, vol. 31, p. 1092. Review of *Sexual Harassment: A Reference Handbook*, by Lynne Eisaguirre.

Winokur, L. A. "The Sexual Harassment Debates." *Progressive*, November 1993, vol. 57: 11, p. 37. Reviews numerous books on sexual harassment, including *Sexual Harassment on the Job: What It Is and How to Stop It*, by William Petrocelli and Barbara Kate Repa; *Sexual Harassment: Women Speak Out*, an anthology of personal accounts; *Harassed: 100 Women Define Inappropriate Behavior in the Workplace*, by Nancy Dodd McCann and Thomas A. McGinn; and *The 9 to 5 Guide to Combating Sexual Harassment: Candid Advice from 9 to 5, National Association of Working Women*, by Ellen Bravo and Ellen Cassedy.

Zvirin, Stephanie. *Booklist*, April 15, 1993, vol. 89, p. 1505. Review of *Sexual Harassment*, edited by Carol Wesseker, Karin L. Swisher and Christina Pierce.

————. *Booklist*, June 1–15, 1993, vol. 89, p. 1804. Review of Elaine Landau's book, *Sexual Harassment*.

NEWS ARTICLES

EDUCATION

Adler, Jerry. "Tale of Sex, Lies and Audiotape." *Newsweek*, October 21, 1991, p. 38. Discusses the sexual harassment charges against Christopher Downs, a professor of psychology at the Clear Lake Branch of the University of Houston in Texas. Downs, who is openly gay, was accused of sexually harassing a gay student. Investigations conducted by the university have found the gay student's charges to be unfounded.

Amiei, Barbara. "Here's Looking at You, Kid" *MacLean's*, April 1987, p. 87. An opinion piece stating that a student's sexual harassment case against a University of Toronto professor trivializes the issue by including winks, leers, and stares in the definition of harassment.

Anand, Geeta. "Students Disect Sexual Harassment" *Boston Globe*, October 16, 1994, sec. WW, p. 1. 11th and 12th graders at Newton North High School in Massachusetts create a video about sexual harassment in school. The film is entitled, "Sexual Harassment and Self-Esteem: Facing Up to Harassment."

————. "Video Tackles a Tough Subject." *Boston Globe*, October 21, 1994, p. 39. A high school teacher in Newton, Massachusetts, brings her students together to tell and reenact their stories of sexual harassment for a video on the subject.

"Campus Watch." *National Review*, February 15, 1993, vol. 45: 3, p. 14. A sexual harassment case filed by four graduate students against the University of Minnesota resulted in mandatory attendance for faculty at sexual harassment workshops.

"Chicago Board of Ed. Explains New Sexual Harassment Policy." *Jet*, July 11, 1994, p. 40. A unique and interesting sexual harassment policy developed by the Chicago Board of Education.

Cockburn, Alexander. "Beat the Devil: And a Final Word from Foucault." *Nation*, April 11, 1994, p. 476. Discusses in detail a female student's sexual harassment charges against Professor Lawrence Jorgensen of Los Angeles Valley College.

"Database." *U.S. News and World Report*, June 14, 1993, p. 22. Give statistics on sexual harassment occuring in schools; the figures take into account girls who claim to be sexually harassed by teachers and peers alike. Describes where harassment is most prone to occur.

Del Borgo, V. and M. Margaronis, et al. "Students on the Move." *Nation*, March 26, 1988, p. 405. Nine articles on student movements in the 1980s, including gay and lesbian rights, South Africa divestment, the new left, African Americans, feminists, and sexual harassment awareness.

Easton, Nina J. "The Law of the School Yard." *Los Angeles Times*, October 2, 1994, sec. MAG, p. 16. A California student takes legal action against a Petaluma school where she claims she was sexually harassed by fellow students who taunted her.

English, Bella. "At Harvard, Teenager Learns a Bitter Lesson." *Boston Globe*, October 5, 1994, p. 3. A teenage woman attending summer school at Harvard was stalked on campus by a fellow classmate. Despite the woman's complaints, Harvard's administration failed to take action.

Evans, Sherrell. "Stemming Sex Harassment in Schools." *Atlanta Journal and Atlanta Constitution (ATCJ)*, November 24, 1994, sec. XJ, p. 14. Discusses discipline and sexual harassment in the Clayton County, Georgia, public school systems.

Fraser, John. "The Mark of Zero (Guidelines for Preventing Harassment and Discrimination in Ontario University)." *Saturday Night*, April 1994. p. 10. A humor piece mocking concerns over sexual harassment in higher education.

"From Studies to Sex." *Maclean's*, November 9, 1992, vol. 105: 45, p. 79. The findings of a Maclean's/Decima national Canadian telephone poll of 500 university students on a wide range of topics, including sexual harassment.

Garret, Echo Montgomery. "What You Need to Know About Sexual Harassment (on College Campuses)." *Money*, Winter 1994, p. 37. Defines sexual harassment, discusses the high incidence of sexual harassment on college campuses, and advises parents and students how to recognize and ward off such behavior.

Gibbs, Nancy, Sharon E. Epperson and Bonnie L. Rochman. "Romancing the Student: Rattled by Lawsuits, Colleges Are Cracking Down on Faculty-Student Love Affairs." *Time*, April 3, 1995, p. 58. Student-teacher romances are not uncommon on college campuses, and they can end in lawsuits like Lisa Topal's suit against English professor Malcolm Woodfield and the University of Pennsylvania. Universities are creating new, more stringent policies to prevent these relationships.

Gleick, Elizabeth and Margaret Nelson. "The Boys on the Bus." *People*, November 30, 1992, p. 125. Sue Mutziger files a sexual harassment suit on behalf of her seven-year-old daughter, whom she feels was sexually harassed by boys on her schoolbus.

Goldin, Davidson. "Harassment Claims Tarnish Cornell Star's Luster." *New York Times*, March 23, 1995, p. B4. Four Cornell University students charged distinguished psychology professor James B. Maas of sexually harassing them, and Cornell's Ethics Committee found him guilty.

"Great Moments in Religion: Theology Professor Who Used Story from the Talmud about Accidental Sex Receives Sexual-Harassment Complaint and Is Disciplined." *Fortune*, May 16, 1994, p. 154. After eight years at the United Church of Christ Seminary, Professor Graydon Snyder was charged with sexual harassment of a student offended by a Talmud story.

Hart, Jordana. "Newton Principal Suspended for Patting Teacher." *Boston Globe*, November 24, 1994, p. 71. Thomas P. O'Neill Jr., principal of a Newton, Massachusetts school, was suspended for stroking a teacher in the workplace. Discusses disciplinary measures schools are taking to curb sexual harassment.

Henneberger, Melinda and Michel Marriott. "For Some, Rituals of Abuse Replace Youthful Courtship." *New York Times*, July 11, 1993. p. 1. A nationwide survey finds that two-thirds of girls and 42% of boys at the junior high and high school levels report being pinched, touched, or grabbed at school. The article discusses the differences in perception between girls and boys in response.

Hentoff, Nat. "Assaulted by the Talmud." *Progressive*, August 1994, p. 16. A member of the Chicago Theological Seminary is accused of sexual harassment by a student as a result of telling a story from the Talmud.

———. "The Banishment of Professor Silva." *Village Voice*, December 21, 1993, p. 22. Examines the issues surrounding the suspension of Professor J. Donald Silva from the University of New Hampshire for sexual harassment.

Hernandez, Raymond. "Three Suspended for Groping at West Point." *New York Times*, November 5, 1994, sec. A, p. 25. Football players at West Point harass female cadets at a pep rally and are suspended from their team for the rest of the year.

Houston, Fiona. "The War on Boys." *Men's Health*, October 1994, vol. 9: 8, p. 108. An attack on the Women's Equity in Education Act, passed by the U.S. Senate in 1994, as an example of the feminist "myth" of women's victimization and men's privilege in education.

Istona, Mildred. "Boys Will Be Boys?" *Chatelaine*, November 1993, p. 6. Editorial about the consequences for teenage girls of daily sexual harassment at school.

Katz, Debra M. "School Districts Formulating Policies on Sexual Harassment." *New York Times*, October 30, 1994, sec. LI, p. 1. Long Island school districts are creating new policies to protect students and staff from sexual harassment.

Kauffman, L.A. "How Political Is the Personal?" *Nation*, March 26, 1988, p. 419. Discusses the failure of university feminists to define the issue of sexual harassment.

Kors, A. C. "Harassment Policies in the University." *Society*, May/June 1991, p. 22. Reviews the efforts of universities to prevent sexual harassment on campus.

Kurth, Peter. "Adam & Eve." *Forbes*, September 26, 1994, p. 53. Mothers are extremely sensitive to sexuality as it relates to their children. Camp counselors are afraid to rub suntan lotion on children, fathers are afraid to hold their children on their laps.

Lewin, Tamar. "If Flames Singe, Who Is to Blame?" *New York Times* (Late New York Edition), September 25, 1994, p. 3. Sexual harassment in cyberspace. Two California students at Santa Rosa Junior College experience sexual discrimination on-line and take legal action.

———. "Students Seeking Damages for Sex Bias." *New York Times* (Late New York Edition), July 15, 1994, p. B7. Details sexual harassment suits by two teenage women in New York and California. The outcome of these suits could set new legal precedents for educators at the primary and secondary levels.

Lewis, Anthony. "Time to Grow Up." *New York Times*, October 14, 1994, sec. A, p. 35. The columnist comments on the case of a professor at Santa Rosa Junior College who is accused of sexual harassment.

Moroney, Tom. "Milford School Official Accused of Sexually Harassing Students." *Boston Globe*, September 28, 1994, p. 24. An assistant principal at Milford High School in Worcester, Massachusetts, is accused of fondling several of his students. The local DA is investigating these allegations.

Paglia, Camille. "The Real Lesson of *Oleanna*." *Los Angeles Times*, November 6, 1994, sec. CAL, p. 6. The anti-feminist author reviews David Mamet's play about sexual harassment involving a professor and a student.

Paylor, Diane. "The He-Man Women-Haters Club." *Sassy*, November 1994, p. 50. Recounts Shannon Richey Faulkner's struggles to enroll as a cadet at South Carolina's military college, the Citadel; the Supreme Court's decision to allow her attendance there; and the subsequent abuse and sexual harassment she endured.

Pochoda, Elizabeth. "Academic License." *Nation*, December 27, 1993, p. 806. Discussion of the November/December 1993 issue of *Lingua Franca*, which featured an article about sexual harassment charges against a literature professor.

"Professor Wins Reinstatement After a Sex Harassment Charge." *New York Times* (Late New York Edition), October 12, 1994, p. B7. A federal court order that reinstated a University of New Hampshire professor accused of verbal sexual harassment sets a precedent on sexual harassment versus freedom of speech in the classroom.

Rabkin, Jeremy. "Rule of Law: New Checks on Campus Sexual-Harassment Cops." *Wall Street Journal*, October 19, 1994, sec. A, p. 21. Explores two cases in which college professors were accused of sexual harassment by their students and punished by the universities. The professors have retaliated by suing the universities.

Roberts, Patricia C. "Explicit Film Prompts Law Suit." *Christianity Today*, November 14, 1994, p. 64. Details a California sexual harassment lawsuit by the Rutherford Institute against a Rio Linda High School teacher. The suit was sparked by a film that the teacher showed in his classroom.

Rollenhagen, Erin. "Skirting the Issue." *Seventeen*, October 1994, p. 122. A report on sexual harassment experienced by female students at Ames Middle School in Ames, Iowa, how they retaliated, and what the administration is doing to resolve the school's battle of the sexes.

Saltzman, Amy. "It's Not Just Teasing: Sexual Harassment Starts Young: Here's How Some Schools Discourage It." *U.S. News & World Report*, October 6, 1993, p. 73. Describes various sexual harassment programs that are being implemented in several states.

Sauerwein, Kristina. "A New Lesson in Schools: Sexual Harassment Is Unacceptable." *Los Angeles Times*, August 1, 1994, sec. E, p. 1. Parents pressure schools and federal agencies by filing complaints about peer sexual harassment experienced by their children in school. Schools struggle to address the issue on a local level.

Shannon, Salley. "Why Girls Don't Want to Go to School." *Working Mother*, November 1993, p. 58. Girls are labeled as troublemakers when they reveal their experiences of sexual harassment in school, which makes them reluctant to report abuse. The article discusses the importance of implementing school policies and creating a safe environment for female students.

"Swarthmore and Sexual Harassment—Again." *U.S. News & World Report*, September 12, 1994, p. 25. A male student accused of sexual harassment by a female classmate is found guilty by the Swarthmore College administration, expelled, then readmitted. The accuser filed suit to prevent her harasser from returning.

Van Gelder, Miranda. "High School Lowdown: Sexism and Racism by High School Teachers." *Ms.*, March/April 1992, p. 94. Students' fears about dealing with teachers who sexually and racially harass them.

Wieseltier, Leon. "Diddler on the Roof." *New Republic*, July 11, 1994, p. 42. Examination of a sexual harassment case against a professor at a theological seminary in Chicago.

GENERAL INFORMATION

Abcarian, Robin. "Sexual Harassment as Pulp Fiction." *Los Angeles Times*, November 20, 1994, p. 1. Discusses men's viewpoints on and feelings about sexual harassment, with reviews of Michael Crichton's novel *Disclosure* and David Mamet's pay *Oleanna*.

"ABC: Boys Will Be Boys." *Teen*, October 1994, p. 104. The magazine article reviews an ABC After School Special called "Boys Will Be Boys" which depicts an episode of sexual harassment.

"Angela Rippon: Sexual Harassment in the UK." ABC's "Good Morning, America," October 18, 1991, program n1395. Joan Lunden interviews British broadcaster Angela Rippon on the issue of sexual harassment.

Ascher-Walsh, Rebecca and Benjamin Svetkey. "He Said She Said: Two Very Different Views on the Making of *Disclosure*." *Entertainment Weekly*, December 16, 1994, p. 22. Interviews with Michael Douglas and Demi Moore, the stars of the film version of Michael Crichton's novel *Disclosure*, in which a male employee is sexually harassed by his female supervisor.

"The Attractiveness Factor." *Psychology Today*, May 1994, p. 16. Considers the role attractiveness plays in sexual harassment incidents and argues that good looks can have a greater effect than rank. Also discussed is the effect of the victim's marital status.

August, Melissa, Philip Elmer-DeWitt, et al. "Sexual Harassment: A Primer." *Time*, June 6, 1994, p. 12. Outlines the revolution in sexual harassment awareness from 1964 to 1993, discussing landmark hearings, ruling, and the evolution of anti-harassment guidelines.

Bain, George. "A Questionable Caterwauling." *MacLean's*, March 1, 1993, p. 46. Asserts that many sexual harassment charges are exaggerated and unfounded, citing a study which found that 81% of female students had experienced sexual harassment defined in vague, loose terms.

Annotated Bibliography

———. "Bargepole." *Punch*, November 6, 1991, p. 44. The columnist argues that women send mixed sexual messages to men, leading them on and then reproaching them for their behavior.

Barry, Rebecca. "You Talking to Me?" *Seventeen*, September 1994, p. 143. Discusses the phenomenon of catcalling and its impact on women.

Berger, Melanie. "What to Do If You're a Victim of Sexual Harassment." *Ladies Home Journal*, January 1992, p. 46. Information on legislation recently passed by the Senate, allowing sexual harassment victims to sue for damages.

Bode, Janet. "Sex for Shelter: When Your Landlord Wants More Than the Rent." *Glamour*, November 1987, p. 318. Sexual harassment of tenants is established as a violation of the Federal Fair Housing Act.

Brawley, Peggy. "And Why Don't Some Men Understand?" *People*, October 28, 1991, p. 48. The different viewpoints on sexual harassment held by men and women are examined in an interview with Deborah Tannen, a linguistics professor at Georgetown University.

Brothers, Dr. Joyce. "Why Men Abuse Women." *Parade*, November 11, 1984, p. 4. The psychologist concludes that men are not aware of the many forms abuse takes, including the more subtle linguistic and psychological ones.

Cammuso, Frank and Hart Seely. "Oldfinger." *New Yorker*, June 21, 1993, p. 102. A satirical look at James Bond-style sexism.

Carlson, Margaret B. "Female Chauvinist Pigs?" *Time*, December 12, 1994, p. 62. Eight men from Boston claim they have suffered sexual discrimination at Jenny Craig International Weight-Loss Centers.

Carton, Barbara. "Muscled Out?: At Jenny Craig, Men Are Ones Who Claim Sex Discrimination." *Wall Street Journal*, November 29, 1994, sec. A, p. 1. Reports alleged sexual harassment of male employees at Jenny Craig International Weight-Loss centers, for which the men sued.

Chapman, Gary. "Flamers." *New Republic*, April 10, 1995, p. 13. An expose of the startlingly widespread harassment of women in cyberspace.

"Chavis Denies Harassment Allegations from Former Administrative Assistant." *Jet*, August 15, 1994, p. 4. The executive director of the National Association for the Advancement of Colored People (NAACP) denies sexually harassing his former administrative assistant, Mary Stansel.

"Chavis Won't Resign NAACP Post: Woman Who Accused Him of Harassment Has History of Filing Lawsuits, Newspaper Reports." *Jet*, August 22, 1994, p. 12. Rumors surface about the woman who has charged the executive director of the NAACP with sexual harassment.

Chemin, Anne. "Rewriting Napoleon's Code." *World Press Review*, June 1994, p. 46. An excerpt from the Paris newspaper *Le Monde* discusses the history of the Napoleonic Code (French law) and attempts to overhaul it, with reference to the issue of sexual harassment.

"Chicago Landlord Agrees to Pay $180,000 to Settle Suit Charging He Sexually Harassed Six Female Tenants. Must Sell Building." *Jet*, December 19, 1994, p. 11. Six female tenants charged their landlord, Gheorghi Nediaikov, with sexual harassment; he has agreed to pay $180,000 in damages.

"City Continues Effort to Prevent Sexual Harassment." *New York Times*, November 21, 1992, p. 21. New York City agencies struggle to create effective policies to deter and punish sexual harassment.

Cornish, Edward S. "Moonlight, Violins, Briefs, and Bytes." *Futurist*, January/February 1987, p. 2. Given the high risk of sexual harassment claims, this article suggests potential lovers may soon draw up contracts to protect their interests.

Crichton, Sarah, Debra Rosenberg, et al. "Sexual Correctness." *Newsweek*, October 25, 1993, p. 52. Exposes the divided opinions of feminists surrounding sexual harassment and date-rape issues.

Davidson, N. "Feminism and Sexual Harassment." *Society*, May/June 1991, p. 39. Purports that sexual harassment is a fanatical feminist issue and suggests that a more rational approach to the subject is warranted.

Deane, Barbara. "At His Mercy." *Redbook*, May 1992, p. 98. The sexual harassment, robbery, and molestation of 21 low-income single women by a building manager of an apartment complex in Fairfield, California, is discussed.

Demak, R. "Athletes and Rape." *Sports Illustrated*, March 23, 1992, p. 4. Discusses the increased news coverage and publicity given sexual harassment and assault charges involving athletes. Questions whether the number of incidents has increased or just the rate at which they are reported.

Dowling, Katherine. "The Sexual Harassment Jackpot." *Los Angeles Times*, September 7, 1994, sec. B, p. 7. The author believes Americans are stretching the meaning of sexual harassment in order to cash in on the issue.

Eagan, Andrea Boroff. "The Girl in 1-A; Sexual Harassment Hits Home." *Mademoiselle*, April 1987, p. 252. Report on the sexual harassment of female tenants by landlords and building managers.

Eastland, Terry. "An American Originalist." *American Spectator*, December 1990, vol. 23: 12, p. 36. This opinion piece discusses allegations of sexual harassment by sportswriter Lisa Olson against members of the New England Patriots football team.

Annotated Bibliography

Epstein, Jack. "Brazilian Women Leaders in Fight for Equal Rights." *National Catholic Reporter*, May 20, 1994, p. 6. Overview of sexual harassment laws in Brazil and in Latin America, and recent legal breakthroughs.

"Even in Prison, Men Get Better Treatment Than Women." *Glamour*, March 1994, p. 80. Investigation of the differential treatment of men and women who are incarcerated. In addition to being sexually harassed by male guards, women receive longer sentences and have fewer civil rights than their male counterparts.

Fields, Suzanne. "Battle of the Sexes Drifts into Dangerous Territory." *Insight on the News*, July 5, 1993, p. 17. Discusses the conflict between men and women regarding sexual harassment.

Gladstone, Mark and Bailey, Eric. "Bill on Rules for Sex Harassment Suits Advances." *Los Angeles Times*, August 26, 1994, sec. A, p. 3. A California bill passes, making sexual harassment lawsuits easier to file.

Gross, Jane. "Suffering in Silence No More: Fighting Sexual Harassment." *New York Times*, July 13, 1992, p. A1. A report on changing attitudes about sexual harassment, rising sensitivity to and awareness of the subject women's rage and indignation in the wake of the Hill-Thomas hearings.

Hazlett, Thomas W. "That's Not Funny!" *Reason*, April 1994, p. 74. The author's assessment of "male bashing" in contemporary society, citing women's reactions to the emasculation of John Wayne Bobbit by his wife.

Heil, Andrea. "Love Sick." *Mademoiselle*, December 1986, p. 128. Report on sexual harassment of women by obsessive former boyfriends and advice on what women can do.

Holmberg, Arthur. "Approaches: The Language of Misunderstanding." *American Theatre*, October 1992, p. 94. An analysis of David Mamet's new play, *Oleanna*, which deals with sexual harassment.

Holmes, Steven A. "Leader Used NAACP Money to Settle a Sex Harassment Case." *New York Times*, July 29, 1994, p. A1. Conflicts mount in the NAACP over sexual harassment charges against its executive director.

———. "NAACP Board Dismisses Group's Executive Director." *New York Times*, August 21, 1994, p. 1. Benjamin F. Chavis Jr. is dismissed for his "inimical" behavior. He settles out of court with Mary E. Stansel to circumbent a sexual harassment lawsuit by his former employee.

Ingrassia, Michele, Melinda Liu, et al. "Abused and Confused." *Newsweek*, October 25, 1993, p. 57. An overview of the ambiguities and pitfalls of determining in legal terms what constitutes sexual harassment. Reports the increased number of claims and discusses how to distinguish a joke from an insult.

James, Caryn. "Tales from the Corner Office." *New York Times* (Late New York Edition), December 11, 1994, p. 1. Analyzes Hollywood's simplified portrayals of sexual harassment in film such as adaptations of the play *Oleanna* and the novel *Disclosure*.

Juffer, Jane. "Abuse at the Border," *Progressive*, April 1988, p. 14. Central American refugee women tell of their experiences of physical and sexual abuse as they tried to enter the United States.

Karlsberg, Elizabeth. "Love Gone Loco: When Breakups Go Too Far." *Teen*, February 1987, p. 36. 1987 statistics indicate that 30% of murdered women are killed by their boyfriends or husbands.

Kunen, James S. "The Dark Side of Love." *People*, October 26, 1987, p. 88. When an intimate relationship deteriorates into obsession, sexual harassment can be a result.

Levin, Susanna. "The High Price of Fame." *Women's Sports & Fitness*, April 1994, p. 23. Because of their public exposure, female athletes face the danger of being stalked and sexually harassed.

Malestic, Susan. "When Love Becomes Obsession." *Single Parent*, Summer 1994, p. 23. Discusses how a woman can protect herself when being stalked. Reveals the state of anti-stalking legislation.

Metz, Holly. "Stopping Sexual Harassment." *Progressive*, April 1994, p. 12. An excerpt from Martha Langelan's book, *Back Off!* The author, an instructor of seminars on self-defense for women, suggests that the best way for women to stop sexual harassment is by confronting the harasser, openly describing the inappropriate behavior and demanding that it stop.

Monroe, Sylvester. "After the Revolution." *Time*, August 29, 1994, p. 40. The NAACP votes to dismiss executive director Benjamin F. Chavis, who was accused of sexually harassing his former administrative assistant. Financial mismanagement of the organization by Chavis is also cited as reason for dismissal.

Morgenson, Getchen. "Advice to Women: Act Like a Freight Train." *Forbes*, May 15, 1989, p. 72. Profiles two women who believe that sexual harassment is brought on by the actions of those who experience it.

"Mutual Respect." *Los Angeles Times*, November 12, 1994, sec. B, p. 7. In an out-of-court settlement, seven women who filed sexual harassment claims against the Newport Beach, California, Police Department will be awarded $1.2 million. The editorial questions government spending on huge sexual harassment settlements.

Nemeth, M., B. Wickens et al. "Chilling the Sexes." *Maclean's*, February 17, 1992, vol. 105: 7, p. 42. In light of the increasing number of sexual harassment cases reported by women in Canada, relations of the sexes have been strained by the vagueness of its definition and men's fears of being falsely accused.

Annotated Bibliography

————. "Claiming the Late-Night Crown." *Ebony*, June 1992, p. 68. Highlights Arsenio Hall's success as a late-night talk-show host and profiles his life and character. Specifically mentions his primarily all-women staff and emphasizes his campaign to combat sexual harassment and racism.

Norton, Helen. "What to Do If You're Harassed." *Hispanic*, January/February 1994, p. 22. A member of the Women's Legal Defense Fund offers helpful and practical guidelines on what a woman can do to defend herself when confronted with sexual harassment.

Paul, Ellen Frankel. "Bared Buttocks and Federal Cases." *Society*, May 1991, p. 4. Despite society's increasing awareness of sexual harassment of women, this article warns that a line must be drawn between injury and offense.

Pollan, Stephen and Mark Levine. "Confronting a Sexual Harasser." *Working Woman*, March 1994, p. 71. How to tell a harasser that his behavior is bothersome, how to ask him to stop.

Richler, Mordecai. "Duck!" *Gentleman's Quarterly*, September 1994, p. 148. A humor piece satirizing sexual harassment and telling men how to protect themselves against women who are protecting themselves.

Roberts, Marjory. "Understanding Rita?" *Psychology Today*, December 1986, p. 14. The American Psychological Association (APA) has found that men often misinterpret women's friendliness as sexual interest.

Robledo, Fred. "Stewards Suspend Jockey." *Los Angeles Times*, September 22, 1994, sec. C, p. 9. Stewards at Fairplex Park in California suspend jockey Brian Long indefinitely for his failure to attend a court hearing addressing sexual harassment charges lodged against him by female jockey Joy Scott.

Rosen, Jeffery. "The Book of Ruth." *New Republic*, August 2, 1993, p. 19. A look at Supreme Court Associate Justice Ruth Bader Ginsburg, speculating on her potential influence in court rulings relating to women.

Rudolph, Ileane. "When Sam Met Regina." *TV Guide*, November 19–25, 1994, p. 40. Review of an episode of the NBC drama "Law & Order" that addressed sexual harassment issues.

Schultz, Ellen E. and Junda Woo. "The Bedroom Ploy: Plaintiffs' Sex Lives Are Being Laid Bare in Harassment Cases." *Wall Street Journal*, September 19, 1994, sec. A, p. 1. Despite the enactment of the Civil Rights Act of 1991, intended to make it easier to lodge sexual harassment complaints, corporate defense lawyers subject plaintiffs to ruthless questioning about their sexual history.

Secunda, Victoria and Jan Buckwald. "After Anita Hill: The New Female Activism." *New Woman*, November 1992, p. 108. The Hill-Thomas hearings spurred support for the women's rights movement and feminism across the country.

"Sexual Harassment." *National Review*, November 4, 1991, vol. 43: 20, p. 14. An analysis of the legal aspects of sexual harassment—whom makes the laws and why.

"Sexual Harassment—Oui ou Non?" *Glamour*, September 1992, p. 150. Reviews the results of a survey taken by a French magazine, *Le Point*, and concludes that French public opinion about sexual harassment has been influenced by America's points of view.

Shannon, Elaine. "The Sex Wars, Continued." *Vogue*, August 1994, p. 76. Sexual harassment cases are on the rise in the United States, mainly filed by women, yet general confusion persists about the definition of sexual harassment.

Shapiro, L., L. Buckley, et al. "Why Women Are Angry." *Newsweek*, October 21, 1991, p. 41. Explains how the Hill-Thomas hearings fanned the flames of women's rage. Comments on the current state of the women's movement.

Simon, John. "Disclosure." *National Review*, December 31, 1994, p. 62. Reviews the movie, *Disclosure*, and discusses its premise: An honest and decent male character is falsely accused of sexual harassment by a jealous, resentful female colleague.

Sloane, Pat. "I Don't See It as Pervasive." *Advertising Age*, October 21, 1991, p. 1. Considers the impact of the Hill-Thomas hearings on the American public. Includes interviews with four top female executives on the issue of sexual harassment.

Smolowe, Jill. "Anita Hill's Legacy." *Time*, October 19, 1992, p. 56. Explores the fears of sexual harassment victims a year after the Hill-Thomas hearings.

Staples, Brent. "Breastly Manners In Cyberspace." *New York Times*, October 13, 1994, sec. A, p. 26. Sexual harassment is a growing problem on the Internet.

Strebeigh, F. "Defining Law on the Feminist Frontier." *New York Times Magazine*, October 6, 1991, p. 28. A profile of Catherine A. MacKinnon, law professor and feminist theorist, who wrote *Sexual Harassment of Working Women: A Case of Discrimination*.

Tibbetts, John C. "*Disclosure* Director Relates to Thriller's Tensions." *Christian Science Monitor*, December 9, 1994, p. 12. An interview with Barry Levinson, director of the film adaptation of Michael Crichton's novel *Disclosure*.

Travers, Peter. "*Oleanna*." *Rolling Stone*, December 1, 1994, p. 132. A review of the film adaptation of David Mamet's play, in which a student accuses her professor of sexual harassment.

Underwood, Nora. "Murder in Arkansas." *Maclean's*, January 11, 1988, p. 27. Mass murderer Ronald Gene Simmons had a history of sexually harassing female relatives and neighbors before he started a string of killings.

"Untitled." *Ms.*, July/August 1993, p. 87. A short piece on the increase in sexual harassment lawsuits since the Hill-Thomas hearings. According to a report by the EEOC, 90% of cases are filed by women.

Weinraub, Bernard. "A Man. A Woman. A Movie. Not a Polemic." *New York Times*, December 6, 1994, p. B1. A review of the recently released movie *Disclosure*, based on the novel by Michael Crichton.

Wexler, Annette. "Self-Help for Victims of Sex Harassment." *New York Times*, July 31, 1994, sec. NJ, p. 1. A profile of the Violet Club, a self-help group for women who have experienced sexual harassment at work.

"Where Do We Stand on Pornography?" *Ms.*, January/February 1994, p. 32. Feminists explore sexual exploitation, harassment, and censorship as they relate to the pornography industry.

Wolff, Craig. "Girl Is Sexually Assaulted in Public Pool in Bronx." *New York Times*, July 6, 1994, p. B3. A description of an episode of "whirlpooling," in which young men surround and attack teenage girls in public pools.

Wright, Robert. "Feminists, Meet Mr. Darwin." *New Republic*, November 28, 1994, p. 34. The author supports the idea that there are scientifically proven biological differences between men and women, discussing the Hill-Thomas hearings and sexual harassment in general within this framework.

Wyden, Peter. "Sexual Harassment." *Good Housekeeping*, July 1993, p. 121. The history of sexual harassment and an analysis of how it has evolved, citing early landmark cases.

Yang, Catherine. "Rudderless at the NAACP." *Business Week*, December 12, 1994, p. 41. The NAACP struggles financially and administratively after the dismissal of its executive director, Benjamin F. Chavis Jr.

Yorkshire, Heidi. "Shirley Temple Black Sets the Record Straight." *McCall's*, March 1987, p. 88. A review of Shirley Temple Black's autobiography and her experiences of being sexually harassed as a child star.

Young, Cathy. "The Frontiers of Flirting." *Men's Health*, October 1994, vol. 9: 8, p. 109. Report on a sexual harassment seminar conducted by Nancy Butler, a gender-equity consultant.

GOVERNMENT

Alter, J. "Why There Isn't a Better Way." *Newsweek*, October 21, 1991, p. 45. Analyzes the process by which Anita Hill's allegations of sexual harassment against Clarence Thomas became public.

"Anita Hill." CBS's "60 Minutes," February 2, 1992, program n2420. An interview with Anita Hill.

"Anita Hill and Clarence Thomas." CNN's "Moneyline," October 11, 1991, program n494. A discussion of the charges by Anita Hill against Clarence Thomas.

"Arkansas Woman to File Clinton Sex Harassment Lawsuit." CNN's "Inside Politics," May 4, 1994, program n574. Report about a former Arkansas state employee who plans to file a sexual harassment lawsuit against President Bill Clinton.

"Author of Book Critical of Anita Hill Defends Work." NPR's "All Things Considered," July 9, 1993, program n1173. David Brock's book, *The Real Anita Hill*, is discussed. Brock claims Hill was coerced and framed into lying by Senate staffers opposed to the nomination of Clarence Thomas.

Baker, Russell. "Pre-pos-terous." *New York Times*, May 28, 1994, p. 19. An opinion piece on the Paula Jones-Bill Clinton lawsuit as an argument for court reforms.

Barron, James. "Magazine Barred from Using Nude Photos of Clinton's Accuser." *The New York Times* (Late New York Edition), November 30, 1994, p. A21. Results of a federal hearing involving *Penthouse* magazine and Paula Jones. *Penthouse* is prohibited from distributing its January 1995 issue, which contains photographs of the plaintiff partially nude.

"Bob Bennett on Paula Jones' Sexual Harassment Case." CNN's "Larry King Live," July 21, 1994, program n1179. President Clinton's personal lawyer discusses the Paula Jones sexual harassment case.

Bogert, Carroll. "Tinker, Tailor, Lecher, Spy." *Newsweek*, September 26, 1994, p. 43. Discusses agent Janine Brookner's sex discrimination battle with the CIA.

Boo, K. "The Organization Woman." *Washington Monthly*, December 1991, p. 44. Examines why it took 10 years for Anita Hill to come forward with her allegations of sexual harassment against Clarence Thomas.

Brockway, D. "The Real Anita Hill." *American Spectator*, March 1992, p. 18. Argues that Anita Hill's charges of sexual harassment against Clarence Thomas are lies. Cites conflicting testimony to underscore the argument.

Broder, John M. and Ronald J. Ostrow. "The CIA's Dirty Little Secret." *Los Angeles Times*, October 10, 1994, sec. A, p. 1. Exposes the agency's long history of sexual discrimination and harassment.

Burleigh, Nina. "The Fall and Rise of Bob Packwood." *Time*, April 3, 1995, p. 47. A report on the Oregon senator's reemergence as an influential legislator despite the numerous sexual harassment claims filed against him; his political future is examined in light of the Senate Ethics Committee's ongoing investigation.

"A Capital Sex Scandal?" CNN's "Crossfire," November 24, 1992, program n709. Panel discussion of sexual harassment allegations against Senator

Annotated Bibliography

Bob Packwood. Commentary by Ellen Bravo of the National Association of Working Women and GOP advisor attorney, Gloria Toote.

Caplan, Lincoln. "Who Lied?" *Newsweek*, November 14, 1994, p. 52. Reviews *Strange Justice*, by Jane Mayer and Jill Abramson, in which the two *Wall Street Journal* reporters argue that Anita Hill was telling the truth.

Carlson, Margaret B. "The Ultimate Men's Club." *Time*, October 21, 1991, p. 50. Describes the prevailing male atmosphere of the U.S. Senate and its slowness to recognize sexual harassment as a serous affront to the rights of women.

"The Case Against Bob Packwood." CNN's "Larry King Live," February 9, 1993, program n759. Bob Packwood speaks out on charges he sexually harassed numerous women in the 1970s and 1980s.

"Charges 'Resolved' in Rift between Flake and Former Female Aide at NY Church." *Jet*, June 6, 1988, p. 10. A sexual harassment case involving Representative Floyd Flake and a former aide at a church in Queens.

"Charles Ogletree." ABC's "Good Morning, America," October 14, 1991, program n1391. An interview with Anita Hill's attorney concerning the Hill-Thomas hearings.

Clift, Eleanor. "Congress: The Ultimate Men's Club." *Newsweek*, October 21, 1991, p. 32. Cites statistics on the ratio of men to women serving in the Capitol. Discusses changes that are being made on the Hill in response to the women's pressure for change.

Clymer, Adam. "Packwood Weighs Quitting the Senate, His Lawyer Asserts." *New York Times*, November 20, 1993, p. 1. The Republican senator from Oregon accused of sexual harassment considers resigning.

———. "Parade of Witnesses Support Hill's Story, Thomas's Integrity." *New York Times*, October 14, 1991. A discussion of testimony by witnesses in the Hill-Thomas hearings.

Dominus, Susan. "Our Women in Washington." *Glamour*, January 1994, p. 120. In the elections of 1994, the number of women candidates voted into the House doubled, and the number of women elected into the Senate increased by four. Many female legislators have championed bills on sexual harassment and sex discrimination.

Eastland, Terry. "Advice and Descent." *National Review*, November 4, 1991, p. 22. Explores possible violations of Senate rules and federal law during the Senate Judiciary Committee's Hill-Thomas hearings.

Engelberg, Stephen and Deborah Sontag. "Behind the Agency's Walls: Misbehaving and Moving Up." *New York Times* (Late New York Edition), December 21, 1994, p. A1+. Exposes the failure of the Immigration and Naturalization Service to crack down on managers accused of sexual harassment. Cites the case of J. William Carter, an immigration officer, who despite his wrongdoing ranks second highest at the Border Patrol.

Ferguson, Andrew. "The Look That Killed." *National Review*, April 4, 1994, p. 80. Before appearing in a television interview, Ohio Representative Martin Hoke was captured on tape remarking on the size of a woman producer's breasts.

Fialka, John J. "CIA Is Charged in Two Legal Actions With Abuse Toward Women, Toleration of Heavy Drinking." *Wall Street Journal*, September 9, 1994, sec. A, p. 16. Over 100 female employees report their experiences of sexual harassment at the CIA.

Ford, Valerie. "Anita Hill Broke the Silence on Harassment, But Will We Listen?" *National Catholic Reporter*, May 29, 1992, vol. 28: 30, p. 19. The Hill-Thomas hearings are discussed to illustrate that sexual harassment must be taken seriously.

Gabriel, Trip. "The Trials of Bob Packwood." *New York Times Magazine*, August 29, 1993, p. 30. A biographical profile of Bob Packwood, the senator accused of sexually harassing female staff and campaign workers.

Garvery, Megan. "Male FAA Worker Sues, Alleging Female 'Gantlet' Demeaned Him." *Washington Post*, September 9, 1994, sec. A, p. 21. An employee of the Department of Transportation files a grievance of sexual harassment, saying he was severely abused by his female co-workers.

Gillespie, Marcia Ann. "We Speak in Tongues . . . African American Women Speak Out Against Sexual Harassment, Refusing to Be Silenced." *Ms.*, January/February 1992. The silence of African-American males during the Hill-Thomas hearings was disgraceful, all the more reason for African-American women to speak out against sexual harassment. @BIB =
Gladstone, Mark. "Sex Harassment Suit Names Areias, Chief Aide." *Los Angels Times*, August 25, 1994, sec. A, p. 3. A California legislative aide was threatened with losing her job after lodging sexual harassment complaints.

Gleick, Elizabeth, Michael Haederle, Margie Bonnett and Fannie Weinstein. "Agent of Change." *People*, November 1, 1993, p. 101. FBI agent Suzane Doucette is suing the FBI after five years of sexual harassment, thereby breaking the agency's stringent code of silence.

Goodman, Ellen. "Who Told the Truth?" *Boston Globe*, November 13, 1994, sec. A, p. 7. An assessment of questions left unanswered by the Hill-Thomas hearings, with a review of *Strange Justice*, a book on the episode by Jane Mayer and Jill Abramson.

Graves, Florence George. "The Other Woman: Remember Angela Wright? Neither Do Most People." *Washington Post*, October 9, 1994, sec. F, p. 1. The story of Angela Wright, the other woman who accused Clarence Thomas of sexual harassment.

Hentoff, Nat. "A Day in Court for Paula Jones." *Washington Post*, November 12, 1994, sec. A, p. 25. An examination of the court brief filed by the American Civil Liberties Union (ACLU) on Paula Jones' behalf, which argues that granting President Clinton immunity from her sexual harassment charges would compromise the dignity of the presidency.

Hewitt, Bill and B. Austin. "She Could Not Keep Silent." *People*, October 28, 1991, p. 40. A biographical profile of Anita Hill and commentary on how her testimony in the Hill-Thomas hearings brought the issue of sexual harassment to the forefront of public awareness.

Hill, Anita. "The Nature of the Beast." *Ms.*, January 1992, p. 32. An excerpt from Hill's comments on sexual harassment before a panel at the National Forum for Women State Legislators. Why so many women remain silent about sexual harassment and how anger can empower women to take action.

Hutton, Lauren. "Anita Hill: Law Professor." *Interview*, January 1992, p. 55. The model and actress praises Hill for her courage in making her sexual harassment charges against Clarence Thomas public, then discusses the abuses women have suffered throughout history.

Jackson, Robert L. "Focus Is Shifting Back to Packwood Probe." *Los Angeles Times*, November 17, 1994, sec. A, p. 14. After a long investigation into sexual harassment charges against Senator Bob Packwood, the Senate Ethics Committee is finally beginning to receive portions of his diaries.

"Jones Will Pursue Suit Against Clinton." *Boston Globe*, October 8, 1994, p. 11. Clinton rejects an out-of-court settlement with the former Arkansas state employee who has charged him with sexual harassment.

Jordan, June. "Can I Get a Witness?" *Progressive*, December 1991, p. 12. The improper treatment of Anita Hill as a witness during the confirmation hearings for Clarence Thomas is examined.

"Judging Thomas." *Nation*, October 28, 1991, p. 501. An editorial piece highlighting Clarence Thomas' prior history of disrespect for women.

"Justice Department Backs Delay for Jones' Suit." *Boston Globe*, August 20, 1994, p. 5. The Justice Department postpones Paula Jones' sexual harassment lawsuit against President Clinton until his presidential term ends.

Kelman, M. "Lessons of the Thomas Affair." *New Leader*, November 4, 1991, p. 5. Suggests that the Hill-Thomas hearings did little to bring out the important issues of the case, focusing instead on political rivalries.

Lewis, Neil A. "Aides at Justice Study Immunity for Presidents." *New York Times*, May 20, 1994, p. A1. The Justice Department tries to decide whether to shield President Clinton from Paula Jones' sexual harassment charges until after he has left office.

———. "Justice Department Sides with Clinton on Woman's Suit." *New York Times*, August 19, 1994, sec. A, p. 18. The Justice Department determines that President Clinton is immune from Paula Jones' civil suit until his term in office is over.

———. "Law Professor Accuses Thomas of Sexual Harassment in 1980s." *New York Times*, October 7, 1991, p. A1. Two days before the Senate Judiciary

Committee is scheduled to vote on the nomination of Clarence Thomas to the Supreme Court, Anita F. Hill's accusations of sexual harassment come to light.

Marshall, Eliot. "AID Acts on Erickson Case." *Science*, October 14, 1988, p. 188. The former director of malaria research for the U.S. Agency for International Development (AID), James M. Erickson, has been charged with sexual harassment and misconduct. Erickson sues to force a decision on his status.

Mayer, Jane and Jill Abramson. "Digging for Drt." *Newsweek*, November 14, 1994, p. 55. An excerpt from *Strange Justice*, the two reporters' book about the Hill-Thomas hearings.

Minerbrook, Scott. "The Case of the Sexual Predator." *US News & World Report*, April 19, 1993, p. 31. The FBI investigates a Tennessee judge who sexually assaults women.

"More Questions." *American Spectator*, September 1994, vol. 27, p. 82. Questions are to whether or not a president should be immune from civil lawsuits while in office, with reference to sexual harassment charges against President Clinton by Paula Jones.

Nelson, Jil. "Anita Hill: No Regrets." *Essence*, March 1992, p. 54. After the hearings, Anita Hill discusses the event and the impact it has had on her life.

"No Class Act." *Cosmopolitan*, December 1994, p. 40. An examination of the political implications and impact of charges that President Bill Clinton had an extramarital affair with Gennifer Flowers and that he sexually harassed Paula Jones.

Pollitt, Katha. "Subject to Debate: Feminist Reaction to Paula Jones." *Nation*, June 13, 1994, p. 824. Considers the challenge to feminists when a pro-choice president is charged with sexual harassment.

"Ocmulgee DA Was Told to Quit, GBI Reports Says." *Atlanta Constitution*, November 11, 1994, sec. B, p. 5. Georgia DA was persuaded to resign when he learned that he had been recorded on tape sexually harassing a female staff member.

Pincus, Walter. "CIA and the 'Glass Ceiling' Secret." *Washington Post*, September 9, 1994, sec. A, p. 25. A top-secret study found that over half of the CIA's female case officers had experienced sexual harassment and racial discrimination.

Ragsdale, Shirley. "When Men Are Sexual-Harassment Victims." *USA Today*, September 22, 1994, sec. A, p. 12. Douglas P. Hartman filed a lawsuit against the Department of Transportation, claiming that his experience of sexual harassment at a cultural diversity training workshop was worse than Paula Coughlin's trauma at the Tailhook convention.

114

Annotated Bibliography

Reed, Julia. "The Burden of Proof." *Vogue*, January 1994, p. 32. Evaluates sexual harassment charges filed by over two dozen women against Senator Bob Packwood and questions whether Packwood's diaries can be legally subpoenaed. Commentary on the charges from a female point of view.

Reed, S. and S. McElwaine. "Full-Court Presser." *People*, October 28, 1994, p. 55. Profile of the career of Nina Totenberg, National Public Radio's legal correspondent, who broke the story of the Anita Hill-Clarence Thomas controversy.

Reinhardt, R. "Anita Hill (Testimony Before Judiciary Committee Against Clarence Thomas)." *People*, December 30, 1991, v. 36, p. 46. Describes the impact that Anita Hill's televised testimony in the Hill-Thomas hearings has had on women and corporate America.

Salholz, Eloise, David A. Kaplan, and Eleanor Clift, "Anatomy of a Debacle." *Newsweek*, October 21, 1991, p. 26. Congress is criticized for its male bias after Hill-Thomas hearings.

"Sex and the CIA." *Washington Post*, September 23, 1994, sec. A, p. 26. The director of the CIA gives his reaction to multiple allegations of sexual harassment and discrimination against the agency.

"Sex Harassment Case: Questions and Politics." *New York Times*, October 25, 1992, p. 1. In New York City, the new deputy chief appointed by Mayor David Dinkins is accused of sexual harassment by a former colleague. Comparisons are made to the Hill-Thomas hearings.

Shalit, Ruth. "A Klutz, Not a Criminal." *Gentlemen's Quarterly*, August 1994, p. 45. Argues that Senator Bob Packwood should be reprimanded, not indicted, for unwanted sexual overtures he made toward women in the past. Asserts that the senator did not create a "hostile environment" or block women's careers.

Shapiro, Bruce. "Believe It: *Strange Justice: The Selling of Clarence Thomas* by Jane Mayer and Jill Abramson/*Resurrection: The Confirmation of Clarence Thomas* by John C. Danforth/*The Complete Transcripts of the Clarence Thomas-Anita Hill Hearings*." *Nation*, December 12, 1994, p. 730. Reviews of two books about the Hill-Thomas hearings, as well as of the published transcripts of those hearings.

Sharpe, R. "Capitol Hill's Worst Kept Secret: Sexual Harassment." *Ms.*, January 1992, vol. 2: 4, p. 28. An investigation of the prevalence of discrimination and sexual harassment of women on Capitol Hill. In response, the Capitol Hill Women's Political Caucus Sexual Harassment Task Force has formed.

"She Said . . . He Said." *Current Events*, October 28, 1991, p. 1. A general overview of the Hill-Thomas hearings, with information from a *USA Today* public opinion poll.

Signorile, Michelangelo. "Queer in America." *Advocate*, April 20, 1993, no. 627, p. 33. An excerpt from the book bearing the same title; discusses a gay man's experience of being sexually harassed by a gay male legislator.

Sullivan, Suzanne L. "Back Off! Stopping Harassers in Their Tracks." *Off Our Backs*, December 1993, vol 23: 11, p. 10. Martha J. Langelan, former president of the Washington, DC, Rape Crisis Center, discusses in an interview the Senate's handling of the Hill-Thomas hearings.

Szep, Paul. "Editorial Cartoon." *Boston Globe*, October 16, 1994, p. 82. A cartoon mocks President Clinton for "mis-handling" foreign policy and international relations—as well as Paula Jones.

Taylor, Elizabeth. "Bad Old Boys of Chicago Politics." *Savvy Woman*, August 1988, p. 16. George Dunne, president of Chicago's Cook County Board of Commissioners, allegedly has been hiring women in exchange for sexual favors.

Thomas, Evan. "There Is Always Something; Does Washington's Scandal Machine Go Too Far?" *Newsweek*, October 21, 1991, p. 33. Excerpts from a new book by Suzanne Garment, *SCANDAL: The Culture of Mistrust in American Politics*, which notes the press's unquenchable thirst for scandal. Discusses the Hill-Thomas hearings as one example.

Thomas, Virginia Lamp. "Breaking Silence." *People*, November 11, 1991, p. 108. Clarence Thomas' wife speaks about her husband and the Hill-Thomas hearings.

"Too Much Immunity in the Jones Case." *New York Times* (Late New York Edition), December 30, 1994, p. A30. Discussion of Paula Jones' lawsuit against President Clinton and the unfairness of his exemption from her charges until after he leaves office.

Toobin, Jeffrey. "The Burden of Clarence Thomas." *New Yorker*, September 27, 1993, p. 38. Justice Clarence Thomas on the Hill-Thomas hearings, more than two years later.

Walker, R. "Becoming the Third Wave." *Ms.*, January 1992, p. 39. The Hill-Thomas hearings had more to do with attitudes toward women's power and credibility than with sexual harassment per se.

Walsh, Kenneth T. "New Mates on a Very Leaky Ship." *U.S. News & World Report*, July 11, 1994, p. 31. Changes in the Clinton administration considered in light of sexual harassment charges made against the president by Paula Jones.

Weiner, Tim. "CIA to Pay $410,000 to Spy Who Says She Was Smeared." *The New York Times* (Late New York Edition), December 8, 1994, p. A1. CIA will pay top spy Janine M. Brookner $410,000 in a sex discrimination suit she filed against the agency. Brookner was demoted as a result of male subordinates' false charges of sexual and other misconduct.

"When Love Letters Become Hated Mail" *Time*, October 21, 1991, p. 63. Details of Kerry Ellison's sexual harassment charges against a colleague at the Internal Revenue Service (IRS). The decision of Ninth Circuit Court of Appeals establishes the reasonable woman standard.

White, Jack E. "The Stereotypes of Race." *Time*, October 21, 1991, p. 66. Discusses the issue of race in the Hill-Thomas hearings.

Will, George F. "Anita Hill's Tangled Web." *Newsweek*, April 19, 1993, p. 74. Review of David Brock's book *The Real Anita Hill*, which explores evidence that Hill's allegations against Clarence Thomas were complete fabrications.

Winternitz, Helen. "Anita Hill: One Year Later." *Working Woman*, September 1992, p. 21. Anita Hill's life in the year following the Hill-Thomas hearings.

Zuckerman, Mortimer B. "Behind the Paula Jones Story." *U.S. News & World Report*, May 23, 1994, p. 82. An assertion that the sexual harassment charges of Paula Jones against President Bill Clinton are insubstantial and inflated.

Zuckman, Jill. "Burke Says Group Spread Assertions on Kennedy." *Boston Globe*, October 26, 1994, p. 23. Reporter Richard Burke denies spreading allegations about Edward M. Kennedy's sexual harassment of his staff and his cocaine use.

———. "Senate Panel Calls Allegations Against Kennedy Baseless." *Boston Globe*, October 25, 1994, p. 1. The Senate Ethics Committee finds a claim of sexual harassment against Senator Edward Kennedy unfounded and clears him of the charges.

HELPING PROFESSIONS

"American Agenda—Sexual Harassment Among Doctors." ABC's "ABC World News Tonight," May 26, 1994, program n4104. An account by George Strait about the domination of the medical establishment by men, and about the frequency of sexual harassment of female patients and co-workers.

Begley, Sharon and Nina Archer Biddle, et al. "Hey Doc, You Got Great Legs." *Newsweek*, January 31, 1994, p. 54. A study published in the *New England Journal of Medicine* has found that it is not uncommon for female physicians to be sexually harassed by their male patients.

Chisholm, Patricia. "Betrayal of Trust." *Maclean's*, December 12, 1995, p. 53. A doctor in British Columbia, Canada, who is accused of sexually harassing a former 19-year-old patient has been found guilty of plotting her murder. Doctor Joseph Charalambous had become obsessed with preventing Sia Simmons, his former patient, from testifying against him.

Emery, M. "A Surgeon Cuts to the Heart of the Matter." *People*, October 28, 1991, p. 50. An interview with Dr. Frances Conley, one of the nation's foremost neurosurgeons, who candidly discusses the sexual harassment she has endured from colleagues over the years.

Majka, L.C. "Sexual Harassment in the Church." *Society*, May/June 1991, p. 14. The problem of sexual harassment in religious institutions.

McDonald, Kim. "Sex Under Glass." *Psychology Today*, March 1988, p. 58. A discussion of liability issues for sexologists.

"A Trail of Abuse." *Christian Century*, December 22, 1993, vol. 110: 37, p. 1,294. Discusses the Roman Catholic Church's reaction to multiple sexual harassment charges filed against priests.

MILITARY

"After Tailhook—Women in the Military." CNN's "Newsmaker Saturday." February 19, 1994, Program n210. How the Tailhook scandal has created opportunities for women in the military. @BIB = "Backlash Against Women from Tailhook Will Continue." NPR's "All Things Considered," October 30, 1994, program n1651. The reporter who brought the Tailhook scandal to the public's attention notes, three years later, that the navy's treatment of women remains basically the same.

Cary, Peter, Bruce B. Auster, et al. "What's Wrong With the Navy?" *U.S. News & World Report*, July 13, 1992, p. 22. The Tailhook scandal has forced the navy to examine existing policies on sexual harassment.

Dowd, Maureen. "Navy Defines Sexual Harassment with the Colors of Traffic Lights." *New York Times*, June 19, 1993, p. 1. The U.S. Navy is beginning to crack down on sexual harassment by educating commanding officers about the issue.

Fusco, Coco. "Army Rules." *Village Voice*, August 11, 1992, vol 37: 32, p. 20. Discussion of the Tailhook scandal and the preponderance of aggressive and patriarchal behavior in the U.S. military.

Grogan, David and Liz McNeil. "Burden of Shame." *People*, April 5, 1993, p. 83. After filing sexual harassment charges against the U.S. Army, Alexis Colon committed suicide. The family has filed a $320 million claim.

Lamar, Jacob V. "Redefining a Woman's Place." *Time*, February 15, 1988, p. 27. Secretary of Defense Frank Carlucci orders military reforms that will make 4,000 additional military posts accessible to women. The move represents a milestone for women in the military.

"Much Too Macho." *Time*, September 28, 1987, p. 28. A study finds a high rate of sexual harassment of women in the U.S. Navy and Marine Corps. Secretary of Defense Caspar Weinberger forms a high-level task force to combat the abuse.

"Paula Coughlin." *News for You*, November 16, 1994, p. 2. Reviews the Supreme Court's decision in favor of Lt. Paula Coughlin in her sexual harassment case against the U.S. Navy and discusses the sexist climate women in the military have had to endure.

Schmitt, Eric. "Airforce Sergeant in a Sex Complaint Tells of Reprisals." *New York Times*, June 10, 1994, p. A1. Sergeant Zenaida Martinez, a police officer at Milden Hall Airbase in England, suffers retaliation from her command after testifying before Congress about sexual harassment.

———. "Handling of Harassment Issues Helps Kill Admiral's Nomination." *New York Times*, June 26, 1994, sec. 1, p. 17. The Defense Department withdrew Stanley R. Arthur's nomination as commander of American forces because of his questionable handling of a sexual harassment case.

———. "Navy Acts Against 10 Male Instructors in Sex Harassment Case." *New York Times* (Late New York Edition), December 16, 1994, p. A27. Report on the court-martial of four male instructors and the punishment of six other officers for attempting to elicit sex from 16 female students enrolled in the navy's computer and communications network courses.

———. "Navy Chief Trying to Make Amends over Harassment." *New York Times*, June 1, 1994, p. A1. Describes sexual abuse at the 1991 Tailhook Convention and the reparations the navy is attempting to make to Lt. Darlene Simmons, one of the victims.

———. "Pentagon Plea: Let an Admiral Keep His Stars." *New York Times*, April 13, 1994, p. A1. Three top Pentagon officials travel to Capitol Hill in an unprecedented move to urge Congress to allow Admiral Kelso to retire with full rank and pension, despite his involvement in the Tailhook scandal.

———. "Senate Panel Says Admiral in Scandal Merits Full Pension." *New York Times*, April 14, 1994, p. A1. Senators debate whether to allow Admiral Frank Kelso to retire from the navy with full rank and pension after his involvement in the Tailhook scandal.

———. "Senate Women Want Admiral to Lose Rank." *New York Times*, April 19, 1994, p. A1. Admiral Frank B. Kelso II, the U.S. Navy's chief of operations, plans to resign, maintaining his four-star rank as admiral. Six out of seven women in the Senate oppose his retirement with full rank due to his role in the Tailhook debacle.

"Two Women Settle Tailhook Suits." *New York Times*, November 6, 1994, sec. 1, p. 46. Wendy Delane and Julie Marler settle their lawsuits against the U.S. Navy and the Las Vegas Hilton for an undisclosed sum. They claim to have been among over two dozen women who were sexually harassed and/or molested during the Tailhook convention in 1991.

Warrick, Pamela. "Tailhook Behind Her, She Starts a New Life." *Los Angeles Times*, November 8, 1994, sec. E, p. 1. The U.S. Navy awards Paula Coughlin $6.7 million for the sexual harassment she endured during the Tailhook convention of 1991.

"Woman Wins $5 Million for Tailhook." *New York Times*, November 1, 1994, sec. A, p. 24. The Las Vegas Hilton, where the Tailhook Convention was held, is ordered to pay a former navy lieutenant $5 million for its failure to provide adequate security.

WORKPLACE

"Activists Discuss Sexual Harassment in the Workplace." NBC's "Good Morning America," July 6, 1992, Program n1581. Sexual harassment in the workplace is discussed in the Joan Lunden interview of NOW Legal and Education fund executive directors Helen Newborne and Letitia Baldridge.

Allen, Bonnie. "Sexual Harassment: One Way Out." *Essence*, August 1987, p. 96. Provides tips on how to cope with sexual harassment on the job. Includes guidelines for making formal legal complaints when other methods fail to mitigate the situation.

Auerbach, Jon and Michael Grunwald. "Four Female Firefighters Sue Department." *Boston Globe*, November 30, 1994, p. 29. Half the women firefighters working for the Boston Fire Department sued their employer over constant sexual harassment by male firefighters.

Bacon, D. "See You In Court." *Nation's Business*, July 1989, p. 16. Speculation about the reasons behind the rapid increase in the number of sexual harassment lawsuits filed by employees against their employers.

Baber, Asa. "The 1995 New Year's Quiz." *Playboy*, January 1995, p. 34. A satirical look at sexual harassment in the form of a quiz.

Balamaci, M., G. Verner, et al. "The Price of Saying No." *People*, October 28, 1991, p. 44. Three women who were sexually harassed in the workplace tell their stories and relate how they fought back.

Balzo, Denise Del. "What Waitresses Are Wearing." *Glamour*, September 1994, p. 144. Readers' opinions on the costumes many waitresses are required to wear and the messages sent by their clothing.

Bargepole. "Bargepole." *Punch*, May 15, 1991, p. 52. The author argues that sexual harassment is nonexistent in the business world and that billions of pounds are needlessly wasted on sexual harassment lawsuits.

"Beer Commercials and Working Women." *Off Our Backs*, January 1992, p. 3. Discusses litigation by five women employees who have filed sexual harassment charges against Stroh Brewey Co. for its sexually suggestive advertising campaign.

"Bimbos in Beer Ads—Spoof of Sexual Harassment?" CNN's "Larry King Live," December 19, 1991, program n455. Discussion of the hostile work environment sexual harassment charges filed by five female employees of Stroh Brewery Co. as a result of its provocative advertising.

"Golden Litigation." *Christian Science Monitor*, September 7, 1994, p. 18. An editorial discussion of *Weeks v. Baker & McKenzie*.

Goldstein, Richard. "Body Politics: Wall of Change." *Village Voice*, November 26, 1991, p. 52. A column addressing the need to consider the feelings of co-workers when hanging posters or pictures in the workplace.

Greene, Richard. "A Pattern of Fornication." *Forbes*, June 16, 1986, p. 66. The U.S. Court of Appeals for the District of Columbia will rule on *Vinson v. Taylor*. The case is discussed in detail.

Greenhouse, Linda. "Court, 9-0, Makes Sex Harassment Easier to Prove." *New York Times*, November 10, 1993, p. A1. Commentary on the Supreme Court's ruling in *Harris v. Forklift Systems, Inc.*, which broadens the definition of sexual harassment and makes it easier for women to make a claim.

Gregory, Deborah. "Sexual Harassment." *Essence*, March 1993, p. 99. Analyzes the psychological impact of sexual harassment and offers suggestions on how to discourage male co-workers from sexually harassing women at work.

Gross, Ciceil L. "Catherine Claxton vs. the UN." *New York Times*, September 15, 1994, sec. A, p. 23. A discussion of U.N. employee Catherine Claxton's three-year battle in a sexual harassment case against her employer.

Gross, Jane. "Jury Awards $7.1 Million in Sex Case." *New York Times* (Late New York Edition), September 2, 1994, p. A16. Rena Weeks, a former secretary at the law firm of Baker & McKenzie, is awarded $7.1 million for sexual harassment while working at the firm.

———. "Law Firms and Harassment." *New York Times*, July 29, 1994. The sexual harassment suit filed by Rena Weeks against the world's largest law firm, Baker & McKenzie.

Halberstam, Joshua. "Flirting with Disaster." *Self*, March 1994, p. 152. Focuses on sexual harassment in the workplace and the varied and subtle forms of behavior that constitute sex discrimination.

Hanna, Janan. "Seven Waitresses File Sex Lawsuit, Allege Bob Chinn's Was a Grab House." *Chicago Tribune*, November 18, 1994, sec. 2NW, p. 6. Female employees at a restaurant in Wheeling, Illinois, sued the owner for sexually harassing them on the job.

Hammonds, Keith H. "Clarifying 'Sexual Harassment.'" *Business Week*, November 22, 1993, p. 52. The legal implications for employers of the Supreme Court's ruling in *Harris v. Forklift Systems, Inc.*

Haskell, Molly. "Managing Your Sexuality." *Working Woman*, August 1994, p. 29. Explores the complexities of human sexuality in the workplace, suggesting that manifestations such as flirtation, teasing, and innuendo constitute power struggles between the sexes.

Henriques, Diana. "Sexual Harassment and a Chief Executive." *New York Times*, March 30, 1995, sec. D, p. 1. The board of directors of W. R. Grace

& Company demands the resignation of chief executive J. P. Bolduc after employees make allegations of sexual harassment.

Hentoff, Nat. "'I Would Prefer Not To.'" *Washington Post*, September 24, 1994, sec. A, p. 27. Describes the case of a New York City accountant at the Department of Housing Preservation and Development who refused to attend a required sexual harassment prevention training course, on moral grounds.

Herring Hubert B. "A Million-Dollar Leer." *New York Times*, September 4, 1994, sec F, p. 2. Jurors' views on *Weeks v. Baker & McKenzie*.

Hewitt, Bill. "Objects of Desire." *People*, December 19, 1994, p. 103. Discusses cases of male employees claiming to have been sexually harassed by women.

"The High Cost of Sex Harassment." *The New York Times*, September 12, 1994, sec. A, p. 14. The Rena Weeks case sends tremors through corporate America.

Holden, Ted. "Revenge of the 'Office Ladies': Sexual Harassment Is Still the Norm, but Japanese Working Women Are Fighting Back." *Business Week*, July 13, 1992, p. 42. What Japanese working women are doing to combat frequent sexual harassment in the workplace.

Janofsky, Michael. "Gay Workers Accuses Male of Harassing Him Sexually." *New York Times*, November 18, 1994, sec. A, p. 24. Philadelphia restaurant worker Warren J. Swage Jr. filed sexual harassment complaints against his male boss.

Jones, Patrica A. "Dealing with Sexual Harassment." *Black Enterprise*, February 1987, vol 17, p. 1084. Examines the corporate world's heightened awareness of sexual harassment in the workplace and notes the difficulty of recognizing subtler forms. Highlights, as a case in point, the Supreme Court's 1986 ruling in *Meritor Savings Bank v. Vinson*.

———. "Stressbusters." *Black Enterprise*, February 1987, vol. 17, p. 106. Enumerates causes of high stress for working women, including sexual harassment.

"Jury Awards $900,000 to Black Female Officer in Detroit Police Case." *Jet*, April 27, 1987, p. 66. Discusses the case of Cheryl Preston, a Detroit police officer, who filed a sexual harassment complaint against her co-workers in 1984, claiming she suffered a nervous breakdown.

Kadetsky, Elizabeth. "The Union." *Ms.*, March/April 1994, p. 33. The Screen Actors Guild protects registered talent agents accused of sexual harassment.

Kantrowitz, B., T. Barett, et al. "Striking a Nerve." *Newsweek*, October 21, 1991, p. 34. Describes the prevalence of sexual harassment of American working women and how the Hill-Thomas hearing have become a catalyst for their rage.

Annotated Bibliography

Kiechel, Walter. "The High Cost of Sexual Harassment." *Fortune*, September 14, 1987, p. 147. Details the hidden costs of sexual harassment in the workplace, such as employee turnover, lowered morale, and declining productivity.

Kilborn, Peter I. "A Sexual Harassment Case Draws Swift Action from an Agency." *New York Times* (Late New York Edition), January 10, 1995, p. A14. Two female employees at the Rock & Roll Hall of Fame in Cleveland file a sexual harassment claim against a co-worker and get an almost immediate response from the EEOC. Within nine months, the perpetrator is convicted of public indecency on three counts, ordered to serve a prison sentence of 30 days, and fined $250.

Kolbert, E. "Sexual Harassment at Work Is Pervasive, Survey Suggests." *New York Times*, October 11, 1991, p. A1. A New York Times/CBS News poll finds that sexual harassment continues to be a problem of significant magnitude in the workplace.

Lanpher, Katherine. "A Bitter Brew." *Ms.*, November 1992, p. 36. An in-depth discussion of the Stroh Brewery sexual harassment lawsuit.

"The Law at Work." *Changing Times*, November 1986, p. 132. Discusses employer-employee relations in light of legal developments in sexual harassment, such as the Supreme Court's ruling in *Meritor Savings Bank v. Vinson*.

Lope, Robert J. "Study of L.A. Fire Department Cites Race, Gender Bias." *Los Angeles Times*, November 12, 1994, sec. A, p. 1. A November 1994 audit concluded that women and minorities employed by the Los Angeles City Fire Department are discriminated against and abused both sexually and racially.

Lublin, Joann S. "Resisting Advances: Employers Act to Curb Sex Harassing on the Job; Lawsuits, Fines Feared; Formal Policies Are Issued, Training Sessions Held; but Policing Is Difficult." *Wall Street Journal*, April 24, 1981, vol. 197, p. 1. What companies are doing to deter sexual harassment in the workplace, which persists despite their efforts.

Malnic, Eric. "Suit Accuses Movie Theatres' Mangers of Sex Harassment." *Los Angeles Times*, August 26, 1994, sec. B, p. 3. A former female employee charges Cineplex Odeon Theatres with sexual harassment.

Maloof, Denise N. "Protesters Charge Houston's With Racism." *Atlanta Journal and Atlanta Constitution (ATCJ)*, November 24, 1994, sec. XJN, p. 31. New Orleans protesters picket Houston's restaurant for racial discrimination and sexual harassment.

Marton, Kati. "An All Too Common Story." *Newsweek*, October 21, 1991, p. 8. A former newswoman's testimony of sexual harassment and the silence she maintaind in order to keep her job.

Matusow, Barbara. "Baby, What'd I Say?" *Washingtonian*, August 1993, vol. 328: 11, p. 60. Discusses the development of office policies and laws designed to prevent sexual harassment.

McLaughlin, Paul, Nancy Stewart and Fern Stimpson. "The Case of the Amourous Associate." *Canadian Business*, January 1990, p. 79. Ways to avoid sexual harassment in the workplace.

Moore, T. S. "Experts Tell Ways Men Can Avoid Sex Harassment Charges." *Jet*, March 30, 1992. Offers tips to men on what kind of behavior to avoid in the office; explains what sexual harassment is and is not.

Morris, Chris and Phyllis Stark. "Biz Faces Sexual Harassment Onus." *Billboard*, November 16, 1991, p. 6. Discusses the prevalence of sexual harassment in the music industry.

Noble, Linda. "My Struggle to Fight Harassment." *Glamour*, May 1994, p. 139. One womans fight against sexual harassment at the Bath Iron Works Corporation.

Nussbaum, Karen. "The Challenges Ahead." *Working Mother*, May 1994, p. 32. Women's advances in the workforce over the past 15 years and the remaining hurdles they face.

"Ocmulgee DA Was Told to Quit, GBI Report Says." *Atlanta Constitution*, November 11, 1994, sec. B, p. 5. A Georgia DA was forced to resign after being tape recorded while sexually harassing a female staff worker.

"Office Intercourse." *Harpers' Bazaar*, October 1994, p. 136. Discusses the subtle nuances of sexist language in the workplace.

Parker-Pope, Tara and Dan Michaels. "Sexual Harassment Campaign Barks Up Controversial Tree." *Wall Street Journal*, November 15, 1994, p. 17A. An advertisement produced by the Amsterdam office of the J. Walter Thompson Company depicts a bedraggled male employee being "sexually harassed" by a dog who mounts his leg.

Pereira, Joseph. "Legal Beat: Free-Speech Rights vs. Sexual Harassment." *Wall Street Journal*, October 3, 1994, sec. B, p. 5. In the workplace, David Heller circulated nude photos from *Hustler* and *Penthouse* magazines with the face of his co-worker Sylvia Smith Bowman pasted on them. Heller's defense is that Bowman was running for local office and therefore was a public figure, which he claims gave him the right to circulate her picture under the auspices of free speech.

Petersen, James R. "Mixed Company." *Playboy*, February 1992, p. 47. Argues that sexual interest is often erroneously interpreted as sexual harassment by feminists in the workplace.

Preston, Julia. "UN Wrestles with Sexual Harassment in Its Ranks." *Washington Post*, September 8, 1994, sec. A, p. 29. Complaints filed against the U.N. by female employees are forcing the agency to address the issue of sexual harassment.

Pristin, Terry. "Firms Wake Up to the Problem of Sex Harassment." *New York Times*, October 14, 1994, sec. B, p. 18. Discusses the impact Rena Weeks' $7.1 million award for punitive damages has had on law firms across the country.

"Quick Quiz: What Qualifies as Sex Discrimination?" *Glamour*, March 1987, p. 89. Exploration of what constitutes sexual harassment on the job, with information on the Supreme Court's ruling in *Meritor Savings Bank v. Vinson*, sex discrimination, and employer awareness.

Rabinowitz, Dorothy. "A Cautionary Tale." *New York*, January 8, 1990, p. 34. A criminal harassment claim is brought against Lewis M. Eisenberg of Goldman, Sachs & Co. by Eisenberg's former assistant, Cathy Abraham.

Richardson, John H. "California Suite—Inside the Business of Hollywood: Moguls, Movies and Money." *Premiere*, June 1992, p. 23. A discussion of the sexual harassment case against Michael Levy of Silver Pictures.

Sandroff, R., G. Baseman, et al. "Sexual Harassment." *Working Woman*, June 1992, p. 47. Results of a survey comparing working women's views and experiences of sexual harassment with the views of corporate management. Includes a 1988 report, "Sexual Harassement in the Fortune 500."

Schmidt, Peggy. "Warning: Men at Work May Be Hazardous to Your Career." *Mademoiselle*, December 1987, p. 178. A discussion of the subtler forms of sexual harassment in the workplace, such as innuendo and sexist humor.

Segal, Troy. "Getting Serious about Sexual Harassment: More Companies Are Addressing It, but There's Still a Long Way to Go." *Business Week*, November 9, 1992, p. 78. The strides being made by companies in combating sexual harassment in the Workplace, the work that remains to be done.

"Sexual Harassment in the Workplace." *World Monitor*, March 1993, p. 9. A worldwide survey conducted by the International Labour Organisation reveals that women in more than 22 industrialized countries have experienced varying degrees of sexual harassment; up to 60% of these cases have gone unreported.

"Sexual Harassment Lands Companies in Court: Working Women Reject Obscenities, Embraces, and Double Entendres." *Business Week*, October 1, 1979, p. 120. What working women are doing to defend and protect themselves against sexual harassment, including filing suit against their employers.

"Sexual Harassment on the Job." *New England Business*, May 20, 1985, p. 25. Since 1980, when the EEOC issued guidelines on sexual harassment, the number of grievances has increased dramatically. Corporations are beginning to establish in-house sexual harassment regulations, but many companies are unsure about how to deal with the problem most effectively.

Simison, Robert L. and Cathy Trost. "Abusive Acts: Sexual Harassment at Work Is a Cause for Growing Concern; Many Incidents Are Violent, and a

Lot Go Unreported." *Wall Street Journal*, June 24, 1986, vol. 207, p. 1. The often violent sexual abuse of women in the workplace, which often goes unnoticed, unreported, and ignored.

Simmons, Connie. "Ending Sexual Harassment." *Vogue*, September 1987, p. 70. The Supreme Court decision in *Meritor Savings Bank v. Vinson* expands the conditions under which Title VII sexual harassment claims can be filed.

Slade, Margot. "Sexual Harassment: Stories from the Field." *New York Times*, March 27, 1994, section 4, p. 1. Cites several cases of sexual harassment and discusses the complexities involved in handling them fairly. Explains why each case must be addressed individually.

Spiro, Leah. "Is Wall Street Finally Starting to Get It?" *Business Week*, September 26, 1994, p. 54. Persistent sexual harassment and racial discrimination within Wall Street institutions and what needs to be done to combat them.

Spiro, Leah and Michele Galen. "The Angry Voices of Kidder." *Business Week (Industrial/Technology Edition)*, February 1, 1993, p. 60. Charges of sexual harassment and discrimination at Kidder, Peabody, and Co., a 127-year-old brokerage house.

Stacey, Michelle. "Can You Work It Out? 5 Worst-Case Office Scenarios." *Mademoiselle*, January 1992, p. 100. Methods for dealing with sensitive situations at work, such as sexual harassment, working with a new boss or an old boyfriend.

"Staffing Audit Burns Fire Department." *Los Angeles Times*, November 19, 1994, Sec. B, p. 7. An editorial on sexual and racial discrimination and harassment at the Los Angeles Fire Department.

Stanley, Alessandra. "Sexual Harassment Thrives in the New Russian Climate." *New York Times*, April 17, 1994, p. 1. Reveals that sexual harassment in the Russian workplace is prevalent and overt.

Stevens, Amy. "Lawyers & Clients: Women Lawyers Harassed by Clients, Too." *Wall Street Journal*, November 4, 1994, sec. B, p. 1. The harassment of women lawyers by their clients is not an uncommon occurrence and is difficult to handle. Most of these incidents go unreported.

"Striking a Nerve." *Newsweek*, October 21, 1991, p. 34. General report on the incidence of sexual harassment in the workplace, citing figures taken from polls.

Strom, S. "Harassment Rules Often Not Pushed." *New York Times*, October 20, 1991, p. 1. Despite the fact that federal law requires companies to institute and enforce policies prohibiting sexual harassment, many employers have yet to do so.

Sutton, Milton, "Safe Sex in the Office; Just Say Sign on the Dotted Line." *Advertising Age*, July 18, 1994, p. 18. Instructs men on how to avoid sexual harassment charges in the workplace. One proposed tactic is to sign a pre-dating agreement when dating colleagues.

Swoboda, Frank. "Employers Find a Tool to End Worker's Right to Sue: Arbitration." *Washington Post*, September 18, 1994, sec. H, p. 8. Companies are asking employees to sign contracts with arbitration clauses, denying them the right to sue for punitive damages in cases of sexual harassment.

"The Sexual Harassment Controversy." *Glamour*, November 1992, p. 112. Discusses the legalities of sexual harassment claims in the workplace.

Torry, Saundra. "Harassment Case Award Strikes a Chord with Firms." *Washington Post*, September 5, 1994, sec. WBIZ, p. 7. The Rena Weeks case alerts corporate America to the seriousness of sexual harassment. Fear of financial losses undelies the anxiety.

Watanabe, Teresa. "Japan's Female Job Applicants Feeling Harassed." *Los Angeles Times*, September 2, 1994, sec. A, p. 5. Women in Japan are beginning to report incidents of sexual harassment.

Will, R. B., S. D. Lydenberg, et al. "Twenty Corporations that Listen to Women." *Ms.*, November 1987, p. 45. Profiles of companies that value women employees and what they are doing to address concerns such as sexual harassment.

Witt, Linda. "Woman Warrior." *Mother Jones*, September/October 1994, p. 15. Karen Nussbaum, director of the Women's Bureau of the U.S. Department of Labor, is taking steps to educate working women about sexual harassment. Her groundbreaking survey, "Working Women Count!" will influence public policy affecting working women.

"Work Week: Same-Sex Harassment." *Wall Street Journal*, November 8, 1994, sec. A, p. 1. A discussion of same-sex harassment cases.

Wyse, Lois. "The Way We Are." *Good Housekeeping*, April 1994, p. 230. An opinion piece providing an in-depth discussion of sexual harassment in the workplace.

SCHOLARLY AND PROFESSIONAL JOURNAL ARTICLES

EDUCATION

"ACE Women in Higher Education Report: Eliminating Sexual Harassment on Campus." *Educational Record*, Winter 1992, p. 50. Covers the discussion of sexual harassment issues at recent meetings of the ACE Office of Women in Higher Education.

Baier, John L. "Sexual Harassment of University Students by Faculty Members at a Southern Research University." *College Student Affairs Journal*, Fall

1990, vol. 10: 2, p. 4. A study finds that 10% of male students and 24% of female students experience sexual harassment.

Barlow, Dudley. "The Right Never to Be Uncomfortable?" *Education Digest*, February 1994, vol. 39, p. 12. A high school teacher describes a lesson he taught in class that could have been misconstrued as sexual harassment and makes the point that teachers should not censor subjects, themes, or topics for fear of being accused of wrongdoing.

Beck, Irene. "Sexual Harassment in Schools: Facing the Issue." *PTA Today*, November/December 1994, vol. 20, p. 22. According to a survey taken by the American Association of University Women, 70% of female students in junior and senior high school report they have been sexually harassed.

Benson, Donna J. and Gregg E. Thomson. "Sexual Harassment on a University Campus: The Confluence of Authority Relations, Sexual Interest and Gender Stratification (Harassment of Female Students by Male Faculty; University of California, Berkeley; Based on a Conference Paper)." *Social Problems*, 1982, vol. 29: 3, p. 236. Examines the causes of sexual harassment of female college students by male instructors.

Bogart, Karen and Nan Stein. "Breaking the Silence: Sexual Harassment in Education." *Peabody Journal of Education*, Summer 1987, vol. 64: 4, p. 146. A discussion of the social dynamics underlying sexual harassment in higher education. Explores legal strategies for prevention.

Carroll, Lynne and Kathryn L. Ellis. "Faculty Attitudes Towards Sexual Harassment: Survey Results, Survey Process." *Initiatives*, Fall 1989, vol. 52: 3, p. 35. A survey indicates that male faculty members at one university are more tolerant of sexual harassment than women faculty members. Some male faculty are opposed to sexual harassment research efforts.

Collison, N. K. "A Sure-Fire Winner Is To Tell Her You Love Her; Women Fall For It All The Time: Men Talk." *Chronicle of Higher Education*, November 13, 1991, p. A1. The efforts of Ronald E. Campbell, director of housing at George Mason University, to educate men on college campuses about sexual harassment and date rape.

"Consensual Amorous Relationships Between Faculty and Students: The Constitutional Right to Privacy." *The Journal of College and University Law*, Summer 1988, vol. 15, p. 21. The legal rights of students and professors regarding romantic relationships with each other.

Cooper, G. Robb, et al. "Sexual Harassment in the Schools." *School Business Affairs*, April 1994, vol. 60: 4, p. 27. Defines sexual harassment and provides suggestions for prevention in schools.

Corbett, Kelly, et al. "Sexual Harassment in High School." *Youth and Society*, September 1993, vol. 25: 1, p. 93. A survey investigates college students' experiences of sexual harassment while in high school.

Decker, Robert H. "Can Schools Eliminate Sexual Harassment?" *The Education Digest*, January 1989, vol. 54, p. 59. Suggestions to help school board members prepare policies and guidelines on sexual harassment.

———. "Eleven Ways to Stamp Out the Potential for Sexual Harassment." *American School Board Journal*, August 1988, vol. 175: 8, p. 28. A "how to" guide, using the Equal Employment Opportunity Commission's guidelines as a starting point.

DeLoughry, Thomas J. and David L. Wilson. "Case of Computer Conference at California College Pits Free Speech against Civil-Rights Protection." *Chronicle of Higher Education*, September 28, 1994, p. A26. Women students at a California junior college charge sexual harassment at an all-male computer conference.

Dziech, Billie Wright. "The Bedevilling Issue of Sexual Harassment." *Chronicle of Higher Education*, December 8, 1993, p. A48. Discusses the increasing complexity of the sexual harassment issue and the controversy surrounding the effects of such harassment upon students.

Eaton, Judith S. "Strategies for Survival: Executive Women in Higher Education." *Liberal Education*, 1981, vol. 67: 3, p. 209. How women administrators in higher education can prevail in six types of power struggle, sexual harassment being one.

Elza, Jane. "Liability and Penalties for Sexual Harassment in Higher Education." *West's Education Law Quarterly*, April 1993, vol. 2: 2, p. 235. A call for colleges and universities to adopt, codify and systematize sexual harassment policies and procedures.

First, Patricia F. and Joan L. Curcio. "Ethical Liability: Are Girls Safe in Your Schools?" *School Business Affairs*, July 1994, vol. 60: 7, p. 37. Describes two cases in which female students were sexually harassed by teachers.

Fischer, Ann R. and Glenn E. Good. "Gender, Self, and Others: Perceptions of the Campus Environment." *Journal of Counseling Psychology*, July 1994, vol. 41, p. 343. A study examines gender roles and sex equity in higher education.

Gaines, Stanley O., Jr. "Sexual Harassment in American Academia." *Proteus*, Fall 1993, vol. 10: 2, p. 29. A general discussion of sexual harassment in higher education.

Gant, Elizabeth J. "Applying Title VII 'Hostile Work Environment' Analysis to Title IX of the Education Amendment of 1972—An Avenue of Relief for Victims of Student-to-Student Sexual Harassment in the Schools." *Dickinson Law Review*, Spring 1994, vol. 98, p. 489. The prevention of sexual harassment among students, with reference to the Civil Rights Act of 1991 and the Education Amendments of 1972. Examines the implications of the hostile work environment concept for Title IX.

Garlick, Rick. "Male and Female Responses to Ambiguous Instructor Behaviors." *Sex Roles*, January 1994, vol. 30: 1–2, p. 135. Male and female students perceive "ambiguous instructor immediacy behaviors" and their appropriateness differently.

Glazer, Sarah. "Sex on Campus." *CQR Researcher*, November 4, 1994, vol. 4: 41, p. 961. A general discussion of sexual harassment in higher education and an evaluation of the effectiveness of new prevention policies.

Gordon, Lynn D. "Women on Campus, 1870–1920: History to Use." *Thought and Action*, Spring 1990, vol. 6: 1, p. 5. An historical review of women in higher education.

Higginson, Nan M. "Addressing Sexual Harassment in the Classroom." *Educational Leadership*, November 1993, p. 93. One teacher's view on how to deal with the topic of sexual harassment in a junior high classroom.

Hoffman, Frances L. "Sexual Harassment in Academia: Feminist Theory and Institutional Practice." *Harvard Educational Review*, May 1986, vol. 56, p. 105. A look at feminist theories of sexual harassment in academia and how institutions actually cope with it.

Jaschik, S. "U.S. Plans Policies to Fight Harassment and Bias at Colleges." *Chronicle of Higher Education*, May 8, 1991, p. A1. Discusses new policies developed by the Education Department's Office for Civil Rights to prevent sexual harassment of students in higher education.

Jumsden, Linda S. "Getting Serious About Sexual Harassment." *ERIC Digest*, October 1992, n75, p. 3. Guidelines for developing sexual harassment policies and procedures in higher education.

Lawton, Millicent. "N.E.A. to Publish Curriculum on Student Harassment." *Education Week*, April 27, 1994. News that the National Education Association has published "Flirting or Hurting?" a curriculum on student-to-student sexual harassment in the schools.

Leatherman, C. "Colleges Seek New Ways to Deal With Sexual Harassment as Victims on Campus Are Reluctant to . . . " *Chronicle of Higher Education*, December 4, 1991, p. A1. Interviews with 24 affirmative action officers at universities throughout the United State indicate that issues of sexual harassment and rape are not being effectively dealt with, despite school policies and procedures.

Leiren, Hall. "Head-Banging for the Cause." *Alberta Report/Western Report*, September 5, 1994, vol. 21: 38, p. 28. Analyzes sexual harassment on Canadian college and university campuses, citing the case of *Krista Scott v. Prince George's College of New Caledonia*. In the case, a female student filed a sexual harassment claim after she allegedly was attacked in a women's restroom; suspicions arose that she fabricated her story and self-inflicted her injuries.

Lott, Bernice. "Sexual Harassment: Consequences and Remedies." *Thought and Action*, Winter 1993, vol. 8: 2, p. 89. An overview of the legal, sociological, and psychological aspects of sexual harassment. Examines the impact of Women Against Sexual Harassment, a group of faculty, staff, and graduate students at the University of Rhode Island founded to deter sexual harassment on campus.

Lydiard, Beverly W. "A Decade of Dealing with Sexual Harassment." *School Administrator*, January 1993, vol. 50: 1, p. 20. A vocational high school in Lexington, Massachusetts, has fought sexual harassment since 1980 with aggressive, proactive policies and educational programs.

Lyle, Katy and Mark Bregman. "I'll Never Look at the World the Same Again." *Scholastic Update*, March 12, 1993, p. 14. A student's personal account of sexual harassment in her high school, discussing her victory in a two-year lawsuit.

Marczely, Bernadette. "A Legal Update on Sexual Harassment in the Public Schools." *Clearinghouse*, July–August 1993, p. 329. Discusses school personnel's liability in sexual harassment claims. Provides sample cases to illustrate the issue.

Martindale, Don. "Patrons and Clients: The Sociology of Academic Advising." *International Journal of Contemporary Sociology*, 1979, vol. 16: 3–4, p. 2. An historical overview of sexual harassment in the context of academic advisorship of students, 1940–1979.

Masland, Susan W. I. "Gender Equity in Classrooms: The Teacher Factor." *Equity & Excellence in Education*, December 1994, vol. 27, p. 19. What teachers can do to eliminate gender bias in the classroom.

McMillen, L. "A Mixed Message for Campuses Seen in Thomas Hearings." *Chronicle of Higher Education*, October 23, 1991, p. A1. Explores the impact of the Hill-Thomas hearings on women in college.

Mentell, Edward J. "What to Do to Stop Sexual Harassment at School." *Educational Leadership*, November 1993, vol. 51: 3, p. 96. A study reveals widespread sexual harassment in schools; followed by a discussion of school administrators' responsibility to ensure a safe school environment.

Messer-Davidow, Ellen. "Changing the System: The Board of Trustees Caper." *Women's Studies Quarterly*, Fall 1990, vol. 18: 3–4, p. 136. Recounts attempts by the Board of Friends of Women's Studies, a group that supports the University of Cincinnati's Center for Women's Studies, to place a feminist on the university's Board of Trustees.

Monaghan, P. "Sex-Harassment Case Challenges University of Washington." *Chronicle of Higher Education*, October 30, 1991, p. A1. Provides a summary of sexual harassment cases at universities across the United States and explores the problems universities have in dealing with these allegations.

Mooney, Carolyn J. "Charges of Sexual Harassment Shake a School at University of Miami." *Chronicle of Higher Education*, March 31, 1993, p. A14. A student brings a sexual harassment case against a professor at the University of Miami.

Myers, Ken. "AALS Group Attempts to Devise Model Sexual Harassment Rules." *National Law Journal*, January 25, 1993, p. 4. A summary of discussions covering law school sexual harassment policies at a convention of the Association of American Law Schools' Section on Women in Legal Education.

Paludi, Michele A. "Ethnicity, Sex, and Sexual Harassment." *Thought and Action*, Winter 1993, vol. 8: 2, p. 105. Deals with the issue of sexual harassment of minority women in education and reviews Hunter College's administrative policies to deter sexual harassment.

Parson, L. Alayne, et al. "The Campus Climate for Women Faculty at a Public University." *Initiatives*, Spring 1991, vol. 54: 1, p. 19. A questionnaire reveals the environment is "chilly" for female faculty at a state school.

Pattullo, Edward L. "Sex and Secrecy at Harvard College: An Argument for Full Disclosure in Sexual Harassment Cases." *Harvard Magazine*, January/February 1992, vol. 94, p. 67. Results of a survey of tenured and non-tenured faculty, graduate students, and undergraduates at Harvard, which shows that many have experienced sexual harassment by people in positions of power.

Peart, Karen N. "At Odds with Ads." *Scholastic Update*, May 7, 1993, p. 16. Discusses the impact on youth of advertising, which often demeans women and depicts sexual harassment in various forms.

Perry, Nancy Walker. "Sexual Harassment on Campus: Are Your Actions Actionable?" *Journal of College Student Development*, November 1993, vol. 34: 6, p. 406. General coverage of sexual harassment on college campuses, with guidelines for defining and curbing it.

Peters, Lori. "A Student's Experience." *Initiatives*, Winter 1990, vol. 52: 4, p. 17. A personal account of one student's experience of sexual harassment in a university, and the actions she took.

Reilly, Timothy, Sandra Carpenter, Valerie Dull and Kim Bartlett. "The Factorial Survey: An Approach to Defining Sexual Harassment on Campus." *Journal of Social Issues*, 1982, vol. 38: 4, p. 99. A survey of undergraduate students and faculty at the University of California determined that the more subtle the harassment, the more difficult it is to define.

Riger, Stephanie. "Gender Dilemmas in Sexual Harassment Policies and Procedures." *American Psychologist*, May 1991, vol. 46: 5, p. 497. Underreporting of sexual harassment in higher education may perpetuate policies that can discourage women from following through with their grievances.

Annotated Bibliography

Robertson, Claire, Constance E. Dyer, and Ann D. Campbell. "Campus Harassment: Sexual Harassment Policies and Procedures at Institutions of Higher Learning." *Signs*, Summer 1988, vol. 13: 4, p. 792. An overview of the results of a 1984 survey of U.S. institutions of higher learning regarding protocols developed for dealing with sexual harassment.

Roscoe, Bruce, Jeremiah S. Strouse, et al. "Sexual Harassment: Early Adolescents' Self-Reports of Experiences and Acceptance." *Adolescence*, Fall 1994, p. 515. A study of teenagers' experiences of sexual harassment by their peers, with commentary on the need for sexual harassment programs in high schools and junior high schools. Suggests several policies that can be incorporated into the educational system.

Rossi, Peter H. and Eleanor Weber-Burdin. "Sexual Harassment on the Campus." *Social Science Research*, 1983, vol. 12: 2, p. 131. A general look at the problem at the university level.

Semonsky, Michael R. and Lawrence B. Rosenfeld. "Perceptions of Sexual Violations: Denying a Kiss, Stealing a Kiss." *Sex Roles*, April 1994, vol. 30: 7, p. 503. A study comparing the perceptions and reactions of male and female undergraduates to a minor sexual violation.

Sharpe, Patricia and Frances E. Mascia-Less. "'Always Believe the Victim,' 'Innocent Until Proven Guilty,' 'There Is No Truth:' The Competing Claims of Feminism, Humanism and Postmodernism in Interpreting Charges of Harassment in the Academy (Part of a Symposium, Constructing Meaningful Dialogue on Difference: Feminism and Postmodernism in Anthropology and the Academy)." *Anthropological Quarterly*, April 1993, vol. 66, p. 87. The theory and reality of sexual harassment in teacher/student relationships and with relation to women professors.

Shoop, Julie Gannon. "Beyond Horseplay: Students Sue Schools Over Sexual Harassment." *Trial*, June 1994, vol. 30: 6, p. 12. Summarizes some early cases in which students charged their schools with sexual harassment.

Somers, Amy. "Sexual Harassment in Academe: Legal Issues and Definitions." *Journal of Social Issues*, 1982, vol. 38: 4, p. 23. Outlines the problem of sexual harassment in universities and colleges and describes its legal implications.

Stein, Nan D. "Breaking Through Casual Attitudes on Sexual Harassment." *Education Digest*, May 1993, vol. 58: 9, p. 7. A guide to handling sexual harassment properly in the school setting.

Stockdale, Margaret S. and Alan Vaux. "What Sexual Harassment Experiences Lead Respondents to Acknowledge Being Sexually Harassed? A Secondary Anylysis of a University Survey." *Journal of Vocational Behavior*, October 1993, vol. 43: 2, p. 221. A survey of more than 1,000 graduate students, undergraduates, and faculty members measures the prevalence of sexual harassment in academe and individuals' response to it.

Straus, Susan. "Sexual Harassment at an Early Age." *Principal*, September 1994, vol. 74, p. 26. Sexual harassment by peers in primary and secondary school is gaining widespread attention, giving rise to the theory that sexually harassing behavior may be a symptom of sexual abuse suffered by the perpetrator.

Valentine-French, Suzanne and Lorraine H. Radtke. "Attributions of Responsibility for an Incident of Sexual Harassment in a University Setting." *Sex Roles*, October 1989, vol. 21: 7–8, p. 545. Sexual harassment in a university setting as perceived by male and female observers.

Walker, Gillian, Lynda Erickson and Lorette Woolsey, eds. "Sexual Harassment: Ethical Research and Clinical Implications in the Academic Setting." *International Journal of Women's Studies*, September/October 1985, vol. 8, p. 424. Discusses the problems of sexual harassment in the academic setting from an ethical point of view.

West, Ellen, et al. "Addressing Sexual Harassment: A Strategy for Changing the Climate in Higher Education." *NASPA Journal*, Winter 1994, vol. 31: 2, p. 130. Summary of sexual harassment on college campuses; one university's strategy for effecting change.

Williams, Elizabeth A., et al. "The Impact of a University Policy on the Sexual Harassment of Female Students." *Journal of Higher Education*, January–February 1992, vol. 63: 1, p. 50. The author describes her experience of sexual harassment at a university and her fight to confront and expose her perpetrator. Examines the power dynamics between students and professors.

Wishmietsky, Dan and Dennis Felder. "Assessing Coach-Student Relationships." *Journal of Physical Education, Recreation & Dance*, September 1989, vol. 60: 7, p. 76. A study of sexual relations and sexual harassment between high school students and their phys-ed teachers and coaches.

Zirkel, Perry A. "Abuse of Students by Students?" *Phi Delta Kappan*, December 1993, p. 344. Exploration of details in *Douglas vs. Cincinnati Board of Education*, in which an assistant principal is said to have inappropriately touched female students.

GENERAL

"The Battle of the Belly-Button." *Economist*, September 24, 1994, p. 39. Reports on advances in women's rights in South Korea, citing the first sexual harassment case won by a woman.

Blakey, Anne. "When 'No' Isn't Enough: How to Handle Sexual Harassment." *Human Rights*, Spring 1993, vol. 20, p. 12. What constitutes sexual harassment, how to prevent and avoid it, and how to cope with it when conventional propriety and decency fail.

Annotated Bibliography

Broom, Dorothy, Marguerite Byrne and Lily Petkovic. "Off Cue: Women Who Play Pool." *Australia and New Zealand Journal of Sociology*, August 1992, vol. 28: 2, p. 175. A discussion of the attitudes and tratment encountered by women who play the traditinally male-dominated sport of pool.

Burrows, Terry. "The Oldest Profession: Sexual Harassment in the Eighties." *Melbourne Journal of Politics*, 1984/1985, vol. 16, p. 20. A general overview of sexual harassment.

Chriss, James J. "Spain on Status and Space: A Comment." *Sociological Theory*, March 1994, vol. 12: 1, p. 106. A sociological theory of sexual harassment and gender stratification.

Cowperthwaite, Margaret. "Sexual Harassment: A Selected Bibliography, 1981–1983." *Association for Communication Administration Bulletin*, October 1983, n46, p. 66. Fifty-seven annotated references on sexual harassment in the workplace and on campus.

"Defense Lawyer Fingers Culprits in Cost Spiral." *National Underwriter*, November 19, 1990, vol. 94: 47, p. 26. At a recent meeting, insurers contemplate the potentially high costs to their companies of sexual harassment, child-molestation, and environmental cases.

Fitzgerald, Mark. "Anomymous Source Debate Begins Anew." *Editor & Publisher*, March 14, 1992, vol. 125: 11, p. 11. American editors discuss the *Seattle Times'* decision to print an article on the alleged sexual harassment of eight women by a U.S. senator, without printing the women's names.

Flynn, Kelly. "Preventive Medicine for Sexual Harassment." *Personnel*, March 1991, vol. 68: 3, p. 17. A five-point procedure for the prevention of sexual harassment.

Gale, Mary Ellen. "On Curbing Racial Speech." *Rights and Responsibilities*, Winter 1990–91, vol 1, p. 47. Explores ways to eliminate abusive and discriminatory language, with reference to sexual as well as racial harassment.

Gehry, Frank, B. J. Hatelay and Susan Rose, presenters, with Madeleine Stoner, moderator. "The Politics of Empowerment, A Paradigm Shift in Thought and Action for Feminists: New Questions Beyond the Feminist Focus on Sexual Harassment—Is It Helping Us Move from Victimhood to Empowerment, or Is It a Diversion?" *American Behavioral Scientist*, August 1994, vol. 37, p. 1122. Feminist theories of sexual harassment.

Glen, Ron. "E-Mail Voyeurism." *Canadian Datasystems*, October 1991, vol. 23: 10, p. 57. Discusses, snooping, tampering, and sexual harassment via e-mail.

Griswold, Robert L. "Sexual Cruelty and the Case for Divorce in Victorian America." *Signs*, Spring 1986, vol. 11: 3, p. 529. Discusses cases of sexual harassment and abuse in Victorian marriages that served as grounds for divorce.

Hernton, Calvin. "Breaking Silences." *Black Scholar*, Winter 1991, vol. 22: 1, p. 42. Sexual harassment and racial oppression of African-American women in the United States, with coverate of the Hill-Thomas hearings.

James, Joy. "Anita Hill: Martyr Heroism & Gender Abstractions." *Black Scholar*, Winter 1991, vol. 22: 1–2, p. 17. Anita Hill's name as a symbol of reverence or ridicule in recent feminist and masculine writing.

Johnson, Kim K. and Jane E. Workman. "Clothing and Attributions Concerning Sexual Harassment." *Home Economics Research Journal*, December 1992, vol. 21: 2, p. 160. A study reveals that students believe provocative clothing can induce sexual harassment.

Langer, Howard J. "The Women's Movement: What N.O.W.?" *Social Education*, 1983, vol. 47: 2, p. 112. The implications of the Women's movement for sexual harassment.

Lichtman, Judith and Holly Fechner. "Almost There: For Women, The Civil Rights Act of 1991 Is a Move in the Right Direction." *Human Rights*, Summer 1992, vol. 19, p. 16. The significance of the Civil Rights Act of 1991 for women's rights.

Menon, Shobha A. and Suresh Kanekar. "Attitudes Toward Sexual Harassment of Women in India." *Journal of Applied Social Psychology*, December 16, 1992, vol. 22, p. 1940. A look at Indian attitudes regarding women as a contributing factor in sexual harassment there.

Monroe, Bill. "Anita Hill Explosion Also Hit the Press." *WJR: Washington Journalism Review*, December 1991, vol. 13: 10, p. 6. Analysis of reporting on the Hill-Thomas hearings by three different papers: the *LA Times*, *The New York Times* and the *Washington Post*.

Nelson, Barbara, et al. "The Women's Caucus For Political Science: Five Views of Its Significance Today." *PS: Political Science & Politics*, 1990, vol. 23: 3, p. 439. Five commentaries on the activity of the Women's Caucus for Political Science since its inception in 1969, including Barbara Nelson's discussion of what the caucus has been doing to combat the sexual harassment of women.

Powell, Gary N. "Sexual Harassment: Confronting the Issue of Definition (Based on a Conference Paper)." *Business Horizons*, July/August 1983, vol. 26, p. 24. An examination of the legal definition of harassment and the behaviors that legitimately represent harassment.

Rosenberg, Richard S. "Free Speech, Pornography, Sexual Harassment and Electronic Networks," *Info-Society*, October/December 1993, vol. 9, p. 285. Proposed guidelines for preventing and coping with sexual harassment in cyberspace.

Staaz, Clarice. "Sexual Harassment." *Queen's Quarterly* (Canada), 1980, vol. 87: 3, p. 481. A brief look at the problem in Canada.

Stanley, John D. "Sexual Harassment: Insight and Abatement (What Characterizes Such Behavior and Methods of Dealing with the Problem)." *Business and Society*, Spring 1984, vol. 23, p. 32. A discussion of sexual harassment; how to identify and deter it.

Thompson, Sandra and Frederic Hayward. "At Issue: Is Sexual Harassment Primarily a 'Woman's Problem?'" *CQ Researcher*, August 9, 1991, p. 553. A look at the idea that women don't report sexual harassment because they are taught from childhood on to make excuses for men's behavior.

Walsh, Doris. "Safe Sex in Advertising." *American Demographics*, April 1994, vol. 16: 4, p. 24. A survey conducted for the journal reveals consumers' attitudes toward sexual imagery in advertising.

Young, Cathy. "Life, Liberty & the ACLU." *Reason*, October 1994, vol. 26: 5, p. 32. An interview with Nadine Strossen, president of the American Civil Liberties Union (ACLU), including discussion of sexual harassment.

GOVERNMENT

Alston, Chuck. "Bush Takes Congress to Task: Democrats Fire Right Back: Senate to Investigate Leaks of Sexual Harassment Charges against Clarence Thomas." *Congressional Quarterly Weekly Report*, October 26, 1991, vol. 49, p. 3106. A report on news leaks of Anita Hill's sexual harassment charges against Supreme Court nominee Clarence Thomas.

Angel, Marina. "Sexual Harassment by Judges." *University of Miami Law Review*, March 1991, vol. 45, p. 817. Addresses sexual harassment committed by judges.

"American Survey: A Not Very Funny Thing on the Way to the Court." *Economist*, October 12, 1991, p. 25. The Senate decides to delay confirmation of Clarence Thomas to the U.S. Supreme Court in order to investigate sexual harassment charges.

"American Survey: Something Awful Has Happened." *Economist*, October 19, 1991, p. 25. Investigation into Anita Hill's charges of sexual harassment by Clarence Thomas has shocked people working on Capitol Hill.

Bell, Ella Louise. "Myths, Stereotypes, and Realities of Black Women: A Personal Reflection." *Behavioral Science and Public Affairs*, February 1995, vol. 28. What the Hill-Thomas hearings did to the image of African-American women.

Bergoffen, Debra. "Being Philosophical About Sexual Harassment." *Women & Laguage*, Fall 1992, vol. 15: 2, p. 35. Discussion of the Hill-Thomas hearings from a philosophical point of view.

"Between the Lines." *National Journal*, December 5, 1992, vol. 24: 29, p. 2801. A spoof of Senator Bob Packwood's sexual harassment of women.

"Beware Bimbos." *Economist*, April 16, 1994, vol. 331: 7859, p. 27. Considers the possibility that Paula Jones will file a sexual harassment case against President Clinton.

Biskupic, J. "Thomas Drama Engulfs Nation: Anguished Senate Faces Vote." *Congressional Quarterly Weekly Report*, October 12, 1991, vol. 49: 41, p. 2948. The Hill-Thomas hearings put pressure on the Senate and may alter the confirmation process for future Supreme Court nominees.

Boo, Katherine. "The Organization Woman: The Real Reason Anita Hill Stayed Silent." *Washington Monthly*, December 1991, vol. 23, p. 44. Evaluates and assesses why Anita Hill remained silent about her sexual harassment by Clarence Thomas for so long.

"The Clarence Thomas Confirmation." *Black Scholar.*, Winter 1991/1992, vol. 22, p. 1. An in-depth discussion of the confirmation of Clarence Thomas to the Supreme Court.

Coleman, Emma Jordan. "Race, Gender, and Social Class in the Thomas Sexual Harassment Hearings: The Hidden Fault Lines in Political Discourse." *Harvard Women's Law Journal*, Spring 1993, vol. 15, p. 1. The political implications of the Hill-Thomas hearings.

Connolly, Ceci. "Court Hearing Set for December 16 on Packwood Subpoena." *Congressional Quarterly Weekly Report*, November 27, 1992, vol. 51, p. 3251. Investigating sexual harassment charges against Senator Bob Packwood, the Senate demands he turn over his diaries as evidence.

"Cornered by His Past." *Economist*, June 4, 1994, vol. 331, p. 13. Measures the impact of the Whitewater and Paula Jones cases on President Clinton's political future.

"Country Matters (Paula Jones Accuses President of Sexual Harassment While He Was Governor)." *Economist*, May 14, 1994, vol. 331, p. 34. A report on Paula Jones' charges of sexual harassment against President Bill Clinton.

"Diary of a Senator." *Economist*, October 30, 1993, vol. 329, p. 28. The legal ramifications of the Supreme Court's decision to allow the Senate to subpoena the diaries of Senator Bob Packwood as evidence in his sexual harassment case.

Donovan, Beth. "Packwood Loses in High Court: Diary Transfer to Begin." *Congressional Quarterly Weekly Report*, March 5, 1994, vol. 52, p. 524. An update on Senator Bob Packwood's sexual harassment lawsuit.

Guy-Sheftall, Beverly. "Breaking the Silence: A Black Feminist Response to the Hill-Thomas hearings (for Audre Lorde)." *Black Scholar*, Winter 1991, vol. 22: 1–2, p. 35. The Hill-Thomas hearings may have violated a cultural taboo by airing black problems in front of whites.

Hook, Janet. "Packwood Loses Again on Protecting Diaries." *Congressional Quarterly Week Report*, February 19, 1994, vol. 52, p. 421. A report on developments in the sexual harassment case against Senator Bob Packwood.

Idelson, Holly. "Packwood Asks Supreme Court to Stop Transfer of Diaries." *Congressional Quarterly Weekly Report*, February 26, 1994, vol. 52, p. 459. Senator Bob Packwood fights to keep his diaries from being used as evidence in the sexual harassment lawsuit against him.

Irwin, V. "A National Drama." *Scholastic Update*, November 1, 1991, p. 20. A discussion of the Hill-Thomas hearings, noting the impact of the case on public attitudes about the nomination of Supreme Court justices.

Jordan, June. "Can I Get a Witness?" *Black Scholar*, Winter 1991, vol. 22: 1–2, p. 56. An analysis of the Hill-Thomas hearings from a perspective sympathetic with Hill.

"Judge Upholds Subpoena of Packwood Diaries (Text of Judge Jackson's Order)." *Congressional Quarterly Weekly Report*, January 29, 1994, vol. 52, p. 201. A court requires Senator Bob Packwood to obey the subpoena of his diaries as evidence in his sexual harassment suit.

Kuntz, Phil. "Ethics Panel Gets Its Members: Packwood Feisty in Defense." *Congressional Quarterly Weekly Report*, January 30, 1993, vol. 51, p. 208.

———. "First Issue for Packwood Case: Can Senators Lie to Win?" *Congressional Quarterly Weekly Report*, May 1, 1993, vol. 51, p. 1062.

———. "Judge Seizes Packwood Diaries as Panel Expands Probe." *Congressional Quarterly Weekly Report*, December 18, 1993, vol. 51, p. 3460.

———. "Oregon Group Asks Senate Not to Seat Packwood." *Congressional Quarterly Weekly Report*, December 19, 1992, vol. 50, p. 3881.

———. "Oregonians Get Tough Hearing in Bid to Unseat Packwood." *Congressional Quarterly Weekly Report*, May 15, 1993, vol. 51, p. 1204.

———. "Packwood Challenges Accuser, Says Resigning No Option." *Congressional Quarterly Weekly Report*, January 8, 1994, vol. 52, p. 15.

———. "Packwood, Coverdell Sworn In Despite Election Challenges." *Congressional Quarterly Weekly Report*, January 9, 1993, vol. 51, p. 61.

———. "Packwood Loses Argument to Protect Diaries." *Congressional Quarterly Weekly Report*, January 29, 1994, vol. 52, p. 157.

———. "Packwood Rebuffs Subpoena for Private Diary Entries: Material Said to Discuss 'Affairs' of Other Lawmakers and Staff." *Congressional Quarterly Weekly Report*, October 23, 1993, vol. 51, p. 2861.

———. "Packwood's Accusers Spared Questions on Sexual Past." *Congressional Quarterly Weekly Report*, February 6, 1993, vol. 51, p. 254.

———. "Packwood Wins the First Round in Post-Election Complaints." *Congressional Quarterly Weekly Report*, May 22, 1993, vol. 51, p. 1275.

———. "Pressure for Prompt Action Leads to Packwood Inquiry." *Congressional Quarterly Weekly Report*, December 5, 1992, vol. 50, p. 3749.

———. "Senate Rebuffs Packwood 94-6; Diary Issue Moves to Court: Senator's New Troubles: Calls for Resignation, Possible Inquiry Into Job Offers for Wife." *Congressional Quarterly Weekly Report*, November 6, 1993, vol. 51, p. 3024.

———. "Senate Shares the Risk in Packwood Probe." *Congressional Quarterly Weekly Report*, March 13, 1993, vol. 51, p. 565.

———. "Showdown Over Packwood Diaries Sure to Leave Senate Wounds." *Congressional Quarterly Weekly Report*, October 30, 1993, vol. 51, p. 2941. Ongoing coverage of the investigation into sexual harassment charges lodged against Senator Bob Packwood.

Kirk, Connie Westerman. "Ending Harassment at City Hall: Policy Initiatives in Large American Cities." *State and Local Government Review*, Fall 1989, vol. 21, p. 100. A look at municipal sexual harassment policies in major cities and their effectiveness.

Lipari, Lisbeth. "As the World Turns: Drama, Rhetoric, and Press Coverage of the Hill-Thomas Hearings." *Political Communication*, July/September 1994, vol. 11, p. 299. Notes from a British symposium on the Hill-Thomas hearings.

Margulies. "Between the Lines." *National Journal*, January 4, 1992, vol. 24: 1, p. 40. A humorous portrayal of the televised Hill-Thomas hearings.

———. "Between the Lines." *National Journal*, December 18, 1993, vol. 25: 51, p. 3016. Poking fun at Senator Bob Packwood, a fictitious female member of the Senate ethics staff responds to a question posed by Lady Justice.

Morse, Claire K., Elizabeth M. Woodward, and Richard L. Zweigenhaft. "Gender Differences in Flashbulb Memories Elicited by the Clarence Thomas Hearings." *The Journal of Social Psychology*, August 1993, vol. 133, p. 453. The different reactions of men and women to the Hill-Thomas hearings.

"Mr. Packwood's Scolding." *The Economist*, February 20, 1993, vol. 326, p. 24. Senator Bob Packwood is reprimanded by the Select Committee on Ethics for sexual improprieties.

Palmer, Elizabeth A. "Packwood Publicly Apologizes, Says He Will Not Resign." *Congressional Quarterly Weekly Report*, December 12, 1992, vol. 50, p. 3797. After initial denials, Senator Bob Packwood makes a public apology for sexual misconduct, but he refuses to resign.

Rosen, R. "Sex, Lies, and Vulnerability." *Tikkun*, January 1992, vol. 7: 1, p. 22. The Hill-Thomas hearings as a catalyst for public debate over long-hidden truths about sexual harassment.

Smith, Barbara. "Ain't Gonna Let Nobody Turn Me Around." *Black Scholar*, Winter 1991, vol. 22: 2, p. 90. A discussion of the Hill-Thomas hearings from an African-American perspective.

Annotated Bibliography

Spencer, Camille. "The Chronology of the Clarence Thomas Confirmation." *Black Scholar*, Winter 1991, vol. 22: 1–2, p. 1. A narrative account of the Hill-Thomas hearings.

"Thomas Drama Engulfs Nation: Anguished Senate Faces Vote: Public Outrage, Anger from Women Could Affect More than Confirmation of the Nominee." *Congressional Quarterly Weekly Report*, October 12, 1991, vol. 49, p. 2948. The Senate is thrown into upheaval by Anita Hill's sexual harassment charges against Supreme Court nominee Clarence Thomas, and by public pressure to respond.

"Thomas' Victory Puts Icing on Reagan-Bush Court: Bruising Fight Over Sexual Harassment Underscores Policy Stakes in Battle between Branches." *Congressional Quarterly Weekly Report*, October 19, 1991, vol. 49, p. 3026. Clarence Thomas' confirmation as a Supreme Court justice has political causes and effects.

Wattenberg, Daniel. "Gunning for Koresh: It Was Only When Their Funding Was Up for Review—And a Pattern of Sexual Harassment Emerged at Their Agency—That the Federal Bureau of Alcohol, Tobacco and Firearms Decided to Make an Example of David Koresh and His Branch Davidian Followers." *American Spectator*, August 1993, vol. 26, p. 31. When charges of sexual harassment within the ATF came to light, the bureau attempted to deflect criticism by taking action against the cult, which was also suspected of sexual harassment.

Wright, Sarah E. "The Anti-Black Agenda." *Black Scholar*, Winter 1991, vol. 22: 1–2, p. 109. Racially based difficulties in accepting Hill as a symbol of women's liberation; racist ramifications of Thomas' Supreme Court confirmation.

Wooley, Susan C. "Anita Hill, Clarence Thomas and the Enforcement of Female Silence." *Women & Therapy*, 1992, vol. 12: 4, p. 3. The Hill-Thomas hearings as an example of gender differences in expression.

Zook, Jim. "U.S. Student-Aid Official Quits Amid Charges He Made Sexual Advances to College Student-Aid . . . " *Chronicle of Higher Education*, May 11, 1994, p. A25. R.W. Evans resigns after being charged with sexual harassment by two of his staff members.

Zuckman, Jill. "Sexual Harassment Complaints Embroil Packwood, Senate." *Congressional Quarterly Weekly Report*, November 28, 1992, vol. 50, p. 3707. Sexual harassment charges against Senator Bob Packwood cause chaos and confusion in the Senate.

HELPING PROFESSIONS

Bell, Carl C. "Books: Sexual Exploitation." *JAMA: The Journal of the American Medical Association*, December 23, 1989, vol. 262: 23, p. 3354. Commentary on "sexual exploitation in professional relationships."

"Hospitals Ready for Sex-Abuse Risk: Consultant." *National Underwriter*, October 21, 1991, vol. 95: 42, p. 3. A hospital consultant discusses the effects of national sexual harassment awareness on health care organizations.

"RNs Differ on Sex Harassment Charge." *American Journal of Nursing*, March 1993, vol. 93: 3, p. 97. Reports case of hostile work environment sexual harassment filed by a nurse against an obstetrician at San Pedro Peninsula Hospital. Reviews the testimony of other female nurses who worked at the hospital at the time of the grievance.

"A Suit For Sex Harassment . . . " *American Journal of Nursing*, March 1993, vol. 93: 3, p. 9. A New Jersey nurse battles to keep her job after filing a sexual harassment complaint and being subject to a retaliatory conspiracy.

Taubman, Stan. "Beyond the Bravado: Sex Roles and the Exploitive Male." *Social Work*, January/February 1986, vol. 31: 1, p. 12. Discusses the sexual exploitation of female outpatients by males working in the mental health services field.

Telles-Irvin, Patricia and Ivy S. Schwartz. "Sexual Harassment Among Female Dentists and Dental Students in Texas." *Journal of Dental Education*, September 1992, vol. 56: 9, p. 612. A Texas survey investigates sexual harassment amongst dental patients and professionals.

Turshen, Meredeth. "The Impact of Sexism on Women's Health and Health Care." *Journal of Public Health Policy*, Summer 1993, vol. 14: 2, p. 164. The potential impact of trends in U.S. affirmative action legislation on women patients.

Zinn, Christopher. "Australian Doctors Get Tough on Sexual Misconduct." *BMJ: British Medical Journal (International Edition)*, May 7, 1994, vol. 308: 6938, p. 1185. The Australian Medical Association holds that common-law courts are too easy on doctors charged with sexual misconduct. These cases should be dealt with by medical tribunals.

LEGAL

Aalberts, Robert J. and Lorne H. Seidman. "Sexual Harassment by Clients, Customers, and Suppliers: How Employers Should Handle an Emerging Legal Problem." *Employee Relations Law Journal*, Summer 1994, vol. 20, p. 85. Presents a model policy for effective handling of employee sexual harassment by third parties. Cites, as a case in point, *Robinson v. Jacksonville Shipyards, Inc.*

Alfred, Steven. "Sexual Harassment: New Grounds for Employer Liability." *Popular Government*, Summer 1987, vol. 53, p. 14. Analyzes existing laws as a legal foundation for determining employers' role and responsibility in sexual harassment cases.

Annotated Bibliography

"An Analysis of Judicial Deference to EEOC Interpretative Guidelines." *Administrative Law Journal*, Summer 1987, vol. 1, p. 213. A discussion of the court's rulings on administrative policy regarding sexual harassment in light of guidelines written by the Equal Employment Opportunity Commission.

"An Employer's Guide to Understanding Liability for Sexual Harassment Under Title VII: *Meritor Savings Bank v. Vinson*." *University of Cincinnati Law Review*, 1987, vol. 55, p. 1181. Reviews the case of *Meritor Savings Bank v. Vinson* and its implications for employees' rights under Title VII.

"Anti-Discrimination Law—Sexual Harassment and Battery: Mutually Exclusive Remedies for Independent Harm—*Wirig v. Kinney Shoe Corp.*, 161 N.W. 2d 371 (MN)." *William Mitchell Law Review*, Spring 1991, vol. 17, p. 627. In the case of *Wirig v. Kinney Shoe Corp.*, Wirig filing a dual complaint against the shoe company for both assault & battery and sexual harassment. A discussion of how these separate injuries were legally addressed.

Apruzzese, Vincent J. "Selected Recent Developments in EEO Law: The Civil Rights Act of 1991, Sexual Harassment and the Emerging Role of ADR." *Labor Law Journal*, vol 43: 6, June 1992. An exploration of the judicial significance for sexual harassment of the Civil Rights Act of 1991 and a discussion of the resulting popularity among employers of alternate dispute resolution procedures.

Backhouse, Constance. "*Bell v. The Flaming Steer Steak House Tavern* (1990 C.H.R.R. D/155 1383–1112): Canada's First Sexual Harassment Decision." *University of Western Ontario Law Review*, May 1981, vol. 19, p. 111. Examines the legal details of *Bell v. The Flaming Steer Steak House.*

"Bad Samaritans Make Dangerous Precedent: The Perils of Holding an Employer Liable for an Employee's Sexual Misconduct." *Alaska Law Review*, June 1991, vol. 8, p. 181. A review of the case of *Doe v. Samaritan Counseling Center.*

Barton, Christopher P. "Between the Boss and a Hard Place: A Consideration of *Meritor Savings Bank, FSB v. Vinson* and the Law of Sexual Harassment." *Boston University Law Review*, May 1987, vol. 67, p. 445. A discussion of the legal impact of *Meritor Savings Bank v. Vinson.*

Bass, Stuart L. "Recent Court Decisions Expand Role of Arbitration in Harassment and Other Title VII Cases." *Labor Law Journal*, January 1995, vol. 46, p. 38. The role of arbitration versus litigation in cases of sexual harassment.

Baxter, Ralph H., Jr. "Sexual Harassment Claims: The Issues." *Legal Economics*, November/December 1982, vol. 8, p. 14. A brief discussion of the legal issues surrounding sexual harassment claims.

Bennett, Alexander and Dawn D. Bennett. "The Supreme Court Finally Speaks on the Issue of Sexual Harassment: What Did It Say?" *Women's Rights Law*

Reporter, Spring 1987, vol. 10, p. 65. Reviews the Supreme Court's first ruling regarding sexual harassment, in *Meritor Savings Bank v. Vinson*.

Bernstein, Anita. "Law, Culture, and Harassment." *University of Pennsylvania Law Review*, April 1991, vol. 142, p. 1227. Compares the sexual harassment laws of America with those of various European countries.

Berthel, K. Lee. "Sexual Harassment in Education Institutions: Procedure for Filing a Complaint with the Office for Civil Rights, Department of Education." *Capital University Law Review*, 1981, vol. 10, p. 585. A guide to filing a Title IX sexual harassment complaint, with a list of federal and state offices that accept claims.

Bloom, Howard. "Beware Sexual Harassment." *New England Business*, April 1991, vol. 13: 4 p. 10. Rulings of two recent federal appeals court cases and their interpretation.

Blum, Andrew. "Assumption of Risk Tested in Hooters Suit." *National Law Journal*, May 24, 1993, vol. 15: 38, p. 7. Six Hooters restaurant waitresses file charges of sexual harassment against the chain.

Bowman, Cynthia Grant. "Street Harassment and the Informal Ghettoization of Women." *Harvard Law Review*, January 1993, vol 106, p. 517. A legal look at the mistreatment of women by men in public.

Brown, Berna L. "Sexual Harassment in Employment: Procedure for Filing a Complaint with the Ohio Civil Rights Commission." *Capital University Law Review*, vol. 10, p. 531. Outlines the rights of Ohio state residents under state and federal laws and gives step-by-step procedures for filing a sexual harassment complaint.

"*Bundy v. Jackson* (611 F. 2d 931): Eliminating the Need to Prove Tangible Economic Job Loss in Sexual Harassment Claims Brought Under Title VII." *Pepperdine Law Review*, May 1982, vol. 9, p. 907. The legal outcome of *Bundy v. Jackson* and the implications it will have on the interpretation of Title VII.

Carter, Victoria A. "Working on Dignity: EC Initiatives on Sexual Harassment in the Workplace." *Northwestern Journal of International Law and Business*, Winter 1992, vol. 12, p. 431. A general legal discussion of sexual harassment in the workplace.

Chema, Richard J. "Arresting Tailhook: The Prosecution of Sexual Harassment in the Military." *Military Law Review*, Spring 1993, vol. 140, p. 1. Discussion of sexual harassment in the military and the legal repercussions of the Tailhook debacle.

Chudacoff, Nancy Fisher. "New EEOC Guidelines on Discrimination Because of Sex: Employer Liability for Sexual Harassment Under Title VII of the Civil Rights Act of 1964." *Boston University Law Review*, March 1981, vol. 61, p. 535. An examination of the EEOC's new guidelines on workplace sexual harassment and their meaning for employers' liability in such cases.

"Civil Rights, Discrimination, Sex: A Title VII Vilation Is Shown When Sexual Harassment of an Employee Is Condoned by the Employer, Even Though the Employee's Tangible Job Benefits Are Not Affected." *University of Cincinnati Law Review*, 1981, vol. 50, p. 414. The significance of *Bundy v. Jackson* with relation to employer liability for violations of Title VII.

Cohen, Cynthia Fryer and Joyce P. Vincelette. "Notice, Remedy and Employer Liability for Sexual Harassment." *Labor Law Journal*, May 1984, vol. 35, p. 301. A discussion of how to properly handle instances of sexual harassment in the workplace. Discusses what employers are legally required to do.

Coles, Frances S. "Sexual Harassment: Complainant Definitions and Agency Responses." *Labor Law Journal*, June 1985, vol. 36, p. 369. Reviews and defines employees' justifiable and legally sound sexual harassment complaints and how they are handled by government agencies.

Cooper, Stacy J. "Sexual Harassment and the Swedish Bikini Team: A Reevaluation of the 'Hostile Environment' Doctrine." *Columbia Journal: Law and Social Problems*, Spring 1993, vol. 26, p. 387. Citing the 1991 lawsuit against Stroh Brewery Company, considers whether a company's advertising should be taken into account in sexual harassment lawsuits brought by employees. Attention to freedom of speech issues.

Dennison, Lynn. "An Argument for the Reasonable Woman Standard in Hostile Environment Claims." *Ohio State Law Journal*, 1993, vol. 54, p. 473. Discusses the legal rights of female employees to be protected from sexual harassment in the workplace, as defined from the standpoint of a "reasonable woman."

Dumas, Kitty. "Senators Target Damages Caps in Sex Discrimination Suits." *Congressional Quarterly Weekly Report*, March 14, 1992, vol. 50, p. 620. The Senate focuses on the size of damage awards that can be granted to victims in sexual harassment cases.

Effron, Seth. "The Angela Wright Case." *Nieman Reports*, Winter 1991, vol. 45: 4, p. 22. A legal account of the actions of the *Charlotte Observer* during the Hill-Thomas hearings, when a former employee complained that Thomas had also harassed her.

Ehrenreich, Nancy S. "Pluralist Myths and Powerless Men: The Ideology of Reasonableness in Sexual Harassment Law." *Yale Law Journal*, April 1990, vol. 99: 6, p. 1177. Discusses the legal ramifications of *Rabidue v. Osceola Refining Co.*

Ellis, Judy Trent. "Sexual Harassment and Race: A Legal Analysis of Discrimination." *Journal of Legislation*, Winter 1981, vol. 8, p. 30. The civil rights of employees and citizens with regard to racial and sexual discrimination and harassment.

Faley, Robert H. "Sexual Harassment: Critical Review of Legal Cases with General Principles and Preventive Measures." *Personnel Psychology*, Fall 1982, vol. 35: 3, p. 583. A review of over four dozen sexual harassment cases that helped to set standards for establishing legal claims under Title VII.

"France: Law Against Sexual Harassment." *International Labour Review*, 1993, vol. 132: 1, p. 5. A review of French laws relevant to sexual harassment.

"Free Speech and Religious, Racial, and Sexual Harassment." *William and Mary Law Review*, Winter 1991, vol. 32, p. 207. An in-depth analysis of the civil liberty of free speech versus the problem of religious, racial and sexual harassment.

Gadlin, Howard. "Careful Maneuvers: Mediating Sexual Harassment." *Negotiation Journal*, April 1991, vol. 7, p. 139. Describes effective methods for mediating sexual harassment disputes.

Garvin, Stacey J. "Employer Liability for Sexual Harassment." *HRMagazine*, June 1991, vol. 36: 6, p. 101. Court rulings on employer liability in cases of sexual harassment.

George, Glenn B. "The Back Door: Legitimizing Sexual Harassment Claims." *Boston University Law Review*, January 1993, vol. 73, p. 1. Legal methods of establishing the legitimacy of sexual harassment claims.

Gilbert, Kathleen. "Sexual Harassment in the Military." *Guild Practitioner: Current Problems: Law and Practice*, Spring 1992, vol. 49, p. 38. Discusses the legal aspects of sexual harassment in the military.

Greenbaum, Marcia L. "Sexual Harassment and Arbitration," an article in *Proceedings of New York University 35th Annual National Conference on Labor, June 9-11, 1982*. New York: New York University Press, 1983, p. 379. Arbitration methods for handling sexual harassment cases.

Hallinan, Kathleen M. "Invasion of Privacy or Protection Against Sexual Harassment: Co-Employee Dating and Employer Liability." *Columbia Journal of Law and Social Problems*, Spring 1993, vol. 26, p. 435. Discusses whether regulations regarding employee dating serve as a legitimate form of protection or if they are an invasion of employees' privacy.

Hartstein, Barry A. "Bosses Take Heed! Harassment May Be Costly." *National Law Journal*, October 31, 1994, vol. 17: 9, p. A21. *Weeks v. Baker & McKenzie*, a sexual harassment case involving the world's largest law firm, is discussed.

Hauck, Vern E. and Thomas G. Pearce. "Sexual Harassment and Arbitration." *Labor Law Journal*, January 1992, vol. 43: 1. A report on how labor arbitrators deal with sexual harassment claims.

148

Annotated Bibliography

Johnson, Kristi J. "*Chiepuzio v. BLT Operating Corporation* (826 F. Supp. 1334 (1993): What Does It Mean to Be Harassed 'Because of ' Your Sex?: Sexual Stereotyping and the 'Bisexual' Harasser Revisited." *Iowa Law Review*, March 1994, vol. 79, p. 731. Examines in detail the case of *Chiepuzio v. BLT Operating Corporation*, which addresses issues of same-sex and opposite-sex harassment.

Juliano, Ann C. "Did She Ask for It? The 'Unwelcome' Requirement in Sexual Harassment Cases." *Cornell Law Review*, Summer 1992, vol. 77, p. 1558. The legal definitions and interpretations of "unwanted" advances, as illustrated by several sexual harassment cases.

Jurlansz, Russell G. "Recent Developments in Canadian Law: Anti-Discrimination Law." *Ottawa Law Revue/Revue de Droit d'Ottawa*, November 3, 1987, vol. 19, p. 447. Newly passed sexual harassment laws in Canada.

Kadar, Marlene. "Sexual Harassment: Where We Stand: Research and Policy." *Windsor Year Book of Access to Justice*, 1983, vol. 3, p. 358. Criticizes the limited scope of sexual harassment law and suggests that the issue must be addressed from both a legal and social point of view. Recommends that trade unions and women's organizations cooperate to educate both workers and employers.

Kirkpatrick, Robert M. and John B. Nason. "Employment Law Litigation and the Changing Limitations on Personnel Management: Three Illustrations." *Journal of Retail Banking*, Fall 1982, vol. 4, p. 62. Offers three examples of labor law litigation on sexual harassment and considers how to handle the problem of sexual harassment in the workplace.

Koen, Clifford N., Jr. "Sexual Harassment Claims Stem from a Hostile Work Environment." *Personnel Journal*, August 1990, vol. 69: 8, p. 88. Analysis of *Meritor Savings Bank v. Vinson*.

Kriger, Linda J. and Cindi Fox. "Evidentiary Issues in Sexual Harassment Litigation." *Berkeley Women's Law Journal*, 1985, vol. 1, p. 115–139. Examines why a plaintiff's past sexual history is inadmissible in court within the existing legal structure, and why a defendant's past is sometimes admissible.

"La Guerre des Sexes" (in French). *Nouv Ovservateur*, May 19–25, 1994, p. 36. Compares French and American laws regarding such issues as sexual harassment and date rape; contains an interview with Elisabeth Badinter.

Laddy, Donna L. "*Burns v. McGregor Electronic Industries* (989 F. 2d 959 (1993): A Per Se Rule Against Admitting Evidence of General Sexual Harassment Claims." *Iowa Law Review*, May 1993, vol. 78, p. 939. Considers the legal implications of the ruling in *Burns v. McGregor Electronic Industries*.

Ledgerwood, Donna E. and Sue Johnson-Dietz. "The EEOC's Foray into Sexual Harassment: Interpreting the New Guidelines for Employer Liability." *Labor Law Journal*, December 1980, vol. 31, p. 741. Analysis and explanation of the EEOC's guidelines on sexual harassment.

Lester, Toni P. "The Yankee Women in King Arthur's Court—What the United States and the United Kingdom Can Learn from Each Other about Sexual Harassment Law." *Boston College International and Comparative Law Review*, Summer 1991, vol. 17, p. 233. Compares the sexual harassment labor laws of the United States with those of Great Britain.

Leventer, Jan C. "Sexual Harassment and Title VII: EEOC Guidelines, Conditions, Litigation and the United States Supreme Court." *Capital University Law Review*, 1981, vol. 10, p. 481. An in-depth look at the history and evolution of EEOC guidelines on sex discrimination in employement.

Levy, Anne C. "The Change in Employer Liability for Supervisor Sexual Harassment after *Meritor (Meritor Savings Bank v. Vinson*, 106 S. Ct., 2399): Much Ado About Nothing." *Arkansas Law Review*, 1989, vol. 12, p. 795. The impact on employers' legal responsibility in cases of sexual harassment of the Supreme Court's ruling in *Meritor Savings Bank v. Vinson*.

Lewis, Darryl M. Halcomb. "Sexual Harassment Under Workers' Compensation Law." *Labor Law Journal*, vol. 44: 5, May 1993. An examination of the ways in which workers' compensation law applies to cases of sexual harassment in the workplace.

McKay, Nellie Y. "Anita Hill and Clarence Thomas: Personal Reflections on Social Equality and the Rights of Black Women." *Sage: A Scholarly Journal on Black Women*, Fall 1990, vol. 7: 2, p. 58. The implications of the Hill-Thomas case for the social equality and rights of black women.

Marmo, Michael. "Arbitrating Sex Harassment Cases." *Arbitration Journal*, 1980, p. 35. Reviews standard types of sexual harassment cases, the legal issues surrounding them and the applicability of arbitration.

MacKinnon, Catharine. "Introduction to Symposium: Sexual Harassment." *Capital University Law Review*, 1981, vol. 10, p. i. Sexual harassment law is the first historical example of law created from a woman's point of view. The speaker notes the need to maintain women's voice in this and other legislative matters.

Matson, Joanne Liebman. "Civil Rights—Sex Discrimiantion in Education: Compensatory Damages Available in a Title IX Sexual Harassment Claim. *Franklin v. Gwinnett County Public Schools*, 112 S. Ct. 1028 (1992)." *University of Arkansas at Little Rock Law Journal*, Winter 1993, vol. 15, p. 271. The implications of the Supreme Court's *Franklin* decision on the award of damages to plaintiffs filing sexual harassment claims under Title IX.

Meads, Melanie A. "Applying the Reasonable Woman Standard in Evaluating Sexual Harassment Claims: Is It Justified?" *Law and Psychology Review*, Spring 1993, vol. 17, p. 209. Discusses the legal notion of the reasonable woman with regard to sexual harassment claims.

Michelsen, Jan. "A Class Act: Forces of Increased Awareness, Expanded Remedies, and Procedural Strategy Converge to Combat Hostile Workplace Environments." *Indiana Law Review*, 1991, vol. 27, p. 607. The use of class-action lawsuits in cases of workplace sexual harassment, as in *Jenson v. Eveleth Taconite Co.*

Monat, Jonathan S. and Angel Gomez. "Decisional Standards Used by Arbitrators in Sexual Harassment Cases." *Labor Law Journal*, October 1986, vol. 37, p. 712. Looks at sexual harassment cases handled by arbitration and the common methods arbitrators have employed to resolve them.

Moore, John W. "The Case of the Hanging Curve Ball." *National Journal*, June 12, 1993, p. 1434. A look at *Harris v. Forklift Systems Inc.*, a case then before the Supreme Court.

Morin, Laurie A. "Civil Remedies for Therapist-Patient Sexual Exploitation." *Golden State University Law Review*, Summer 1989, vol. 19, p. 401. Possible remedies in sexual harassment cases brought against therapists by their clients.

Murray, P. J. "Employer: Beware of 'Hostile Environment' Sexual Harassment." *Duquesne Law Review*, 1987/88, vol. 26, p. 461. Focuses on hostile work environment sexual harassment in the workplace, suggesting that the courts must define verbal abuse as thoroughly as they have defined physical abuse.

Nelson, Richard R. "State Labor Legislation Enacted in 1980." *Monthly Labor Review*, 1981, vol. 104: 1, p. 21. A report on recent labor legislation, including sexual harassment laws passed in several states.

———. "State Labor Legislation Enacted in 1992." *Monthly Labor Review*, January 1993, vol. 116, p. 35. A report on recent labor legislation, including sexual harassment laws, passed in several states.

O'Neill, Catherine A. "Sexual Harassment Cases and the Law of Evidence: A Proposed Rule." *University of Chicago Legal Forum*, 1989, p. 219. Argues that, as in rape cases, women who have been sexually harassed should not be questioned about their past sexual history.

Pellicciotti, Joseph M. "Canada's Approach to Eradicating Workplace Sexual Harassment: The Canadian Supreme Court's *Janzen v. Platy Enterprises, Ltd.* (33 D.L.R. 4th 32) and Its Relationship to the United States Supreme Court's *Meritor v. Vinson* (106 S. Ct. 2399)." *Loyola of Los Angeles International and Comparative Law Journal*, February 1992, vol. 14, p. 237. Compares rulings in two major cases as illustrations for differences and similarities in Canadian and American sexual harassment law.

Petersen, Donald J. and Douglas P. Massengill. "Sexual Harassment Cases Five Years after *Meritor Savings Bank v. Vinson.*" *Employee Relations Law Journal*, Winter 1992/1993, vol. 18, p. 489. A look at the landmark sexual harassment ruling and subsequent cases, evaluating changes that have taken place, legally, and what has remained relatively unchanged.

Pollack, Wendy. "Sexual Harassment: Women's Experience vs. Legal Definitions." *Harvard Women's Law Journal*, Spring 1990, vol. 13, p. 35. An in-depth ananlysis of the dichotomy between women's experiences of sexual harassment and the law's perspective on those experiences.

Redford, Mary F. "By Invitation Only: The Proof of Welcomeness in Sexual Harassment Cases." *North Carolina Law Review*, March 1991, vol. 72, p. 499. A discussion of where the burden of proof of "welcomeness" lies in sexual harassment cases.

"Report of the Missouri Task Force on Gender and Justice." *Missouri Law Review*, Summer 1993, vol. 58, p. 489. A report on discrimination against women in the Missouri courts; considers the potential bias of judges and court personnel in cases of criminal law, family law, and domestic violence.

Reuben, Richard C. "Award a Lesson for Firms." *ABA Journal*, November 1994, vol. 80, p. 19. Discusses the outcome of *Weeks v. Baker & MacKenzie* and its impact on law firms across the country.

Rosario, Louise do. "Profile: Mizuho Fukushima: Petite Lady Lawyer Fights Sex Harassment." *Far Eastern Economic Review*, August 12, 1993, vol. 156, p. 86. A profile of one woman who fought back against harassment in Japan sheds light on Japanese sexual harassment laws and civil rights for women there.

Rosen, Helen D. "Employer Liability for Sexual Harassment in the Work Place Under Title VII of the Civil Rights Act of 1964." *New York Law School Human Rights Annual*, Fall 1984, vol. 2, p. 151. A discussion of the legal responsibilities of employers under Title VII of the Civil Rights Act of 1964.

Schneider, Ann. "Sexual Harassment Brief Bank and Bibliography." *Women's Rights Law Reporter*, 1985, vol. 8, p. 267. Presents summaries of 182 sexual harassment cases dating from the mid-1970s to 1985.

Schupp, Robert W. "Sexual Harassment Under Title VII of the Civil Rights Act of 1964." *Labor Law Journal*, April 1981, vol. 32, p. 238. An overview of employer's Title VII responsibilities with regard to sexual harassment in the workplace; analysis of employees' civil rights and liberties in this area.

Seymour, William C. "Sexual Harassment: Finding a Cause of Action Under Title VII (the Civil Rights Act of 1964) and State Tort Laws as Potential Remedies for Sexual Harassment of Women Employees." *Labor Law Journal*, March 1979, vol. 30, p. 139. Evaluates Title VII of the Civil Rights Act of 1964 and several state tort laws as possible protections for women in the workplace.

Shanley, Mary Jo. "Perceptions of Harm: The Consent Defense in Sexual Harassment Cases." *Iowa Law Review*, May 1986, vol. 71, p. 1109. Examines the notion of consent in sexual harassment cases.

Annotated Bibliography

Sherman, Rorie. "Claims of Bias at NIH Bolstered." *National Law Journal*, December 9, 1991, vol. 14: 14, p. 3. Analysis of *Johnson v. Sullivan*, which aired allegations against the National Institutes of Health concerning discrimination against women and the handicapped.

Shoop, Robert J. "The Reasonable Woman in a Hostile Work Environment." *West's Education Law Quarterly*, July 1992, vol. 1: 3, p. 218. Discusses the evolution of the legal concept of hostile work environment sexual harassment and of the reasonable woman standard.

Silbergeld, Arthur F. "Reasonable Victim Test for Judging Hostile Environment Sexual Harassment Cases" *Employment Relations Today*, Summer 1991, vol. 18: 2, p. 257. Discussion and interpretation of the results of *Ellison v. Brady*, a 1991 sexual harassment case.

Simon, Howard A. "Ellison v. Brady: A 'Reasonable Woman' Standard for Sexual Harassment." *Employee Relations Law Journal*, Summer 1991, vol. 17: 1, p. 71. Explores the U.S. Court of Appeals' decision in *Ellison v. Brady*.

Smith, Bruce Chandler. "When Should an Employer Be Held Liable for the Sexual Harassment by a Supervisor Who Creates a Hostile Work Environment? A Proposed Theory of Liability." *Arizona State Law Journal*, November 2, 1987, vol. 19, p. 285. An overview of the legal approach to the question of when employers should be held liable for sexual harassment experienced by their employees at work.

Smith, J. Clay, Jr. "Prologue to the EEOC Guidelines on Sexual Harassment." *Capital University Law Review*, 1981 vol. 10, p. 471. A history of the legal evolution of sexual harassment at the federal level.

Sperry, Martha. "Hostile Environment Sexual Harassment and the Imposition of Liability Without Notice: A Progressive Approach to Traditional Gender Roles and Power Based Relationships." *New England Law Review*, 1990, vol. 24, p. 917. Examines the outcomes of several sexual harassment cases and highlights the first case that recognized sexual harassment as gender discrimination.

Stanley-Elliott, Lynne E. "Sexual Harassment in the Workplace: Title VII (of the Civil Rights Act of 1964)'s Imperfect Relief." *Journal of Corporation Law*, Spring 1981, vol. 6, p. 625. The flaws and loopholes in Title VII of the Civil Rights Act of 1964.

Strauss, Marcy. "Sexist Speech in the Workplace." *Harvard Civil Rights & Civil Liberties Law Review*, Winter 1990, vol. 25, p. 1. Speech as a tool of sexual discrimination in the workplace; the legalities of this type of behavior.

Sullivan, George M. and William A. Nowlin, "Critical New Aspects of Sex Harassment Law." *Labor Law Journal*, September 1986, vol. 37, p. 617. An update on recent developments in labor law that cover sexual harassment.

Sexual Harassment

"Symposium: The Civil Rights Act of 1991: Theory and Practice." *Notre Dame Law Review*, November 5, 1993, vol. 68, p. 911. Focuses on sexual harassment legislation passed during the Bush administration.

"Symposium on Women and the Law." *Notre Dame Journal of Law, Ethics & Public Policy*, November 2, 1992, vol. 6, p. 283. An in-depth discussion of women and the law.

Taub, Nadine. "Keeping Women in Their Place: Stereotyping Per Se as a Form of Discrimination." *Boston College Law Review*, January 1980, vol. 21, p. 345. The illegality of sexual harassment by virtue of its nature as a form of sexual discrimination.

Teinowitz, Ira and Bob Geiger. "Suits Try to Link Sex Harassment, Ads." *Advertising Age*, November 18, 1991, vol. 62: 49, p. 48. Discusses the sexual harassment case filed against Stroh Brewery Co., which attempted to link provocative advertising with sexual harassment at the firm.

Terpstra, David E. "Outcomes of Federal Court Decisions on Sexual Harassment." *The Academy of Management Journal*, March 1992, vol. 35: 1. A quantitative analysis of the impact of federal court rulings in sexual harassment cases.

———. "The Process and Outcomes of Sexual Harassment Claims." *Labor Law Journal*, October 1993, vol. 44: 10. A narrative analysis of the legal implications of sexual harassment claims for workers and employers.

"United States: Supreme Court Rules on Harassment in Workplace." Facts On File, November 11, 1993, vol. 53: 2763, p. 843. Discusses *Harris v. Forklift Systems Inc.*, citing excerpts from the Supreme Court's ruling.

Vermeulen, Joan. "Employer Liability Under Title VII for Sexual Harassment by Supervisory Employees." *Capital University Law Review*, 1981, vol. 10, p. 499. Evaluates the legal liability of employers for sexual harassment by managers of subordinates.

Vinciguerra, Marlisa. "The Aftermath of Meritor: A Search for Standards in the Law of Sexual Harassment." *Yale Law Journal*, June 1989, vol. 98: 8, p. 1717. Discussion of the Supreme Court's decision in *Meritor Savings Bank v. Vinson*, and the concepts of quid pro quo and hostile work environment harassment.

Warren, Jerry K. "Sexual Harassment in the Employment Context: An Analysis of the New Title VII Cause of Action." *Baylor Law Review*, Fall 1980, vol. 32, p. 605. A look at evolving interpretations of Title VII and how they will affect both employers and employees.

Winston, Judith A. "Mirror, Mirror on the Wall: Title VII, Section 1981, and the Intersection of Race and Gender in the Civil Rights Act of 1990." *California Law Review*, May 1991, vol. 79: 3, p. 775. Civil rights laws governing sexual harassment are of particular interest to women of color.

Annotated Bibliography

Wittenburg, Russell W. "Sexual Harassment: A Jurisprudential Analysis." *Capital University Law Review*, 1981, vol. 10, p. 607. Summarizes the specifics of sexual harassment law and measures its effectiveness in curtailing the problem.

MILITARY

"Between the Lines." *National Journal*, August 1, 1992, vol. 24: 31, p. 1800. Sexual harassment in the military is depicted in a cartoon.

Chema, Richard J. "Arresting Tailhook: The Prosecution of Sexual Harassment in the Military." *Military Law Review*, Spring 1993, vol. 140, p. 1. Debate over whether the criminalization of sexual harassment is a necessary, effective, and adequate way to handle sexual misconduct in the military.

"The Curious Logic Behind Women in Combat." *Alberta Report/Western Report*, September 5, 1994, p. 12. Discusses the Tailhook case and cites other instances of sexual harassment in the military.

Morrison, David C. "Belatedly, the Navy's on a New Course." *National Journal*, July 11, 1992, vol. 24: 28, p. 1635. Questions the impact of Tailhook on the navy's future treatment of women.

Palmer, Elizabeth. "Committee Opposes Penalizing Admiral Kelso Over Tailhook: Administration Looks to Next Hurdle in Push to Let Top Officer Retire with Full Benefits." *Congressional Quarterly Weekly Report*, April 16, 1994, vol. 52, p. 905. The U.S. Senate Armed Services Committee recommends that Admiral Frank B. Kelso II, a central figure in the Tailhook scandal, be permitted to retire with full pension and rank.

———. "Senate Backs Admiral's Pension Over Women's Opposition." *Congressional Quarterly Weekly Report*, April 23, 1994, vol. 52, p. 1014. Despite protest from women in Congress, the Senate accepts the Armed Services Committee's recommendation that Admiral Frank B. Kelso retire with full benefits, despite his role in the Tailhook scandal.

Peters, Mike. "Between the Lines." *National Journal*, May 8, 1993, vol. 25: 19, p. 1131. A satirical look at the navy's Tailhook scandal.

Rowe, Mary P. "The Post-Tailhook Navy Designs an Integrated Dispute Resolution System." *Negotiation Journal*, July 1993, vol. 9, p. 207. Enactment of a "red-light, green-light" sexual harassment prevention program by the navy in the wake of the Tailhook scandal.

PSYCHOLOGY

Barr, Paula A. "Perception of Sexual Harassment." *Sociological Inquiry*, Fall 1993, vol. 63: 4, p. 460. Study participants read two short stories containing gender-related themes and answer a questionnaire; results show that men and women perceive and react to sexual harassment on the basis of gender and socialization.

Carr, Rey A. "Addicted to Power: Sexual Harassment and the Unethical Behavior of University Faculty." *Canadian Journal of Counselling*, October 1991, vol. 25: 4, p. 447. States that the source of sexual harassment is the imbalance of power, rather than moral or ethical issues. Analyzes the subject within an addiction framework.

Glaser, Robert D. and Joseph S. "Unethical Intimacy: A Survey of Sexual Contact and Advances Between Psychology Educators and Female Graduate Students." *American Psychologist*, January 1986, vol. 41: 1, p. 43. Presents three theories of individual perception of sexual harassment, as derived from cases involving psychology students.

Gutek, Barbara A. "Sexual Harassment: Rights and Responsibilities." *Employee Responsibilities and Rights Journal*, December 1993, vol. 6, p. 325. Evaluates employees' legal and civil rights with regard to sexual harassment in the workplace. Considers the rights of victims, alleged harassers, and companies.

Gutek, Barbara and Mary P. Koss. "Changed Women and Changed Organizations: Consequences of and Coping with Sexual Harassment." *Journal of Vocational Behavior*, February 1993, vol. 42: 1, p. 28. Addresses the psychological impact of sexual harassment and victims' coping strategies.

Gutek, Barbara and Bruce Morasch. "Sex-Ratios, Sex-Role Spillover, and Sexual Harassment of Women at Work." *Journal of Social Issues*, Winter 1982, vol. 38: 4, p. 55. Asserts that women who work with other women are less likely to recognize sex discrimination and harassment because all are treated in a similar fashion.

Hemming, Heather. "Women in a Man's World: Sexual Harassment." *Human Relations*, January 1, 1985, vol. 38, p. 67. Examines the psychodynamics of sexual harassment.

McKinney, Kathleen. "Contrapower Sexual Harassment: The Effects of Student Sex and Type of Behavior on Faculty Perceptions." *Sex Roles*, December 1992, vol. 27, p. 627. Analysis of the influence of student gender and behavior upon the demeanor of instructors.

Marks, Michelle A. and Eileen S. Nelson. "Sexual Harassment on Campus: Effects of Professor Gender on Perception of Sexually Harassing Behaviors." *Sex Roles*, February 1993, vol. 28, p. 207. Analysis of the influence of instructor gender on students' interpretations of sexual harassment.

Murrell, Audrey J. and Beth L. Dietz-Uhler. "Gender Identity and Adversarial Sexual Beliefs as Predictors of Attitudes toward Sexual Harassment." *Psychology of Women Quarterly*, June 1993, vol. 17: 2, p. 169. Explores the correlation between sexist beliefs and tolerance of sexual harassment.

Popovich, Paula M., DeeAnn N. Gehlauf, et al. "Perception of Sexual Harassment as a Function of Sex of Rater and Incident Form and Consequence." *Sex Roles*, December 1992, p. 609. A questionnaire distributed to 198 students reveals perceptual differences between male and female students concerning examples of sexual harassment.

Schnuder, Beth E. "Consciousness about Sexual Harassment among Heterosexual and Lesbian Women Workers." *Journal of Social Issues*, Winter 1982, vol. 38: 4, p. 75. A study finds that lesbians in the workplace are more likely to feel sexually harassed than their heterosexual counterparts.

Stockdale, Margaret S. and Alan Vaux. "What Sexual Harassment Experiences Lead Respondents to Acknowledge Being Sexually Harassed? A Secondary Analysis of a University Survey." *Journal of Vocational Behavior*, October 1993, vol. 43: 2, p. 221. A survey indicates that past experiences of sexual violation lead to greater sensitivity in detecting sexually inappropriate behavior.

Thacker, Rebecca A. and Stephen F. Gohmann. "Sexual Harassment: 'Reasonable' Assumptions?" *Public Personnel Management*, Fall 1993, vol. 22: 3, p. 461. Reveals that men and women define and perceive sexual harassment differently and analyzes gender differences in psychological impact.

Woody, Robert Henley and Nancy Walker Perry. "Sexual Harassment Victims: Psycholegal and Family Therapy Considerations." *American Journal of Family Therapy*, Summer 1993, vol. 21: 2, p. 136. Discusses the psychological impact of sexual harassment on victims and explores clinical treatment options.

Workman, Jane E. and Kim K. Johnson. "The Role of Cosmetics in Attributions about Sexual Harassment." *Sex Roles*, June 1991, vol. 24: 11–12, p. 739. The significance attributed to the use of cosmetics by victims of sexual harassment.

WORKPLACE

Acken, Brenda T., Kent St. Pierre and Peter Veglahn. "Limiting Sexual Harassment Liability." *Journal of Accountancy*, June 1991, vol. 171: 6, p. 42. Procedures and policies to limit sexual harassment liability in the workplace.

Aggarwal, Arjun P. "Arbitral Review of Sexual Harassment in the Canadian Workplace." *The Arbitration Journal*, March 1991, vol. 16, p. 1. Comments on the handling of charges of sexual harassment in the Canadian workplace. Specific cases are cited.

"A.M. Radio: Laughs or Lawsuits." *Broadcasting*, May 8, 1989, p. 58. The verbal harassment of newswomen by male morning radio announcers.

"Back to the Bench." *New Scientist*, January 27, 1990, vol. 125: 1, p. 23. Notes the shortage of women scientists in the U.K. and conjectures that it may be attributed to the fear of sexual harassment in a predominantly male discipline.

Brazen, Cheryl Blackwell. "The Internal Sexual Harassment Investigation: Self-Evaluation Without Self-Discrimination." *Employee Relations Law Journal*, Spring 1990, vol. 15: 4, p. 551. Advises employers how to conduct a proper internal investigation of sexual harassment, with an anecdotal incident as an example.

Bularzik, Mary. "Sexual Harassment at the Workplace: Historical Notes." *Radical America*, 1978, vol. 12: 4, p. 24. An historical overview of sexual harassment in the workplace up through 1978.

Burleigh, Nina and Stephanie B. Goldberg. "Breaking the Silence." *ABA Journal*, August 1989, vol. 75, p. 46. Sexual harassment of women in law firms.

Caughey, Bernard. "News Sources as Sexual Harassers of Reporters." *Editor & Publisher*, November 2, 1991, vol. 124: 44, p. 48. A discussion of the problems faced by female reporters when their news sources become sexual harassers.

Champagne, Paul J. and Bruce R. McAfee. "Auditing Sexual Harassment." *Personnel Journal*, June 1989, vol. 68: 6, p. 124. Litigative status of sexual harassment in the courts as regards corporate liability for the actions of managers.

"Combating Sexual Harassment at Work." *Conditions of Work Digest*, vol. 11: 1. Geneva: International Labour Office, 1992. A 300-page document covering laws and regulations that protect working women from sexual harassment, in the United States and in other countries.

Connell, Dana S. "Effective Sexual Harassment Policies: Unexpected Lessons from Jacksonville Shipyards." *Employee Relations Law Journal*, Autumn 1991, vol. 17: 2, p. 191. In reviewing a noted lawsuit, the article evaluates the sexual harassment policies of the courts and of the EEOC.

Clark, C. S. "Sexual Harassment." *CQ Researcher*, August 9, 1991, p. 537. An overview of the power struggles between men and women at work and how men and women perceive sexual harassment differently. Describes inappropriate behavior of male bosses toward female employees and reports on the increased number of grievances filed by women.

Collins, Eliza G., C. Blodgett and B. Timothy. "Sexual Harassment: Some See It, Some Won't—A Survey of HBR Subscribers Reveals That the Biggest Issue Is Not Defining Sexual Harassment but Recognizing It When It Occurs." *Harvard Business Review*, March/April 1981, vol. 59, p. 76. A survey conducted by the *Review* indicates that personnel managers understand the literal definition of sexual harassment but have difficulty applying it to actual cases.

158

Annotated Bibliography

Daily, Bill and Miriam Finch. "Benefiting from Non-Sexist Language in the Workplace." *Business Horizons*, March 1993, vol. 36: 2, p. 30. Sexist language as a form of sexual harassment in the workplace.

Dauer, Christopher. "Policy Offered for Sexual Harassment Defense." *National Underwriter*, November 4, 1991, vol. 95: 44, p. 15. How organizations can protect themselves when charged with sexual harassment.

Deutschman, Alan. "Dealing with Sexual Harassment." *Fortune*, November 4, 1991, vol. 124: 11, p. 145. A study of sexual harassment within corporations.

Dolecheck, Carolyn C. and Maynard M. Dolecheck. "Sexual Harassment: A Problem for Small Businesses." *American Journal of Small Business*, January/March 1983, vol. 7, p. 45. Discusses the threats to and problems of small businesses in dealing with sexual harassment in the workplace.

Duncan, Jack W., Larry R. Sneltzer and Terry L. Leap. "Humor and Work: Applications of Joking Behavior to Management." *Journal of Management*, June 1990, vol. 16: 2, p. 255. Considers the role of humor in the workplace and the risks that it can cross the line to sexual harassment.

Eller, Martha E. "Sexual Harassment: Prevention, Not Protection." *Cornell Hotel & Restaurant Administration Quarterly*, February 1990, vol. 30: 4, p. 84. Proposes that the hospitality industry focus on preventing sexual harassment rather than dealing with it after it has already occurred.

English, Linda. "Business and Professional Ethics." *Australian Accountant*, February 1990, vol. 60: 1, p. 18. The Australian business community's concern with ethics and harassment.

Escobedo, Duwayne. "Utilities Taking Steps to Halt Sexual Harassment." *Public Utilities Fortnightly*, November 15, 1991, vol. 128: 10, p. 9. A discussion of the development of sexual harassment programs within public utility companies.

Esposito, Michael D. "Directors Are Liable for Discrimination." *Journal of Compensation & Benefits*, January/February 1991, vol. 6: 4, p. 41. Predicts changes that will occur in the workplace by the year 2000. Lists strategies that employers should consider to create a healthy, liability-free work environment.

———. "Get Your Act Together." *Executive Excellence*, November 1991, vol. 8: 11, p. 6. Ways to attract, retain, motivate, and promote women and minorities in the workplace.

Estrich, Susan. "Sex at Work." *Stanford Law Review*, April 1991, vol. 43, p. 813. An overview of sex in the workplace, its legal implications and ramifications.

Faivush, Margot Frank. "The Key to Employee Leasing Is Benefits." *Financial Manager*, March/April 1990, vol. 3: 2, p. 70. Discusses the advantages of hiring a leasing firm to handle responsibilities such as personnel administration, payroll, and benefits.

Sexual Harassment

Filipczak, Bob. "Is It Getting Chilly in Here? Men and Women at Work." *Training*, February 1994, vol. 31: 2, p. 25. Developing a better office environment in light of the problem of sexual harassment.

Garvey, Margaret S. "The High Cost of Sexual Harassment Suits." *Personnel Journal*, January 1986, vol. 65, p. 75. Assesses the tremendous expenses some companies have incurred in sexual harassment cases.

Gibson, Virginia M. "Beyond Legal Compliance: What's Next?" *HR Focus*, July 1993, vol. 70: 7, p. 17. Discusses the difficulties of changing the attitudes and opinions of employees regarding sexual harassment and argues that lack of tolerance and awareness are responsible for inappropriate behavior.

Giuffre, Patti A. and Christine L. Williams. "Boundary Lines: Labeling Sexual Harassment in Restaurants." *Gender & Society*, September 1994, vol. 8: 3, p. 378. Interviews with 18 waitpeople in Texas who work in sex-charged environments; the study compares and contrasts how different people define and perceive sexual harassment.

Goldberg, Jan. "Socializing on the Job." *Career World*, May 1994, p. 4. The pitfalls of friendships and romantic relations with colleagues. Advocates strong boundaries between social and professional life.

Hass, Marsha E. and Dorothy P. Moore. "Company Uniforms: Vulnerability in People-Packaging." *Employment Relations Today*, Spring 1990, vol. 17: 1, p. 37. The implications and risks of requiring employees to wear certain types of uniforms or clothing.

Hosseini, Jamshid C. and Robert L. Armacost. "Randomized Responses: A Better Way to Obtain Sensitive Information." *Business Horizons*, May/June 1990, vol. 33: 3, p. 82. Discusses the different methods by which employers obtain sensitive information from employees regarding sexual harassment.

Ireland, Karin. "The Ethics Game." *Personnel Journal*, March 1991, vol. 70: 3, p. 72. A discussion of Citicorp policies on employee ethics.

Jossem, Jared H. "investigating Sexual Harassment Complaints." *Personnel*, July 1991, vol. 68: 7, p. 9. A guide for the investigation of sexual harassment complaints in the workplace.

Juergens, Jennifer. "Unwelcomed Advances: Why Women Get Harassed at Meetings." *Successful Meetings*, March 1991, vol. 40: 3, p. 44. The particular vulnerability of career women when attending meetings with groups of men.

Katz, David M. "WC Sex Cases Help to Fuel Frequency Rise, Lawyer Says." *National Underwriter*, November 26, 1990, vol. 94: 48, p. 2. Workers' compensation liability of employers in sexual harassment.

Kauppinen-Toropainen, Kaisa and James E. Gruber. "Antecedents and Outcomes of Woman-Unfriendly Experiences: A Study of Scandinavian, Former Soviet, and American Women." *Psychology and Women Quarterly*,

December 1993, vol. 17: 4, p. 431. Analysis of male harassment of women and its impact in three cultures.

Kay, Douglas R. "Running a Gauntlet of Sexual Abuse: Sexual Harassment of Female Naval Personnel in the United States Navy." *California Western Law Review*, Fall 1992, vol. 29, p. 307. A discussion of the sexual harassment of female navy personnel.

Laabs, Jennifer J. "New Sexual-Harassment Bill Is Proposed." *Personnel Journal*, September 1993, p. 156. Governor Mario Cuomo of New York proposes a bill that requires employers to create and enforce policies against sexual harassment in the workplace.

Lan, Seekay. "Sexual Harassment: An International Problem—Japanese Businessman Produces Video to Prevent Lawsuits." *Japan Times Weekly International Edition*, November 11–17, 1991, vol. 31: 45, p. 8. An exploration of the differences between what is acceptable in Japan regarding sexual harassment, and what is acceptable among Japanese businessman working in the United States.

Leap, Terry L. and Edmund R. Gray. "Corporate Responsibilities in Cases of Sexual Harassment." *Business Horizons*, October 1980, vol. 28, p. 58. A review of corporate legal responsibility to employees on the issue of sexual harassment on the job.

Lewis, Kathryn E. and Pamela R. Johnson. "Preventing Sexual Harassment Complaints Based on Hostile Work Environments." *SAM Advanced Management Journal*, Spring 1991, vol. 56: 2, p. 21. How management can prevent the development of a hostile work environment.

Levin, Gary. "How Industry Views Harassment." *Advertising Age*, October 21, 1991, vol. 62: 45, p. 55. The impact of the Hill-Thomas hearings on marketers, media, and agencies.

Linenberger, Patricia. "What Behavior Constitutes Sexual Harassment?" *Labor Law Journal*, April 4, 1983, vol. 34, p. 238. Information for personnel executives on the definition of sexual harassment.

Lissy, William E. "Investigation of Sexual Harassment Charges." *Supervision*, December 1992, vol. 53: 12, p. 20. Suggestions to managers on how to handle charges of sexual harassment in the workplace.

Machson, Robert A. and Joseph P. Montelone. "Insurance Coverage for Wrongful Employment Practices Claims Under Various Liability Policies." *Business Lawyer*, February 1994, vol. 49, p. 689. Liability insurance coverage available to businesses for discrimination, sexual harassment, and wrongful discharge claims.

McCalla, Robert K. "Stopping Sexual Harassment Before It Begins." *Management Review*, April 1991, vol. 80: 4, p. 44. Management strategies for averting workplace sexual harassment.

McKibben, Jenny. "Powerful Barrier to Equality." *Industrial Society*, December 1990, p. 16. A survey by the Alfred Marks Bureau of businesses in the U.K. shows how men abuse their authority over female employees, especially through sexual harassment.

McQueen, Iris. "Sexual Harassment: Are You Protected?" *Security Management*, December 1990, vol. 34: 12, p. 57. Advises what management can do to avoid sexual harassment lawsuits.

Moskal, Brian S. "Sexual Harassment: An Update." *Industry Week*, November 18, 1991, vol. 240: 22, p. 37. An update on sexual harassment in the workplace and management handling of sexual harassment complaints.

Niven, Daniel and Cheryl Wang. "The Case of the Hidden Harassment." *Harvard Business Review*, March 1992, vol. 70: 2, p. 12. A discussion of sexual harassment in the workplace includes a case study.

Overman, Stephanie. "A Delicate Balance Protects Everyone's Rights." *HRMagazine*, November 1990, vol. 35: 11, p. 36. Discusses rifts between employers and employees regarding such controversial issues as drug-testing and sexual harassment.

Perry, Phillip M. "Avoid Costly Lawsuits for Sexual Harassment." *Editor & Publisher*, August 10, 1991, vol. 124: 32, p. 44. A look at the increasing number of sexual harassment cases in the workplace, and some suggestions about procedures and policies that may be helpful preventatives.

———. "Sexual Harassment: Not a Laughing Matter." *Dealerscope Merchandising*, September 1991, vol. 33: 9, p. 72. A discussion of the potential losses arising from sexual harassment, both for the employee and for the company involved.

Pierce, Patricia A. "Sexual Harassment: Frankly, What Is It?" *Journal of Intergroup Relations*, Winter 1994, vol. 20: 4, p. 3. Describes how the federal definition of sexual harassment has evolved. Suggests preventative measures for employers.

Polansky, E. "Sexual Harassment at the Workplace: The Behavior That Our Culture Condones and the Law Prohibits Makes It Profoundly Difficult to Enforce Title VII." *Human Rights*, 1980, vol. 8, p. 14. An overview of the history and development of sexual harassment awareness and law. Notes the similarities between rape and sexual harassment—their impact on the victims and the motives of the perpetrators. Notes the dichotomy of what seems acceptable to society and what is illegal in court.

Rubenstein, Michael. "Devising a Sexual Harassment Policy." *Personnel Management*, February 1991, vol. 23: 2, p. 34. Ideas for employers and trade unions on creating sexual harassment policy.

Savage, J. A. "Harassment Issue Not Burning IS." *Computer World*, November 18, 1991, vol. 25: 46, p. 65. A look at sexual harassment in the information systems (IS) industry.

Annotated Bibliography

Sawyer, Sandra and Arthur A. Whatley. "Sexual Harassment: A Form of Sex Discrimination: Several Critical Court Cases Indicate the Kinds of Management Policy Needed in This Sensitive Area." *Personnel Administrator*, January 1980, vol. 25, p. 36. Based on an analysis of several key sexual harassment court cases, the article offers suggestions to personnel managers on how to create effective sexual harassment policies.

Segal, Jonathan A. "Ignorance Is No Defense." *HRMagazine*, April 1990, vol. 35: 4, p. 93. The benefits to employers of sensitivity to the feelings and attitudes of employees; advises employers on how to compose a constructive questionnaire for this purpose.

———. "Safe Sex: A Workplace Oxymoron?" *HRMagazine*, June 1990, vol. 35: 6, p. 175. Discusses what is necessary to prevent sexual harassment.

———. "The Sexlessness of Harassment." *HRMagazine*, August 1991, vol. 36: 8, p. 71. The different forms of sexual harassment in the workplace represent problems of power rather than sex.

Seymour, Sally. "The Case of the Mismanaged Ms." *Harvard Business Review*, November 1987, vol. 65: 6, p. 77. Sexual harassment as it applies to managers.

Shair, David I. "A Novel Approach to Sexual Harassment." *HR Focus*, June 1994, p. 24. Michael Crichton's take on sexual harassment in his novel *Disclosure*.

Slovak, Patricia Costello. "Sex in the Workplace—from Romance to Harassment." *Human Resources Professional*, Spring 1991, vol. 3: 3, p. 9. Discusses the liability of employers for sexual harassment in the workplace.

Spann, Jeri. "Dealing Effectively with Sexual Harassment: Some Practical Lessons from One City's Experience." *Public Personnel Management*, Spring 1990, vol. 19: 1, p. 53. The city of Madison, Wisconsin, has created effective policies to combat sexual harassment of city employees.

St. Lifer, Evan and Michael Rogers. "Cartoon Causes Strife." *Library Journal*, March 1, 1994, vol. 119: 4, p. 26. Discusses the removal of a cartoon from the workstation of a cataloger in a library in Minnetonka, Minnesota. The cartoon was said to be a form of sexual harassment.

Stein, M. L. "Female Sportswriters and Sexual Harassment." *Editor & Publisher*, October 26, 1991, vol. 124: 43, p. 8. Sexual harassment as it applies to female sportswriters.

Stringer, Donna M., Helen Remick, Jan Salisbury, and Angela B. Ginorio. "The Power and Reasons Behind Sexual Harassment: An Employer's Guide to Solutions." *Public Personnel Management*, Spring 1990, vol. 19: 1, p. 43. Examines the possible causes of sexual harassment in the workplace and offers employers solutions.

Sunoo, Brenda Paik. "Court Declines Sexual Harassment Issue." *Personnel Journal*, November 1994, vol. 73: 11 p. 126. The Supreme court refuses to review a lower court's decision on the sexual harassment case *Haribian v. Columbia University.*

Thomann, Daniel A. and Donald E. Strickland. "Lane Managers and the Daily Round of Work: The Front-Line Defense Against Sexual Harassment." *Industrial Management*, May/June 1990, vol. 32: 3, p. 14. Outlines what managers can do to fight sexual harassment.

Tuttle, Cliff. "Sexual Harassment Is No Joke." *Management Review*, August 1990, vol. 79: 8, p. 44. Warns management about the seriousness of sexual harassment and cites instances where a "joke" can lead to large losses for a company.

Verespej, Michael A. "Arbitration: The Newest Legal Option." *Industry Week*, July 15, 1991, vol. 240: 14, p. 56. Discusses employers' options in sexual harassment lawsuits.

Watstein, Sarah Barbara. "Disturbances in the Field—Sexual Harassment and Libraries: Stories from the Front." *Wilson Library Bulletin*, November 1993, vol. 68: 3, p. 43. Investigates sexual harassment amongst library workers.

"What's Your Opinion?" *Personnel Journal*, June 1994, vol. 73: 6, p. 14. A summary of a survey about the prevention of sexual harassment in the workplace.

Webster, George D. "Directors Are Liable for Discrimination." *Association Management*, January 1991, vol. 43: 1, p. 88. Citing *Mayo v. Questech Inc.*, the article points out the dangers to executive directors when a board member has been accused of inappropriate behavior. The article then outlines preventive measures directors can take to avoid such risks.

Weinstein, Sarah Barbara and Rosalyn Wilcots. "Policies and Procedures of Selected National Organizations." *Wilson Library Bulletin*, September 1994, p. 26. Sexual harassment policies and procedures developed and enforced by several national organizations are compared to those developed by the American Library Association.

White, Shelby. "The Office Pass: Women Workers Are Beginning to Speak Up About Sexual Harassment and Even File Suits; They Charge Sexual Discrimination but Is It That or Rather an 'Outrageous Use of Power?'" *Across the Board*, April 1977, vol. 14, p. 17. Whether the growing number of sexual harassment complaints are legitimate, or whether they represent an abuse of women's civil liberties and legal rights.

"Why Managers Should Investigate Harassment Complaints." *Workfile Report*, 1991, vol. 8: 2, p. 11. Describes the consequences faced by a manager who failed to investigate a female employee's sexual harassment grievance. Advises managers how to address sexual harassment issues as they arise.

Annotated Bibliography

GOVERNMENT DOCUMENTS

Attenborough, Susan and National Union of Provincial Government Employees. *Sexual Harassment at Work.* Ottawa, Ontario, Canada: National Union of Provincial Government Employees, 1981. A report on sexual harassment of provincial government employees in Canada.

Bureau of National Affairs, Inc. *Corporate Affairs: Nepotism, Office Romance & Sexual Harassment.* Washington, DC: BNA Books, 1988. Information about corporate personnel issues, such as nepotism, sexual harassment, ethics, and personnel management.

Bureau of National Affairs, Inc. *Sexual Harassment: Employer Policies and Problems.* Washington, DC: BNA Books, 1987. Addresses sexual harassment from the employer's point of view, examining what policies presently exist to deter it and to provide coverage for corporations.

Bureau of National Affairs, Inc. *Sexual Harassment and Labor Relations.* Washington, DC: BNA Books, 1981. Sexual discrimination and sexual harassment in the workplace.

Unwanted Sexual Attention and Sexual Harassment: Results of a Survey of Canadians. Canadian Human Rights Commission, Research and Special Studies Branch, 1983. Statistics relating to sexual harassment of women in Canada.

Clode, Dianne. *Sexual Harassment in the Federal Government: An Update.* Washington, DC: U.S. Merit Systems Protection Board, 1988. A report to the president and Congress updating a 1981 study of sexual harassment within the federal government.

Gomez, Barney L. *Alcohol, Tobacco and Firearms Bureau's Handling of Sexual Harassment and Related Complaints: A Statement for the Record by Barney L. Gomez, Assistant Director Office of Special Investigations, Before the Committee on Governmental Affairs, U.S. Senate/United States General Accounting Office.* Washington, DC: The Office, 1993. Text of a statement on sexual harassment within the ATF.

In the Supreme Court of the United States, October Term, 1985: Meritor Savings Bank, FSB, Petitioner v. Mechelle Vinson, on Writ of Certiorari to the United States Court of Appeals for the District of Columbia Circuit: Brief for the United States and the Equal Employment Opportunity Commission as Amici Curiae. Washington, DC: U.S. Supreme Court, 1985. Testimony in the landmark sexual harassment case.

Maryland Commission for Women. Baltimore, MD: Maryland Commission for Women, in Cooperation with the Maryland Department of Personnel, 1980. A study of sexual harassment of women in the state of Maryland.

Massachusetts Advisory Committee to the U.S. Commission on Civil Rights. *Sexual Harassment on the Job: A Guide for Employers.* Washington, DC: U.S.

Commission on Civil Rights, 1984. A 21-page manual for employers on the issue of sexual harassment in the workplace.

National Renewable Energy Laboratory (US). *Crossing the Line: How to Recognize and Deal with Sexual Harassment in the Workplace*. Golden, CO: National Renewable Energy Laboratory, 1991. An in-depth study of sexual harassment in the workplace.

New Hampshire Advisory Committee to the U.S. Commission on Civil Rights, with the assistance of the New Hampshire Commission for Human Rights and the New Hampshire Commission on the Status of Women. *Sexual Harassment on the Job: A Guide for Employers*. Washington, DC: U.S. Commission on Civil Rights, 1982. A guidebook to help employers in New Hampshire deal with issues of sexual harassment in the workplace.

New Jersey Committee on Sex Discrimination in the Statutes. *Sex Discrimination in Education: A Report*. Trenton, NJ. New Jersey Committee on Sex Discrimination, 1991. A report on the occurrence of sex discrimination in the New Jersey Public School System.

New York State Governor's Task Force on Sexual Harassment. *Sexual Harassment, Building a Consensus for Change: The Governor's Task Force on Sexual Harassment: Final Report/ Submitted to Governor Mario M. Cuomo*. Albany, NY: New York State Division for Women (Distributor), 1993. A report delivered to the governor of New York outlining what can be done to stop sexual harassment in New York state.

North Carolina State Department of Public Education. *Affirmative Action Plan, November 1987*. Raleigh: The Department, 1987. Details the aggressive affirmative-action policies adopted by the North Carolina State Department of Public Instruction.

Northwest Women's Law Center, with assistance from the Office for Equity Education, Superintendent of Public Instruction, State of Washington. *Sexual Harassment in the Schools: A Statewide Project for Secondary and Vocational Schools*. Seattle, WA: Northwest Women's Law Center, 1986. The Northwest Women's Law Center reports on sexual harassment within the schools of Washington state, specifically at the vocational and high school levels.

Pennsylvania Commission for Women. *Sexual Harassment on the Job: A Guide for Managers and Employees*. Harrisburg, PA: Pennsylvania Commission for Women, 1993. Covers federal and state sexual harassment law as it applies to the Pennsylvania workplace.

Rearman, Marilyn I. and Mary T. Labrato. *Sexual Harassment in Employment: Investigator's Guidebook*. Sacramento, CA: California State Commission on the Status of Women, 1984. A handbook for investigating sexual harassment complaints in the California workplace.

Annotated Bibliography

Richey, Charles R. and the U.S. Federal Judicial Center. *Manual on Employment Discrimination Law and Civil Rights Actions in the Federal Courts.* Washington, DC: GPO, 1988. Legal matters surrounding sexual harassment, such as the right to sue and the right to a jury trial. Cites other sources and relevant case law.

Rubensten, Michael and the European Communities Commission. *The Dignity of Women at Work: A Report on the Problem of Sexual Harassment in the Member States of the European Communities.* Luxembourg: European Communities Official Publications Office, 1988. The prevalence of sexual harassment in member states of the European communities.

Tailhook 91. Washington, DC: Department of Defence, distributed by the U.S. GPO, 1992. Findings of a Pentagon investigation of the 35th Annual Tailhook Symposium in Las Vegas, 1991, and subsequent investigations by the navy.

Till, Frank J. *Sexual Harassment: A Report on the Sexual Harassment of Students.* Washington, DC: U.S. Department of Education, 1980. Addresses the sexual harassment of female college students.

U.S. Army. *Training in the Prevention of Sexual Harassment: Employee Training.* Washington, DC: Department of the Army, 1984. Describes the sexual harassment preventive training program for employees of the U.S. Army.

U.S. Army. *Training in the Prevention of Sexual Harassment: Supervisory Training.* Washington, DC: Department of the Army, 1984. The army's manual for supervisory training in the prevention of sexual harassment.

U.S. Coast Guard. *Women in the Coast Guard Study.* Washington, DC: GPO 1990. A report on the treatment of women in the U.S. Coast Guard, including recruitment and training, attitudes of men and women, fraternization, and sexual harassment.

U.S. Congress House Committee on Armed Services. *Women in the Military: The Tailhook Affair and Problem of Sexual Harassment: Report of the Military Personnel and Compensation Subcommittee and Defense Policy Panel of the Committee on Armed Services, House of Representatives, 102nd Cong., 2nd Sess.* Washington, DC: U.S. GPO, 1992. Text of testimony on sexual harassment in the military, with discussion of the Tailhook scandal.

U.S. Congress House Committee on Armed Services, Military Personnel and Compensation Subcommittee. *Gender Discrimination in the Military: Hearings Before the Military Personnel and Compensation Subcommittee and the Defense Policy Panel of the Committee on Armed Services, House of Representatives, 102nd Cong., 2nd sess., Held July 29 and 30, 1992.* Washington, DC: U.S. GPO, 1992. Text of hearings on sex discrimination and sexual harassment of women in the armed forces.

U.S. Congress House Committee on Armed Services, Military Personnel and Compensation Subcommittee. *Sexual Harassment of Military Women and*

Sexual Harassment

Improving the Military Complaint System: Hearing Before the Committee on Armed Services, House of Representatives, 103rd Cong., 2nd sess., Hearing Held March 9, 1994. Washington, DC: U.S. GPO, 1994. A 276-page document addressing the sexual harassment of women in the military. Discusses complaints received in conjunction with military law and reviews other crimes committed against women.

U.S. Congress House Committee on Armed Services, Military Personnel and Compensation Subcommittee. *Women in the Military, Hearings. 100th Cong., 1st and 2nd sess., October 1, 1987–February 4, 1988.* Washington, DC: U.S. GPO, 1988. Testimony on contributions made and conditions faced by women in the military, including sexual harassment.

U.S. Congress House Committee on Armed Services, Military Personnel and Compensation Subcommittee. *Women in the Military: Hearings. 101st Cong., 2nd sess., March 20, 1990.* Washington, DC: GPO, 1990. Testimony on contributions made and conditions faced by women in the military, including sexual harassment.

U.S. Congress House Committee on Education and Labor. *Civil Rights and Women's Equity in Employment Act of 1991: Report Together with Minority, Additional, and Dissenting Views (to Accompany H.R. 1 Which . . . Was Referred Jointly to the Committee on Education and Labor and the Committee on the Judiciary) (Including Cost Estimate of the Congressional Budget Office).* Washington, DC: U.S. GPO, 1991. Sexual harassment in the workplace.

U.S. Congress House Committee on Education and Labor. *Hearings on H.R. 4000, the Civil Rights Act of 1990. 101st Cong., 2nd sess., 1990, volumes 1–3.* Washington, DC: GPO, 1990. Three volumes of testimony on employment discrimination given in hearings on the proposed Civil Rights Act of 1990, including reports on sexual harassment of women in the workplace and the need to protect women's legal and civil rights.

U.S. Congress House Committee on Education and Labor, Subcommittee on Employment Opportunities. *Hearing on Sexual Harassment in Non-Traditional Occupations: Hearing Before the Subcommittee on Employment Opportunities of the Committee on Education and Labor, House of Representatives, 102nd Cong., 2nd Sess., Hearing Held in Washington DC, June 25, 1992.* Washington, DC: U.S. GPO, 1992. Documentation of a 1992 hearing on sexual harassment experienced by women in non-traditional jobs.

U.S. Congress House Committee on Education and Labor, Subcommittee on Employment Opportunities. *Women in the Workplace: Supreme Court Issues: Hearing Before the Subcommittee on Employment Opportunities of the Committee on Education and Labor, House of Representatives, 99th Cong., 2nd Sess., Hearing Held in Washington DC, on December 30, 1986.* Washington, DC: U.S. GPO, 1986. A 118-page transcript of hearings on the changing status of women in the workforce. Focuses on affirmative action and addresses the prevalence of sex discrimination against women of color, including sexual harassment.

U.S. Congress House Committee on Education and Labor, Subcommittee on Employment Opportunities, and U.S. Congress House Committee on Post Office and Civil Service, Subcommittee on Civil Service. *Joint Oversight Hearing on the Federal Equal Employment Opportunity Complaint Process, Joint Hearing. 101st Cong., 2nd sess., August 1, 1990.* Washington, DC: U.S. GPO, 1990. A 68-page document detailing instances of sexual harassment in federal agencies and discussing the government's failure to protect victims.

U.S. Congress House Committee on Government Operations, Commercial and Consumer. *Followup on Investigation of Senior-Level Employee Misconduct and Mismanagement at the Internal Revenue Service: Hearing, May 9, 1990.* Washington, DC: U.S. GPO, 1991. Sexual misconduct by senior-level employees in the IRS.

U.S. Congress House Committee on Government Operations, Employment and Housing Subcommittee. *Alleged Retaliation by Sumitomo Corp. of America Against Employee Who Testified Before Congress About Sexual Harassment and Discrimination: Hearing Before the Employment and Housing Subcommittee of the Committee on Government Operations, House of Representatives, 102nd Cong., 2nd. Sess., February 26, 1992.* Washington, DC: U.S. GPO, 1993. Testimony on the retaliation of Sumitomo Corporation against an employee who charged the company with sexual harassment in a congressional hearing.

U.S. Congress House Committee on the Judiciary. *Civil Rights Act of 1990, Report Together with Minority and Additional Views to Accompany H.R. 4000. House of Representatives 101–644, part 2, 101st Cong., 2nd sess., 1990.* Washington, DC: U.S. GPO, 1990. Analysis of the proposed Civil Rights Act of 1990, with criticism of recent Supreme Court decisions on sexual harassment cases that have undermined Title VII. An 80-page summary.

U.S. Congress House Committee on Post Office and Civil Service, Subcommittee on Oversight and Investigations. *Oversight Hearing on Sexual Harassment Within the Federal Law Enforcement Agencies: Hearing Before the Subcommittee on Oversight and Investigations of the Committee on Post Office and Civil Service, House of Representatives, 103rd Cong., 2nd Sess., March 8, 1994.* Washington, DC: U.S. GPO, 1994. Text of hearings on the abuse of women within the civil service, including law enforcement agencies, the Drug Enforcement Administration, and the Bureau of Alcohol, Tobacco and Firearms.

U.S. Congress House Committee on Post Office and Civil Service, Subcommittee on Oversight and Investigations. *Sexual Harassment in the Federal Government, Hearings, 96th Cong., 1st sess, 1979.* Washington, DC: U.S.

GPO, 1979. Sexual harassment of women employees in the federal government; the need for training to eliminate such behavior.

U.S. Congress House Committee on Post Office and Civil Service Subcommittee on Oversight and Investigations. *Sexual Harassment in the Federal Government, Hearings. 96th Cong., 2nd sess., 1980.* Washington, DC: U.S. GPO, 1980. Sexual harassment in the federal government, how to prevent such behavior and why many instances go unreported. A bibliography of books, journals, and articles on sexual harassment is also provided.

U.S Congress House Committee on Post Office Service. *Racial Discrimination and Sexual Harassment in U.S. Postal Service: Hearings, July 1, 1981.* Washington, DC: U.S. GPO, 1982. Addresses instances of sexual harassment and racial discrimination within the United States Post Office.

U.S. Congress House Committee on Standards of Official Conduct. *In the Matter of Representative Gus Savage, Report. H. Rept. 101–397, 101st Cong., 2nd sess., 1990.* Washington, DC: U.S. GPO, 1990. A 19-page report on the committee's investigation into Representative Gus Savage's sexual misconduct during a visit to Zaire.

U.S. Congress House Committee on Standards of Official Conduct. *In the Matter of Representative Jim Bates, Report. H. Rept. 101–293, 101st Cong., 1st sess., October 18, 1989.* Washington, DC: U.S. 1989. A 58-page report on sexual harassment charges filed against Representative Jim Bates.

U.S. Congress House Committee on Veteran's Affairs, Subcommittee on Oversight and Investigations. *Sexual Harassment in the VA Workplace and VA Healthcare for Women Veterans: Hearing Before the Subcommittee on Oversight and Investigations of the Committee on Veteran's Affairs, House of Representatives, 102nd Cong., 2nd Sess., September 17, 1992.* Washington, DC: U.S. GPO, 1993. Hearings to investigate the sexual harassment of women in the Veteran's Administration.

U.S. Congress Senate Committee on Armed Services. *Honor Systems and Sexual Harassment at the Service Academies: Hearing Before the Committee on Armed Service, United States Senate, 103rd Cong., 2nd Sess., February 3, 1994.* Washington, DC: U.S. GPO, 1994. Testimony on the prevention of sexual harassment of women within the armed forces, including a U.S. government investigation of honor systems and sexual harassment at the service academies.

U.S. Congress Senate Committee on Governmental Affairs, Subcommittee on Governmental Efficiency and the District of Columbia. *District of Columbia Sexual Assault Laws: Hearing Before the Subcommittee on Governmental Efficiency and the District of Columbia of the Committee on Governmental Affairs, United States Senate, 97th Cong., 1st Sess., on S. Res. 207, September 30, 1981.* Washington, DC: U.S 1983. Describes the sexual assault laws of the District of Columbia. Also includes information on the sexual harassment of children.

U.S. Congress Senate Committee on the Judiciary. *The Complete Transcripts of the Clarence Thomas-Anita Hill Hearings, October 11, 12, 13, 1991*, preface by Nina Totenberg, edited by Anita Miller. Chicago: Academy Chicago Publishers, 1994. Full transcript of the Senate Judiciary Committee's October 1991 hearings.

U.S. Congress Senate Committee on the Judiciary. *Nomination of Judge Clarence Thomas to Be Associate Justice of the Supreme Court of the United States: Hearings, September 10–October 13, 1991*. Washington, DC: U.S. GPO,1993. A detailed account of Thomas' confirmation hearings, including Anita Hill's charges of sexual harassment.

U.S. Congress Senate Committee on Labor and Human Resources. *Employment Non-Discrimination Act of 1994: Hearing of the Committee on Labor and Human Resources, United States Senate, 103rd Cong., 2nd sess., on S. 2238 to Prohibit Employment Discrimination on the Basis of Sexual Orientation, July 29, 1994*. Washington, DC: U.S. GPO, 1994. Testimony on discrimination and sexual harassment of gay and lesbian employees of the federal government.

U.S. Congress Senate Committee on Labor and Human Resources. *Sex Discrimination in the Workplace, 1981: Hearings Before the Committee on Labor and Human Resources, United States Senate, 97th Cong., 1st Sess. on Examination on Issues Affecting Women in Our Nation's Labor Force, January 28 and April 21, 1981*. Washington, DC: U.S. GPO, 1981. Documents the 1981 hearings on sexual harassment in the workplace.

U.S. Congress Senate Committee on Labor and Human Resources. *University Responses to Racial and Sexual Harassment on Campuses: Hearing Before the Committee on Labor and Human Resources, United States Senate, 102nd Cong., 2nd Sess., September 10, 1992*. Washington, DC: U.S. GPO, 1992. Text of hearings on the responses of universities to racial and sexual harassment on campus.

U.S. Congress Senate Select Committee on Ethics. *Refusal of Senator Bob Packwood to Produce Documents Subpoenaed by the Select Committee on Ethics: Report (to accompany S. Res. 153)*. Washington, DC: U.S. GPO, 1993. The committee's debate on Packwood's refusal to deliver diaries covering the years during which he allegedly sexually harassed more than two dozen women.

U.S. Customs Service, Special Assistant to the Commissioner. *Equal Employment Opportunity—Managerial Function*. Washington, DC: U.S. Customs Service, 1987. A 64-page report on workplace sexual harassment and the process by which complaints are handled.

U.S. Defense Fuel Supply Center. *Equal Employment Opportunity Handbook*. Washington, DC: U.S. GPO, 1990. A handbook that details the Defense

Fuel Supply Center's enactment of the EEOC's sexual harassment guidelines, with a review of the Hispanic Employment program and the Federal Women's Program.

U.S. Departments of the Army and Air Force, National Guard Bureau. *Prevention of Sexual Harassment, Guidelines for Commanders, Managers, and Supervisors.* Washington, DC: U.S. GPO, 1982. A 9-page manual for National Guard commanders, managers, and supervisors that defines sexual harassment, outlines existing military policies, and presents several illustrative court cases.

U.S. General Accounting Office. *Coast Guard: Information Needed to Assess the Extent of Sexual Assaults on Ships: Report to the Honorable Mike Lowry, House of Representatives/U.S. General Accounting Office.* Washington, DC: U.S. GAO, 1988. A report on sexual harassment in the Coast Guard.

U.S. General Accounting Office. *Federal Employment: Inquiry into Sexual Harassment Issues at Selected VA Medical Centers: Report to Congressional Requesters.* Washington, DC: U.S. GAO 1993. A report on sexual harassment at several VA medical centers.

U.S. Merit Systems Protection Board. *Sexual Harassment in the Federal Government: An Update.* Washington, DC: U.S. GPO, 1988. A 61-page comparison of the results of 1980 and 1987 studies on the level of sexual harassment in the federal workplace.

U.S. Merit Systems Protection Board, Office of Merit Systems Review and Studies. *Sexual Harassment in the Federal Workplace: Is it a Problem?* Washington, DC: U.S. GPO, 1981. A 204-page study of sexual harassment in the federal workplace and the cost of possible remedies.

U.S. Office of Personnel Management. *Workshop on Sexual Harassment: Participant Materials.* Washington, DC: U.S. GPO, 1980. A 30-page handbook for participants in sexual harassment workshops, with exercises designed to heighten sexual harassment awareness and background on federal sexual harassment laws and policies.

U.S. Office of Personnel Management. *Workshop on Sexual Harassment: Trainer's Manual.* Washington, DC: U.S. GPO, 1980. An 82-page manual designed for leaders of training workshops on sexual harassment, with information of sexual harassment policies for federal employees and statements made by government officials on sexual harassment.

U.S. Small Business Administration, Office of Equal Employment Opportunity. *Reference Manual for the Prevention of Sexual Harassment/Prepared by Special Emphasis Program Manager, U.S. Small Business Administration, Office of Equal Employment Opportunity.* Washington, DC: U.S. Small Business Administration, Office of Equal Employment Opportunity, 1993. A manual designed to help small businesses prevent workplace sexual harassment.

U.S. Veterans Administration, Office of Personnel and Labor Relations. *Supervisory Training Program: The Supervisor and EEO/Affirmative Action—Unit XII.* Washington, DC: U.S. VA, Office of Personnel and Labor Relations, 1988. A 55-page training manual to familiarize VA management with EEOC sexual harassment guidelines and their legal and personnel management implications.

GOVERNMENT BROCHURES AND PAMPHLETS

Caution, Sexual Harassment Is Illegal. Washington, DC: Office for Human Resources, U.S. Fish and Wildlife Service, 1991. A pamphlet warning against sexual harassment and outlining its various forms.

Dealing with Sexual Harassment. Washington, DC: Department of the Treasury, U.S. Customs Service, 1988. Information about sexual harassment in the United States.

Facts about Sexual Harassment. Washington, DC: U.S. Equal Employment Opportunity Commission, 1990. A factual guide for women about sexual harassment.

"Not for Women Only": a Guide Toward an Environment Free of Sexual Harassment. Washington, DC: U.S. Department of Health and Human Services, Office of the Assistant Secretary for Personnel Administration, Federal Women's Program, 1992. A pamphlet focusing on the prevention of sexual harassment.

Sexual Harassment. Bethesda, MD: Health Care Financing Administration, Equal Opportunity Office, 1991. A fact sheet on the sexual harassment of women within the work environment.

Sexual Harassment in the Workplace: It Is a Problem. Washington, DC: Alcohol, Drug Abuse, and Mental Health Administration, Federal Women's Program, Office of Equal Employment Opportunity, 1984. Discusses the sexual harassment of working women in the United States.

Sexual Harassment: It's Not Academic. Washington, DC: U.S. Department of Education, Office for Civil Rights, 1988. A 1988 report on sexual harassment from the U.S. Department of Education.

Sexual Harassment: Know Your Rights. Washington, DC: U.S. Department of Labor, Office of the Secretary, Women's Bureau, 1994. General and legal information about sexual harassment and the legal and civil rights of the United States citizens.

Understanding Sexual Harassment. Portland, OR: U.S. Department of Agriculture, Forest Service, Pacific Northwest Region, 1981. A pamphlet defining the different types of sexual harassment.

U.S. Army, Belvoir Research Development and Engineering Center. *Equal Opportunity*. For Belvoir, VA: Belvoir Research Development and Engineering Center, 1987. A booklet addressing sexual harassment and affirmative action. Focuses primarily on civilian employees.

U.S. Department of Agriculture. *Sexual Harassment: Sexual Harassment Is Prohibited and Can Be Stopped*. Washington, DC: Department of Agriculture, 1989. An anti-sexual harassment poster designed by the Department of Agriculture.

U.S. Department of Defense, American Forces Information Service. *It's Shocking! It's Disgusting! It Makes Your Hair Stand on End!: Don't Call It Hands-On Management! It's Sexual Harassment! Let It go and You Could Create a Monster! Defense Billboard no. 27*. Alexandria, VA: U.S. DOD, American Forces Information Service, 1990. A visual warning against sexual harassment designed by the U.S. Department of Defense.

U.S. Equal Employment Opportunity Commission. *Facts About Sexual Harassment*. Washington, DC: U.S. EEOC, 1990. A 2-page pamphlet explaining what sexual harassment is and how to defend oneself against it.

U.S. Internal Revenue Service, National EEO Office. *EEO Notebook*. Washington, DC: U.S. GPO 1989. A 12-page booklet describing the Internal Revenue Service's policy on sexual harassment.

Vermont Advisory Committee to the U.S. Commission on Civil Rights. *Sexual Harassment on the Job: A Guide for Employers*. Washington, DC: U.S. GPO 1982. A 23-page manual for employers, outlining sexual harassment laws and offering techniques for handling sexual harassment in the workplace.

Which Picture Doesn't Belong? Alexandria, VA: American Forces Information Service, DOD, 1988. A poster depicting the sexual harassment of women.

A Working Woman's Guide to Her Job Rights. Washington, DC: U.S. Department of Labor, Women's Bureau, U.S. GPO, 1978. A woman's guide to sexual harassment and job rights in the workplace.

Wyoming Advisory Committee to the U.S. Commission on Civil Rights. *Corporate Reactions to Workplace Conditions in Wyoming*. Washington, DC: U.S. GPO, 1982. A 15-page report on executive responses to problems faced by women and minorities employed in the Rocky Mountain region; some corporate managers denied any difficulties, others acknowledged problems and offered suggestions for improving workplace conditions.

Wyoming Advisory Committee to the U.S. Commission on Civil Rights. *Workplace Conditions in Wyoming: Women and Minorities in the Mineral Extraction Industries*. Washington, DC: U.S. Commission on Civil Rights, 1982. A 58-page report on workplace conditions for women and minorities in the mineral-extraction industries.

Annotated Bibliography

AUDIOVISUAL MATERIALS

All the Wrong Moves: A Story of Sexual Harassment in the Workplace. Dartnell Corp., 1987. Video.

Blaming the Sexual Harassment Victim. Video, 28 min. An adaptation of a "Phil Donahue" show questioning why female victims of sexual harassment are blamed, while their abusers are not.

Clarence Thomas and Anita Hill: Public Hearing, Private Pain. Alexandria, VA: PBS Video, 1992. Video, 58 min. Originally aired as a segment of "Frontline," the piece by Ofra Bikel looks at the Hill-Thomas hearings from African-American points of view and considers the impact the hearings have had on the community.

Date Rape: Behind Closed Doors. Cambridge Educational Group, Inc. Video, 1990.

The EEOC's Sexual Harassment Package. EEOC. Video.

How Far Is Too Far? Dist. by Coronet, the Multimedia Company, 1988. Video 18 min. Explores recent court decisions in sexual harassment cases.

Handling the Sexual Harassment Complaint and *Sexual Harassment in the Workplace: Identify, Stop, Prevent.* American Media Incorporated, 1990. Video, two programs, 20 min. each. Provides managers with ways to identify and cope with incidents of sexual harassment in the workplace. Focuses on sexual harassment as a form of illegal sex discrimination.

It's No Game. A Mountain View Production (developed by the Center for Women in Government), 1987. Video, 33 min. A simulated training session shows how employees and supervisors can be taught about sexual harassment in the workplace. Uses scenes from the television series, "Cagney and Lacey."

It's Not Just Courtesy—It's the Law. Advantage Media, Inc., 1990. Video, 26 min., 30 sec. Education piece that presents sexual harassment as a pervasive and serious issue.

Lures of Death. MTI Teleprograms, 1984. Video, 15 min. A study of crimes against children. Suggests possible methods to teach children how to avoid potentially dangerous situations, including sexual harassment.

Making Advances: What Organizations Must Do About Sexual Harassment. Distributed by Coronet, the Multimedia Company, 1988. Video, 30 min. Discusses what can be done to achieve and maintain a harassment-free work environment.

Monsieur Hire. Orion Pictures, Orion Home Video, 1991. Video, 88 min. A film adaptation of the novel by Georges Simenon, in which a woman discovers that a neighbor has been spying on her; she decides to become the aggressor.

Sexual Harassment

The Power Pinch. Integrated Video Services, 1981. Video, 28 min. A documentary discussing the various definitions of sexual harassment and various preventive measures.

Race, Gender and Power in America. Sponsored by the Georgetown University Law Center, 1992. Video, 393 min. A documentary on the sexual harassment of, and racial discrimination against, women.

Respect: Sexual Harassment (Teens-at-Risk Series). Derry, NH: Chip Taylor Communications, 1994. Video, 8 min.

Sex, Power and the Workplace. Community Television of Southern California/KCET, 1992 Video, 58 min. A presentation of several sexual harassment cases in the workplace and a general discussion of possible remedies.

Sexual Harassment. Video, 19 min. Addresses the consequence of sexual harassment and possible solutions.

Sexual Harassment ("Soapbox with Tom Cottle" Series). Produced by WGBY-TV, Distributed by PBS Video. Video, 28 min.

Sexual Harassment Awareness Programs. Philips Office Associates, 1983. Videos, 20 min. A three-part training series for managers and employees that provides a comprehensive overview of the legal dangers of sexual harassment: "Sexual Harassment—A Threat to Your Profits"; "Sexual Harassment—That's Not My Job Description"; "Sexual Harassment—What It Is and What We Can Do to Stop It."

Sexual Harassment: Crossing the Line. Cambridge Educational Productions, 1992. Video, 30 min. Addresses questions, confusion and feelings of anxiety about sexual harassment and suggests specific methods to cope with them.

Sexual Harassment from 9 to 5. Video, 26 min. Discusses various aspects of sexual harassment in the workplace.

Sexual Harassment: Handling the Complaint. Audio Graphics Training Systems, 1993. Video, 30 min. Instructions to employers for dealing with charges of sexual harassment in the workplace.

Sexual Harassment: How to Protect Yourself and Your Organization. Cambridge Career Products, 1993. Videos, 126 min. Designed for personnel managers, the training package shows how to effectively handle incidents of sexual harassment in the workplace.

Sexual Harassment in Healthcare: Relearning the Rules. Videolearning Resource Group. Video, 15 min.

Sexual Harassment Is Bad Business. J. M. Glasc, 1987. Video, 22 min. An analysis of sexual harassment in the workplace and the legal liability of employers. Presents the views of victims, managers, and co-workers affected by sexual harassment.

Annotated Bibliography

Sexual Harassment Manual for Managers and Supervisors: How to Prevent and Resolve Sexual Harassment Complaints in the Workplace. Commerce Clearing House. Video.

Sexual Harassment, The New Rules. Management Briefing and Employee Awareness Training. Commonwealth Films, Inc., 1993. Videos, two programs, 37 min. ea. A two-part program dealing with sexual harassment, providing guidelines for appropriate behavior in the post Hill-Thomas era. Titles include: 1. "A Management Briefing." 2. "Employee Awareness Training."

Sexual Harassment: No Laughing Matter. Advantage Media Inc., 1984. Video, 15 min. Clarifies, for employers, the legal definition of sexual harassment and alerts them to problems for which they may be liable.

Sexual Harassment: No Place in the Workplace. Michigan Media, 1979. Video, 29 min. Lynn Farley and Gloria Steinem discuss the problems of sexual harassment in the workplace.

Sexual Harassment of Men by Women. Video, 28 min. Phil Donahue hosts a show in which male guests describe how they have been sexually harassed by women.

Sexual Harassment 101, Parts 1 and 2 (Gender Jeopardy Series). Select Media. Video, approx. 30 min.

Sexual Harassment on the Job. Video, 28 min. Phil Donahue's guest, Susan Meyer, talks about how to cope with sexual harassment in the workplace.

Sexual Harassment on the Job. Films for the Humanities and Sciences, Video, 28 min. Deals with the sexual harassment of women and sex discrimination on the job.

Sexual Harassment: The Other Point of View. United Training Media, 1987. Video, 33 min. Illustrates what types of behavior constitute sexual harassment and advises what to do when encountering it; also, how to stop it before it starts.

Sexual Harassment: Prevention, Recognition and Correction. Bureau of Business Practice, 1993. Video, 25 min. Defines actions and behavior that constitute illegal sexual harassment and provides practical suggestions on how to prevent it.

Sexual Harassment: Shades of Grey. United Training Media, 1990. Videos, five programs, 13 min. ea. Workplace training program; titles include: 1. "What Are We Doing Here?" 2. "What Is Sexual Harassment?" 3. "Why Should I Worry About It?" 4. "What Does the Law Say?" 5. "What Am I Supposed to Do?"

Sexual Harassment: Understanding the Law. Audio Graphics Training Systems, 1992 Video, 30 min. A two-part series on the legal definition of sexual harassment and its legal repercussions.

Sexual Harassment: Walking the Corporate Fine Line. NOW Legal Defense and Education Fund, 1987. Video, 22 min. An overview of sexual harassment, its history, definition, and impact. Instructs personnel management how to effectively and sensitively investigate a sexual harassment complaint.

Sexual Harassment: What Every Manager Must Know. Black Ravan Corp., 1991 Video, 60 min.

Sexual Harassment: What Every Woman Must Know. Black Ravan Corp., 1991 Video, 60 min.

Sexual Politics at Work. WNET/Alvin H. Perlmutter, Inc., 1993. Video, 60 min. A debate led by Fred Graham on issues of conduct between men and women on the job.

Stop Sexual Harassment on Campus. Old Dominion University, Center for Instructional Services, 1988. Video, 24 min. Dramatizations of sexual harassment incidents on campus, with possible preventative techniques.

Thomas Confirmation Hearing. Purdue University, Public Affairs Video Archives, 1991. Video, 122 min. A compilation of testimony by Anita Hill and Clarence Thomas before the Senate Judiciary Committee in October 1991.

Thomas-Hill Hearings. C-SPAN, 1991. Video (3 cassettes), 1,071 min. Contains the complete testimony from the Hill-Thomas hearings.

Town Meeting: A Process Run Amok, Thomas/Hill Hearings. MPI Home Video, 1991. Video, 90 min. Focuses on media coverage of the sexual harassment allegations in the Hill-Thomas hearings. Originally appeared on "ABC's Nightline" with Ted Koppel.

U.S. Congress. Senate Committee on the Judiciary. Sexual Harassment Hearing Compilation. West Lafayette, Indiana: Purdue University, Public Affairs Video Archives, 1991. Video, 1 cassette, 122 min. Originally available as *Thomas-Hill Hearings* from C-SPAN, 1991. Excerpts and highlights from the confirmation hearings.

What Is Sexual Harassment? The Learning Seed, 1994. Video, 23 min. Defines sexual harassment and discusses its presence in our everyday lives. Also outlines possible strategies for ending it.

CHAPTER 7

ORGANIZATIONS AND AGENCIES

PRIVATE ORGANIZATIONS

Ad Hoc Sexual Harassment Coalition
c/o Lauren Wechsler
Ms. Foundation for Women
141 Fifth Avenue
New York, NY 10010
(212) 353-8580

A coalition of women's and civil rights groups dedicated to fighting sexual harassment.

American Association of University Women Legal Advocacy Fund
111 16th Street, NW
Washington, DC 20036
(202) 785-7744

Provides support for sexual harassment suits against colleges and universities.

American Society for Training and Development
1640 King Street
Alexandria, VA 22313
(703) 683-8100

A national professional group that provides information for anti-harassment training in the workplace.

Association for Union Democracy Women's Project
500 State Street
Brooklyn, NY 11217
(718) 855-6650

Referrals, counseling, and group assistance for women union members; anti-harassment training.

Business and Professional Women/USA
2012 Massachusetts Avenue, NW
Washington, DC 20036
(202) 293-1100

An association of working women that publishes position papers on sexual harassment. More than 3,000 local chapters.

Catalyst
250 Park Avenue South
New York, NY 10002-1459
(212) 777-8900

A research and advisory group committed to opening opportunities and solving problems for women in corporate careers.

Center for the Prevention of Sexual and Domestic Violence
1914 North 34th Street, Suite 105

Seattle, WA 98103
(206) 634-1903

Offers information and support for victims of sexual harassment by members of the clergy.

**Center for Research on Women
Sexual Harassment in Schools
Project**
Wellesley College
Wellesley, MA 02181
(616) 283-2500

Studies sexual harassment in school systems and ways to stop it.

Center for Research on Women
Clement Hall
Memphis State University
Memphis, TN 38152
(901) 678-2770

Advances research in women's studies, especially with regard to southern women and women of color. Maintains the Research Clearinghouse, a database of sources.

Center for Women in Government
University of Albany
Draper Hall 310
135 Western Avenue
Albany, NY 12222
(518) 442-3900

Offers sexual harassment information to workers nationwide.

Center for Women's Policy Studies
2000 P Street, NW, Suite 508
Washington, DC 20036
(202) 872-1770

Studies the impact of government policy on the status of women and publishes information on sexual harassment for students.

Center for Working Life
600 Grand Avenue, Suite 305

Oakland, CA 94610
(510) 893-7343

A nonprofit organization that provides sexual harassment training and counseling for victims of harassment.

Clearinghouse on Women's Issues
P.O. Box 70603
Friendship Heights, MD 20813

A coalition of women's groups focusing on issues of sex discrimination.

Coalition of Labor Union Women
15 Union Square
New York, NY 10003
(212) 242-0789

Legal referrals, workplace policies, and contract language concerning sexual harassment of union members.

Equal Rights Advocates
1663 Mission Street, Suite 550
San Francisco, CA 94130
(415) 621-0672

Basic sexual harassment information and referrals, in English and Spanish.

Federally Employed Women
400 Eye Street, NW, Suite 425
Washington, DC 20005
(202) 898-0994

An organization for women employed by the federal government.

**Federation of Organizations for
Professional Women**
2001 S Street, NW, Suite 500
Washington, DC 20009
(202) 328-1415

A coalition that addresses issues such as sexual harassment, offers counseling, and operates the Professional Women's Legal Fund.

Fund for the Feminist Majority
1600 Wilson Boulevard

180

Arlington, VA 22209
(703) 522-2214

Conducts research, provides information, and publishes information on sexual harassment.

**Institute for Women and Work
School of Industrial and Labor
  Relations
Cornell University
15 East 26th Street, 4th floor
New York, NY 10010
(212) 340-2812**

Publishes a list of sexual harassment resources, offers training seminars.

**National Association for Women
  in Education
1325 18th Street, NW, Suite 210
Washington, DC 20036
(202) 659-9330**

Publishes information on campus harassment.

**National Council for Research
  on Women
The Sara Delano Roosevelt
  Memorial House
47-49 East 65th Street
New York, NY 10021
(212) 570-5000**

Offers research resources, educational programs, and policy analysis on issues affecting women.

**National Employment Law Project
236 Massachusetts Avenue, NE
Washington, DC 20002
(202) 544-2185**

Tracks developments in employment law issues such as sexual harassment.

**National Employment Lawyers
  Association
535 Pacific Avenue**

San Francisco, CA 94133
(415) 227-4655

Publishes a national directory of member attorneys.

**National Federation of Business
  and Professional Women's Clubs
2012 Massachusetts Avenue, NW
Washington, DC 20036
(202) 293-1200**

A research and education organization that maintains a library of information on working women and lobbies for improvements in conditions faced by working women.

**National Lawyers Guild
  Anti-Sexism Committee
131 George Street
San Jose, CA 95110
(408) 287-1916**

Provides referrals to member attorneys, including those who specialize in sexual harassment.

**National Women's Law Center
1616 P Street, NW, Suite 100
Washington, DC 20007
(202) 328-5160**

A nonprofit organization conducts research on legal issues affecting women.

**National Women's Political Caucus
1275 K Street, NW, Suite 750
Washington, DC 20005
(202) 898-1100**

Tracks the voting records of senators and representatives on sexual harassment issues and publishes a model sexual harassment policy.

**9 to 5, the National Association of
  Working Women
614 Superior Avenue, NW**

Cleveland, OH 44113
(216) 566-9308

Nonprofit organization with chapters nationwide that provides information and advice about sexual harassment. Publishes a newsletter.

**NOW Legal Defense and
  Education Fund**
99 Hudson Street, 12th floor
New York, NY 10013
(212) 925-6635

Addresses legal issues of concern to women, consults with corporations, and publishes a list of sexual harassment sources and a Legal Resource Kit for victims of harassment.

**Project of the Center for the Study
  of Communication**
**University of Massachusetts
  Foundation for Media Education**
P.O. Box 2008
Amherst, MA 01004-2002
(413) 545-2341

Publishes information on gender-related subjects.

**Society for Human Resource
  Management**
606 N. Washington Street
Alexandria, VA 22314
(703) 548-3440

A membership organization of personnel managers; provides information on formulating sexual harassment policies, training programs, and grievance procedures.

Tradeswomen, Inc.
P.O. Box 40664
San Francisco, CA 94140
(415) 821-7335

A support and networking group for women in non-traditional jobs; publishes a magazine and a newsletter.

United States Student Association
815 15th Street, NW, Suite 838

Washington, DC 20005
(202) 347-8772

Advocates for student rights, including sexual harassment prevention.

Wider Opportunities for Women
1325 G Street, NW
Washington, DC 20005
(202) 638-3143

A nonprofit group dedicated to advancing the cause of women in non-traditional employment. Publishes sexual harassment information and assists employers with sexual harassment training.

Women Employed Institute
22 West Monroe, Suite 1400
Chicago, IL 60603
(312) 782-3902

A membership organization that offers sexual harassment counseling, training, and referral, and fact sheets in the Chicago area.

**Women for Racial and Economic
  Equality**
198 Broadway, Room 606
New York, NY 10038
(212) 385-1103

An organization working toward passage of a Women's Bill of Rights to end racial and economic discrimination against women.

**Women's Action for Good
  Employment Standards**
**c/o Institute for Research on Women's
  Health**
1616 18th Street, NW, #109B
Washington, DC 20009
(202) 483-8643

Among other workplace issues of concern to this organization is sexual harassment.

Women's Alliance for Job Equity
1422 Chestnut Street, Suite 1100

Philadelphia, PA 19102
(215) 561-1873

A group that offers sexual harassment information, support, training, and referrals in the Philadelphia area.

Women's Law Project
125 South 9th Street, Suite 401
Philadelphia, PA 19107
(215) 928-9801

Philadelphia-area information and referrals on sexual harassment.

Women's Legal Defense Fund
1875 Connecticut Avenue, NW,
** Suite 710**
Washington, DC 20009
(202) 986-2600

A non profit sexual harassment organization offering education, information, and advocacy.

Women Organized Against
** Sexual Harassment**
P.O. Box 4768
Berkeley, CA 84704
(415) 642-7310

Gathers information and plans strategies to end sexual harassment.

Women's Rights Litigation
** Clinic**
Rutgers University Law School
15 Washington Street
Newark, NJ 07102
(201) 648-5637

Offers legal information, counselling, and support on the issue of sexual harassment.

Women Students' Sexual
** Harassment Caucus**
Department of Applied
** Psychology**
Ontario Institute for Studies in
** Education**
252 Bloor Street West

Toronto, Ontario M5S 1V6
(416) 923-6641

Studies ways to end sexual harassment at colleges and universities.

W.R.A.T.H. (Women Refusing to
Accept Tenant Harassment)
607 Elmira Road, Suite 299
Vacaville, CA 95687

Offers support to victims of sexual harassment in housing.

GOVERNMENT
AGENCIES

Commission on the Economic
** Status of Women**
State Office Building, Room 85
100 Constitution Avenue
St. Paul, MN 55155
(612) 296-8590

A legislative advisory panel that researches issues affecting the economic status of women.

National Association of
** Commissions for Women**
c/o D.C. Commission for Women
N-345 Reeves Center
2000 14th Street, NW
Washington, DC 20009
(202) 628-5030

A coalition of government organizations that monitor the status of women.

U.S. Department of Labor
** Women's Bureau**
200 Constitution Avenue, NW,
** Room S3311**
Washington, DC 20210
(202) 523-6665

The department's office for working women publishes a list of sexual harassment resources.

FAIR EMPLOYMENT PRACTICE AGENCIES

The following agencies handle discrimination complaints under state or municipal laws. State agencies are listed first, followed by local offices. All state agencies are included, regardless of complaint procedures or enforcement powers.

ALASKA

State Commission for Human Rights
431 West 7th Avenue, Suite 101
Anchorage, AK 99501
(907) 276-7474

Anchorage Equal Rights Commission
620 East 10th Avenue, Suite 204
Anchorage, AK 99501

Human Rights Commission
Southcentral Region
P.O. Box AH, 314 Goldstein
Boulevard
Juneau, AK 99811
(907) 465-3560

ARIZONA

Civil Rights Division, Attorney
General's Office
1275 West Washington Street
Phoenix, AZ 85007
(602) 255-5263

Southern Arizona Office
402 West Congress Street, Suite 315
Tucson, AZ 85701

Governor's Office of Affirmative
Action
1700 West Washington Street, State
Capitol Room 804
Phoenix, AZ 85007

CALIFORNIA

Department of Fair Employment and
Housing
1201 I Street, Suite 211
Sacramento, CA 95814
(916) 445-9918

California District and Field Offices,
Department of Fair Employment and
Housing
1529 "F" Street
Bakersfield, CA 93301
(805) 395-2728

1900 Mariposa Mall
Suite 130
Fresno, CA 93721
(209) 445-5373

322 West First Street
Room 2126
Los Angeles, CA 90012
(213) 620-2610

1111 Jackson Street
Oakland, CA 94607
(415) 464-4095 375 West Hospitality Lane
Room 280
San Bernardino, CA 92408
(714) 383-4711

110 West C Street
Suite 1702
San Diego, CA 92101
(619) 237-7405

30 Van Ness Avenue
San Francisco, CA 94102
(415) 557-2005

888 North First Street
Room 316
San Jose, CA 95112
(408) 227-1264

28 Civic Center Plaza
Room 330
Santa Ana, CA 92701
(714) 558-4159

5730 Ralston Street
Room 302
Ventura, CA 93003
(805) 654-4513

Organizations and Agencies

COLORADO

Civil Rights Commission,
Room 600C
State Services Building
1525 Sherman Street
Denver, CO 80203
(303) 866-2621

Colorado Branch Offices, Civil Rights Commission

2860 South Circle Drive
North Building
Suite 2103
Colorado Springs, CO 80906

222 South 6th Street
Room 417
Grand Junction, CO 81501
(303) 248-7329

800 8th Avenue
Suite 223
Greeley, CO 80631
(303) 356-9221

720 North Main
Suite 222
Pueblo, CO 81003
(303) 545-3520

CONNECTICUT

Commission on Human Rights and
    Opportunities
Central Office
90 Washington Street
Hardford, CT 06115
(203) 566-3350

Connecticut Regional Offices, Commission on Human Rights and Opportunities

Capital Region
1229 Albany Avenue
Hartford, CT 06112

West Central Region
232 North Elm Street
Waterbury, CT 06702

Eastern Region
302 Captain's Walk
New London, CT 06320

Southwest Region
1862 East Main Street
Bridgeport, CT 06610

DELAWARE

Department of Labor,
    Anti-Discrimination Section
Wilmington State Office Building
820 North French Street, 6th Floor
Wilmington, DE 19801
(302) 571-2900

State Human Relations Commission
William Service Center
805 River Road
Dover, DE 19910
(302) 736-4567

Georgetown Service Center
Route 113-Bradford Street Extension
Georgetown, DE 19947

DISTRICT OF COLUMBIA

D.C. Office of Human Rights
2000 14th Street NW, 3rd Floor
Washington, DC 20009
(202) 939-8740

FLORIDA

Commission of Human Relations
325 John Knox Road
Suite 240, Building F
Tallahassee, FL 32399
(904) 488-7082 or (800) 342-8170

Lee County Department of Equal
    Opportunity
P.O. Box 398
Fort Myers, FL 33902-0398
(813) 334-2166

Sexual Harassment

GEORGIA

Georgia Office of Fair Employment
  Practices
156 Trinity Avenue SouthWest,
  Suite 208
Atlanta, GA 30303
(404) 656-1736

Governor's Council on Human
  Relations
State Capitol, Room 249
Atlanta, GA 30334
(404) 656-6757

Augusta/Richmond County
Human Relations Commission
Suite 400, 500 Building
Augusta, GA 30902

HAWAII

Department of Labor & Industrial
  Relations
Enforcement Division
888 Mililani Street, Room 401
Honolulu, HI 96813
(808) 548-3976

IDAHO

Commission on Human Rights
450 West State Street
Boise, ID 83720
(208) 334-2873

ILLINOIS

Department of Human Rights
One Illinois Center
100 West Randolph Street, Suite 10-100
Chicago, IL 60601
(312) 917-6200

Springfield Regional Office
Stratton Office Building, Room 623
Springfield, IL 62706
(217) 785-5100

INDIANA

Civil Rights Commission
32 East Washington Street, Suite 900
Indianapolis, IN 46204
(317) 232-2600

IOWA

Civil Rights Commission
211 East Maple Street
2nd Floor, State Office Building
Des Moines, IA 50319
(515) 281-4121 or (800) 457-4416

KANSAS

Commission on Civil Rights, Landon State
Office Building
900 South West Jackson, 8th Floor,
Suite 851S
Topeka, KS 66612
(913) 296-3206

Kansas Branch Offices, Commission on Civil Rights

212 South Market
Wichita, KS 67202
(913) 265-7466

Wichita Civil Rights and Equal
  Employment Opportunity Commission
455 North Main Street, 10th Floor
Wichita, KS 67202

KENTUCKY

Commission on Human Rights
701 West Muhammad Ali
  Boulevard
P.O. Box 69
Louisville, KY 40201
(502) 588-4024

832 Capital Plaza Tower
Frankfort, KY 40601
(502) 564-3550

MAINE

Human Rights Commission
State House, Station No. 51
Augusta, ME 04333
(207) 289-2326

MARYLAND

Commission on Human Relations
20 East Franklin Street
Baltimore, MD 21202
(301) 333-1700

514 Race Street
Cambridge, MD 21613
(301) 228-0112

Professional Arts Building
Room 305, 5 Public Square
Hagerstown, MD 21740

MASSACHUSETTS

Commission Against Discrimination
McCormack State Office Building
1 Ashburton Place
Boston, MA 02108
(617) 727-3990

Massachusetts District Offices,
Commission Against Discrimination

145 State Street
Springfield, MA 01103

222 Union Street
New Bedford, MA 02740

22 Front Street
P.O. Box 8008
Worcester, MA 01614

MICHIGAN

Department of Civil Rights
303 West Kalamazoo

Lansing, MI 48913
(517) 334-6079

Department of Civil Rights
Michigan Plaza Building
Detroit, MI 48226
(313) 256-2663

Michigan District Offices,
Department of Civil Rights

221 East Roosevelt
Battle Creek, MI 49017

Grand Rapids State
   Office Building
350 Ottawa Street, NW
Grand Rapids, MI 49502

State Office Building
125 East Union Street
Flint, MI 48502

State Office Building
301 East Louis B. Glick Highway
Jackson, MI 49201

309 N. Washington Square
Leonard Plaza Building
Room 103
Lansing, MI 48913

State Office Building
411 East Genesee
Saginaw, MI 48605

242 Pipestone
Benton Harbor, MI 49022

2542 Peck
Muskegon Heights, MI 49444

Pontiac State Bank Building
28 North Saginaw
10th Floor
Pontiac, MI 48058

L'Anse-Baraga
Upper Peninsula, U.S. 41
Arnheim, Pelkie, MI 49958

187

Sexual Harassment

MINNESOTA

Department of Human Rights
500 Bremer Building
7th and Robert Streets
St. Paul, MN 55101
(612) 296-5663

MISSOURI

Commission on Human Rights
315 Ellis Boulevard
P.O. Box 1129
Jefferson City, MO 65102
(314) 751-3325

Missouri Regional Offices, Commission on Human Rights

625 North Euclid
Suite 605
St. Louis, MO 63108
(314) 444-7590

1601 East 18th Street
Suites 320 and 340
Kansas City, MO 64108
(816) 472-2491

526 D South Main
Sikeston, MO 63801
(314) 471-7185

MONTANA

Human Rights Commission
Room C-317, Cogswell Building
Capital Station, Box 1728
Helena, MT 59624
(406) 444-2884

NEBRASKA

Nebraska Equal Opportunity Commission
P.O. Box 94934
301 Centennial Mall South
Lincoln, NE 68509
(402) 471-2024

Nebraska Branch Offices, Equal Opportunity Commission

5620 Ames Avenue
Suite 110
Omaha, NE 68104

4500 Avenue I
Box 1500
Scottsbluff, NE 69361

Lincoln Commission on Human Rights
129 North 10th Street, Room 318
Lincoln, NE 68508

Omaha Human Relations Dept.
1819 Farnam Street, Suite 505
Omaha, NE 68102

NEVADA

Equal Rights Commission
515 East Tropicana
Suite 590
Las Vegas, NV 89158
(702) 386-5304

668 Galletti Way
Sparks, NV 89431
(702) 789-0288

NEW HAMPSHIRE

Commission for Human Rights
61 South Spring Street
Concord, NH 03301
(603) 271-2767

NEW JERSEY

Division on Civil Rights, Department
of Law & Public Safety
Headquarters Office
1100 Raymond Boulevard
Newark, NJ 07102
(201) 648-2700

New Jersey Branch Offices, Division on Civil Rights, Department of Law & Public Safety
436 East State Street
Trenton, NJ 08608
(609) 292-4605

130 Broadway
Camden, NJ 08102
(609) 757-2850

370 Broadway
Paterson, NJ 07501
(201) 345-1465

NEW MEXICO
Human Rights Commission
930 Baca Street
Santa Fe, NM 87501
(505) 827-6420

NEW YORK
State Division of Human Rights
55 West 125th Street
New York, NY 10027
(212) 870-8400 or (800) 427-2773

New York Branch Offices, State Division of Human Rights
Alfred East Smith
State Office Building
25th Floor
Albany, NY 12225
(518) 474-2705

364 Hawley Street
Binghamton, NY 13901
(607) 773-7713

349 East 149th Street
Bronx, NY 10451

1360 Fulton Street
4th Floor

Brooklyn, NY 11216
(718) 622-4600

69 Delaware Avenue
Buffalo, NY 14202
(716) 847-3713

State Office Building
Veterans Highway
Hauppauge, NY 11787
(516) 360-6434

100 Main Street
2nd Floor
Hempstead, NY 11550
(516) 538-1360

270 Broadway
9th Floor
New York, NY 10007
(212) 587-5041

NYS Harlem Office Building
163 West 125th Street
2nd Floor
New York, NY 10027

120-55 Queens Boulevard
Kew Gardens, NY 11424
(718) 520-3373

259 Monroe Avenue
Rochester, NY 14607
(716) 238-8250

351 South Warren Street
Syracuse, NY 13202
(315) 428-4633

30 Glenn Street
3rd Floor
White Plains, NY 10603
(914) 949-4394

NORTH CAROLINA
Human Relations Council
121 West Jones Street

Raleigh, NC 27603
(919) 733-7996

Office of Administrative Hearing
424 North Blount
Raleigh, NC 27601
(919) 733-2691

NORTH DAKOTA

Department of Labor
State Capitol, 5th Floor
Bismarck, ND 58505
(701) 224-2660

OHIO

Civil Rights Commission
220 Parsons Avenue
Columbus, OH 43215
(614) 466-2785

Ohio Branch Offices, Civil Rights Commission

615 West Superior Avenue, NW
Cleveland, OH 44113
(215) 622-3150

Southeast Regional Office
220 Parsons Avenue
Columbus, OH 43215
(614) 466-5928

North-Southwest
  Regional Office
800 Miami Tower
40 West Fourth Street
Dayton, OH 45402
(513) 228-3612

Northwest Regional Office
510 Gardner Building
506 Madison and Superior
Toledo, OH 43604
(419) 241-9164

Southwest Regional Office
Masonry Office Building
2nd Floor
707 Race Street

Cincinnati, OH 45202
(513) 852-3344

South-Northeast Regional Office
302 Peoples Federal
  Building
39 East Market Street
Akron, OH 44308
(216) 253-3167

OKLAHOMA

Human Rights Commission, Room 480
2101 North Lincoln Boulevard
Oklahoma City, OK 73105
(405) 521-2360

OREGON

Bureau of Labor and Industries
Civil Rights Division,
State Office Building
1400 SouthWest Fifth Avenue
Portland, OR 97201
(503) 229-5900 or (800) 452-7813

Oregon Branch Offices, Bureau of Labor and Industries

165 East 7th Street
Room 220
Eugene, OR 97401

3865 Wolverine Street, NE
Building E-1
Salem, OR 97310

700 East Main
Medford, OR 97504

PENNSYLVANIA

Human Relations Commission
101 South Second Street, Suite 300

Harrisburg, PA 17105-3145
(717) 787-4410

Pennsylvania Branch Offices, Human Relations Commission
State Office Building
11th Floor
300 Liberty Avenue
Pittsburgh, PA 15222

711 State Office Building
Broad & Spring Garden
Philadelphia, PA 19130
(215) 238-6940

3405 North 6th Street
Harrisburg, PA 17110
(717) 787-9780

PUERTO RICO

Department of Labor and Human
  Resources
Anti-Discrimination Unit
505 Munoz Rivera Avenue
Hato Rey, PR 00918
(809) 754-5353

RHODE ISLAND

Commission for Human Rights
10 Abbott Park Place
Providence, RI 02903
(401) 277-2661

SOUTH CAROLINA

Human Affairs Commission
2611 Forest Drive
Columbia, SC 29204
(803) 737-6570

SOUTH DAKOTA

Division on Human Rights
State Capitol Building
222 East Capitol, Suite 11

Pierre, SD 57501
(605) 773-3177

TENNESSEE

Human Development Commission
Capitol Boulevard Building, Suite 602
226 Capitol Boulevard
Nashville, TN 37219
(615) 741-2424

Tennessee Field Offices, Human Development Commission
170 North Main Street
Room 1113
Memphis, TN 38103

540 McCallie Avenue
6th Floor West, Room 605
Chattanooga, TN 37402

TEXAS

Commission on Human Rights
P.O. Box 13493
Capitol Station
Austin, TX 78711
(512) 475-1178

Austin Human Relations Commission
P.O. Box 1088
Austin, TX 78767

Corpus Christi Human Relations
  Commission
101 North Shoreline
Corpus Christi, TX 78408

Forth Worth Human Relations
  Commission
1000 Throckmorton Street
Forth Worth, TX 76102

UTAH

Industrial Commission
Anti-Discrimination Division
160 East 3rd Street South

Salt Lake City, UT 84151
(801) 530-6801

VERMONT

Attorney General of Vermont
Civil Rights Division, Pavilion Office
  Building
109 State Street
Montpelier, VT 05602
(802) 828-3171

VIRGINIA

Department of Labor and Industry
P.O. Box 12064
Richmond, VA 23241
(804) 786-2376

Alexandria Human Rights Office
405 Cameron Street
Alexandria, VA 22313

Fairfax County Human Rights
  Commission
Circle Towers Office Building
Suite 206
9401 Lee Highway
Fairfax, VA 22030

VIRGIN ISLANDS

Department of Labor
P.O. Box 3159 53A, 54A & B
Kronprindfens Code
Charlotte Amalie
St. Thomas, VI 00801
(809) 776-3700

WASHINGTON

Washington State Human Rights
  Commission
402 Evergreen Plaza Building
711 South Capitol Way
Mail Stop FJ-41

Olympia, WA 98504
(206) 753-6770

Washington Branch Offices, State Human Rights Commission

Columbia Building
1516 2nd Avenue
Suite 400
Seattle, WA 98101
(206) 464-6500

West 905 Riverside Avenue
Suite 416
Spokane, WA 99201
(509) 456-4473

32 North 3rd Street,
Suite 441
Yakima, WA 98901
(509) 545-2379

WEST VIRGINIA

Human Rights Commission
1036 Quarrier Street
215 Professional Building
Charleston, WV 25301
(304) 348-2616

WISCONSIN

Department of Industry, Labor, and
  Human Relations
Equal Rights Division
201 East Washington Avenue
Madison, WI 53702
(608) 266-6860

Wisconsin Branch Offices, Department of Industry, Labor, and Human Relations, Equal Rights Division

819 North 6th Street
Room 25

Milwaukee, WI 53203
(414) 224-4384

424 South Monroe Street
Green Bay, WI 54301
(414) 497-4170

718 West Clairemont Avenue
Eau Claire, WI 54701
(715) 836-5135

1328 Schofield Avenue
Schofield, WI 54476
(715) 359-0471

WYOMING

Fair Employment Commission
Hathaway Building
Cheyenne, WY 82002
(307) 777-7261

135 North Ash Street
Room 180
Casper, WY 82601
(307) 234-8650

Commission of Labor & Statistics
Herschler Building
Cheyenne, WY, 82002

U.S. EQUAL EMPLOYMENT OPPORTUNITY COMMISSION

The Equal Employment Opportunity Commission (EEOC) aims to eliminate discrimination in the workplace. To achieve this purpose, the commission investigates cases of alleged discrimination, including cases of sexual harassment; helps victims prosecute cases; and offers educational programs for employers and community organizations. The EEOC publishes a packet of information about sexual harassment.

1801 L Street, NW
Washington, DC 20507
(202) 663-4900

(800) USA-EEOC
(800) 872-3362 (Spanish also)

Equal Employment Opportunity
   Commission
Administrative Offices
2401 E Street, NW
Washington, DC 20507
(202) 634-6922 or (800) USA-EEOC

EEOC DISTRICT, AREA, AND LOCAL OFFICES

Following is an alphabetical directory of EEOC's "full-service" district offices, and the area and local offices serving those districts.

Albuquerque Area Office
(Phoenix District)
Western Bank Building, Suite 1105
505 Marquette, NW
Albuquerque, NM 87101
(505) 766-2061

Atlanta District Office
Citizens Trust Building, Suite 1100
75 Piedmont Avenue, NE
Atlanta, GA 30335
(404) 331-6091

Baltimore District Office
109 Market Place, Suite 4000
Baltimore, MD 21202
(301) 962-3932

Birmingham District Office
212 Eight Avenue North, Suite 824
Birmingham, AL 35203
(205) 254-0082

Boston Area Office
(New York District)
JFK Building, Room 409-B
Boston, MA 02203
(617) 223-4535

Buffalo Local Office
(New York District)
Guaranty Building,

28 Church Street
Buffalo, NY 14202
(716) 846-4441

Charlotte District Office
5500 Central Avenue
Charlotte, NC 28212
(704) 567-7100

Chicago District Office
Federal Building, Room 930-A
536 South Clark Street
Chicago, IL 60605
(312) 353-2713

Cincinnati Area Office
(Cleveland District)
Federal Building, Room 7015
550 Main Street
Cincinnati, OH 45202
(513) 684-2851

Cleveland District Office
1375 Euclid Avenue, Room 600
Cleveland, OH 44115
(216) 522-7425

Dallas District Office
8303 Embrock Drive
Dallas, TX 75247
(214) 767-7015

Dayton Area Office
(Cleveland District)
Federal Building, Room 60
200 West 2nd Street
Dayton, OH 45402
(513) 225-2753

Denver District Office
1845 Sherman Street, 2nd Floor
Denver, CO 80203
(303) 837-2771

Detroit District Office
Patrick V. MacNamara Federal
   Building, Room 1540
477 Michigan Avenue

Detroit, MI 48226
(313) 226-7636

El Paso Local Office (Dallas District)
First National Building, Suite 1112
109 North Oregon Street
El Paso, TX 79901
(915) 541-7596

Fresno Area Office
(San Francisco District)
1313 P Street, Suite 103
Fresno, CA 93721
(209) 487-5793

Greensboro Local Office
(Charlotte District)
324 West Market Street, Room B-27
Post Office Box 3363
Greensboro, NC 27402
(910) 333-5174

Greenville Local Office
(Atlanta District)
Century Plaza, Suite 109-B
211 Century Drive
Greenville, SC 29607
(803) 233-1791

Houston District Office
405 Main Street, Sixth Floor
Houston, TX 77002
(713) 226-2601

Indianapolis District Office
Federal Building, U.S. Courthouse
46 East Ohio Street, Room 456
Indianapolis, IN 46204
(317) 269-7212

Jackson Area Office
(Birmingham District)
McCoy Federal Office Building
100 West Capitol Street, Suite 721
Jackson, MS 39269
(601) 965-4537

Kansas City Area Office
(St. Louis District)
911 Walnut, 10th Floor

Kansas City, MO 94106
(816) 374-5773

Little Rock Area Office
(New Orleans District)
Savers Building, Suite 621
320 West Capitol Avenue
Little Rock, AR 72201
(501) 378-5060

Los Angeles District Office
3660 Wilshire Boulevard, 5th Floor
Los Angeles, CA 90010
(213) 251-7278

Louisville Area Office
(Memphis District)
601 West Broadway, Room 104
Louisville, KY 40202
(502) 582-6082

Memphis District Office
1407 Union Avenue, Suite 502
Memphis, TN 38104
(902) 521-2617

Miami District Office, Metro Mall
1 Northeast First Street, 6th Floor
Miami, FL 33132
(305) 536-4491

Milwaukee District Office
310 West Wisconsin Avenue,
Suite 800
Milwaukee, WI 53203
(414) 291-1111

Minneapolis Local Office
(Milwaukee District)
110 South Fourth Street, Room 178
Minneapolis, MN 55401
(612) 349-3495

Nashville Area Office
(Memphis District)
Parkway Towers, Suite 1100
Nashville, TN 37219
(615) 251-5820

Newark Area Office
(New York District)

60 Park Place, Room 301
Newark, NJ 07102
(201) 645-6383

New Orleans District Office
F. Edward Herbert Federal Building
600 South Maestri Place, Room 528
New Orleans, LA 70130
(504) 589-2329

New York District Office
90 Church Street, Room 1505
New York, NY 10007
(212) 264-7161

Norfolk Area Office
(Baltimore District)
Federal Building, Room 412
200 Granby Mall
Norfolk, VA 23510
(804) 441-3470

Oakland Local Office
(San Francisco District)
Wells Fargo Bank Building
1333 Broadway, Room 430
Oakland, CA 94612
(415) 273-7588

Oklahoma Area Office
(Dallas District)
Alfred P. Marrah Federal Building
200 NW Fifth Street, Room 703
Oklahoma City, OK 73102
(405) 231-4911

Philadelphia District Office
127 North 4th Street, Suite 300
Philadelphia, PA 19106
(215) 597-7784

Phoenix District Office
135 North Second Avenue,
Fifth Floor
Phoenix, AZ 85003
(602) 261-3882

Pittsburgh Area Office
(Philadelphia District)
Federal Building, Room 2038A

1000 Liberty Avenue
 Pittsburgh, PA 15222
(412) 644-3444

Raleigh Area Office
(Charlotte District)
178 West Hargett Street, Suite 500
Raleigh, NC 27601
(919) 856-4064

Richmond Area Office
(Baltimore District)
400 North 8th Street, Room 6206
Richmond, VA 23240
(804) 771-2692

San Antonio Area Office
(Houston District)
727 East Durango, Suite 601-B
San Antonio, TX 78206
(512) 229-6051 San Diego Local Office
(Los Angeles District)
San Diego Federal Building
880 Front Street
San Diego, CA 92188
(619) 293-6288

San Francisco District Office
10 United Nations Plaza,
Fourth Floor

San Francisco, CA 94102
(415) 556-0260

San Jose Local Office
(San Francisco District)
U.S. Courthouse and Federal
  Building
280 South First District, Room 4150
San Jose, CA 95113
(408) 291-7352

Seattle District Office
Arcade Plaza Building
1321 Second Avenue, 7th Floor
Seattle, WA 98101
(206) 442-0968

St. Louis District Office
625 North Euclid Street
St. Louis, MO 63108
(314) 425-6585

Tampa Area Office (Miami District)
700 Twiggs Street, Room 302
Tampa, FL 33602
(813) 228-2310

Washington Area Office
(Baltimore District)
1717 H Street, NW, Suite 400
Washington, DC 20006
(202) 653-6197

APPENDICES

APPENDIX A

TITLE VII OF THE 1964 CIVIL RIGHTS ACT

DISCRIMINATION BECAUSE OF RACE, COLOR, RELIGION, SEX, OR NATIONAL ORIGIN

Sec. 703 [42 U.S.C. § 2000e-2]. (a) It shall be an unlawful employment practice for an employer —

(1) to fail or refuse to hire or to discharge any individual, or otherwise, to discriminate against any individual with respect to his compensation, terms, conditions, or privileges of employment, because of such individual's race, color, religion, sex, or national origin; or

(2) to limit, segregate, or classify his employees or applicants for employment in any way which would deprive or tend to deprive any individual of employment opportunities or otherwise adversely affect his status as an employee, because of such individual's race, color, religion, sex, or national origin.

(b) It shall be an unlawful employment practice for an employment agency to fail or refuse to refer for employment, or otherwise to discriminate against, any individual because of his race, color, religion, sex or national origin, or to classify or refer for employment any individual on the basis of his race, color, religion, sex, or national origin.

APPENDIX B

EEOC GUIDELINES ON SEXUAL HARASSMENT, FROM THE 1990 GUIDELINES ON DISCRIMINATION BECAUSE OF SEX

§ 1604.11 SEXUAL HARASSMENT.

(a) Harassment on the basis of sex is a violation of Sec. 703 of Title VII.[1] Unwelcome sexual advances, requests for sexual favors, and other verbal or physical conduct of a sexual nature constitute sexual harassment when (1) submission to such conduct is made either explicitly or implicitly a term or condition of an individual's employment, (2) submission to or rejection of such conduct by an individual is used as the basis for employment decisions affecting such individual, or (3) such conduct has the purpose or effect of unreasonably interfering with an individual's work performance or creating an intimidating, hostile, or offensive working environment.

(b) In determining whether alleged conduct constitutes sexual harassment, the Commission will look at the record as a whole and at the totality of the circumstances, such as the nature of the sexual advances and the context in which the alleged incidents occurred. The determination of the legality of a particular action will be made from the facts, on a case by case basis.

(c) Applying general Rule VII principles, an employer, employment agency, joint apprenticeship committee or labor organization (hereinafter collectively referred to as "employer") is responsible for its acts and those of its agents and supervisory employees with respect to sexual harassment regardless of whether the specific acts complained of were authorized or even forbidden by the employer and regardless of whether the employer knew or should have known of their occurrence. The Commission will examine the circumstances of the particular employment relationship and the job functions performed by the individual in determining whether an individual acts in either a supervisory or agency capacity.

---

[1]The principles involved here continue to apply to race, color, religion or national origin.

(d) With respect to conduct between fellow employees, an employer is responsible for acts of sexual harassment in the workplace where the employer (or its agents or supervisory employees) knows or should have known of the conduct, unless it can show that it took immediate corrective action.

(e) An employer may also be responsible for the acts of nonemployees, with respect to sexual harassment of employees in the workplace, where the employer (or its agents or supervisory employees) knows or should have known of the conduct and fails to take immediate and appropriate corrective action. In reviewing these cases the Commission will consider the extent of the employer's control and any other legal responsibility which the employer may have with respect to the conduct of such non-employees.

(f) Prevention is the best tool for the elimination of sexual harassment. An employer should take all steps necessary to prevent sexual harassment from occurring, such as affirmatively raising the subject, expressing strong disapproval, developing appropriate sanctions, informing employees of their right to raise and how to raise the issue of harassment under Title VII, and developing methods to sensitize all concerned.

(g) Other related practices: Where employment opportunities or benefits are granted because of an individual's submission to the employer's sexual advances or requests for sexual favors, the employer may be held liable for unlawful sex discrimination against other persons who were qualified for but denied that employment opportunity or benefit.

APPENDIX C

TITLE IX OF THE 1972 EDUCATION AMENDMENTS

§ 1681. SEX

(a) No person in the United States shall, on the basis of sex, be excluded from participation in, be denied the benefits of, or be subjected to discrimination under any education program or activity receiving Federal financial assistance, except that:

(1) in regard to admissions to educational institutions, this section shall apply only to institutions of vocational education, professional education, and graduate higher education, and to public institutions or undergraduate higher education;

(2) in regard to admissions to educational institutions, this section shall not apply (A) for one year from June 23, 1972, nor for six years after June 23, 1972, in the case of an educational institution which has begun the process of changing from being an institution which admits only students of one sex to being an institution which admits students of both sexes, but only if it is carrying out a plan for such a change which is approved by the Secretary of Education or (B) for seven years from the date an educational institution begins the process of changing from being an institution which admits only students of only one sex to being an institution which admits students of both sexes, but only if it is carrying out a plan for such a change which is approved by the Secretary of Education, whichever is the later;

(3) this section shall not apply to an educational institution which is controlled by a religious organization if the application of this subsection would not be consistent with the religious tenets of such organization;

(4) this section shall not apply to an educational institution whose primary purpose is the training of individuals for the military services of the United States, or the merchant marine;

(5) in regard to admissions this section shall not apply to any public institution of undergraduate higher education which is an institution that traditionally and continually from its establishment has had a policy of admitting only students on one sex.

APPENDIX D

---

42 U.S.C. § 1983

42 U.S.C. § 1983. Civil Action for Deprivation of Rights.

Every person who, under color of any statute, ordinance, regulation, custom, or usage, of any State or Territory or the District of Columbia, subjects, or causes to be subjected, any citizen of the United States or other persons within the jurisdiction thereof to the deprivation of any rights, privileges or immunities secured by the Constitution and laws, shall be liable to the person injured in an action of law, suit in equity, or other proper proceedings for redress. For purposes of this section, any Act of Congress applicable exclusively to the District of Columbia shall be considered to be a statute of the District of Columbia.

APPENDIX E

18 U.S.C. § 241 AND 242

18 U.S.C. § 241. Conspiracy Against Rights.

If two or more persons conspire to injure, oppress, threaten, or intimidate any inhabitant of any State, Territory, or District in the free exercise or enjoyment of any right or privilege secured to him by the Constitution or laws of the United States, or because of his having so exercised the same; or

If two or more persons go in disguise on the highway, or on the premises of another, with intent to prevent or hinder his free exercise or enjoyment of any right or privilege so secured —

They shall be fined no more than $10,000 or imprisoned not more then ten years, or both; and if death results, they shall be subject to imprisonment for any term of years or for life.

18 U.S.C. § 242. Deprivation of Rights Under Color of Law.

Whoever, under color of any law, statute, ordinance, regulation, or custom, willfully subjects any inhabitant of any State, Territory, or District to the deprivation of any rights, privileges, or immunities secured or protected by the Constitution or laws of the United States, or to different punishments, pains, or penalties, on account of such inhabitant being an alien, or by reason of his color, or race, than are prescribed for the punishment of citizens, shall be fined not more than $1,000 or imprisoned not more than one year, or both; and if bodily injury results shall be fined under this title or imprisoned not more than ten years, or both; and if death results shall be subject to imprisonment for any term of years or for life.

APPENDIX F

U.S. SUPREME COURT RULING: FRANKLIN V. GWINNETT COUNTY PUBLIC SCHOOLS

Christine FRANKLIN, Petitioner,
v.
GWINNETT COUNTY PUBLIC SCHOOLS
and William Prescott.
No. 90-918.

Argued Dec. 11, 1991.
Decided Feb. 26, 1992.

WHITE, J., delivered the opinion of the Court, in which BLACKMUN, STEVENS, O'CONNOR, KENNEDY, and SOUTER, JJ., joined. SCALIA, J., filed an opinion concurring in the judgment, in which REHNQUIST, C.J., and THOMAS, J., joined.

Joel I. Klein, Washington, D.C., for petitioner.

Albert M. Pearson, III, Athens, Ga., for respondents.

Stephen L. Nightingale, Washington, D.C., for respondents as amicus curiae.

Justice WHITE delivered the opinion of the Court.

This case presents the question whether the implied right of action under Title IX of the Education Amendments of 1972, 20 U.S.C. §§ 1681–1688 (Title IX), [FN1] which this Court recognized in Cannon v. University of Chicago, 441 U.S. 677, 99 S.Ct. 1946, 60 L.Ed.2d 560 (1979), supports a claim for monetary damages.

> *FN1. This statute provides in pertinent part that "No person in the United States shall, on the basis of sex, be excluded from participation in, be denied the benefits of, or be subjected to discrimination under any education program or activity receiving Federal financial assistance." 20 U.S.C. § 1681(a).*

I

Petitioner Christine Franklin was a student at North Gwinnett High School in Gwinnett County, Georgia, between September 1985 and August 1989. Respondent Gwinnett County School District operates the high school and receives federal funds. According to the complaint filed on December 29, 1988 in the United States District Court for the Northern District of Georgia, Franklin was subjected to continual sexual harassment beginning in the autumn of her tenth grade year (1986) from Andrew Hill, a sports coach and teacher employed by the district. Among other allegations, Franklin avers that Hill engaged her in sexually-oriented conversations in which he asked about her sexual experiences with her boyfriend and whether she would consider having sexual intercourse with an older man, Complaint ¶ 10; First Amended Complaint, Exh. A, p. 3; [FN2] that Hill forcibly kissed her on the mouth in the school parking lot, Complaint ¶ 17; that he telephoned her at her home and asked if she would meet him socially, Complaint, ¶ 21; First Amended Complaint, Exh. A, pp. 4–5; and that, on three occasions in her junior year, Hill interrupted a class, requested that the teacher excuse Franklin, and took her to a private office where he subjected her to coercive intercourse. Complaint ¶¶ 25, 27, 32. The complaint further alleges that though they became aware of and investigated Hill's sexual harassment of Franklin and other female students, teachers and administrators took no action to halt it and discouraged Franklin from pressing charges against Hill. Complaint ¶¶ 23, 24, 35. On April 14, 1988, Hill resigned on the condition that all matters pending against him be dropped. Complaint ¶¶ 36, 37. The school thereupon closed its investigation. Complaint ¶ 37.

FN2. This exhibit is the report of the United States Department of Education's Office of Civil Rights based on that office's investigation of this case. Franklin incorporated this exhibit into her amended complaint.

In this action, [FN3] the District Court dismissed the complaint on the ground that Title IX does not authorize an award of damages. The Court of Appeals affirmed. Franklin v. Gwinnett Cty. Public Schools, 911 F.2d 617 (CA11 1990). The court noted that analysis of Title IX and Title VI of the Civil Rights Act of 1964, 42 U.S.C. § 2000d et seq. (Title VI), has developed along similar lines. Citing as binding precedent Drayden v. Needville Independent School Dist., 642 F.2d 129 (CA5 1981), a decision rendered prior to the division of the Fifth Circuit, the court concluded that Title VI did not support a claim for monetary damages. The court then analyzed this Court's decision in Guardians Assn. v. Civil Service Comm'n of New York City 463 U.S. 582, 103 S.Ct. 3221, 77 L.Ed.2d 866 (1983), to determine whether it implicitly overruled Drayden. The court stated that the absence of a majority opinion left unresolved the question whether a court could award such relief upon a showing of intentional discrimination. As a second basis for its holding that monetary damages were unavailable, the court reasoned that Title IX was enacted under Congress' Spending Clause powers and that "[u]nder such statutes, relief may frequently be limited to that which is equitable in nature, with the recipient of federal funds thus retaining the option of terminating such receipt in order to rid itself of an injunction." Franklin, 911 F.2d, at 621. [FN4] The court closed by observing it would "proceed with extreme care" to afford compensatory relief absent express provision by Congress or clear direction from this Court. Id., at 622. Accordingly, it held that an action for monetary damages could not be sustained for an alleged intentional violation of Title IX, and affirmed the District Court's ruling to that effect. Ibid. [FN5]

FN3. Prior to bringing this lawsuit, Franklin filed a complaint with the Office of Civil Rights of the United States Department of Education (OCR) in August 1988. After investigating these charges for several months, OCR concluded that the school district had violated Franklin's rights by subjecting her to physical and verbal sexual harassment and by interfering with her right to complain about conduct proscribed by Title IX. OCR determined, however, that because of the resignations of Hill and respondent William Prescott and the implementation of a school grievance procedure, the district had come into compliance with Title IX. It then terminated its investigation. First Amended Complaint, Exh. A, pp. 7–9.

FN4. The court also rejected an argument by Franklin that the terms of outright prohibition of Title VII, 42 U.S.C. §§ 2000e to 2000e-17, apply by analogy to Title IX's antidiscrimination provision, and that the remedies available under the two statutes should also be the same. Franklin, 911 F.2d, at 622. Because Franklin does not pursue this contention here, we need not address whether it has merit.
FN5. Judge Johnson concurred specially, writing that the result was controlled by Drayden v. Needville Independent School Dist., 642 F.2d 129 (CA5 1981), and that there was no need to address whether Titles VI and IX are grounded solely in the Spending Clause and whether Title VII analysis should apply to an action under Titles VI or IX. See Franklin, supra, at 622–623 (Johnson, J., concurring specially).

Because this opinion conflicts with a decision of the Court of Appeals for the Third Circuit, see Pfeiffer v. Marion Center Area School Dist., 917 F.2d 779, 787–789 (1990), we granted certiorari, 501 U.S.———, 111 S.Ct. 2795, 115 L.Ed.2d 969 (1991). We reverse.

II

[1][2] In Cannon v. University or Chicago, 441 U.S. 677, 99 S.Ct. 1946, 60 L.Ed.2d 560 (1979), the Court held that Title IX is enforceable through an implied right of action. We have no occasion here to reconsider that decision. Rather, in this case we must decide what remedies are available in a suit brought pursuant to this implied right. As we have often stated the question of what remedies are available under a statute that provides a private right of action is "analytically distinct" from the issue of whether such a right exists in the first place. Davis v. Passman, 442 U.S. 228, 239, 99 S.Ct. 2264, 2274, 60 L.Ed.2d 846 (1979). Thus, although we examine the text and history

Appendices

of a statute to determine whether Congress intended to create a right of action, Touche Ross & Co. v. Redington, 442 U.S. 560, 575–576, 99 S.Ct. 2479, 2489, 61 L.Ed.2d 82 (1979), we presume the availability of all appropriate remedies unless Congress has expressly indicated otherwise. Davis, supra, 442 U.S., at 246–47, 99 S.Ct., at 2277–2278. This principle has deep roots in our jurisprudence.

A

[3] "[W]here legal rights have been invaded, and a federal statute provides for a general right to sue for such invasion, federal courts may use any available remedy to make good the wrong done." Bell v. Hood, 327 U.S. 678, 684, 66 S.Ct. 773, 777, 90 L.Ed. 939 (1946). The Court explained this longstanding rule as jurisdictional, and upheld the exercise of the federal court's power to award appropriate relief so long as a cause of action existed under the Constitution or laws of the United States. Ibid.

The Bell Court's reliance on this rule was hardly revolutionary. From the earliest years of the Republic, the Court has recognized the power of the judiciary to award appropriate remedies to redress injuries actionable in federal court, although it did not always distinguish clearly between a right to bring suit and a remedy available under such a right. In Marbury v. Madison, 5 U.S. (1 Cranch) 137, 163, 2 L.Ed. 60 (1803), for example, Chief Justice Marshall observed that our government "has been emphatically termed a government of laws, and not of men. It will certainly cease to deserve this high appellation, if the laws furnish no remedy for the violation of a vested legal right." This principle originated in the English common law, and Blackstone described "it is a general and indisputable rule, that where there is a legal right, there is also a legal remedy, by suit or action at law, whenever that right is invaded." 3 W. Blackstone, Commentaries 23 (1783). See also Ashby v. White, 1 Salk. 19, 21, 87 Eng.Rep. 808, 816 (Q.B1702) ("If a statute gives a right, the common law will give a remedy to maintain that right . . .").

In Kendall v. United States, 37 U.S. (12 Pet.) 524, 9 L.Ed. 1181 (1838), the Court applied these principles to an act of Congress that accorded a right of action in mail carriers to sue for adjustment and settlement of certain claims for extra services but which did not specify the precise remedy available to the carriers. After surveying possible remedies, which included an action against the postmaster general for monetary damages, the Court held that the carriers were entitled to a writ of mandamus compelling payment under the terms of the statute. "It cannot be denied but that congress had the power to command that act to be done," the Court stated; "and the power to enforce the performance of the act must rest somewhere, or it will present a case which has often been said to involve a monstrous absurdity in a well organized government, that there should be no remedy, although a clear and undeniable right should be shown to exist. And if the remedy cannot be applied by the circuit court of this district, it exists nowhere." Id., at 624. Dooley v. United States, 182 U.S. 222, 229, 21 S.Ct. 762, 764, 45 L.Ed. 1074 (1901), also restated "the principle that a liability created by statute without a remedy may be enforced by a common-law action."

The Court relied upon this traditional presumption again after passage of the Federal Safety Appliance Act of 1893, ch. 196, 27 Stat. 531. In Texas & Pacific R. Co. v. Rigsby, 241 U.S. 33, 36 S.Ct. 482, 60 L.Ed. 874 (1916), the Court first had to determine whether the act supported an implied right of action. After answering that question in the affirmative, the Court then upheld a claim for monetary damages: "A disregard of the command of the statute is a wrongful act, and where it results in damage to one of the class for whose especial benefit the statute was enacted, the right to recover the damages from the party in default is implied, according to a doctrine of the common law. . . ." Id., at 39, 36 S.Ct., at 484. The foundation upon which the Bell v. Hood Court articulated this traditional presumption, therefore, was well settled. See also Texas & New Orleans R. Co. v. Railway & Steamship Clerks, 281 U.S. 548, 569, 50 S.Ct. 427, 433, 74 L.Ed. 1034 (1930).

B

Respondents and the United states as amicus curiae, however, maintain that whatever the traditional presumption may have been when the Court decided Bell v. Hood, it has disappeared in succeeding decades. We do not agree. In J.I. Case Co. Borak, 377 U.S. 426, 84 S.Ct. 1555, 12 L.Ed.2d 423 (1964), the Court adhered to the general rule that all appropriate relief is available in an action brought to vindicate a federal right when Congress has given no indication of its purpose with respect to remedies. Relying on Bell v. Hood, the Borak Court specifically rejected an argument that a court's remedial power to redress violations or the Securities Exchange Act of 1934 was limited to a declaratory judgment. 377 U.S., at 433–434, 84 S.Ct., at 1560. The Court concluded that the federal courts "have the power to grant all necessary remedial relief" for violation of the Act. Id., at 435, 84 S.Ct., at 1561. As Justice Clark's opinion for the Court observed, this holding closely followed the reasoning of a similar case brought under the Securities Act of 1933, in which the Court had stated:

"'The power to enforce implies the power to make effective the right to recovery afforded by the Act. And the power to make the right of recovery effective implies the power to utilize any of the procedures or actions normally available to the litigant according to the exigencies of the particular case.'" Id., at 433–434, 84 S.Ct. at 1560 (quoting

Appendices

Deckert v. Independence Shares Corp., 311 U.S. 282, 288, 61 S.Ct. 229, 233, 85 L.Ed. 189 (1940)).

That a statute does not authorize the remedy at issue "in so many words is no more significant than the fact that it does not in terms authorize execution to issue on a judgment." Id., at 288, 61 S.Ct., at 233. Subsequent cases have been true to this position. See, e.g., Sullivan v. Little Hunting Park, Inc., 396 U.S. 299, 239, 90 S.Ct. 400, 405, 24 L.Ed.2d 386 (1969), stating that the "existence of a statutory right implies the existence of all necessary and appropriate remedies"; Carey v. Piphus, 435 U.S. 247, 255, 98 S.Ct. 1042, 1048, 55 L.Ed.2d 252 (1978), upholding damages remedy under 42 U.S.C. § 1983 even though the enacting Congress had not specifically provided such relief.

The United States contends that the traditional presumption in favor of all appropriate relief was abandoned by the Court in Davis v. Passman, 442 U.S. 288, 99 S.Ct. 2264, 60 L.Ed.2d 846 (1979), and that the Bell v. Hood rule was limited to actions claiming constitutional violations. The United States quotes language in Davis to the effect that "the question of who may enforce a statutory right is fundamentally different from the question of who may enforce a right that is protected by the Constitution." Davis, 442 U.S., at 241, 99 S.Ct., at 2275. The Government's position, however, mirrors the very misunderstanding over the difference between a cause of action and the relief afforded under it that sparked the confusion we attempted to clarify in Davis. Whether Congress may limit the class of persons who have a right of action under Title IX is irrelevant to the issue in this lawsuit. To reiterate, "the question whether a litigant has a 'cause of action' is analytically distinct and prior to the question of what relief, if any, a litigant may be entitled to receive." Id., at 239, 99 S.Ct., at 2274. Davis, therefore, did nothing to interrupt the long line of cases in which the Court has held that if a right of action exists to enforce a federal right and Congress is silent on the question of remedies, a federal court may order any appropriate relief. See id., 247, n. 26, 99 S.Ct., at 2278, n. 26 (contrasting Brown v. General Services Administration, 425 U.S. 820, 96 S.Ct. 1961, 48 L.Ed.2d 402 (1976)). [FN6]

FN6. Cases cited by respondents and the United States since Davis are inapposite, either because they involved holdings that plaintiffs had no right of action, see, e.g., Virginia Bankshares, Inc. v. Sandberg, 501 U.S.———, 111 S.Ct. 2749, 115 L.Ed.2d 929 (1991); Karahalios v. National Federation of Fed. Employees, Local 1263, 489 U.S. 527, 109 S.Ct. 1282, 103 L.Ed.2d 539 (1989); Thompson v. Thompson, 484 U.S. 174, 108 S.Ct. 513, 98 L.Ed.2d 512 (1988); Texas Industries, Inc. v. Radcliff Materials Inc., 451 U.S. 630, 101 S.Ct. 2061, 68, L.Ed.2d 500 (1981); California v. Sierra Club, 451 U.S. 287, 101 S.Ct. 1772, 68 L.Ed.2d 101 (1981); Northwest Airlines, Inc. v. Transport Workers, 451 U.S. 77, 101. S.Ct. 1571, 67 L.Ed.2d 750 (1981); Touche Ross & Co. v. Redington, 442 U.S. 560, 99 S.Ct. 2479, 61 L.Ed.2d 82 (1979); Securities

---

Investor Protection Corp. v. Barbour, 421 U.S. 412, 95 S.Ct. 1733, 44 L.Ed.2d 263 (1975); or because the Court rejected a claim for damages under a statute that expressly enumerated the remedies available to plaintiffs. Massachusetts Mut. Life Ins. Co. v. Russell, 473 U.S. 134, 105 S.Ct. 3085, 87 L.Ed.2d 96 (1985).

[4] Contrary to arguments by respondents and the United States that Guardians Assn. v. Civil Service Comm'n of New York City, 463 U.S. 582, 103 S.Ct. 3221, 77 L.Ed.2d 866 (1983), and Consolidated Rail Corp. v. Darrone, 465 U.S. 624, 104 S.Ct. 1248, 79 L.Ed.2d 568 (1984), eroded this traditional presumption, those cases in fact support it. Though the multiple opinions in Guardians suggest the difficulty of inferring the common ground among the Justices in that case, a clear majority expressed the view that damages were available under Title VI in an action seeking remedies for an intentional violation, and no Justice challenged the traditional presumption in favor of a federal court's power to award appropriate relief in a cognizable cause of action. See Guardians, 463 U.S., at 595, 103 S.Ct., at 3229 (WHITE, J., joined by REHNQUIST, J.); id., at 607–611, 103 S.Ct., at 3235–3237 (Powell, J., concurring in judgment, joined by Burger, C.J.); id., at 612, and n. 1, 103 S.Ct., at 3227, and n. 1 (O'CONNOR, J., concurring in judgment); id., at 624–628, 103 S.Ct., at 3244–3246 (Marshall, J., dissenting); id., at 636, 103 S.Ct., at 3250 (STEVENS, J.,dissenting, joined by Brennan and BLACK-MUN, JJ.). The correctness of this inference was made clear the following Term when the Court unanimously held that the 1978 amendment to § 504 of the Rehabilitation Act of 1973—which had expressly incorporated the "remedies, procedures, and rights set forth in title VI" (29 U.S.C. § 794a(a)(2))—authorizes an award of backpay. In Darrone, the Court observed that a majority in Guardians had "agreed that retroactive relief is available to private plaintiffs for all discrimination . . . that is actionable under Title VI." 465 U.S., at 630, n. 9, 104 S.Ct., at 1252 n. 9. The general rule, therefore is that absent clear direction to the contrary by Congress, the federal courts have the power to award any appropriate relief in a cognizable cause of action brought pursuant to a federal statute.

III

[5] We now address whether Congress intended to limit application of this general principle in the enforcement of Title IX. See Bush v. Lucas, 462 U.S. 367, 378, 103 S.Ct. 2404, 2411–2412, 76 L.Ed.2d 648 (1983); Wyandotte Transp. Co. v. United States, 389 U.S. 191, 200, 88 S.Ct. 379, 385, 19 L.Ed.2d 407 (1967). Because the cause of action was inferred by the Court in Cannon, the usual recourse to statutory text and legislative history in the period prior to that decision necessarily will not enlighten our analysis. Respondents and the United States fundamentally misunderstand the nature

Appendices

of the inquiry, therefore, by needlessly dedicating large portions of their briefs to discussions of how the text and legislative intent behind Title IX are "silent" on the issue of available remedies. Since the Court in Cannon concluded that this statute supported no express right of action, it is hardly surprising that Congress also said nothing about the applicable remedies for an implied right of action.

During the period prior to the decision in Cannon, the inquiry in any event is not "'basically a matter of statutory construction,'" as the United States asserts. Brief for United States as Amicus Curiae 8 (quoting Transamerica Mortgage Advisors, Inc. v. Lewis, 444 U.S. 11,15, 100 S.Ct. 242, 245, 62 L.Ed.2d 146 (1979)). Rather, in determining Congress's intent to limit application of the traditional presumption in favor of all appropriate relief, we evaluate the state of the law when the legislature passed Title IX. Cf. Merrill Lynch, Pierce, Fenner & Smith, Inc. v. Curran, 456 U.S. 353, 378, 102 S.Ct. 1825, 1839, 72 L.Ed.2d 182 (1982). In the years before and after Congress enacted this statute, the Court follow[ed] a common-law tradition [and] regarded the denial of a remedy as the exception rather than the rule." Id., at 375, 102 S.Ct., at 1837 (footnote omitted). As we outlined in Part II, this has been the prevailing presumption in our federal courts since at least the early nineteenth century. In Cannon, the majority upheld an implied right of action in part because in the decade immediately preceding enactment of Title IX in 1972, this Court had found implied rights of action in six cases. [FN7] In three of those cases, the Court had approved a damages remedy. See, e.g., J.I. Case Co., 377 U.S., at 433, 84 S.Ct., at 1560, Wyandotte Transp. Co., supra, 389 U.S., at 207, 88 S.Ct., at 389; Sullivan v. Little Hunting Park, Inc., 396 U.S. 229, 90 S.Ct. 400, 24 L.Ed.2d 386 (1969). Wholly apart from the wisdom of the Cannon holding, therefore, the same contextual approach used to justify an implied right of action more than amply demonstrates the lack of any legislative intent to abandon the traditional presumption in favor of all available remedies.

FN7. J.I. Case Co. v. Borak, 377 U.S. 426, 84 S.Ct. 1555, 12 L.Ed.2d 423 (1964); Wyandotte Transp. Co. v. United States, 389 U.S. 191, 88 S.Ct. 379, 19 L.Ed.2d 407 (1967); Jones v. Alfred H. Mayer Co., 392 U.S. 409, 88 S.Ct. 2186, 20 L.Ed.2d 1189 (1968); Allen v. State Bd. of Elections, 393 U.S. 544, 89 S.Ct. 817, 22 L.Ed.2d 1 (1969); Sullivan v. Little Hunting Park, Inc., 396 U.S. 229, 90 S.Ct. 400, 24 L.Ed.2d 386 (1969); and Superintendent of Ins. of New York v. Bankers Life & Casualty Co., 404 U.S. 6, 92 S.Ct. 165, 30 L.Ed.2d 128 (1971).

In the years after the announcement of Cannon, on the other hand, a more traditional method of statutory analysis is possible, because Congress was legislating with full cognizance of that decision. Our reading of the two amendments to Title IX enacted after Cannon leads us to conclude that

Congress did not intend to limit the remedies available in a suit brought under Title IX. In the Civil Rights Remedies Equalization Amendment of 1986, 42 U.S.C. § 2000d-7, Congress abrogated the States' Eleventh Amendment immunity under Title IX, Title VI, § 504 of the Rehabilitation Act of 1973, and the Age Discrimination Act of 1975. This statute cannot be read except as a validation of Cannon's holding. A subsection of the 1986 law provides that in a suit against a State, "remedies (including remedies both at law and in equity) are available for such a violation to the same extent as such remedies are available for such a violation in the suit against any public or private entity other than a State." 42 U.S.C. § 2000d-7(a)(2). While it is true that this savings clause says nothing about the nature of those other available remedies, cf. Milwaukee v. Illinois, 451 U.S. 304, 329, n. 22, 101 S.Ct. 1784, 1798–1799 n. 22, 68 L.Ed.2d 114 (1981), absent any contrary indication in the text or history of the statute, we presume Congress enacted this statute with the prevailing traditional rule in mind.

In addition to the Civil Rights Remedies Equalization Amendment of 1986, Congress also enacted the Civil Rights Restoration Act of 1987, Pub.L. 100-259, 102 Stat. 28 (1988). Without in any way altering the existing rights of action and the corresponding remedies permissible under Title IX, Title VI, § 504 of the Rehabilitation Act, and the Age Discrimination Act, Congress broadened the coverage of these antidiscrimination provisions in this legislation. In seeking to correct what it considered to be an unacceptable decision on our part in Grove City College v. Bell, 465 U.S. 555, 104 S.Ct. 1211, 79 L.Ed.2d 516 (1984), Congress made no effort to restrict the right of action recognized in Cannon and ratified in the 1986 Act or to alter the traditional presumption in favor of any appropriate relief for violation of a federal right. We cannot say, therefore, that Congress has limited the remedies available to a complainant in a suit brought under Title IX.

IV

Respondents and the United States nevertheless suggest three reasons why we should not apply the traditional presumption in favor of appropriate relief in this case.

A

[6] First, respondents argue that an award of damages violates separation of powers principles because it unduly expands the federal courts' power into a sphere properly reserved to the Executive and Legislative Branches. Brief for Respondents 22–25. In making this argument, respondents misconceive the difference between a cause of action and a remedy. Unlike the finding of a cause of action, which authorizes a court to hear a case or controversy, the

212

discretion to award appropriate relief involves no such increase in judicial power. See generally Note, Federal Jurisdiction in Suits for Damages Under Statutes Not Affording Such Remedy, 48 Colum.L.Rev. 1090, 1094–1095 (1948). Federal courts cannot reach out to award remedies when the Constitution or laws of the United States do not support a cause of action. Indeed, properly understood, respondents' position invites us to abdicate our historic judicial authority to award appropriate relief in cases brought in our court system. It is well to recall that such authority historically has been thought necessary to provide an important safeguard against abuses of legislative and executive power, see Kendall v. United States, 37 U.S. (12 Pet.) 524, 9 L.Ed. 1181 (1838), as well as to insure an independent judiciary. See generally Katz, The Jurisprudence of Remedies: Constitutional Legality and the Law of Torts in Bell v. Hood, 117 U.Pa.L.Rev. 1, 16–17 (1968). Moreover, selective abdication of the sort advocated here would harm separation of powers principles in another way, by giving judges the power to render inutile causes of action authorized by Congress through a decision that no remedy is available.

B

[7] Next, consistent with the Court of Appeals's reasoning, respondents and the United States contend that the normal presumption in favor of all appropriate remedies should not apply because Title IX was enacted pursuant to Congress's Spending Clause power. In Pennhurst State School and Hospital v. Halderman, 451 U.S. 1, 28–29, 101 S.Ct. 1531, 1545–1546, 67 L.Ed.2d 694 (1981), the Court observed that remedies were limited under such Spending Clause statutes when the alleged violation was unintentional. Respondents and the United States maintain that this presumption should apply equally to intentional violations. We disagree. The point of not permitting monetary damages for an unintentional violation is that the receiving entity of federal funds lacks notice that it will be liable for a monetary award. See id. at 17, 101 S.Ct., at 1540. This notice problem does not arise in a case such as this, in which intentional discrimination is alleged. Unquestionably, Title IX placed on the Gwinnett County Schools the duty not to discriminate on the basis of sex, and "when a supervisor sexually harasses a subordinate because of the subordinate's sex, that supervisor 'discriminate[s]' on the basis of sex." Meritor Savings Bank, FSB v. Vinson, 477 U.S. 57, 64, 106 S.Ct. 2399, 2404, 91 L.Ed.2d 49 (1986). We believe the same rule should apply when a teacher sexually harasses and abuses a student. Congress surely did not intend for federal monies to be expended to support the intentional actions it sought by statute to proscribe. Moreover, the notion that Spending Clause statutes do not authorize monetary awards for intentional violations is belied by our unanimous holding in Darrone. See 465 U.S., at 628, 104 S.Ct., at 1251. Respondents and the United

States characterize the backpay remedy in Darrone as equitable relief, but this description is irrelevant to their underlying objection: that application of the traditional rule in this case will require state entities to pay monetary awards out of their treasuries for intentional violations of federal statutes. [FN8]

> *FN8. Franklin argues that, in any event, Title IX should not be viewed solely as having been enacted under Congress' Spending Clause powers and that it also rests on powers derived from § 5 of the Fourteenth Amendment. See Brief for Petitioner 19, n. 10. Because we conclude that a money damages remedy is available under Title IX for an intentional violation irrespective of the constitutional source of Congress' power to enact the statute, we need not decide which power Congress utilized in enacting Title IX.*

C

[8][9] Finally, the United States asserts that the remedies permissible under Title IX should nevertheless be limited to backpay and prospective relief. In addition to diverging from our traditional approach to deciding what remedies are available for violation of a federal right, this position conflicts with sound logic. First, both remedies are equitable in nature, and it is axiomatic that a court should determine the adequacy of a remedy in law before resorting to equitable relief. Under the ordinary convention, the proper inquiry would be whether monetary damages provided an adequate remedy, and if not, whether equitable relief would be appropriate. Whitehead v. Shattuck, 138 U.S. 146, 150, 11 S.Ct. 276, 276, 34 L.Ed. 873 (1891). See generally C. McCormick, Law of Damages 1 (1935). Moreover, in this case the equitable remedies suggested by respondent and the Federal Government are clearly inadequate. Backpay does nothing for petitioner, because she was a student when the alleged discrimination occurred. Similarly, because Hill—the person she claims subjected her to sexual harassment—no longer teaches at the school and she herself no longer attends a school in the Gwinnett system, prospective relief accords her no remedy at all. The government's answer that administrative action helps other similarly-situated students in effect acknowledges that its approach would leave petitioner remediless.

V

In sum, we conclude that a damages remedy is available for an action brought to enforce Title IX. The judgment of the Court of Appeals, therefore, is reversed and the case is remanded for further proceedings consistent with this opinion.

So ordered.

Justice SCALIA, with whom THE CHIEF JUSTICE and Justice THOMAS join, concurring in the judgment.

Appendices

The substantive right at issue here is one that Congress did not expressly create, but that this Court found to be "implied." See Cannon v. University of Chicago, 441 U.S. 677, 99 S.Ct. 1946, 60 L.Ed.2d 560 (1979). Quite obviously, the search for what was Congress's remedial intent as to a right whose very existence Congress did not expressly acknowledge is unlikely to succeed, see ante, at 1035–1036; it is "hardly surprising," as the Court says, ibid., that the usual sources yield no explicit answer.

The court finds an implicit answer, however, in the legislators' presumptive awareness of our practice of using "any available remedy" to redress violations of legal rights. Bell v. Hood, 327 U.S. 678, 684, 66 S.Ct. 773, 777, 90 L.Ed. 939 (1946); see ante, at 1035–1036. This strikes me as question-begging. We can plausibly assume acquiescence in our Bell v. Hood presumption when the legislature say nothing about remedy in expressly creating a private right to action; perhaps even when it says nothing about remedy in creating a private right of action by clear textual implication; but not, I think, when it says nothing about remedy in a statute in which the courts divine a private right of action on the basis of "contextual" evidence such as that in Cannon, which charged Congress with knowledge of a court of appeals' creation of a cause of action under a similarly worded statute. See Cannon, supra, 441 U.S., at 696–698, 99 S.Ct., at 1957–58. Whatever one thinks of the validity of the last approach, it surely rests on attributed rather than actual congressional knowledge. It does not demonstrate an explicit legislative decision to create a cause or action, and so could not be expected to be accompanied by a legislative decision to alter the application of Bell v. Hood. Given the nature of Cannon and some of our earlier "implied right of action" cases, what the Court's analytical construct comes down to is this: Unless Congress expressly legislates a more limited remedial policy with respect to rights of action it does not know it is creating, it intends the full gamut of remedies to be applied.

In my view, when rights of action are judicially "implied," categorical limitations upon their remedial scope may be judicially implied as well. Cf. Cort v. Ash, 442 U.S. 66, 84–85, 95 S.Ct. 2080, 2091, 45 L.Ed.2d 26. Although we have abandoned the expansive rights-creating approach exemplified by Cannon, see Touche Ross & Co. v. Redington, 442 U.S. 560, 575–576, 99 S.Ct. 2479, 2489, 61 L.Ed.2d 82 (1979); Transamerica Mortgage Advisors, Inc. v. Lewis, 444 U.S. 11, 18, 23–24, 100 S.Ct. 242, 249, 62 L.Ed.2d 146 (1979)—and perhaps ought to abandon the notion of implied causes of action entirely, see Thompson v. Thompson, 484 U.S. 174, 191, 108 S.Ct. 513, 522, 98 L.Ed.2d 512 (1988) (SCALIA, J., concurring in judgment)— causes of action that came into existence under the ancien regime should be limited by the same logic that gave them birth. To require, with respect to a right that is not consciously and intentionally created, that any limitation of remedies must be express, is to provide, in effect, that the most questionable of private rights will also be the most expansively remediable. As the United States puts it, "[w]hatever the merits of 'implying' rights of action may be there is no justification for treating [congressional] silence as the equivalent of the broadest imaginable grant of remedial authority." Brief for United States as Amicus Curiae 12–13.

I nonetheless agree with the Court's disposition of this case. Because of legislation enacted subsequent to Cannon, it is too late in the day to address whether a judicially implied exclusion of damages under Title IX would be appropriate. The Civil Rights Remedies Equalization Amendment of 1986, 42 U.S.C. § 2000d-7(a)(2), must be read, in my view, not only "as a validation of Cannon's holding," ante, at 1036, but also as an implicit acknowledgement that damages are available. See 42 U.S.C. § 2000-7(a)(1) (withdrawing the States' Eleventh Amendment immunity); § 2000-7(a)(2) (providing that, in suits against States, "remedies (including remedies both at law and in equity) are available for [violations of Title IX] to the same extent as such remedies are available for such a violation in the suit against any public or private entity other than a State"). I therefore concur in the judgment.

APPENDIX G

U.S. SUPREME COURT RULING: HARRIS V. FORKLIFT SYSTEMS, INC.

Teresa HARRIS, Petitioner,
v.
FORKLIFT SYSTEMS, INC.
No. 92-1168.

Argued Oct. 13, 1993
Decided Nov. 9, 1993

O'CONNOR, J., delivered the opinion for a unanimous Court. SCALIA, J., and GINSBURG, J., filed concurring opinions.

Irwin Venick, Nashville, TN, for petitioner.

Jeffrey P. Minear, Washington, DC, for U.S. as amicus curiae, by special leave of the Court.

Stanley M. Chernau, Nashville, TN, for respondent.

Justice O'CONNOR delivered the opinion of the Court.

In this case we consider the definition of a discriminatorily "abusive work environment" (also known as a "hostile work environment") under Title VII of the Civil Rights Act of 1964, 78 Stat. 253, as amended, 42 U.S.C. § 2000e et seq. (1988 ed., Supp. III).

I

Teresa Harris worked as a manager at Forklift Systems, Inc., an equipment rental company, from April 1985 until October 1987. Charles Hardy was Forklift's president.

The Magistrate found that, throughout Harris' time at Forklift, Hardy often insulted her because of her gender and often made her the target of unwanted sexual innuendos. Hardy told Harris on several occasions, in the presence of other employees, "You're a woman, what do you know" and "We need a man as the rental manager"; at least once, he told her she was "a dumb ass woman." App. to Pet. for Cert. A-13. Again in front of others, he suggested that the two of them "go to the Holiday Inn to negotiate [Harris'] raise." Id., at A-14. Hardy occasion-

217

ally asked Harris and other female employees to get coins from his front pants pocket. Ibid. He threw objects on the ground in front of Harris and other women, and asked them to pick the objects up. Id., at A-14 to A-15. He made sexual innuendos about Harris' and other women's clothing. Id., at A-15.

In mid-August 1987, Harris complained to Hardy about his conduct. Hardy said he was surprised that Harris was offended, claimed he was only joking, and apologized. Id., at A-16. He also promised he would stop, and based on this assurance Harris stayed on the job. Ibid. But in early September, Hardy began anew: While Harris was arranging a deal with one of Forklift's customers, he asked her, again in front of other employees, "What did you do, promise the guy . . . some [sex] Saturday night?" Id., at A-17. On October 1, Harris collected her paycheck and quit.

Harris then sued Forklift, claiming that Hardy's conduct had created an abusive work environment for her because of her gender. The United States District Court for the Middle District of Tennessee, adopting the report and recommendation of the Magistrate, found this to be "a close case," id., at A-31, but held that Hardy's conduct did not create an abusive environment. The court found that some of Hardy's comments "offended [Harris], and would offend the reasonable woman," id., at A-33, but that they were not

> *"so severe as to be expected to seriously affect [Harris'] psychological well-being. A reasonable woman manager under like circumstances would have been offended by Hardy, but his conduct would not have risen to the level of interfering with that person's work performance.*
>
> *"Neither do I believe that [Harris] was subjectively so offended that she suffered injury. . . . Although Hardy may at times have genuinely offended [Harris], I do not believe that he created a working environment so poisoned as to be intimidating or abusive to [Harris]." Id., at A-34 to A-35.*

In focusing on the employee's psychological well-being, the District Court was following Circuit precedent. See Rabidue v. Osceola Refining Co., 805 F.2d 611, 620 (CA6 1986), cert. denied, 481 U.S. 1041, 107 S.Ct. 1983, 95 L.Ed.2d 823 (1987). The United States Court of Appeals for the Sixth Circuit affirmed in a brief unpublished decision, 976 F.2d 733. (CA6 1992)

We granted certiorari, 507 U.S. ——, 113 S.Ct. 1382, 122 L.Ed.2d 758 (1993), to resolve a conflict among the Circuits on whether conduct, to be actionable as "abusive work environment" harassment (no quid pro quo harassment issue is present here), must "seriously affect [an employee's] psychological well-being" or lead the plaintiff to "suffe[r] injury." Compare Rabidue (requiring serious effect on psychological well-being); Vance v. Southern Bell Telephone & Telegraph Co., 863 F.2d 1503, 1510 (CA11 1989) (same); and Downes v. FAA, 775 F.2d 288, 292 (CA Fed.1985) (same),

Appendices

with Ellison v. Brady, 924 F.2d 872, 877–878 (CA9 1991) (rejecting such a requirement).

II

[1][2] Title VII of the Civil Rights Act of 1964 makes it "an unlawful employment practice for an employer . . . to discriminate against any individual with respect to his compensation, terms, conditions, or privileges of employment, because of such individual's race, color, religion, sex, or national origin." 42 U.S.C. § 2000e-2(a)(1). As we made clear in Meritor Savings Bank v. Vinson, 477 U.S. 57, 106 S.Ct. 2399, 91 L.Ed.2d 49 (1986), this language "is not limited to 'economic' or 'tangible' discrimination. The phrase 'terms, conditions, or privileges of employment' evinces a congressional intent 'to strike at the entire spectrum of disparate treatment of men and women' in employment," which includes requiring people to work in a discriminatorily hostile or abusive environment. Id., at 64, 106 S.Ct., at 2404, quoting Los Angeles Dept. of Water and Power v. Manhart, 435 U.S. 702, 707, n. 13, 98 S.Ct. 1370, 1374, 55 L.Ed.2d 657 (1978) (some internal quotation marks omitted). When the workplace is permeated with "discriminatory intimidation, ridicule, and insult," 477 U.S., at 65, 106 S.Ct., at 2405, that is "sufficiently severe or pervasive to alter the conditions of the victim's employment and create an abusive working environment," id., at 67, 106 S.Ct., at 2405 (internal brackets and quotation marks omitted), Title VII is violated.

[3] This standard, which we affirm today, takes a middle path between making actionable any conduct that is merely offensive and requiring the conduct to cause a tangible psychological injury. As we pointed out in Meritor, "mere utterance of a . . . epithet which engenders offensive feelings in a employee," ibid. (internal quotation marks omitted) does not sufficiently affect the conditions of employment to implicate Title VII. Conduct that is not severe or pervasive enough to create an objectively hostile or abusive work environment—an environment that a reasonable person would find hostile or abusive—is beyond Title VII's purview. Likewise, if the victim does not subjectively perceive the environment to be abusive, the conduct has not actually altered the conditions of the victim's employment, and there is no Title VII violation.

[4][5] But Title VII comes into play before the harassing conduct leads to a nervous breakdown. A discriminatorily abusive work environment, even one that does not seriously affect employees' psychological well-being, can and often will detract from employees' job performance, discourage employees from remaining on the job, or keep them from advancing in their careers. Moreover, even without regard to these tangible effects, the very fact that the discriminatory conduct was so severe or pervasive that it created a work

environment abusive to employees because of their race, gender, religion, or national origin offends Title VII's broad rule of workplace equality. The appaling conduct alleged in Meritor, and the reference in that case to environments " 'so heavily polluted with discrimination as to destroy completely the emotional and psychological stability of minority group workers.' " supra, at 66, 106 S.Ct., at 2405, quoting Rogers v. EEOC, 454 F.2d 234, 238 (CA5 1971), cert. denied, 406 U.S. 957, 92 S.Ct. 2058, 32 L.Ed.2d 343 (1972), merely present some especially egregious examples of harassment. They do not mark the boundary of what is actionable.

[6] We therefore believe the District Court erred in relying on whether the conduct "seriously affect[ed] plaintiff's psychological well-being" or led her to "suffe[r] injury." Such an inquiry may needlessly focus the factfinder's attention on concrete psychological harm, an element Title VII does not require. Certainly Title VII bars conduct that would seriously affect a reasonable person's psychological well-being, but the statute is not limited to such conduct. So long as the environment would reasonably be perceived, and is perceived, as hostile or abusive, Meritor, supra, 477 U.S., at 67, 106 S.Ct., at 2405, there is no need for it also to be psychologically injurious.

[7] This is not, and by its nature cannot be, a mathematically precise test. We need not answer today all the potential questions it raises, nor specifically address the EEOC's new regulations on this subject, see 58 Fed.Reg. 51266 (1993) (proposed 29 CFR §§ 1609.1, 1609.2); see also 29 CFR § 1604.11 (1993). But we can say that whether an environment is "hostile" or "abusive" can be determined only by looking at all the circumstances. These may include the frequency of the discriminatory conduct; its severity; whether it is physically threatening or humiliating, or a mere offensive utterance; and whether it unreasonably interferes with an employee's work performance. The effect on the employee's psychological well-being is, of course, relevant to determining whether the plaintiff actually found the environment abusive. But while psychological harm, like any other relevant factor, may be taken into account, no single factor is required.

III

[8] Forklift, while conceding that a requirement that the conduct seriously affect psychological well-being is unfounded, argues that the District Court nonetheless correctly applied the Meritor standard. We disagree. Though the District Court did conclude that the work environment was not "intimidating or abusive to [Harris]," App. to Pet. for Cert. A-35, it did so only after finding that the conduct was not "so severe as to be expected to seriously affect plaintiff's psychological well-being," id., at A-34, and that Harris was not "subjectively so offended that she suffered injury," ibid. The District Court's

application of these incorrect standards may well have influenced its ultimate conclusion especially given that the court found this to be a "close case," id., at A-31.

We therefore reverse the judgment of the Court of Appeals, and remand the case for further proceedings consistent with this opinion.

So ordered.

Justice SCALIA, concurring.

Meritor Savings Bank v. Vinson, 477 U.S. 57, 106 S.Ct. 2399, 91 L.Ed.2d 49 (1986), held that Title VII prohibits sexual harassment that takes the form of a hostile work environment. The Court stated that sexual harassment is actionable if it is "sufficiently severe or pervasive 'to alter the conditions of the [victim's] employment and create an abusive work environment.'" Id., at 67, 106 S.Ct., at 2405 (quoting Henson v. Dundee, 682 F.2d 897, 904 (CA11 1982)). Today's opinion elaborates that the challenged conduct must be severe or pervasive enough "to create an objectively hostile or abusive work environment—an environment that a reasonable person would find hostile or abusive." Ante, at 370.

"Abusive" (or "hostile," which in this context I take to mean the same thing) does not seem to me a very clear standard—and I do not think clarity is at all increased by adding the adverb "objectively" or by appealing to a "reasonable person's" notion of what the vague word means. Today's opinion does list a number of factors that contribute to abusiveness, see ante, at 371, but since it neither says how much of each is necessary (an impossible task) nor identifies any single factor as determinative, it thereby adds little certitude. As a practical matter, today's holding lets virtually unguided juries decide whether sex-related conduct engaged in (or permitted by) an employer is egregious enough to warrant an award of damages. One might say that what constitutes "negligence" (a traditional jury question) is not much more clear and certain than what constitutes "abusiveness." Perhaps so. But the class of plaintiffs seeking to recover for negligence is limited to those who have suffered harm, whereas under this statute "abusiveness" is to be the test of whether legal harm has been suffered, opening more expansive vistas of litigation.

Be that as it may, I know of no alternative to the course the Court today has taken. One of the factors mentioned in the Court's nonexhaustive list—whether the conduct unreasonably interferes with an employee's work performance—would, if it were made an absolute test, provide greater guidance to juries and employers. But I see no basis for such a limitation in the language of the statute. Accepting Meritor's interpretation of the term "conditions of employment" as the law, the test is not whether work has been impaired, but whether working conditions have been discriminatorily altered. I know of no test more faithful to the inherently vague statutory language than the one the Court today adopts. For these reasons, I join the opinion of the Court.

Justice GINSBURG, concurring.

Today the Court reaffirms the holding of Meritor Savings Bank v. Vinson, 477 U.S. 57, 66, 106 S.Ct. 2399, 2405, 91 L.Ed.2d 49 (1986): "[A] plaintiff may establish a violation of Title VII by proving that discrimination based on sex has created a hostile or abusive work environment." The critical issue, Title VII's text indicates, is whether members of one sex are exposed to disadvantageous terms or conditions of employment to which members of the other sex are not exposed. See 42 U.S.C. § 2000e-2(a)(1) (declaring that it is unlawful to discriminate with respect to, inter alia, "terms" or "conditions" of employment). As the Equal Employment Opportunity Commission emphasized, see Brief for United States and Equal Employment Opportunity Commission as Amici Curiae 9–14, the adjudicator's inquiry should center, dominantly, on whether the discriminatory conduct has unreasonably interfered with the plaintiff's work performance. To show such interference, "the plaintiff need not prove that his or her tangible productivity has declined as a result of the harassment." Davis v. Monsanto Chemical Co., 858 F.2d 345, 349 (CA6 1988). It suffices to prove that a reasonable person subjected to the discriminatory conduct would find, as the plaintiff did, that the harassment so altered working conditions as to "ma[k]e it more difficult to do the job." See ibid. Davis concerned race-based discrimination, but that difference does not alter the analysis; except in the rare case in which a bona fide occupational qualification is shown, see Automobile Workers v. Johnson Controls, Inc., 499 U.S. 187, 200–207, 111 S.Ct. 1196, 1204–08, 113 L.Ed.2d 158 (1991) (construing 42 U.S.C. § 2000e-2(e)(1)), Title VII declares discriminatory practices based on race, gender, religion, or national origin equally unlawful. [FN*]

FN* *Indeed, even under the Court's equal protection jurisprudence, which requires "an exceedingly persuasive jurisdiction" for a gender-based classification, Kirchberg v. Feenstra, 450 U.S. 455, 461, 101 S.Ct. 1195, 1199, 67 L.Ed.2d 428 (1981) (internal quotation marks omitted), it remains an open question whether "classifications based upon gender are inherently suspect." See Mississippi Univ. for Women v. Hogan, 458 U.S. 718, 724, 102 S.Ct. 3331, 3336, 73 L.Ed.2d 1090, and n. 9 (1982).*

The Court's opinion, which I join, seems to me in harmony with the view expressed in this concurring statement.

APPENDIX H

U.S. DISTRICT COURT FOR THE DISTRICT OF MINNESOTA: JENSON V. EVELETH TACONITE COMPANY

Lois E. JENSON, et al., Plaintiffs,
EVELETH TACONITE COMPANY, et al., Defendants.
Civ. No. 5-88-163.
United States District Court,
D. Minnesota,
Third Division.
May 14, 1993.

Paul Sprenger and Jean Boler, Sprenger & Lang, Minneapolis, MN, for plaintiffs.

Mary Stumo and David Goldstein, Faegre & Benson, Minneapolis, MN, for defendants Eveleth Taconite Co., Eveleth Expansion Co., Oglebay Norton Co. and Oglebay Norton Taconite Co., d/b/a Eveleth Mines.

Scott Higbee, Peterson, Engberg & Peterson, Minneapolis, MN, for defendant U.S. Workers of America, Local 6860.

MEMORANDUM OPINION AND ORDER

KYLE, District Judge.

INTRODUCTION

This matter came on for trial before the undersigned on December 21–23 and 28–30, 1992 and February 2, 1983. The Plaintiff Class, [FN1] consisting of women who applied for employment or were employed in hourly positions at a taconite mining facility owned and operated by defendants Eveleth Taconite Company, Eveleth Expansion Company, Oglebay Norton Company, and Oglebay Norton Taconite Company (collectively, "Eveleth Mines"), [FN2] alleged that Eveleth Mines violated Title VII of the Civil Rights Act of 1964, 42 U.S.C. s 2000e-2 (Title VII), and the Minnesota Human Rights Act,

Minn.Stat. s 363.03, subd. 1(2) (1988) ("MHRA"), by discriminating against women on the basis of their sex, including engaging in acts of sexual harassment. [FN3]

FN1. *See Jenson v. Eveleth Mines, 139 F.R.D. 657, 667 (D.Minn.1991).*

FN2. *On March 26, 1993 Eveleth Mines filed and served a Motion for Entry of Judgment and Dismissal From Further Proceedings on behalf of defendants Eveleth Taconite Company, Eveleth Expansion Company, and Oglebay Norton Company. That motion will heard in conjunction with the status conference to be held on June 22, 1993. See Order dated May 14, 1993.*

FN3. *Defendants United Steel Workers of America, Local 6860 (the "Union"), has been named as a defendant in this case only for purposes of formulating appropriate injunctive relief, if such relief is awarded. The Union is the certified bargaining representative for a unit of Eveleth Mines' hourly employees. Plaintiffs press no claims against the Union. Amended Complaint, P 5.*

On Motion of the Plaintiff Class, the litigation was bifurcated into two phases: (1) a "liability" phase to determine whether the defendants violated Title VII and/or MHRA; and if liability was established, (2) a "recovery" phase to determine the eligibility of individual class members for compensatory relief. Craik v. Minnesota State Univ. Bd., 731 F.2d 465, 470 (8th Cir.1984).

PLAINTIFF'S ALLEGATIONS

The Plaintiff Class (hereinafter, "Plaintiffs") allege that Eveleth Mines has engaged in a pattern of discriminatory practices, including discrimination in hiring, and in terms and conditions of employment such as job assignment, promotion, compensation, discipline and training. Plaintiffs also allege sexual discrimination based upon sexual harassment—the existence of a work environment that is hostile to women.

DEFENDANTS' ALLEGATIONS

Eveleth Mines and the Union deny the Plaintiffs' claims and state that hiring practices at Eveleth Mines, as well as the terms and conditions of employment, are conducted in a non-discriminatory manner. Eveleth Mines further alleges that it has had a practice of immediately investigating and correcting sexual harassment when it knows or reasonably should know of its existence, and that it has adhered to that practice at all relevant times.

Appendices

MEMORANDUM OPINION

Based upon the admissible evidence [FN4] adduced at trial [FN5] and upon all the files, records and proceedings herein, as well as the arguments of counsel, the court issues the following Memorandum Opinion, which shall constitute the Court's Findings of Fact and Conclusions of law, in accordance with Fed.R.Civ.P. 529(a). [FN6]

FN4. The class certification hearing in this action was held between May 13, 1991, and June 3, 1991. By agreement of counsel, the evidence adduced at the class certification hearing was considered as having been introduced as part of the case-in-chief; accordingly, the record of the class certification proceedings was also part of the trial in this action.

FN5. Prior to the December, 1992 portion of the trial, the Court directed the parties to summarize the record from the class certification hearing and designate those portions of the record that the parties considered relevant to issues of liability. The defendants have made numerous objections to many of Plaintiffs' designations. The Court has reviewed those objections and has overruled them.

In addition, the defendants also made numerous objections to the plaintiffs' deposition designations under Fed.R.Civ.P. 32. The Court has reviewed those objections and also concluded that they will be overruled.

FN6. Contained herein are citations to the record of both the 1991 proceedings and the December, 1992 and February, 1993 proceedings. Citations to the 1991 proceedings appear in Roman numerals (representing the specific volume of the transcribed proceedings) and page numbers, e.g., "III, 45." Citations to the transcript of the 1992/1993 proceedings appear in page numbers, e.g., "T. Tr., 45."

I. Procedural Posture

As stated above, this matter was brought pursuant to Title VII and MHRA. Jurisdiction and venue are proper in this Court.

A. The Named Plaintiffs

Named plaintiff Lois Jenson began her employment with Eveleth Mines on March 24, 1975. As of the 1992/1993 proceedings, Jenson was on medical leave from Eveleth Mines.

Named plaintiff Patricia Kosmach began her employment with Eveleth Mines on January 21, 1976. As of the 1992/1993 proceedings, Kosmach, who suffers from arterial lateral sclerosis was no longer working at Eveleth Mines. Named plaintiff Kathleen O'Brien Anderson began her employment with Eveleth Mines on July 6, 1976. As of the 1992/1993 proceedings, Anderson was on medical leave from Eveleth Mines.

Jenson filed a charge of sex discrimination with the Minnesota Department of Human Rights ("MDHR") on October 26, 1984. The charge was also filed with the Equal Employment Opportunity Commission("EEOC"). On March 7, 1985, the MDHR issued a memorandum stating that there was probable cause to credit Jenson's allegation of unfair discriminatory practice by Eveleth Mines, in violation of MHRA. [FN7] Jenson received a Right to Sue Notice from the EEOC on August 4, 1988.

FN7. On March 24, 1987 the Commissioner of MDHR caused Eveleth Mines to be served with an administrative complaint alleging that it had discriminated against Jenson, Kosmach, and all those similarly situated on the basis of their sex. The complaint further alleged that Eveleth Mines had maintained and continued to maintain a policy of sex discrimination including, but not limited to, a pattern of sexual harassment. Amended Complaint, P 9. The administrative complaint was dismissed without prejudice upon receiving notice of the named plaintiffs' intent to file a private action.

Kosmach filed a charge of discrimination with the EEOC on April 13, 1988. Kosmach's charge of discrimination included allegations of class-wide discrimination against female employees and applicants. Kosmach received a Right to Sue Notice from the EEOC on August 4, 1988.

Anderson filed a charge of discrimination with the EEOC on November 11, 1988. Anderson received a Right to Sue Notice from the EEOC on December 8, 1988.

The named plaintiffs are employees within the definition of 42 U.S.C. s 2000e(f), and Minn.Stat. s 363.01, subd. 16.

B. The Defendants

Defendants Eveleth Taconite Company ("ETCO") and Eveleth Expansion Company ("EXCO") do business under the name Eveleth Mines. Eveleth Mines' labor force is employed by defendant Oglebay Norton Taconite Company ("ONTAC"), a subsidiary of defendant Oglebay Norton Company ("ONCO"), which manages the operation for Eveleth Mines.

The defendant Union is a labor organization representing all of Eveleth Mines' hourly employees.

Eveleth Mines is an employer within the definition of 42 U.S.C. s 2000e(b), and Minn.Stat. s 363.01, subd. 17.

C. The Litigation

Jenson and Kosmach filed their class action Complaint on August 15, 1988. On March 14, 1989, they filed an Amended Complaint, adding Anderson as a named plaintiff and joining the Union as a defendant.

On December 9, 1991, the named plaintiffs filed a Motion to Amend their Amended Complaint to add claims for compensatory and punitive damages. This Motion was withdrawn on February 3, 1992; it has not been renewed.

A hearing on the named plaintiffs' Motion for Class Certification and a Preliminary Injunction was held in May and June of 1991. On December 16, 1991, this Court [FN8] certified [FN9] the plaintiff class to consist of:

FN8. Hon. James M. Rosenbaum.

FN9. Jenson v. Eveleth Taconite Co., 139 F.R.D. 657 (D.Minn.1991).

Appendices

All women who have applied for, or have been employed in hourly positions at Eveleth Mines at any time since December 30, 1983, and who have been, are being, or as the result of the operation of current practices, will be discriminated against with regard to the terms and conditions of their employment because of their sex.

139 F.R.D. at 667. The Court denied the Plaintiffs' request for a preliminary injunction. Id.

II. The Work Place

Eveleth Mines mines and processes crude taconite ore into pellets that are sixty-five percent (65%) iron. These pellets are then sold for purposes of being processed into pig iron and, ultimately, steel.

Eveleth Mines' mining operations are divided between two open pit mines covering 8,600 acres (the "Thunderbird Mine"). Ore from the Thunderbird Mine is uncovered, loaded into trucks and then brought to the "primary crusher," where it is reduced in size. The ore is then transported, by rail, approximately ten miles to Eveleth Mines' processing facility (the "Fairlane Plant"), where it is converted to taconite pellets. The Thunderbird Mine also has a warehouse facility which serves the mining operation.

The Fairlane Plant consists of several large buildings spread out over a large area. When the ore arrives at the Fairlane Plant, it first goes to the "fine crusher" where it is reduced to gravel-sized pieces. Next, the crushed ore proceeds to the "fine ore surge," where it is stored until processing. Beneath the fine ore surge are rows of conveyor belts and hoppers known as "Mexican feeders." [FN10] The Mexican feeders route the crushed ore to the "concentrator." The area around the Mexican feeders is known as "Mexico."

FN10. Apparently, the belts and hoppers are known as "Mexican" feeders because they resemble an upside-down sombrero.

In the concentrator, the ore is mixed with water and ground in mills until it reaches the consistency of sand. This powder is then sent over revolving drums containing magnets which capture the iron-bearing grains of ore, thereby separating them from waste rock. [FN11] The concentrate proceeds to the "pellet plant," where it is rolled in revolving drums and sprayed with a bonding agent to produce pellets approximately one-half inch in diameter. The pellets are then fire-hardened in a kiln. After cooling, the pellets are loaded for rail shipment to Duluth and other destinations.

FN11. The iron-bearing grains of ore are known as "concentrate." The material not containing iron is known as "tailings." Tailings are divided into "coarse" and "fine" tailings. Fine tailings are left as slurry and are emptied into tailings ponds located behind the buildings. Coarse tailings are used to form dikes around the tailings ponds.

Quality control is an important component of the production process. To that end, pellets are routinely sampled and analyzed at the Fairlane Plant's laboratory to assure their quality.

During periods relevant to this action, the named plaintiffs and Plaintiffs worked at both the Thunderbird Mine and Fairlane Plant, although the majority of Plaintiffs worked at the Fairlane Plant. Plaintiffs worked in all areas of the Fairlane Plant.

Eveleth Mine's work force consists of both hourly and salaried employees. All of the hourly employees are employed in production-related jobs and work at both the Thunderbird Mine and the Fairlane Plant. The hourly workers are divided into two main areas: (1) Maintenance; and (2) Operations. Maintenance workers are required to have craft or technical training, and work as electricians, mechanics, etc. Operations workers are not required to have any special training or education. [FN12]

> FN12. *With one exception, Maintenance employees were men. Until 1982, Eveleth Mines had an apprenticeship program, by which employees could qualify to become Maintenance workers by completing a designed program. When the program was terminated in 1982, one woman had completed a significant portion of the program. No Maintenance employees were hired from 1982 to 1988. In 1988, Eveleth Mines filled Maintenance positions by hiring individuals who had the requisite education of training. In addition, current employees were permitted to enter Maintenance positions by taking a practical skills test. No women applied for Maintenance positions in 1988, nor did any women seek to take the skills test.*

Job assignments and pay are controlled by the terms of the Collective Bargaining Agreement ("CBA"). [FN13] (Plfs' Exh. No. 9.) All hourly employees work in specific job classifications, which are based upon the job that the employee performs. Base pay varies by job class; the higher the job class number, the greater the hourly wage paid to an employee. Most Operations workers begin as Laborers, which along with Janitors, are the positions occupying the lowest job classification, Job Class 2.

> FN13. *Under the CBA, work assignments and other terms of employment are controlled by a seniority system; when an employee begins her employment, she is assigned a job starting date.*

Most Operations positions are organized into sequences of specific jobs. Gaining entry into a sequence is based solely on an employee's job seniority; of those persons interested in obtaining the position, the person with the earliest job starting date receives the position. [FN14] [T. Tr., 713.]

> FN14. *For jobs not located in a sequence and jobs at the bottom of a sequence, job openings are posted for seven days. During that period, those persons interested in obtaining the position sign a "bid sheet" and submit it for consideration. At the end of the seven days, the assignment is made. Job openings within a sequence are not posted.*

Appendices

Once in a sequence, an employee is assigned a sequence starting date. When an opening occurs in a sequence position other than the bottom position in the sequence, the position is offered to the person in the next lower job class with the earliest sequence starting date. (T. Tr., 714.) If that person accepts the position, that person's former position is offered to the most senior person in the next lower sequence job, and so on. If all sequence employees refuse to advance to an open position, the least senior member of the sequence can be forced into the position. Sequence employees may decline any and all opportunities to advance in a sequence by "freezing in" to their current positions; that is, when offered a job higher in the sequence, they refuse the position. Both male and female employees choose to "freeze in" and several reasons explain an individual's decision to do so, including an unwillingness to work the job and/or desiring to remain on the same shift.

Until 1975, Eveleth Mines' hourly work force was composed entirely of men. Thereafter, women began to be hired as hourly employees, beginning with those women who headed households. Eventually women were hired without regard to their domestic status. From 1981 through 1990, women comprised from three to five percent (3–5%) of Eveleth Mines' hourly work force.

In the early 1980's the taconite industry experienced a wrenching downturn. Eveleth Mines responded to the industry crisis by closing one of its production lines and laying off a significant portion of its hourly work force. Layoffs were handled according to seniority: those employees who were least senior were laid off first. In some cases, employees with a low job starting date, but with a high sequence starting date, lost their sequence jobs, but were able to remain on the job; they were "demoted" into the general pool of laborers.

The layoff lasted several years. In 1986 and 1987, Eveleth Mines began to recall workers who had been laid off. In 1988, Eveleth Mines, projecting increasing demand for taconite pellets, decided to reopen its shuttered production line. Maintenance workers were hired in 1988 to prepare the facility for production. In 1989, forty-six (46) individuals were hired into the Operations area; all 46 were hired as laborers. Forty-four (44) were men, two (2) were women. No Operations workers were hired between 1989 and 1992.

III. Claims of Sex Discrimination

A. Legal Standards

Title VII makes it an unlawful employment practice for an employer . . . to discriminate against any individual with respect to his compensation, terms, conditions or privileges of employment, because of such persons's race, color, religion, sex, or national origin.

42 U.S.C. s 2000e-2(a)(1). MHRA makes it an unfair employment practice
... (2) for an employer, because of race, color, creed, religion, national origin,
[or] sex . . . to discriminate against a person with respect to hiring, tenure,
compensation, terms, upgrading, conditions, facilities, or privileges of employment. Minn.Stat. s 363.03, subd. 1(2)(c).

[1][2] In an employment discrimination case tried as a class action, the
burden of proof in a class action differs from cases involving individual
plaintiffs. A class of plaintiffs must establish by a preponderance of the
evidence that the defendant engaged in a "pattern or practice of unlawful
discrimination in various company policies." [FN15] Craik v. Minnesota State
Univ. Bd., 731 F.2d 465, 470 (8th Cir.1984). A pattern or practice is present
when "the discriminatory acts were not isolated, insignificant or sporadic, but
were repeated, routine, or of a generalized nature." Catlett v. Missouri
Highway and Transp. Comm'n, 828 F.2d 1260, 1265 (8th Cir, 1987), cert.
denied, 485 U.S. 1021, 108 S.Ct. 1574, 99 L.Ed.2d 889 (1988); in other words,
"discrimination was the company's standard operating procedure—the regular rather than the unusual practice." [FN16] International B'hood of Teamsters v. United States, 431 U.S. 324, 360-62, 97 S.Ct. 1843, 1867–68, 52
L.Ed.2d 396 (1977).

*FN15. Liability for employment discrimination under the MHRA is interpreted with
reference to Title VII. Danz v. Jones, 263 N.W.2d 395, 398–99 (Minn.1978).
Accordingly, the discussion of liability for sexual discrimination under the MHRA will
be subsumed in the discussion of liability under Title VII.*

*FN16. The language "pattern or practice" was not intended as a word of art, and the
words reflect only their usual meaning. Teamsters, 431 U.S. 336 n. 16, 97 S.Ct. at
1855 n. 16 (quoting statement of Senator Humphrey during consideration of Title
VII).*

[3][4] In the "ordinary" case, the plaintiff class will produce statistical proof
as circumstantial evidence showing some disparity between similarly situated
protected and unprotected employees with respect to some term or condition
of employment. [FN17] The statistical proof usually is supplemented with
other evidence, such as testimony about specific incidents of discrimination.
Although statistical evidence is most common, evidence of specific incidents
of discrimination, where available, is important; it may bring "cold numbers
convincingly to life." Teamsters, 431 U.S. at 339, 97 S.Ct. at 1856. Either
type of proof alone may be sufficient to establish a pattern or practice of
discrimination. Catlett v. Missouri Highway and Transp. Comm'n, 828 F.2d
1260, 1265 (8th Cir.1987).

*FN17. To be of value, however, statistical evidence must reflect "valid comparisons of
similarly situated people." Holden v. Burlington Northern, Inc., 665 F.Supp. 1398,*

Appendices

1409 (D.Minn.1987). *If the factual bases of the statistical conclusions are faulty or suspect, the conclusions themselves are of little utility.*

In rebuttal, the defendant employer will attempt to show that the plaintiff class' "proof is either inaccurate or insignificant." Teamsters, 431 U.S. at 361, 97 S.Ct. at 1867. If the defendant fails, the "trial court may then conclude that a violation has occurred and determine the appropriate remedy." [FN18] Teamsters, 431 U.S. at 361, 97 S.Ct. at 1867. If the defendant fails, the "trial court may then conclude that a violation has occurred and determine the appropriate remedy." [FN18] Teamsters, 431 U.S. at 361, 97 S.Ct. at 1867.

> *FN18. If a pattern or practice of discrimination is established, the plaintiff class is entitled to appropriate prospective relief. In addition, a prima facie case is made out with regard to the recovery phase of the action, in which individuals' right to relief is determined. Craik, 731 F.2d at 470. At the recovery phase, the court presumes that the employer unlawfully discriminated against individual members of the plaintiff class; the defendant has the burden of persuasion and must show by a preponderance of the evidence that it did not unlawfully discriminate against the specific class member seeking relief. Id.*

[5] Class action discrimination claims can be brought under either of two theories—disparate treatment or disparate impact—or both. [FN19] In a "disparate treatment" case, the plaintiff claims the existence of a disparity between men and women in selection rates for a particular job or job benefit and further claims that the disparity is due to unlawful bias against women. See Palmer v. Schultz, 815 F.2d 84, 980 (D.C.Cir.1987). Sometimes the disparity is expressed as the difference between the number of women actually selected and the number of women "one would expect to have been selected, assuming equality in selection rates for men and women." Id. at 90.

> *FN19. With the sole exception of their claim of discrimination in hiring, Plaintiffs have not specified whether their individual claims are brought under either "disparate treatment" or "disparate impact" theories, or both. The hiring claim is premised on both theories.*

[6] If a disparity is found, proof that the disparity was caused by discriminatory animus can be shown by direct or circumstantial evidence. Two types of circumstantial proof may be relied upon: (1) statistical evidence; and (2) anecdotal evidence of incidents of discrimination. Each may alone justify an inference of discriminatory animus, Teamsters, 431 U.S. at 335 n. 15, 97 S.Ct. at 1854 n. 15, putting the burden on the defendant to rebut the proof. However, unless statistical proof shows that the disparity is "gross," Hazlewood School Dist. v. United States, 433 U.S. 299, 307–08, 97 S.Ct. 2736, 2741, 53 L.Ed.2d 768 (1977), anecdotal evidence of discrimination will be an essential teammate in establishing a pattern or practice of disparate treatment. [FN20] 2 Arthur

---

Larson & Lex K. Larson, Employment Discrimination, s 50.83(a), at 10–138 (1993) [hereinafter Larson].

FN20. The Supreme Court, in Hazlewood School Dist. v. United States, 433 U.S. 299, 97 S.Ct. 2736, 53 L.Ed.2d 768 (1977), stated that "[w]here gross statistical disparities can be shown, they alone may in a proper case constitute prima facie proof of a pattern and practice of discrimination." Id. at 307–08, 97 S.Ct. at 2741. Accordingly, except in cases where statistical proof shows a wide disparity of treatment, claims of disparate treatment will usually require both statistical and anecdotal proof.

APPENDIX I

SUPREME COURT OF NEW JERSEY RULING: LEHMANN V. TOYS 'R' US, INC.

Theresa LEHMANN, Plaintiff-Appellant and Cross-Respondent,

v.

TOYS 'R' US, INC., a corporation, Don
Baylous, and Jeffrey Wells, Defendants-
Respondents and Cross-Appellants.

Supreme Court of New Jersey.
Argued Feb. 1, 1993.
Decided July 14, 1993.

Fredric J. Gross, Mount Ephraim, for appellant and cross-respondent.

James R. Williams, New York City, a member of the New York bar, for respondents and cross-appellants (Greenberg, Dauber & Epstein, Newark, attorneys, Mr. Williams, Scott T. Baken, New York City, a member of the New York bar, and Ina B. Lewisohn, Trenton, of counsel).

Alexander P. Waugh, Jr., Asst. Atty. Gen., for amicus curiae Attorney General of New Jersey (Robert J. Del Tufo, Atty. Gen., Jeffrey C. Burstein, Deputy Atty. Gen., on the brief).

Nadine Taub and Michelle Joy Munsat, Newark, submitted a brief on behalf of amici curiae Women's Rights Litigation Clinic and NOW-NJ.

Paul I. Weinder, Roseland, submitted a brief on behalf of amicus curiae Employment Law Council (Timins & Weiner, attorneys).

The opinion of the Court was delivered by

GARIBALDI, J.

This appeal presents this Court with two questions concerning hostile work environment sexual harassment claims under the New Jersey Law Against Discrimination, N.J.S.A. 10:5-1 to -42 (LAD). First, what are the standards for stating a cause of action for hostile work environment sex discrimination claims? Second, what is the scope of an employer's liability for a supervisor's sexual harassment that results in creating a hostile work environment? We hold that a plaintiff states a cause of action for hostile work environment sexual harassment when he or she alleges discriminatory conduct that a reasonable person of the same sex in the plaintiff's position would consider sufficiently severe or pervasive to alter the conditions of employment and to create an intimidating, hostile, or offensive working environment.

We further hold that in the determination of an employer's liability for damages when an employee raises a hostile work environment discrimination claim against a supervisor: (1) an employer will be strictly liable for equitable damages and relief; (2) an employer may be vicariously liable under agency principles for compensatory damages that exceed equitable relief; and (3) an employer will not be liable for punitive damages unless the harassment was authorized, participated in, or ratified by the employer.

I

A. Procedural History

Plaintiff, Theresa Lehmann, brought a civil action in the Law Division against her former employer, Toys 'R' Us, Inc. (Toys 'R' Us); her former supervisor, Don Baylous; and Jeffrey Wells, a human resources manager at Toys 'R' Us. Plaintiff's principal allegations were that defendants subjected her to a hostile work environment on the basis of her sex in violation of the LAD. She asserted that sexual harassment perpetrated and condoned by the defendants had caused her to suffer damages including loss of wages and pension benefits, anxiety, detriment to her health, medical expenses, humiliation, and pain and suffering, and also that she had been required to expend attorneys' fees and to incur other litigation costs. She also alleged various other claims, separate from her LAD claims, including battery, negligence, intentional interference with contractual relations, and intentional infliction of emotional distress.

After a six-day bench trial, the trial court dismissed all of plaintiff's causes of action against defendants except her battery claim against Baylous, for which it awarded her $5,000 as damages.

Plaintiff's appeal to the Appellate Division resulted in the filing of three separate opinions. The Appellate Division unanimously affirmed that the trial court's dismissal of plaintiff's non-LAD claims for invasion of privacy, intentional infliction of emotional distress, reprisal, and tortious interference with contractual relations. Lehmann v. Toys 'R' Us, 255 N.J.Super. 616, 605 A.2d 1125 (1992). The court also unanimously reversed the trial court's dismissal of plaintiff's hostile work environment sexual harassment claim and remanded the matter to the trial court for further fact-finding. Although the court agreed that the trial court had applied the wrong legal standards in evaluating plaintiff's LAD claim, it was unable to agree (splitting three ways) on the standards that should applied on remand to determine the sufficiency of Lehmann's hostile work environment claim and the standard that should be applied to determine Toys 'R' Us's liability for sexual harassment by its supervisor. Judge Shebell, writing for the majority, felt that a "more structured test is required at this juncture," 255 N.J.Super. at 642, 605 A.2d 1125. He therefore adopted, with significant modifications, the first four prongs of the test set forth in Andrews v. City of Philadelphia, 895 F.2d 1469 (3d Cir.1990). However, he rejected the Andrews court's use of respondeat superior principles to assess an employer's liability for hostile work environment sexual harassment by a supervisor, instead holding that an employer was strictly liable.

Judge D'Annunzio, in a brief separate concurrence, stated his "general agreement" with the majority's approach, but disagreed on the matter of an employer's vicarious liability for sexual harassment by a supervisory employee.

Judge Skillman, concurring in part and dissenting in part, rejected the Andrews test, and advocated instead that hostile work environment sexual harassment claims be evaluated under a more flexible standard based on the Equal Employment Opportunity Commission's Guidelines on Discrimination Because of Sex, 29 C.F.R. §§ 1604.1 to 1604.11 (EEOC Guidelines). Judge Skillman also stated that agency principles, rather than strict liability, ought to govern an employer's various liability for sexual harassment by a supervisory employee.

In response to the conflicting opinions rendered by the Appellate Division, both parties filed appeals as of right pursuant to Rule 2:2-1(a), requesting this Court to identify the legal standards for stating an actionable claim of hostile work environment sexual harassment under the LAD and to define the standard for imposing liability on an employer for sexual harassment by its supervisor. Those are the only issues before this Court. We denied plaintiff's petition for certification, which addressed her non-LAD claims. 130 N.J. 19, 611 A.2d 657 (1992).

B. Facts

The following facts were adduced at trial. Lehmann testified that she began working for Toys 'R' Us in August 1981 as a file clerk in the Purchasing Department. She received various promotions to supervisory positions.

In November 1985, defendant Don Baylous joined Toys 'R' Us as Director of Purchasing Administration. Baylous supervised approximately thirty people, including Lehmann, who held the position of Purchase Order Management Supervisor. Baylous and Lehmann worked closely together on a daily basis, and at least once a week Lehmann met with Baylous in his office. Lehmann received favorable evaluations and promotions under Baylous's supervision, and was promoted to Systems Analyst for the Purchasing Department in September of 1986.

In or around December 1986, plaintiff began to notice what she considered offensive sexual comments and touchings from Baylous directed at other female employees. Plaintiff witnesses Baylous walk up behind a female employee at the company Christmas party and put his hands on her. The female employee evidently found his touching offensive because she told him loudly and in angry terms to get his hands off her. The record is replete with other instances of Lehmann witnessing Baylous touch and grab other female employees, although the chronology of those events is somewhat unclear.

The first incident directly involving Lehmann occurred in January 1987. Lehmann testified that Baylous directed her to reject a 300-page purchase order and to tell the employee to rewrite it, and that she replied that the employee would be very angry. Lehmann testified that Baylous told her to "just lean over his desk and show him your tits, implying that that way Frank couldn't get upset at me." Lehmann testified that Baylous had, at various times, directed her to "stick your tits out at" a new boss, and to "write a memo to cover your ass * * * because you have such a cute little ass."

On another occasion in January 1987, Lehmann was in Baylous's office with him. She testified that

> *Don stood up and walked around his desk and stood by the door. I rose and went to my right a little, and I noticed something out of the corner of my eye out of the window, and I said, what's going on out there? At this Don lifted the back of my shirt up over my shoulders. I know my bra strap was exposed, and said, give them a show. And I pulled my shirt down, ran out of the office crying, and I remember running to Marlene Pantess.*

Ms. Pantess's testimony corroborated that Lehmann ran out of Baylous's office crying and that she stated that Baylous had lifted up her shirt.

Lehmann testified that on January 22, 1987, she went to Baylous's immediate boss, Bill Frankfort, to complain about Baylous's conduct. Lehmann requested that she not be identified to Baylous as the complainant. She stated that Frankfort told her to handle it herself, and that she replied that she did not feel she could do so because she had been too afraid to confront Baylous up to that point. Lehmann also testified that Frankfort told her not to report the harassment to Howard Moore, the Executive Vice President in charge of purchasing, because he "was very straight-laced, and he was a family man." Several days later, Lehmann wrote and delivered a letter to Frankfort concerning her complaints of sexual harassment, but Frankfort did not open the letter until after Lehman's resignation.

On January 26, 1987, Eric Jonas, Toys 'R' Us's Manager of Employee Relations, called Lehmann and a female co-worker who also had had problems with Baylous to his office to discuss Baylous's conduct. Lehmann testified that she told Jonas of the specific incidents and gave him a list of names of other women who had experienced inappropriate touchings or comments from Baylous. Lehmann told Jonas that she did not want Baylous fired but wanted his inappropriate behavior stopped. Jonas assured her that he would speak to Baylous. Several days later, Frankfort told Lehmann that Baylous had been spoken to about his conduct.

However, according to Lehmann, Baylous's inappropriate conduct did not cease. In early February 1987, Lehmann was in Baylous's office and began to feel faint. She testified that she asked him to "just kick me into the hall" if she passed out, and that he replied that he would "take advantage of [her]" instead. She reported the incident to Jonas, who instructed her to keep a journal of such incidents. In the following weeks, Lehmann observed Baylous make a comment to a female employee about her anatomy. Lehmann's sister, also a Toys 'R' Us employee, told Lehmann that Baylous had come up behind her and rubbed her shoulders.

In early March 1987, Lehmann informed both Jonas and Frankfort that Baylous had not stopped touching employees and making inappropriate comments. She testified that Jonas told her that she was "paranoid." Jonas also offered Lehmann a transfer within the company, but Lehmann rejected that suggestion because, she said, she loved her job and had not done anything wrong and did not think she was the one who should be transferred.

The following week, Lehmann testified, Baylous grabbed her on the arm and she observed him touching and grabbing other female employees as well. She also was present at a meeting at which Baylous gratuitously announced that the reason that both he and another female employee had colds was not due to sexual intimacy.

Dissatisfied with the results of Jonas's and Frankfort's efforts to control Baylous's conduct, Lehmann took her complaints to Howard Moore, the Executive Vice President in charge of purchasing, on April 6. Lehmann told him that she felt she was being forced out of the company. Moore was dismayed that such conduct was going on without his knowledge.

Later that same day, Lehmann was called to personnel to meet with Laurie Lambert. Lehmann related to Lambert all that had occurred. Lambert offered Lehmann a transfer, but Lehmann again protested "why should I have to transfer when I worked so hard for this job that I love after six years of being in this company?"

The next day, Lehmann gave Baylous two weeks notice of her resignation, stating that it was for personal reasons. She was against summoned to meet with Lambert. Lambert again offered Lehmann a transfer, and recommended that Lehmann confront Baylous directly with her allegations to clear the air. Lehmann rejected both suggestions.

Lehmann testified that a few minutes later, Baylous entered the room. She related to him her complaints. She testified that he was apologetic at first, but that he grew angry and she became increasingly upset. Following the confrontation, Lehmann left Toys 'R' Us and did not return to complete her final two-week period.

Baylous denies that he ever engaged in sexually harassing conduct. He admits that he was formerly a "touchy" person, using pats on the back to convey approval and tapping people to get their attention. However, he denies that he ever touched any employee in a sexual manner, and vigorously denies the "sweater-lifting incident." He also admits to having made some suggestive comments, such as asking one employee if she had gone home for a "quickie" and telling another employee that she had a "cute rump," but he maintained that those comments were intended and interpreted as jokes. He denied ever telling Lehmann to "stick out" or "show" her "tits" or telling her that she had "a cute ass."

Jeffrey Wells, Toys 'R' Us's head of personnel, testified that he had made inquiries and discovered that there had been no window washing undertaken on the building January 1987. That evidence was offered to refute Lehmann's statement that she saw scaffolding outside Baylous's window at the time of the shift-lifting incident. Wells also testified that the company had continued investigating the allegations after Lehmann's departure, and that it had concluded that Baylous had not engaged in sexual harassment. Wells's conclusions about Baylous's conduct were consistent with Baylous's testimony about himself.

Eric Jonas testified that he had monitored Baylous's conduct by making unannounced visits to Baylous's department. He also stated that he had interviewed four of the women whom Lehmann had identified as able to corroborate her complaints, and that none could do so.

Lehmann contended that Toys 'R' Us's investigation was inadequate. She asserted that despite the fact that Toys 'R' Us has a written corporate policy against sexual harassment requiring all claims to be fully investigated, the investigation documented, and those responsible subject to discipline or discharge, Jonas did not keep any substantive written records and failed to question key witnesses about important events. The trial court agreed.

> [T]his court wishes to note that it was unimpressed with Toys 'R' Us investigation of plaintiff's complaints. It appears from the testimony that the Toys 'R' Us employees in charge of investigating this matter did not properly and thoroughly attend to plaintiff's allegations, thus exacerbating plaintiff's problems.

Although Lehmann and defendants disagree about whether Baylous engaged in sexually harassing conduct, all agree and stipulated that Baylous did not attempt to obtain any sexual advantage from any employee of Toys 'R' Us.

The trial court, for the most part, declined to resolve the factual dispute between the parties. Instead, it assumed that all of Lehmann's allegations were true and held that nonetheless she had failed to state a claim for hostile work environment sexual harassment. The Appellate Division unanimously agreed that a hostile work environment in violation of LAD would be established if plaintiff's factual allegations were credited by a finder of fact. We affirm the Appellate Division's judgment that the trial court's dismissal of plaintiff's LAD claims must be reversed and the matter remanded for further fact-finding.

II. Sexual Harassment and The Law Against Discrimination

The New Jersey Law Against Discrimination was first enacted in 1945. Its purpose is "nothing less than the eradication 'of the cancer of discrimination.'" Fuchilla v. Layman, 109 N.J. 319, 334, 537 A.2d 652 (quoting Jackson v. Concord Co., 54 N.J. 113, 124, 253 A.2d 793 (1969), cert. denied sub nom. University of Medicine & Dentistry of N.J. v. Fuchilla, 488 U.S. 826, 109 S.Ct. 75, 102 L.Ed.2d 51 (1988). The opportunity to obtain employment "is recognized as and declared to be a civil right." N.J.S.A. 10:5-4.

The LAD was enacted to protect not only the civil rights of individual aggrieved employees but also to protect the public's strong interest in a discrimination-free workplace. Fuchilla, supra, 109 N.J. at 335, 537 A.2d 652. Freedom from discrimination is one of the fundamental principles of our society. Discrimination based on gender is "peculiarly repugnant in a society which prides itself on judging each individual by his or her merits." Grigoletti v. Ortho Pharmaceutical Corp., 118 N.J. 89, 96, 570 A.2d 903 (1990) (citation omitted).

The LAD specifically prohibits employment discrimination based on sex. N.J.S.A. 10:5-12 provides:

> It shall be unlawful employment practice, or, as the case may be, an unlawful discrimination:
>
> a. For an employer, because of the race, creed, color, national origin, ancestry, age, marital status, affectional or sexual orientation, sex * * * of any individual, * * * to refuse to hire or employ or to bar or to discharge * * * from employment such individual or to discriminate against such individual in compensation or in terms, conditions or privileges of employment * * *.

The legislative history of the LAD is silent on the subject of sexual harassment.

In construing the terms of the LAD, this Court has frequently looked to federal precedent governing Title VII of the Civil Rights Act of 1964, 42 U.S.C.A. § 2000e to § 2000e-17 ("Title VII"), as "a key source of interpretive authority." Grigoletti, supra, 118 N.J. at 97, 570 A.2d 903. Although the "substantive and procedural standards that we have developed under the State's LAD have been markedly influenced by the federal experience," ibid., we have

Sexual Harassment

"applied the Title VII standards with flexibility" and "have not hesitated to depart" from federal precedent "if a rigid application of its standards is inappropriate under the circumstances." Id. at 107, 570 A.2d 903.

Sexual harassment is a form of sex discrimination that violates both Title VII and the LAD. See Meritor Sav. Bank v. Vinson, 477 U.S. 57, 106 S.Ct. 2399, 91 L.Ed.2d 49 (1986) (holding that when supervisor sexually harasses a subordinate because of subordinate's sex, that supervisor discriminates on basis of sex in violation of Title VII); Erickson v. Marsh & McLennan Co., 117 N.J. 539, 555–56, 569 A.2d 793 (1990) (suggesting that sexual harassment that creates hostile environment is prohibited under LAD).

[1][2] Sexual harassment jurisprudence generally divides sexual harassment cases into two categories. Quid pro quo sexual harassment occurs when an employer attempts to make an employee's submission to sexual demands a condition of his or her employment. It involves an implicit or explicit threat that if the employee does not accede to the sexual demands, he or she will lose his or her job, receive unfavorable performance reviews, be passed over for promotions, or suffer other adverse employment consequences. Hostile work environment sexual harassment, by contrast, occurs when an employer or fellow employees harass an employee because of his or her sex to the point at which the working environment becomes hostile.

Plaintiff Lehmann does not charge that defendant Baylous engaged in quid pro quo sexual harassment. Rather, she alleged that his sexually-charged offensive conduct towards her and other women in the workplace created a hostile work environment.

Quid pro quo sexual harassment is more easily recognized and more clearly defined and well-established as a cause of action. Hostile work environment sexual harassment, on the other hand, has only recently been recognized as actionable sexual harassment. Because of the relatively recent recognition of the harm, some confusion, remains in the minds of employers and employees concerning what sorts of conduct constitute hostile work environment sexual harassment.

[3] In the majority of hostile work environment cases, the harassing conduct takes the form of unwelcome sexual touchings and comments. However, the harassing conduct need not be sexual in nature; rather, its defining characteristic is that the harassment occurs because of the victim's sex. See Muench v. Township of Haddon, 255 N.J.Super. 288, 605 A.2d 242 (App.Div.1992) (holding defendant employer liable for hostile work environment sexual harassment where employees harassed dispatcher because she was female although harassment was not sexual in nature).

Although we recognized in Erickson, supra, 117 N.J. at 155–57, 569 A.2d 793, that allegations of a sexually hostile work environment state a claim under the LAD, we have not yet been called on to define the elements of a hostile work environment sexual harassment cause of action. In fashioning a standard we acknowledge that the hostile work environment claim is still evolving. Conduct considered normal and non-discriminatory twenty years ago may well be considered discriminatory today.

Like all courts, we are reluctant to penalize behavior that was not previously understood or intended to be wrongful. However, we cannot deny legal redress to the victims of discrimination and harassment merely because the perpetrators may be unaware of the illegality of their conduct. In order to ensure fairness for all, both employees and employers must be able to understand what constitutes a claim for gender-hostile work environment. A clear and intelligible legal standard will protect employees from the damage wrought by a hostile working environment and will enable employers to conform their conduct to the law.

We therefore agree with the majority below that a structured definition of the cause of action is preferable at this early stage in the development of the law concerning hostile work environment sexual harassment. However, we are sensitive to the concern expressed by Judge Skillman in his dissent below that the standard must be "sufficiently flexible to recognize the wide variety of forms which hostile work environment sexual discrimination may take and to allow for the evolution of this new area of law." 255 N.J.Super. at 648, 605 A.2d 1125.

We find that the standards expressed in the EEOC Guidelines, while helpful, are insufficiently structured to define the cause of action at this stage in the development of the law. However, we agree with the dissent below that the Third Circuit's Andrews test employed by the majority below contains too many analytical difficulties and deficiencies to be usefully employed here.

Rather than risking confusion by engrafting major revisions to the Andrews test, we announce a new test in the hope of creating a standard that both employees and employers will be able to understand and one that employers can realistically enforce. We cannot overstate the importance we place on a test that allows employees to know their rights in a given set of circumstances and that allows employers to set policies and procedures that comply with that test.

[4] To state a claim for hostile work environment sexual harassment, a female plaintiff must allege conduct that occurred because of her sex and that a reasonable woman would consider sufficiently severe or pervasive to alter the conditions of employment and create an intimidating, hostile, or offensive working environment. For the purposes of establishing and examining a cause of action, the test can be broken down into four prongs: the complained-of conduct (1) would not have occurred but for the employee's gender; and it was (2) severe or pervasive enough to make a (3) reasonable woman believe that (4) the conditions of employment are altered and the working environment is hostile or abusive. However, the second, third, and fourth prongs, while separable to some extent, are interdependent. One cannot inquire whether the

alleged conduct was "severe or pervasive" without knowing how severe or pervasive it must be. The answer to that question lies in the other prongs: the conduct must be severe or pervasive enough to make a reasonable woman believe that the conditions of employment are altered and her working environment is hostile.

In this case, we discuss the standard assuming a female plaintiff, because in both the present case and majority of cases, the plaintiff is a woman. However, the standard we announce today applies to sexual harassment of women by men, men by women, men by men, and women by women. The LAD protects both men and women and bars both heterosexual and homosexual harassment. The only difference in the standard would be that a male plaintiff would have to allege conduct that a reasonable man would believe altered the conditions of his employment and created a working environment that was hostile to men.

III. Harassment Because of Plaintiff's Sex

The first element of the test is discrete from the others. It simply requires that in order to state a claim under the LAD, a plaintiff show by a propenderance of the evidence that she suffered discrimination because of her sex. Common sense dictates that there is no LAD violation if the same conduct would have occurred regardless of the plaintiff's sex. For example, if a supervisor is equally crude and vulgar to all employees, regardless of their sex, no basis exists for a sex harassment claim. Although the supervisor may not be a nice person, he is not abusing a plaintiff because of her sex.

[5] The LAD is not a fault- or intent-based statute. A plaintiff need not show that the employer intentionally discriminated or harassed her, or intended to create a hostile work environment. The purpose of the LAD is to eradicate discrimination, whether intentional or unintentional. Although unintentional discrimination is perhaps less morally blameworthy than intentional discrimination, it is not necessarily less harmful in its effects, and it is at the effects of discrimination that the LAD is aimed. Therefore, the perpetrator's intent is simply not an element of the cause of action. Plaintiff need show only that the harassment would not have occurred but for her sex.

[6] When the harassing conduct is sexual or sexist in nature, the but-for element will automatically be satisfied. Thus when a plaintiff alleges that she has been subjected to sexual touchings or comments, or where she has been subjected to harassing comments about the lesser abilities, capacities, or the "proper role" of members of her sex, she has established that the harassment occurred because of her sex.

However, not all sexual harassment is sex-based on its face. In Andrews, supra, 895 F.2d 1469, for example, the plaintiff female police officers alleged,

242

among other things, that male officers hostile to women on the force stole their case files and vandalized their personal property. When the form of the harassment is not obviously based on the victim's sex, the victim must make a prima facie showing that the harassment occurred because of her sex. See also Muench, supra, 255 N.J.Super. 288, 605 A.2d 242 (holding that woman police dispatcher was subject to non-sexual harassment that constituted sexual discrimination under LAD).

[7] In such non-facially sex-based harassment cases a plaintiff might show that such harassment was accompanied by harassment that was obviously sex-based. Alternatively, she might show that only women suffered the non-facially sex-based harassment. All that is required is a showing that it is more likely than not that the harassment occurred because of the plaintiff's sex. For a female plaintiff, that will be sufficient to invoke the rebuttable presumption that the harassment did in fact occur because of the plaintiff's sex. A male plaintiff, in order to invoke the presumption, must make the additional showing that the defendant employer is the rare employer who discriminates against the historically-privileged group. Erickson, supra, 117 N.J. at 551, 569 A.2d 793 ("In reverse discriminating cases, the rationale supporting the rebuttable presumption of discrimination embodied in the prima facie elements does not apply. Thus, when a complainant is not a member of a minority, courts have generally * * * require[d] the plaintiff to show that he has been victimized by an unusual employer who discriminates against the majority." (citation omitted)).

[8] In the case at bar, of course, the harassing conduct alleged by Lehmann consisted of sexual comments and touchings. Such allegations satisfy the requirement that the plaintiff show that the conduct occurred because of her sex.

IV. "Severe or Pervasive"

[9] We turn next to the requirement that the alleged harassing conduct be "severe or pervasive." We emphasize that it is the harassing conduct that must be severe or pervasive, not its effect on the plaintiff or on the work environment. Ellison v. Brady, 924 F.2d 872, 878 (9th Cir.1991).

The disjunctive "severe or pervasive" standard is in conformity with federal Title VII law. The United States Supreme Court in Meritor held that "for sexual harassment to be actionable, it must be sufficiently severe or pervasive" to cause the requisite harm. 477 U.S. at 67, 106 S.Ct. at 2405, 91 L.Ed.2d at 60 (emphasis added). We specifically reject the "regular and pervasive" standard created in Andrews, supra, 895 F.2d 1469, and adopted by the majority below. First, the formulation is incompatible with the "severe or pervasive" standard set forth by the Supreme Court in Meritor. Second, a "regular and pervasive" standard would bar actions based on a single, extremely severe incident or, perhaps, even those based on multiple but randomly-occurring incidents of harassment. We find that result improper. Although it will be a rare and extreme case in which a single incident will be so severe that it would, from the perspective of a reasonable woman, make the working environment hostile, such a case is certainly possible. The LAD was designed to prevent the harm of hostile working environments. No purpose is served by allowing that harm to go unremedied merely because it was brought about by a single, severe incident of harassment rather than by multiple incidents of harassment.

The fact patterns of many reported cases suggest, however, that most plaintiffs claiming hostile work environment sexual harassment allege numerous incidents that, if considered individually, would be insufficiently severe to state a claim, but considered together are sufficiently pervasive to make the work environment intimidating or hostile. "[T]he required showing of severity or seriousness of the harassing conduct varies inversely with the pervasiveness or frequency of the conduct." Ellison, supra 924 F.2d at 878.

Rather than considering each incident in isolation, courts must consider the cumulative effect of the various incidents, bearing in mind "'that each successive episode has its predecessors, that the impact of the separate incidents may accumulate, and that the work environment created may exceed the sum of the individual episodes.'" Burns v. McGregor Elec. Indus., 955 F.2d 559, 564 (8th Cir.1992) (quoting Robinson v. Jacksonville Shipyards, 760 F.Supp. 1486, 1524 (M.D.Fla.1991)). "A play cannot be understood on the basis of some of its scenes but only on its entire performance, and similarly, a discrimination analysis must concentrate not on individual incidents butt on the overall scenario." Andrews, supra, 895 F.2d at 1484.

V. The Requisite Level of Harm

[10] We next consider the level of harm a plaintiff must show to state a valid hostile work environment LAD claim. This is a subject on which there has been considerable disagreement among the federal courts. The United States Supreme Court has granted certiorari to resolve the split among the federal circuits on this question. See Harris v. Forklift Sys., —-U.S. ——, 113 S.Ct. 1382, 122 L.Ed.2d 758 (1993).

On one side of the split are those circuits that hold that in order to state a claim of hostile work environment sexual harassment, the plaintiff must allege conduct that "had the effect of unreasonably interfering with the plaintiff's work performance and creating an intimidating, hostile, or offensive work environment that affected seriously the psycho logical [sic] well-being of the plaintiff * * *." Rabidue v. Osceola Refining Co., 805 F.2d 611 (6th Cir.1986), cert. denied, 481 U.S. 1041, 107 S.Ct. 1983, 95 L.Ed.2d 823 (1987); accord

Appendices

Wilson v. Zapata Off-Shore Co., 939 F.2d 260 (5th Cir.1991); Brooms v. Regal Tube Co., 881 F.2d 412 (7th Cir.1989); Paroline v. Unisys Corp., 879 F.2d 100 (4th Cir.1989), aff'd in relevant part, rev'd in part, 900 F.2d 27 (1990); Sparks v. Pilot Freight Carriers, 830 F.2d 1554 (11th Cir.1987).

The courts on the other side of the split hold that a plaintiff must show that the complained-of conduct was "sufficiently severe or pervasive to alter the conditions of the victim's employment and create an abusive working environment." Ellison, supra, 924 F.2d at 876; accord Meritor, supra, 477 U.S. at 67, 106 S.Ct. at 2405, 91 L.Ed.2d at 60 ("for sexual harassment to be actionable, it must be sufficiently severe or pervasive to alter the conditions of [the victim's] employment and create an abusive working environment" (citations omitted)); Kotcher v. Rosa & Sullivan Appliance Ctr., 957 F.2d 59 (2d Cir.1992); Andrews, supra, 895 F.2d 1469; Lipsett v. University of Puerto Rico, 864 F.2d 881 (1st Cir.1988); Minteer v. Auger, 844 F.2d 569 (8th Cir.1988); Vinson v. Taylor, 753 F.2d 141 (D.C.Cir.1985).

We find the latter line of cases more consistent with the purposes of the LAD. Although psychological damage to victims of harassment is one of the harms the LAD seeks to prevent, it is by no means the only one. The Legislature has found that because of illegal discrimination, of which sexual harassment is a form, "people suffer personal hardships, and the State suffers a grievous harm." N.J.S.A. 10:5-3. Among the personal hardships noted by the Legislature are

*economic loss; time loss; physical and emotional stress; and in some cases severe emotional trauma, illness, homelessness or other irreparable harm resulting from the strain of employment controversies; relocation, search and moving difficulties; anxiety caused by lack of information, uncertainty, and resultant planning difficulty; career, education, family and social disruption; and adjustment problems * * *.*

[Ibid.]

Sex discrimination and sexual harassment also cause serious economic harms. Dr. Freada Klein, a researcher and consultant to large companies on sexual harassment, has estimated that the cost of sexual harassment for a typical Fortune 500 service or manufacturing company of 23,784 employees is over $6.7 million per year, exclusive of costs of litigation, processing state or federal charges, and destructive behavior or sabotage. The $6.7 million figure derived from the costs of employee turnover, absenteeism, reduced productivity, and the use of internal complaint mechanisms. The Civil Rights Act of 1991: Hearings on H.R. 1 Before the House Committee on Education and Labor, 102nd Cong., 1st Sess. 168, 207–214 (1991) (statement of Dr. Freada Klein) (hereinafter Klein). That harm to the productivity and profitability of corporations necessarily harms the economy of the State and the welfare of its citizens.

Moreover, the Legislature has declared that discrimination is "a matter of concern to the government of the State, and that such discrimination threatens not only the rights and proper privileges of the inhabitants of the State but menaces the institutions and foundation of a free democratic State." N.J.S.A. 10:5-3.

Given the breadth of individual and societal harms the flow from discrimination and harassment, to limit the LAD's application to only those cases in which the victim suffered, or could have suffered, serious psychological harm would be contrary to its remedial purpose. We find no support in the statute for a requirement of serious psychological harm before a plaintiff can state a claim. It is the harasser's conduct, not the plaintiff's injury, that must be severe or pervasive. We agree with the Ellison court that "[s]urely, employees need not endure sexual harassment until their psychological well-being is seriously affected to the extent that they suffer anxiety or delibitation" before they can bring a claim. 924 F.2d at 878; see also Carrero v. New York City Hous. Auth., 890 F.2d 569, 578 (2d Cir.1989) ("a female employee need not subject herself to an extended period of demeaning and degrading provocation before being entitled to seek the remedies provided under Title VII").

Of course, if a plaintiff suffers psychological harm and wishes to collect damages for that injury, she must allow that she suffered psychological harm and to what extent. However, that proof goes to the amount of her damages, not to whether she states a cause of action.

Nor need a plaintiff show that she suffered an economic loss. The plaintiff's injury need be no more tangible or serious than that the conditions of employment have been altered and the work environment has become abusive. Although the LAD provides for compensatory and punitive damages, it is not primarily a tort scheme; rather, its primary purpose is to end discrimination. Because discrimination itself is the harm that the LAD seeks to eradicate, additional harms need not be shown in order to state a claim under the LAD. In a claim of hostile work environment sexual harassment, the hostile work environment is the legally recognized harm. Therefore a plaintiff in a hostile work environment sexual harassment case establishes the requisite harm if she shows that her working conditions were affected by the harassment to the point at which a reasonable woman would consider the working environment hostile.

[11] In making that showing, the plaintiff may use evidence that other women in the workplace were sexually harassed. The plaintiff's work environment is affected not only by conduct directed at herself but also by the treatment of others. A woman's perception that her work environment is hostile to women will obviously be reinforced if she witnesses the harassment

246

of other female workers. Therefore, we hold that the plaintiff need not personally have been the target of each or any instance of offensive or harassing conduct. Evidence of sexual harassment directed at other women is relevant to both the character of the work environment and its effects on the complainant.

> *The few courts that have addressed this issue have generally concluded that incidents involving employees other than the plaintiff are relevant in establishing a generally hostile work environment. In Vinson, the District of Columbia Court of Appeals concluded that the trial court's rejection of evidence of harassment of female employees other than the plaintiff was improper. "Evidence tending to show Taylor's harassment of other women working alongside Vinson is directly relevant to the question whether he created an environment violative of Title VII." [Vinson v. Taylor, supra, 753 F.2d] at 146. The court held that no evidence of sexual harassment directed specifically toward the plaintiff was necessary for a claim under Title VII: "Even a woman who was never herself the object of harassment might have a Title VII claim if she were forced to work in an atmosphere where such harassment was pervasive." Id. at 146. This view finds support in racial discrimination cases brought under Title VII. See Rogers v. Equal Employment Opportunity Comm'n, 454 F.2d 234 (5th Cir.1971), cert. denied, 406 U.S. 957, 92 S.Ct. 2058, 32 L.Ed.2d 343 (1972).*

[Hicks v. Gates Rubber Company, 833 F.2d 1406, 1416 (10th Cir.1987).]

Accord Hall v. Gus Constr., 842 F.2d 1015 (8th Cir.1988) ("Although [the plaintiff] was not subjected to sexual propositions and offensive touching, evidence of sexual harassment directed at employees other than the plaintiff is relevant to show a hostile work environment.").

VI. The Reasonable Woman Standard

In evaluating whether the harassment alleged was sufficiently severe or pervasive to alter the conditions of employment and to create a hostile or intimidating work environment for a female plaintiff, the finder of fact shall consider the question from the perspective of a reasonable woman. If the plaintiff is male, the perspective used shall be that of a reasonable man. We choose an objective and gender-specific perspective for a number of reasons.

We choose an objective standard, first, because as we explained above, the LAD is not primarily a tort scheme but rather is aimed at eradicating discriminatory conduct. An objective reasonableness standard better focuses the court's attention on the nature and legality of the conduct rather than on the reaction of the individual plaintiff, which is more relevant to damages.

Secondly, an objective standard provides flexibility. As we noted above, much conduct that would have been considered acceptable twenty or thirty years ago would be considered sexual harassment today. As community standards evolve, the standard of what a reasonable woman would consider harassment will also evolve.

However, incorporating community standards through the use of a reasonableness standard brings dangers against which courts must guard. We emphasize that the LAD is remedial legislation. Its very purpose is to change existing standards of conduct. Thus, the reasonableness requirement must not be used to hold that the prevailing level of discrimination is per se reasonable, or that a reasonable woman would expect sexual harassment on entering a historically male-dominated workplace. The LAD is designed to remediate conditions of hostility and discrimination, not to preserve and immunize pre-existing hostile work environments.

Thirdly, we choose an objective rather than a subjective viewpoint because the purpose of the LAD is to eliminate real discrimination and harassment. "It would not serve the goals of gender equality to credit a perspective that was pretextual or wholly idiosyncratic." Kathryn Abrams, Gender Discrimination and the Transformation of Workplace Norms, 42 Vand.L.Rev. 1183, 1210 (1989). A hypersensitive employee might have an idiosyncratic response to conduct that is not, objectively viewed, harassing. Allegations of such non-harassing conduct do not state a claim, even if the idiosyncratic plaintiff perceives her workplace to be hostile, because the complained-of conduct, objectively viewed, is not harassment, and the workplace, objectively viewed, is not hostile.

Conversely, an extraordinarily tough and resilient plaintiff might face harassing conduct that was, objectively viewed, sufficiently severe or pervasive to make the working environment hostile or intimidating, but because of her toughness, she might not personally find the workplace hostile or intimidating. Under our objective standard, such a plaintiff would state a claim even if she personally did not experience the workplace as hostile or intimidating. Sexual harassment is illegal even if the victim is strong enough not to be injured. Because such tough employees are perhaps the most likely to be strong enough to challenge harassers, the remedial purposes of the LAD are furthered by permitting claims by emotionally resilient plaintiffs without regard to subjective injury.

Of course, the subjective reaction of the plaintiff and her individual injuries remain relevant to compensatory damages. However, a plaintiff's subjective response is not an element of a hostile work environment sexual harassment cause of action.

We emphasize that only claims based on the idiosyncratic response of a hypersensitive plaintiff to conduct that is not objectively harassing would be barred by the reasonable woman standard. The category of reasonable women is diverse and includes both sensitive and tough people. A woman is not unreasonable merely because she falls toward the more sensitive side of the broad spectrum of reasonableness. Nor should "reasonable" be read as the opposite of "emotional." Perhaps because "reasonable" contains the word "reason," some have interpreted reasonableness as requiring a Vulcan-like rationality and absence of feeling. The reasonable woman standard should not be used to reject as unreasonable an emotional response to sexual harassment. On the contrary, such a response is normal and common. Only an idiosyncratic response of a hypersensitive plaintiff to conduct that a reasonable woman would not find harassing is excluded by the reasonable woman standard.

We turn now to our reasons for choosing a gender-specific standard. We believe that in order to fairly evaluate claims of sexual harassment, courts and finders of fact must recognize and respect the difference between male and female perspectives on sexual harassment. The reasonable person standard glosses over that difference, which is important here, and it also has a tendency to be male-biased, due to the tendency of courts and our society in general to view the male perspective as the objective or normative one.

Although there is far from a uniform female perspective on sexual harassment, nonetheless, the research and literature on sexual harassment suggest that there are differences in the way sexual conduct on the job is perceived by men and women. Kathryn Abrams argues that men consider sexual comments and conduct as "comparatively harmless amusement." Abrams, supra, 42 Vand.L.Rev. at 1203 (citing Barbara Gutek, Sex and the Workplace 47–54 (1985)). When sexual comments or conduct are directed at them, men are apt to find it harmless and perhaps even flattering, but they are unlikely to consider it insulting or intimidating. Id. at 1206. Women, on the other hand, are more likely to find sexual conduct and comments in the workplace offensive and intimidating. Ibid. Abrams is speaking here only about heterosexual sexual harassment; she notes that "[t]hese conclusions might be different if a man were harassed by a gay male employer or supervisor." Id. at 1206 n. 97. Indeed, our general observation of a current social debate suggests to us that many men find the prospect of sexual harassment by other men extremely insulting and intimidating and not at all a "comparatively harmless amusement."

Two societal realities may underlie the difference in male and female perspectives. First, women live in a world in which the possibility of sexual violence is ever-present. Given that background, women may find sexual conduct in an inappropriate setting threatening. As the Ellison court perspectively wrote,

> *because women are disproportionately victims of rape and sexual assault, women have a stronger incentive to be concerned with sexual behavior. Women who are victims of mild forms of sexual harassment may understandably worry whether a harasser's conduct is merely a prelude to violent sexual assault. Men, who are rarely victims of sexual assault, may view sexual conduct in a vacuum without a full appreciation of the social setting or the underlying threat of violence that a woman may perceive.*

[924 F.2d at 879.]

Second, in many areas of the workforce, women still represent a minority and are relatively recent entrants into the field. Because of their predominantly junior and minority status, for some women it is more difficult than it is for men to win credibility and respect from employers, coworkers, and clients or customers. That can make women's position in the workplace marginal or precarious from the start. Sexual harassment operates to further discredit the female employee by treating her as a sexual object rather than as a credible co-worker. That can both undermine the women's self-confidence and interfere with her ability to be perceived by others as a capable worker with the potential to advance and succeed. Abrams, supra, 42 Vand.L.Rev. at 1208–09. Because of women's different status in the workplace, conduct that may be "just a joke" for men may have far more serious implications for women.

Those and other differences between the experiences of men and women shape the different perspectives of men and women. Finders of fact applying the gender-specific reasonableness standard must understand and respect those different perspectives.

VII. Employer Liability

If a plaintiff establishes that she was sexually harassed by her supervisor, then the question remains whether the employer is vicariously liable for the supervisor's harassment. This case is the first to present the question of employer liability for sexual harassment since the LAD was amended in 1990 to provide that "all remedies available in common law tort actions shall be available to prevailing plaintiffs" in Superior Court actions. N.J.S.A. 10:5-13 (as amended by L.1990 c. 12). Prior to those amendments, although some compensatory relief (including damages for emotional distress resulting from discrimination) was available under the LAD, see, e.g., Jackson, supra, 54 N.J. at 125–28, 253 A.2d 793; Gray v. Serruto Builders, 110 N.J.Super. 297, 317, 265 A.2d 404 (Ch.Div.1970), the primary form of relief available was equitable in nature. See Shaner v. Horizon Bancorp, 116 N.J. 433, 436–37, 561 A.2d 1130 (1989).

Today, therefore, we must decide what standards to apply to assess employer liability not only for equitable remedies but also for compensatory damages and punitive damages. The Appellate Division unanimously agreed that employers should be strictly liable for all equitable damages and relief arising from hostile work environment claims, and that an employer should not be automatically liable for punitive damages resulting from hostile work environment sexual harassment by a supervisor. However, the Appellate Division was unable to agree on the employer's liability for compensatory damages in a supervisory hostile work environment claim. One judge would

250

impose strict liability on an employer for such compensatory damages, 255 N.J. Super. at 641, 605 A.2d 1125, while the others would apply principles of general agency law to determine the scope of an employer's liability in hostile work environment cases, id. at 644, 660, 605 A.2d 1125.

[12] When the LAD dealt primarily with equitable relief, there was little need to address the issue of employer liability for wrongful conduct of a supervisor. The LAD's remedial purpose of eliminating discrimination and harassment in the workplace was served by holding the employer directly responsible, without regard to fault, for restoring an aggrieved employee to the terms, conditions, and privileges of employment the employee would have enjoyed but for the workplace discrimination or harassment. For the remedial purpose of the LAD to be fulfilled, the employer must take action, because generally the employer is the party with the power and responsibility to hire, promote, reinstate, provide back pay, and take other remedial action. Likewise, only the employer can impose prospective measures to prevent future discrimination and harassment in the workplace. For those reasons, both the courts and the Director of the Division on Civil Rights have imposed liability for equitable relief directly on employers. We see no reason to alter that sound policy. Therefore, we reaffirm that in cases of supervisory sexual harassment, whether the harassment is of the quid pro quo or the hostile work environment type, the employer is directly and strictly liable for all equitable damages and relief. Equitable damages may include hiring or reinstating the harassment victim, disciplining, transferring, or firing the harasser, providing back pay and/or front pay, and taking preventative and remedial measures at the workplace. This list is not intended to be exclusive.

However, different considerations apply to determine the proper standards of employer liability for compensatory and punitive damages. Unlike the situation with equitable damages, the employer is not necessarily the only one capable of providing compensatory relief and is not necessarily the party whose conduct is sufficiently outrageous to warrant punitive damages. Moreover, the Legislature, in amending the LAD to allow "all remedies available in common law tort actions," implied that "common law rules of liability," including general principles of agency law" should apply. Lehmann v. Toys 'R' Us, supra, 255 N.J.Super. at 660, 605 A.2d 1125 (Skillman, J.A.D., dissenting). Using agency law to govern employer liability for compensatory damages in also consistent with the United States Supreme Court's directive that agency principles be applied in Title VII cases.

In Meritor Savings Bank v. Vinson, supra, a majority of the Supreme Court rejected the rule of automatic strict liability for supervisory sexual harassment in hostile work environment cases. Although the majority declined "to issue a definitive rule on employer liability," it suggested that "Congress wanted courts to look to agency principles for guidance in this area." 477 U.S. at 72, 106, S.Ct. at 2408, 91 L.Ed.2d at 63. The majority wrote:

> *While such common-law principles may not be transferable in all their particulars to Title VII, Congress' decision to define "employer" to include any "agent" of an employer surely evinces an intent to place some limits on the acts of employees for which employers under Title VII are to be held responsible. For this reason, we hold that the Court of Appeals erred in concluding that employers are always automatically liable for sexual harassment by their supervisors. See generally Restatement (Second) of Agency §§ 219–237 (1958).*

[Ibid.]

The majority did not expand on how agency principles would be applied to sexual harassment cases. However, later lower court cases have interpreted Meritor as holding that employer liability is governed by strict liability in quid pro quo cases and by agency principles in hostile work environment cases.

Justice Marshall wrote a separate concurring opinion in Meritor, in which Justices Brennan, Blackmun, and Stevens joined. The minority would have adopted the strict liability standard. 477 U.S. at 74, 106 S.Ct. at 2409, 91 L.Ed.2d at 64 (citing 29 C.F.R. § 1604.11(c) (emphasis added)). The concurrence rejected the distinction between quid pro quo and hostile work environment cases urged by the Solicitor General. The minority found that position "untenable," explaining that

> *[a] supervisor's responsibilities do not begin and end with the power to hire, fire, and discipline employees, or with the power to recommend such actions. Rather, a supervisor is charged with the day-to-day supervision of the work environment and with ensuring a safe, productive workplace. There is no reason why abuse of the latter authority should have different consequences than abuse of the former. In both cases it is the authority vested in the supervisor by the employer that enables him to commit the wrong: it is precisely because the supervisor is understood to be clothed with the employer's authority that he is able to impose unwelcome sexual conduct on subordinates.*

[Id. at 76–77, 106 S.Ct. at 2410, 91 L.Ed.2d at 65–66 (Marshall, J., concurring).]

Justice Stevens also joined in the majority opinion. He wrote a separate concurrence, which stated in its entirely: "Because I do not see any inconsistency between the two opinions, and because I believe the question of statutory construction that Justice Marshall has answered is fairly presented by the record, I join both the Court's opinion and Justice Marshall's opinion." Id. at 73, 106 S.Ct. 2409, 91 L.Ed.2d at 64.

[13] We agree with Justice Stevens that there is no inherent contradiction between the majority's adoption of agency principles and Justice Marshall's

observation that a supervisor's delegated authority often goes beyond the power to hire and fire. We are satisfied that agency principles are sufficiently well-established to provide employers with notice of their potential liability and also sufficiently flexible to provide just results in the great variety of factual circumstances presented by sexual harassment cases and to accomplish the purposes of the LAD. Accordingly, we hold that employer liability for supervisory hostile work environment sexual harassment shall be governed by agency principles.

Section 219 of the Restatement (Second) of Agency outlines the liability of a master for the torts of a servant.

> *(1) A master is subject to liability for the torts of his servant committed while acting in the scope of their employment.*
>
> *(2) A master is not subject to liability for the torts of his servants acting outside the scope of their employment, unless:*
> *(a) the master intended the conduct or the consequences, or*
> *(b) the master was negligent or reckless, or*
> *(c) the conduct violated a non-delegable duty of the master, or*
> *(d) the servant purported to act or to speak on behalf of the principal and there was reliance upon apparent authority, or he was aided in accomplishing the tort by the existence of the agency relation.*

[14] Applying those principles, we declare that under § 219(1) an employer, whose supervisory employee is acting within the scope of his or her employment, will be liable for the supervisor's conduct in creating a hostile work environment. Moreover, even in the more common situation in which the supervisor is acting outside the scope of his or her employment, the employer will be liable in most cases for the supervisor's behavior under the exceptions set forth in § 219(2). For example, if an employer delegates the authority to control the work environment to a supervisor and that supervisor abuses that delegated authority, then vicarious liability under § 219(2)(d) will follow. See Katherine S. Anderson, Note, Employer Liability Under Title VII for Sexual Harassment After Meritor Savings Bank v. Vinson, 87 Colum.L.Rev. 1258, 1274 (1987) (suggesting vicarious liability may follow from agency principles when supervisor acts as "employer's surrogate in the day-to-day management of his subordinates"); see also Note, Sexual Harassment Claims of Abusive Work Environment Under Title VII, 97 Harv.L.Rev. 1449, 1461 (1984) (arguing that where employer gives supervisor the power to "structur[e] the work environment—setting a tone and disciplining offenders," employer is vicariously liable for supervisor's abuse of that authority to create hostile work environment).

The determination of whether a supervisor who creates a hostile work environment was aided in accomplishing that tort by the power delegated to him or her to control the day-to-day working environment requires a detailed fact-specific analysis. Specifically, the finder of fact must decide:

1. Did the employer delegate the authority to the supervisor to control the situation of which the plaintiff complains * * * ?
2. Did the supervisor exercise that authority?
3. Did the exercise of authority result in a violation of [the LAD]?
4. Did the authority delegated by the employer to the supervisor aid the supervisor in injuring the plaintiff?

[Bruce Chandler Smith, When Should an Employer Be Held Liable For The Sexual Harassment by a Supervisor Who Creates a Hostile Work Environment? A Proposed Theory of Liability, 19 Ariz.St.L.J. 285, 321 (1987).]

When the answer to each of those questions is yes, then the employer is vicariously liable for the supervisor's harassment under § 219(2)(d).

Another basis for employer liability under agency law is negligence, as set forth in § 219(2)(b). While we decline to set forth a standard of negligence governing sexual harassment claims, we note that common sense suggests that sexual harassment at the workplace is foreseeable, even where anti-harassment policies exist. Although estimates of the incidence of sexual harassment in the workplace vary, all estimates indicate that the problem is widespread. Estimates include: 53% of women having experienced sexual harassment at some point, Abrams, supra, 42 Vand.L.Rev. at 1197–98; 50% of women and 15% of men, Lipsett, supra, 864 F.2d at 898; 42% of women and 15% of men employed by the federal government, U.S. Merit Systems Protection Board, Sexual Harassment in the Federal Workplace: Is It a Problem? 3 (1981); 15% of women and 5% of men each year, The Civil Rights Act of 1991: Hearings on H.R. 1 Before the House Committee on Education and Labor, 102nd Cong., 1st Sess. 168 (1991) (statement of Dr. Freada Klein).

In light of the known prevalence of sexual harassment, plaintiff may show that an employer was negligent by its failure to have in place well-publicized and enforced anti-harassment policies, effective formal and informal complaint structures, training, and/or monitoring mechanisms. We do not hold that the absence of such mechanisms automatically constitutes negligence, nor that the presence of such mechanisms demonstrates the absence of negligence. However, the existence of effective preventative mechanisms provides some evidence of due care on the part of the employer.

Employers that effectively and sincerely put five elements into place are successful at surfacing sexual harassment complaints early, before they escalate. The five elements are: policies, complaint structures, and that includes both formal and informal structures; training, which has to be mandatory for supervisors and managers and needs to be offered for all members of the organization; some effective sensing or monitoring mechanisms, to find out if the policies and complaint structures are trusted; and then, finally, an unequivocal commitment from the top that is not just in words but backed up by consistent practice.

[Klein, supra, at 171.]

Similarly, given the foreseeability that sexual harassment may occur, the absence of effective preventative mechanisms will present strong evidence of an employer's negligence.

Employer liability through agency law may also be found under § 219(2)(a) if the employer intended the conduct. If a plaintiff can show that an employer had actual knowledge of the harassment and did not promptly and effectively act to stop it, liability under that section may be appropriate. However, such conduct would also more clearly qualify as negligence or recklessness, thus triggering liability under § 219(2)(b).

Federal courts have used agency principles to hold employers liable for the acts of their supervisors, even when the acts are outside the scope of employment, in a number of circumstances. In many cases, the courts appear to find vicarious liability using a negligence rubric. Those cases speak of the employer's constructive knowledge and its absence of effective grievance procedures. See EEOC v. Hacienda Hotel, 881 F.2d 1504, 1516 (9th Cir.1989) (holding employer liable and imputing constructive knowledge to employer because if reasonable care exercised, employer should have known about harassment); Yates v. Avco Corp., 819 F.2d 630, 636 (6th Cir.1987) (finding that harassment was foreseeable and that management should have known about it on reasonably diligent inquiry); Robinson, supra, 760 F.Supp. at 1531 (imputing constructive knowledge to employer because acts of harassment were "too pervasive to have escaped the notice of reasonably alert management").

Other Title VII cases suggest that the basis for finding vicarious liability through agency law was intent, under§ 219(2)(b), or, more probably, apparent authority, under § 219(2)(d). In those cases, the harassed employees reasonably believed that the harassment was tolerated by upper management. See Yates, supra, 819 F.2d at 635–36 (vicarious liability where employees had substantiated belief that grievance procedure was ineffective and harasser's conduct tolerated by management). The EEOC's Policy Guidance on Current Issues of Sexual Harassment, 8 Lab.Rel.Rep. (BNA) ¶ 405.6682 (1990), would apply the Restatement § 219(2)(d) to those situations in which there was an inadequate harassment policy, or a policy was improperly enforced.

If the employer has not provided an effective avenue to complain, then the supervisor has unchecked, final control over the victim and it is reasonable to impute his abuse of this power to the employer. The Commission generally will find an employer liable for "hostile environment" sexual harassment by a supervisor when the employer failed to establish *environment" sexual harassment by a supervisor when the employer failed to establish an explicit policy against sexual harassment and did not have a reasonably available avenue by which victims of sexual harassment could complain to someone with authority to investigate and remedy the problem.*

Both of those situations could give rise to a reasonable inference that the supervisor's harassing conduct was tacitly approved by upper management, thus triggering liability under § 219(2)(d).

Although an employer's liability for sexual harassment of which the employer knew or should have known can be seen to flow from agency law, it also can be understood as direct liability. When an employer knows or should know of the harassment and fails to take effective measures to stop it, the employer has joined with the harasser in making the working environment hostile. The employer, by failing to take action, sends the harassed employee the message that the harassment is acceptable and that the management supports the harasser. See Anderson, supra, 87 Colum.L.Rev. at 1274–75. "Effective" remedial measures are those reasonably calculated to end the harassment. The "reasonableness of an employer's remedy will depend on its ability to stop harassment by the person who engaged in harassment." Ellison, supra, 924 F.2d at 882.

We recognize that although we have declined to hold employers strictly liable for hostile work environment sexual harassment by supervisors, we have created a standard that may often result in employers being held vicariously liable for such harassment. We note that there is an important difference between strict liability and vicarious liability under agency law. Under a strict liability standard, an employer would always be liable for supervisory hostile work environment sexual harassment, regardless of the specific facts of the case. We think that in some cases strict liability would be unjust—for example, "where a supervisor rapes one of his subordinates in the workplace." Lehmann v. Toys 'R' Us, supra, 255 N.J.Super. at 661, 605 A.2d 1125 (Skillman, J.A.D., dissenting).

Under agency law, an employer's liability for a supervisor's sexual harassment will depend on the facts of the case. An employer will be found vicariously liable if the supervisor acted within the scope of his or her employment. Moreover, even if the supervisor acted outside the scope of his or her employment, the employer will be vicariously liable if the employer contributed to the harm through its negligence, intent, or apparent authorization of the harassing conduct, or if the supervisor was aided in the commission of the harassment by the agency relationship. Thus, an employer can be held liable for compensatory damages stemming from a supervisor's creation of a hostile work environment if the employer grants the supervisor the authority to control the working environment and the supervisor abuses that authority to create a hostile work environment. An employer may also be held vicariously liable for compensatory damages for supervisory sexual harassment that occurs outside the scope of the supervisor's authority, if the employer had actual or constructive notice of the harassment, or even if the employer did not have actual or constructive notice, if the employer negligently or recklessly failed to have an explicit policy that bans sexual harassment and that provides an effective procedure for the prompt investigation and remediation of such claims.

[15] Concerning punitive damages, we agree with the Appellate Division that a greater threshold than mere negligence should be applied to measure employer liability. Punitive damages are to be awarded "when the wrongdoer's conduct is especially egregious." Leimgruber v. Claridge Assocs., 73 N.J. 450, 454, 375 A.2d 652 (1977). Hence, the employer should be liable for punitive damages only in the event of actual participation by upper management or willful indifference. Shrout v. Black Clawson Co., 689 F.Supp. 774 (S.D.Ohio 1988) (finding that under Ohio law, employer can be liable for punitive damages for sexual harassment by supervisor where employer ratified, participated in, or acquiesced in wrongdoing); Security Aluminum Window Mfg. v. Lehmann Assocs., 108 N.J.Super. 137, 146, 260 A.2d 248 (App.Div.1970); Winkler v. Hartford Accident and Indem. Co., 66 N.J.Super. 22, 29, 168 A.2d 418 (App.Div.) (holding that "[e]xemplary damages may not be recovered against an employer for the wrongful act of an employee, unless the act was specifically authorized, participated in, or ratified by the master"), certif. denied, 34 N.J. 581, 170 A.2d 544 (1961); Kay v. Peter Motor Co., 483 N.W.2d 481, 485 (Minn.App.1992) (holding punitive damages appropriate only when employer's "willful indifference" to misconduct proven).

Essentially, we view the issue of the scope of an employer's liability for compensatory and punitive damages as a question of public policy. Arguments abound on both sides of the issue. We view the crucial issue to be which position provides the most effective intervention and prevention of employment discrimination. The Attorney General, representing the New Jersey Division on Civil Rights, recommends that general agency principles of common law be applied. The Division on Civil Rights, as the agency that enforces the LAD, is entitled to great deference, especially when its position is supported by the statutory language and is consistent with the history of the LAD and in conformity with the United States Supreme Court and most courts that have discussed this issue. Courtrooms are not the best place to prevent or remedy a hostile work environment.

Litigation is vastly disruptive of the plaintiffs' relations with others in the workplace. Such disruption occurs even in areas of employment discrimination in which plaintiffs' allegations are less emotionally charged than in the context of sexual harassment. The sexual harassment plaintiff typically is subjected to further or intensified harassment as she pursues her claim, and her relationships with both men and women in the workplace may be severed beyond repair, a form of damage that even legal victory cannot undo. Moreover, changes in behavior that are compelled by judicial decree, rather than voluntarily introduced and advocated by the employer, may produce lingering resentment among male workers that affects not only their receptivity to subsequent female coworkers, but also their behavior toward the other women in their lives. Strategies to end sexual harassment should not require all women to make the difficult choice between enduring continued harassment and seeking costly victory in the courts.

Litigation can also be a comparatively blunt tool for producing changes in workplace norms. Judgments—and even opinions—in sexual harassment cases give employers only an anecdotal notion of what behavior is unacceptable, and otherwise fail to direct employers toward more satisfactory behavior. Nor do these decisions, in and of themselves, organize or educate employees to produce the necessary changes in conduct. An adverse judgment also may put supervisors on the defensive, rather than engaging them as participants in bringing about change. For the protection of women and the education of those who victimize them, it is necessary to explore less coercive means of normative change.

[Abrams, supra, 42 Vand.L.Rev. at 1183 (footnotes omitted)]

The most important tool in the prevention of sexual harassment is the education of both employees and employers. Consensus among employees and employers should be the goal. We think that providing employers with the incentive not only to provide voluntary compliance programs but also to insist on the effective enforcement of their programs will do much to ensure that hostile work environment discrimination claims disappear from the workplace and the courts.

To summarize, in determining an employer's liability for compensatory and punitive damages when an employee raises a hostile work environment discrimination claim against a supervisor, a three-part standard should be employed. First, strict liability should apply for relief that is equitable in nature. Second, agency principles, which include negligence, should be applied to decide if an employer is liable for compensatory damages that exceed that equitable relief. Third, a higher level of culpability than mere negligence should be required for punitive damages. The issue of Toys 'R' Us's liability should not have been dismissed on a summary judgment motion. On remand, its liability must be reassessed.

VIII. Conclusion

The judgment of the Appellate Division is affirmed as modified. The matter is remanded for findings of fact and further proceedings consistent with this opinion.

For modification, affirmance and remandment —Chief Justice WILENTZ, and Justices CLIFFORD, O'HERN, GARIBALDI and STEIN—5.

Opposed —None.

APPENDIX J

U.S. SUPREME COURT RULING: MERITOR SAVINGS BANK V. VINSON

MERITOR SAVINGS BANK, FSB,
Petitioner

v.

Mechelle VINSON et al.
No. 84-1979.

Argued March 25, 1986.
Decided June 19, 1986.
REHNQUIST, J., delivered the opinion of the Court, in which BURGER, C.J., and WHITE, POWELL, STEVENS, and O'CONNOR, JJ., joined. STEVENS, J., filed a concurring opinion, post. p. —-, MARSHALL, J., filed an opinion concurring in the judgment, in which BRENNAN, BLACK-MUN, and STEVENS, JJ., joined post, p. —-.

F. Robert Troll, Jr., Hyattville, Md., for petitioner.

Patricia J. Barry, Grover City, Cal, for respondents.

Justice REHNQUIST delivered the opinion of the Court.

This case presents important questions concerning claims of workplace "sexual harassment" brought under Title VII of the Civil Rights Act of 1964, 78 Stat. 253, as amended, 42 U.S.C. § 2000e et seq.

I

In 1974, respondent Mechelle Vinson met Sidney Taylor, a vice president of what is now petitioner Meritor Savings Bank (bank) and manager of one of its branch offices. When respondent asked whether she might obtain employment at the bank, Taylor gave her an application, which she completed and returned the next day; later that same day Taylor called her to say that she had been hired. With Taylor as her supervisor, respondent started as a teller-trainee, and thereafter was promoted to teller, head teller, and assistant branch manager. She worked at the same branch for four years, and it is undisputed that her advancement there was based on merit alone. In September 1978, respondent notified Taylor that she was taking sick leave for an indefinite period. On November 1, 1978, the bank discharged her for excessive use of that leave.

Respondent brought this action against Taylor and the bank, claiming that during her four years at the bank she had "constantly been subjected to sexual harassment" by Taylor in violation of Title VII. She sought injunctive relief, compensatory and punitive damages against Taylor and the bank, and attorney's fees.

At the 11-day bench trial, the parties presented conflicting testimony about Taylor's behavior during respondent's employment. [FN] Respondent testified that during her probationary period as a teller-trainee, Taylor treated her in a fatherly way and made no sexual advances. Shortly thereafter, however, he invited her out to dinner and, during the course of the meal, suggested that they go to a motel to have sexual relations. At first she refused, but out of what she described as fear of losing her job she eventually agreed. According to respondent, Taylor thereafter made repeated demands upon her for sexual favors, usually at the branch, both during and after business hours; she estimated that over the next several years she had intercourse with him some 40 or 50 times. In addition, respondent testified that Taylor fondled her in front of other employees, followed her into the women's restroom when she went there alone, exposed himself to her, and even forcibly raped her on several occasions. These activities ceased after 1977, respondent stated, when she started going with a steady boyfriend.

> *FN Like the Court of Appeals, this Court was not provided a complete transcript of the trial. We therefore rely largely on the District Court's opinion for the summary of the relevant testimony.*

Respondent also testified that Taylor touched and fondled other women employees of the bank, and she attempted to call witnesses to support this charge. But while some supporting testimony apparently was admitted without objection, the District Court did not allow her "to present wholesale evidence of a pattern and practice relating to sexual advances to other female employees in her case in chief, but advised her that she might well be able to present such evidence in rebuttal to the defendants' cases." Vinson v. Taylor, 22 EPD ¶ 30,708, p. 14,693, n. 1, 23 FEP Cases 37, 38–39, n. 1 (DC 1980). Respondent did not offer such evidence in rebuttal. Finally, respondent testified that because she was afraid of Taylor she never reported his harassment to any of his supervisors and never attempted to use the bank's complaint procedure.

Taylor denied respondent's allegations of sexual activity, testifying that he never fondled her, never made suggestive remarks to her, never engaged in sexual intercourse with her, and never asked her to do so. He contended instead that respondent made her accusations in response to a business-related dispute.

The bank also denied respondent's allegations and asserted that any sexual harassment by Taylor was unknown to the bank and engaged in without its consent or approval.

The District Court denied relief, but did not resolve the conflicting testimony about the existence of a sexual relationship between respondent and Taylor. If found instead that

> "[i]f [respondent] and Taylor did engage in an intimate or sexual relationship during the time of [respondent's] employment with [the bank], that relationship was a voluntary one having nothing to do with her continued employment at [the bank] or her advancement or promotions at that institution." Id., at 14,692 23 FEP Cases, at 42 (footnote omitted).

The court ultimately found that respondent "was not the victim of sexual harassment and was not the victim of sexual discrimination" while employed at the bank. Ibid., 23 FEP Cases, 43.

Although it concluded that respondent had not proved a violation of Title VII, the District Court nevertheless went on to address the bank's liability. After noting the bank's express policy against discrimination, and finding that neither respondent nor any other employee had ever lodged a complaint about sexual harassment by Taylor, the court ultimately concluded that "the bank was without notice and cannot be held liable for the alleged actions of Taylor." Id., at 14,691 23 FEP Cases, at 42.

The Court of Appeals for the District of Columbia Circuit reversed. 243 U.S.App.D.C. 323 753 F.2d 141 (1985). Relying on its earlier holding in Bundy v. Jackson, 205 U.S.App.D.C. 444, 641 F.2d 934 (1981), decided after the trial in this case, the court stated that a violation of Title VII may be predicated on either of two types of sexual harassment: harassment that involves the conditioning of concrete employment benefits on sexual favors, and harassment that, while not affecting economic benefits, creates a hostile or offensive working environment. The court drew additional support for this position from the Equal Employment Opportunity Commission's Guidelines on Discrimination Because of Sex, 29 CFR § 1604.11(a) (1985), which set out these two types of sexual harassment claims. Believing that "Vinson's grievance was clearly of the [hostile environment] type," 243 U.S.App.D.C., at 327, 753 F.2d, at 145, and that the District Court had not considered whether a violation of this type had occurred, the court concluded that a remand was necessary.

The court further concluded that the District Court's finding that any sexual relationship between respondent and Taylor "was a voluntary one" did not obviate the need for a remand. "[U]ncertain as to precisely what the [district] court meant" by this finding, the Court of Appeals held that if the evidence otherwise showed that "Taylor made Vinson's toleration of sexual harassment a condition of her employment," her voluntariness "had not materiality whatsoever." Id., at 328, 753 F.2d, at 146. The court then surmised that the District Court's finding of voluntariness might have been based on "the voluminous testimony regarding respondent's dress and personal fantasies," testimony that the Court of Appeals believed "had no place in this litigation." Id., at 328, n. 36, 753 F.2d, at 146, n. 36.

As to the bank's liability, the Court of Appeals held that an employer is absolutely liable for sexual harassment practiced by supervisory personnel, whether or not the employer knew or should have known about the misconduct. The court relied chiefly on Title VII's definition of "employer" to include "any agent of such a person," 42 U.S.C. § 2000e(b), as well as on the EEOC Guidelines. The court held that a supervisor is an "agent" of his employer for Title VII purposes, even if he lacks authority to hire, fire, or promote, since "the mere existence—or even the appearance—of a significant degree of influence in vital job decisions gives any supervisor the opportunity to impose on employees," 243 U.S.App.D.C., at 332, 753 F.2d, at 150.

In accordance with the foregoing, the Court of Appeals reversed the judgment of the District Court and remanded the case for further proceedings. A subsequent suggestion for rehearing en banc was denied, with three judges dissenting. 245 U.S.App.D.C. 306, 760 F.2d 1330 (1985). We granted certiorari, 474 U.S. 1047, 106 S.Ct. 57, 88 L.Ed.2d 46 (1985), and now affirm but for different reasons.

II

Title VII of the Civil Rights Act of 1964 makes it "an unlawful employment practice for an employer . . . to discriminate against any individual with respect to his compensation, terms, conditions, or privileges of employment, because of such individual's race, color, religion, sex, or national origin." 42 U.S.C. § 2000e-2(a)(1). The prohibition against discrimination based on sex was added to Title VII at the last minute on the floor of the House of Representatives. 110 Cong.Rec. 2577–2584 (1964), The principal argument in opposition to the amendment was that "sex discrimination" was sufficiently different from other types of discrimination that it ought to receive separate legislative treatment. See id., at 2577 (statement of Rep. Celler quoting letter from United States Department of Labor); id., at 2584 (statement of Rep. Green). This argument was defeated, the bill quickly passed as amended, and we are left with little legislative history to guide us in interpreting the Act's prohibition against discrimination based on "sex."

Respondent argues, and the Court of Appeals held, that unwelcome sexual advances that create an offensive or hostile working environment violate Title VII. Without question, when a supervisor sexually harasses a subordinate because of the subordinate's sex, that supervisor "discriminate[s]" on the basis of sex. Petitioner apparently does not challenge this proposition. It contends instead that in prohibiting discrimination with respect to "compensation, terms, conditions, or privileges" of employment, Congress was concerned with what petitioner describes as "tangible loss" of "an economic character," not "purely psychological aspects of the workplace environment." Brief for Petitioner 30–31, 34. In support of this claim petitioner observes that in both the legislative history of Title VII and this Court's Title VII decisions, the focus has been on tangible, economic barriers erected by discrimination.

We reject petitioner's view. First, the language of Title VII is not limited to "economic" or "tangible" discrimination. The phrase "terms, condition, or privileges of employment" evinces a congressional intent" 'to strike at the entire spectrum of disparate treatment of men and women" in employment. Los Angeles Dept. of Water and Power v. Manhart, 435 U.S. 702, 707, n. 13, 98 S.Ct. 1370, 1375, n. 13, 55 L.Ed.2d 657 (1978), quoting Sprogis v. United Air Lines, Inc., 444 F.2d 1194, 1198 (CA7 1971). Petitioner has pointed to nothing in the Act to suggest that Congress contemplated the limitation urged here.

Second, in 1980 the EEOC issued Guidelines specifying that "sexual harassment," as there defined, is a form of sex discrimination prohibited by Title VII. As an "administrative interpretation of the Act by the enforcing agency," Griggs v. Duke Power Co., 401 U.S. 424, 433–434, 91 S.Ct. 849, 855, 28 L.Ed.2d 158 (1971), these Guidelines, "'while not controlling upon the courts by reason of their authority, do constitute a body of experience and informed judgment to which courts and litigants may properly resort for guidance,'" General Electric Co. v. Gilbert, 429 U.S. 125, 141–142, 97 S.Ct. 401, 410–411, 50 L.Ed.2d 343 (1976), quoting Skidmore v. Swift & Co., 323 U.S. 134, 140, 65 S.Ct. 161, 164, 89 L.Ed.2d 124 (1944). The EEOC Guidelines fully support the view that harassment leading to noneconomic injury can violate Title VII.

In defining "sexual harassment," the Guidelines first describe the kinds of workplace conduct that may be actionable under Title VII. These include "[u]nwelcome sexual advances, requests for sexual favors, and other verbal or physical conduct of a sexual nature." 29 CFR § 1604.11(a) (1985). Relevant to the charges at issue in this case, the Guidelines provide that such sexual misconduct constitutes prohibited "sexual harassment," whether or not it is directly linked to the grant or denial of an economic quid pro quo, where "such conduct has the purpose or effect of unreasonably interfering with an individual's work performance or creating an intimidating, hostile, or offensive working environment."§ 1604.11(a)(3).

In concluding that so-called "hostile environment" (i.e., non quid pro quo) harassment violates Title VII, the EEOC drew upon a substantial body of

Appendices

judicial decisions and EEOC precedent holding that Title VII affords employees the right to work in an environment free from discriminatory intimidation, ridicule, and insult. See general 45 Fed.Reg. 74676 (1980). Rogers v. EEOC, 454 F.2d 234 (CA5 1971), cert. denied, 406 U.S. 957, 92 S.Ct. 2058, 32 L.Ed.2d 343 (1972), was apparently the first case to recognize a cause of action based upon a discriminatory work environment. In Rogers, the Court of Appeals for the Fifth Circuit held that a Hispanic complainant could establish a Title VII violation by demonstrating that her employer created an offensive work environment for employees by giving discriminatory service to its Hispanic clientele. The court explained that an employee's protections under Title VII extend beyond the economic aspects of employment:

> *"[T]he phrase 'terms, conditions or privileges of employment' in [Title VII] is an expansive concept which sweeps within its protective ambit the practice of creating a working environment heavily charged with ethnic or racial discrimination. . . . One can readily envision working environments so heavily polluted with discrimination as to destroy completely the emotional and psychological stability of minority group workers. . . ." 454 F.2d, at 238.*

Courts applied this principle to harassment based on race, e.g., Firefighters Institute for Racial Equality v. St. Louis, 549 F.2d 506, 514–515 (CA8), cert. denied sub nom. Banta v. United States, 434 U.S. 819, 98 S.Ct. 60, 54 L.Ed.2d 76 (1977); Gray v. Greyhound Lines, East, 178 U.S.App.D.C. 91, 98, 545 F.2d 169, 176 (1976), religion, e.g., Compston v. Borden, Inc., 424 F.Supp. 157 (SD Ohio 1976), and national origin, e.g., Cariddi v. Kansas City Chiefs Football Club, 568 F.2d 87, 88 (CA8 1977). Nothing in Title VII suggests that a hostile environment based on discriminatory sexual harassment should not be likewise prohibited. The Guidelines thus appropriately drew from, and were fully consistent with, the existing case law.

[1] Since the Guidelines were issued, courts have uniformly held, and we agree, that a plaintiff may establish a violation of Title VII by proving that discrimination based on sex has created a hostile or abusive work environment. As the Court of Appeals for the Eleventh Circuit wrote in Henson v. Dundee, 682 F.2d 897, 902 (1982):

> *"Sexual harassment which creates a hostile or offensive environment for members of one sex is every bit the arbitrary barrier to sexual equality at the workplace that racial harassment is to racial equality. Surely, a requirement that a man or woman run a gauntlet of sexual abuse in return for the privilege of being allowed to work and make a living can be as demeaning and disconcerting as the harshest of racial epithets."*

Accord, Katz v. Dole, 709 F.2d 251, 254–255 (CA4 1983); Bundy v. Jackson, 205 U.S.App.D.C., at 444–454, 641 F.2d, at 934–944; Zabkowicz v. West Bend Co., 589 F.Supp. 780 (ED. Wis.1984).

265

[2][3] Of course, as the courts in both Rogers and Henson recognized, not all workplace conduct that may be described as "harassment" affects a "term, condition, or privilege" of employment within the meaning of Title VII. See Rogers, v. EEOC, supra, at 238 ("mere utterance of an ethnic or racial epithet which engenders offensive feelings in an employee" would not affect the conditions of employment to sufficiently significant degree to violate Title VII); Henson, 682 F.2d, at 904 (quoting same). For sexual harassment to be actionable, it must be sufficiently severe or pervasive "to alter the conditions of [the victim's] employment and create an abusive working environment." Ibid. Respondent's allegations in this case—which include not only pervasive harassment but also criminal conduct of the most serious nature—are plainly sufficient to state a claim for "hostile environment" sexual harassment.

[4][5] The question remains, however, whether the District Court's ultimate finding that respondent "was not the victim of sexual harassment," 22 EPD ¶ 30,708, at 14,692–14,693, 23 FEP Cases, at 43, effectively disposed of respondent's claim. The Court of Appeals recognized, we think correctly, that this ultimate finding was likely based on one or both of two erroneous views of the law. First, the District Court apparently believed that a claim for sexual harassment will not lie absent an economic effect on the complainant's employment. See ibid. ("It is without question that sexual harassment of female employees in which they are asked or required to submit to sexual demands as a condition to obtain employment or to maintain employment or to obtain promotions falls within protection of Title VII") (emphasis added). Since it appears that the District Court made its findings without ever considering the "hostile environment" theory of sexual harassment, the Court of Appeals' decision to remand was correct.

[6] Second, the District Court's conclusion that no actionable harassment occurred might have rested on its earlier "finding" that "[i]f [respondent] and Taylor did engage in an intimate or sexual relationship . . ., that relationship was a voluntary one." Id., at 14,692, 23 FEP Cases, at 42. But the fact that sex-related conduct was "voluntary," in the sense that the complainant was not forced to participate against her will, is not a defense to a sexual harassment suit brought under Title VII. The gravamen of any sexual harassment claim is that the alleged sexual advances were "unwelcome." 29 CFR § 1604.11(a) (1985). While the question whether particular conduct was indeed unwelcome presents difficult problems of proof and turns largely on credibility determinations committed to the trier of fact, the District Court in this case erroneously focused on the "voluntariness" of respondent's participation in the claimed sexual episodes. The correct inquiry is whether respondent by her conduct indicated that the alleged sexual advances were unwelcome, not whether her actual participation in sexual intercourse was voluntary.

[7][8] Petitioner contents that even if this case must be remanded to the District Court, the Court of Appeals erred in one of the terms of its remand. Specifically, the Court of Appeals stated that testimony about respondent's "dress and personal fantasies." 243 U.S.App.D.C., at 328, n. 36, 753 F.2d, at 146 n. 36, which the District Court apparently admitted into evidence, "had no place in this litigation." Ibid. The apparent ground for this conclusion was that respondent's voluntariness vel non in submitting to Taylor's advances was immaterial to her sexual harassment claim. While "voluntariness" in the sense of consent is not a defense to such a claim, it does not follow that a complainant's sexually provocative speech or dress is irrelevant as a matter of law in determining whether he or she found particular sexual advances unwelcome. To the contrary, such evidence is obviously relevant. The EEOC Guidelines emphasize that the trier of fact must determine the existence of sexual harassment in light of "the record as a whole" and "the totality of circumstances, such as the nature of the sexual advances and the context in which the alleged incidents occurred." 29 CFR § 1604.11(b) (1985). Respondent's claim that any marginal relevance of the evidence in question was outweighed by the potential for unfair prejudice is the sort of argument properly addressed to the District Court. In this case the District Court concluded that the evidence should be admitted, and the Court of Appeals' contrary conclusion was based upon the erroneous, categorical view that testimony about provocative dress and publicly expressed sexual fantasies "had no place in this litigation." 243 U.S.App.D.C., at 328, n. 36, 753 F.2d, at 146, n. 36. While the District Court must carefully weigh the applicable considerations in deciding whether to admit evidence of this kind, there is no per se rule against its admissibility.

III

Although the District Court concluded that respondents had not proved a violation of Title VII, it nevertheless went on to consider the question of the bank's liability. Finding that "the bank was without notice" of Taylor's alleged conduct, and that notice to Taylor was not the equivalent of notice to the bank, the court concluded that the bank therefore could not be held liable for Taylor's alleged actions. The Court of Appeals took the opposite view, holding that an employer is strictly liable for a hostile environment created by a supervisor's sexual advances, even though the employer neither knew nor reasonably could have known of the alleged misconduct. The court held that a supervisor, whether or not he possesses the authority to hire, fire, or promote, is necessarily an "agent" of his employer for all Title VII purposes, since "even the appearance" of such authority may enable him to impose himself on his subordinates.

The parties and amici suggest several different standards for employer liability. Respondent, not surprisingly, defends the position of the Court of

Appeals. Noting that Title VII's definition of "employer" includes any "agent" of the employer, she also argues that "so long as the circumstance is work-related, the supervisor is the employer and the employer is the supervisor." Brief for Respondent 27. Notice to Taylor that the advances were unwelcome, therefore, was notice to the bank.

Petitioner argues that respondent's failure to use its established grievance procedure, or to otherwise put in on notice of the alleged misconduct, insulates petitioner from liability for Taylor's wrongdoing. A contrary rule would be unfair, petitioner argues, since in a hostile environment harassment case the employer often will have no reason to know about, or opportunity to cure, the alleged wrongdoing.

The EEOC, in its brief as amicus curiae, contends that courts formulating employer liability rules should draw from traditional agency principles. Examination of those principles has led the EEOC to the view that where a supervisor exercises the authority actually delegated to him by his employer, by making or threatening to make decisions affecting the employment status of his subordinates, such actions are properly imputed to the employer whose delegation of authority empowered the supervisor to undertake them. Brief for United States and EEOC as Amici Curiae 22. Thus, the courts have consistently held employers liable for the discriminatory discharges of employees by supervisory personnel, whether or not the employer knew, should have known, or approved of the supervisor's actions. E.g., Anderson v. Methodist Evangelical Hospital, Inc., 464 F.2d 723, 725 (CA6 1972).

The EEOC suggests that when a sexual harassment claim rests exclusively on a "hostile environment" theory, however, the usual basis for a finding of agency will often disappear. In that case, the EEOC believes, agency principles lead to

> *"a rule that asks whether a victim of sexual harassment had reasonably available an avenue of complaint regarding such harassment, and, if available and utilized, whether that procedure was reasonably responsive to the employee's complaint. If the employer has an expressed policy against sexual harassment and has implemented a procedure specifically designed to resolve sexual harassment claims, and if the victim does not take advantage of that procedure, the employer should be shielded from liability absent actual knowledge of the sexually hostile environment (obtained, e.g., by the filing of a charge with the EEOC or a comparable state agency). In all other cases, the employer will be liable if it has actual knowledge of the harassment or if, considering all the facts of the case, the victim in question had no reasonably available avenue for making his or her complaint known to appropriate management officials." Brief for United States and EEOC as Amici Curiae 26.*

As respondent points out, this suggested rule is in some tension with the EEOC Guidelines, which hold an employer liable for the acts of its agents without regard to notice. 29 CFR & 1604.11(c) (1985). The Guidelines do require, however, an "examin[ation of] the circumstances of the particular employment relationship and the job [f]unctions performed by the individual in determining whether an individual acts in either a supervisory or agency capacity." Ibid.

This debate over the appropriate standard for employer liability has a rather abstract quality about it given the state of the record in this case. We do not know at this stage whether Taylor made any sexual advances toward respondent at all, let alone whether those advances were unwelcome, whether they were sufficiently pervasive to constitute a condition of employment, or whether they were " so pervasive and so long continuing . . . that the employer must have become conscious of [them]," Taylor v. Jones, 653 F.2d 1193, 1197–1199 (CA8 1981) (holding employer liable for racially hostile working environment based on constructive knowledge).

[9][10] We therefore decline the parties' invitation to issue a definitive rule on employer liability, but we do agree with the EEOC that Congress wanted courts to look to agency principles for guidance in this area. While such common-law principles may not be transferable in all their particulars to Title VII, Congress' decision to define "employer" to include any "agent" of an employer, 42 U.S.C. § 2000e(b), surely evinces an intent to place some limits on the acts of employees for which employers under Title VII are to be held responsible. For this reason, we hold that the Court of Appeals erred in concluding that employers are always automatically liable for sexual harassment by their supervisors. See generally Restatement (Second) of Agency §§ 219–237 (1958). For the same reason, absence of notice to an employer does not necessarily insulate that employer from liability. Ibid.

[11] Finally, we reject petitioner's view that the mere existence of a grievance procedure and a policy against discrimination, coupled with respondent's failure to invoke that procedure, must insulate petitioner from liability. While those facts are plainly relevant, the situation before us demonstrates why they are not necessarily dispositive. Petitioner's general nondiscrimination policy did not address sexual harassment in particular, and thus did not alert employees to their employer's interest in correcting that form of discrimination. App. 25. Moreover, the bank's grievance procedure apparently required an employee to complain first to her supervisor, in this case Taylor. Since Taylor was the alleged perpetrator, it is not altogether surprising that respondent failed to invoke the procedure and report her grievance to him. Petitioner's contention that respondent's failure should insulate it from liability might be substantially stronger if its procedures were better calculated to encourage victims of harassment to come forward.

IV

In sum, we hold that a claim of "hostile environment" sex discrimination is actionable under Title VII, that the District Court's findings were insufficient to dispose of respondent's hostile environment claim, and that the District Court did not err in admitting testimony about respondent's sexually provocative speech and dress. As to employer liability, we conclude that the Court of Appeals was wrong to entirely disregard agency principles and impose absolute liability on employers for the acts of their supervisors, regardless of the circumstances of a particular case.

Accordingly, the judgment of the Court of Appeals reversing the judgment of the District Court is affirmed, and the case is remanded for further proceedings consistent with this opinion.

It is so ordered.

Justice STEVENS, concurring.

Because I do not see any inconsistency between the two opinions, and because I believe the question of statutory construction that Justice MARSHALL has answered is fairly presented by the record, I join both the Court's opinion and Justice MARSHALL's opinion.

Justice MARSHALL, with whom Justice BRENNAN, Justice BLACK-MUN, and Justice STEVENS join, concurring in the judgment.

I fully agree with the Court's conclusion that workplace sexual harassment is illegal, and violates Title VII. Part III of the court's opinion, however, leaves open the circumstances in which an employer is responsible under Title VII for such conduct. Because I believe that question to be properly before us, I write separately.

The issue the Court declines to resolve is addressed in the EEOC Guidelines on Discrimination Because of Sex, which are entitled to great deference. See Griggs v. Duke Power Co., 401 U.S. 424 433–434, 91 S.Ct. 849, 854–55, 28 L.Ed.2d 158 (1971) (EEOC Guidelines on Employment Testing Procedures of 1966); see also ante, at 2404. The Guidelines explain:

"Applying general Title VII principles, an employer . . . is responsible for its acts and those of its agents and supervisory employees with respect to sexual harassment regardless of whether the specific acts complained of were authorized or even forbidden by the employer and regardless of whether the employer knew or should have known of their occurrence. The Commission will examine the circumstances of the particular employment relationship and the job [f]unctions performed by the individual in determining whether an individual acts in either a supervisory or agency capacity.

"With respect to conduct between fellow employees, an employer is responsible for acts of sexual harassment in the workplace where the employer (or its agents or supervisory employees) knows or should have known of the conduct, unless it can show that it took immediate and appropriate corrective action." 29 CFR §§ 1604.11(c), (d) (1985).

The Commission, in issuing the Guidelines, explained that its rule was "in keeping with the general standard of employer liability with respect to agents and supervisory employees. . . . [T]he Commission and the courts have held for years that an employer is liable if a supervisor or an agent violates the Title VII, regardless of knowledge or any other mitigating factor." 45 Fed.Reg. 74676 (1980). I would adopted the standard set out by the Commission.

An employer can act only through individual supervisors and employees; discrimination is rarely carried out pursuant to a formal vote of a corporation's board of directors. Although an employer may sometimes adopt companywide discriminatory policies violative of Title VII, acts that may constitute Title VII violations are generally effected through the actions of individuals, and often an individual may take such a step even in defiance of company policy. Nonetheless, Title VII remedies, such as reinstatement and backpay, generally run against the employer as an entity. [FN1] The question thus arises as to the circumstances under which an employer will be held liable under Title VII for the acts of its employees.

FN1. *The remedial provisions of the Title VII were largely modeled on those of the National Labor Relations Act (NLRA). See Albemarle Paper Co. v. Moody, 422 U.S. 405, 419, and n. 11, 95 S.Ct. 2362, 2372, and n. 11 (1975); see also Franks v. Bowman Transportation Co., 424 U.S. 747, 768–770, 96 S.Ct. 1251, 1266–67, 47 L.Ed.2d 444 (1976).*

The answer supplied by general Title VII law, like that supplied by federal labor law, is that the act of a supervisory employee or agent is imputed to the employer. [FN2] Thus, for example, when a supervisor discriminatorily fires or refuses to promote a black employee, that act is, without more, considered the act of the employer. The courts do not stop to consider whether the employer otherwise had "notice" of the action, or even whether the supervisor had actual authority to act as he did. E.g., Flowers v. Crouch-Walker Corp., 552 F.2d 1277, 1282 (CA7 1977); Young v. Southwestern Savings and Loan Assn., 509 F.2d 140 (CA5 1975); Anderson v. Methodist Evangelical Hospital, Inc., 464 F.2d 723 (CA6 1972). Following that approach, every Court of Appeals that has considered the issue has held that sexual harassment by supervisory personnel is automatically imputed to the employer when the harassment results in tangible job detriment to the subordinate employee. See Horn v. Duke Homes, Inc., Div. of Windsor Mobile Homes, 755 F.2d 599, 604–606 (CA7 1985); Craig v. Y & Y Snacks, Inc., 721 F.2d 77, 80–81 (CA3 1983); Katz v. Dole, 709 F.2d 251, 255, n. 6 (CA4 1983); Henson v. Dundee, 682 F.2d 897, 91 (CA11 1982); Miller v. Bank of America, 600 F.2d 211, 213 (CA9 1979).

FN2. *For NLRA cases, see, e.g., Graves Trucking, Inc. v. NLRB, 692 F.2d 470 (CA7 1982); NLRB v. Kaiser Agricultural Chemical, Division of Kaiser Aluminum & Chemical Corp., 473 F.2d 374, 384 (CA5 1973); Amalgamated Clothing Workers of America v. NLRB, 124 U.S.App.D.C. 365, 377, 365 F.2d 898, 909 (1966).*

The brief filed by the Solicitor General on behalf of the United States and EEOC in this case suggests that a different rule should apply when a supervisor's harassment "merely" results in a discriminatory work environment. The Solicitor General concedes that sexual harassment that affects tangible job benefits is an exercise of authority delegated to the supervisor by the employer, and thus gives rise to employer liability. But, departing from the EEOC Guidelines, he argues that the case of a supervisor merely creating a discriminatory work environment is different because the supervisor "is not exercising, or threatening to exercise, actual or apparent authority to make personnel decisions affecting the victim." Brief for United States and EEOC as Amici Curiae 24. In the latter situation, he concludes, some further notice requirement should therefore be necessary.

The Solicitor General's position is untenable. A supervisor's responsibilities do not begin and end with the power to hire, fire, and discipline employees, or with the power to recommend such actions. Rather, a supervisor is charged with the day-to-day supervision of the work environment and with ensuring a safe, productive workplace. There is no reason why abuse of the latter authority should have different consequences than abuse of the former. In both cases it is the authority vested in the supervisor by the employer that enables him to commit the wrong: it is precisely because the supervisor is understood to be clothed with the employer's authority that he is able to impose unwelcome sexual conduct on subordinates. There is therefore no justification for a special rule, to be applied only in "hostile environment" cases, that sexual harassment does not create employer liability until the employee suffering the discrimination notifies other supervisors. No such requirement appears in the statute, and no such requirement can coherently be drawn form the law of agency.

Agency principles and the goals of Title VII law make appropriate some limitation on the liability of employers for the acts of supervisors. Where, for example, a supervisor has no authority over an employee, because the two work in wholly different parts of the employer's business, it may be improper to find strict employer liability. See 29 CFR § 1604.11(c) (1985). Those considerations, however, do not justify the creation of a special "notice" rule in hostile environment cases.

Further, nothing would be gained by crafting such a rule. In the "pure" hostile environment case, where an employee files an EEOC complaint alleging sexual harassment in the workplace, the employee seeks not money damages but injunctive relief. See Bundy v. Jackson, 205 U.S.App.D.C. 444,

456, n. 12, 641 F.2d 934, 946, n. 12 (1981). Under Title VII, the EEOC must notify an employer of charges made against it within 10 days after receipt of the complaint. 42 U.S.C. § 2000e-5(b). If the charges appear to be based on "reasonable cause," the EEOC must attempt to eliminate the offending practice through "informal methods of conference, conciliation, and persuasion." Ibid. An employer whose internal procedures assertedly would have redressed the discrimination can avoid injunctive relief by employing these procedures after receiving notice of the complaint or during the conciliation period. Cf. Brief for United States and EEOC as Amici Curiae 26. Where a complainant, on the other hand, seeks backpay on the theory that a hostile work environment effected a constructive termination, the existence of an internal complaint procedure may be a factor in determining not the employer's liability but the remedies available against it. Where a complainant without good reason bypassed an internal complaint procedure she knew to be effective, a court may be reluctant to find constructive termination and thus to award reinstatement or backpay.

I therefore reject the Solicitor General's position. I would apply in this case the same rules we apply in all other Title VII cases, and hold that sexual harassment by a supervisor of an employee under his supervision, leading to a discriminatory work environment, should be imputed to the employer for Title VII purposes regardless of whether the employee gave "notice" of the offense.

INDEX

A

Adams, Brock 19, 62, 64
Ad Hoc Sexual Harassment Coalition 179
Air Force Academy, U.S. (Colorado Springs, Colorado) 22
airline stewardesses 57
Alabama 28, 38
Alaska 184
Alcott, Louisa May 56, 64
Alexander v. Yale University (1977) 10, 26, 58
AMA *see* American Management Association
American Association of University Women 21, 179
American Management Association (AMA) 29
American Psychological Association 4
American Society for Training and Development 179
Anderson, Kathleen O'Brien 48, 49
Annis v. County of Westchester (1983) 38
anti-harassment policies 29, 31, 39
anti-harassment training 29, 39

Arizona 184
armed forces 9, 22, 23, 32, 57 *see also specific branch (e.g.,* Navy)
Army Aviation and Troop Command (St. Louis, Missouri) 18, 62
Army Reserve Personnel Center (St. Louis, Missouri) 18, 62
assault 39
Association for Union Democracy Women's Project 179
Association of American Colleges 13
Australia 28
Austria 12

B

Bagley, Sarah 8, 64
Baker & McKenzie (law firm) 20, 21, 63, 68
Barnes v. Costle (1977) 10, 26, 58
Barnes v. Train (1975) 9, 10, 26, 58
battery (harmful or offensive touching) 39
Baylous, Don 51, 52
Biden Jr., Joseph R. 15, 64
birth-control pill 8
blackmail 39

Boston Herald (newspaper) 15, 61, 67
Broderick v. Ruder (1988) 13, 27, 60
Brookner, Janine M. 23, 63, 64
Brown v. City of Guthrie (1980) 11, 27, 40, 59
Bundy v. Jackson (1981) 11, 27, 40, 59
Bush, George
  Civil Rights Act signed by 16, 38, 61
  Tailhook scandal 17, 62
  Thomas nominated to Supreme Court by 15, 65, 66, 68
Business and Professional Women/USA 179
Business & Legal Reports (periodical) 29

C

California 28, 39, 184
Canada 28
Carter, Jimmy 10, 58, 65
Catalyst (research and advisory group) 179
Celia (slave) 7, 56, 65
Center for Research on Women 180

Center for the Prevention of Sexual and Domestic Violence 179–180

Center for Women in Government 180

Center for Women's Policy Studies 180

Center for Working Life 180

Central Intelligence Agency (CIA) 23, 63, 64

Cheney, Richard B. 17, 62, 65

CIA *see* Central Intelligence Agency

Civil Rights Act (1964) 9, 36, 57 *see also* Title VII

Civil Rights Act (1991) 16, 27, 38, 61, 65

Civil Service Reform Act (1978) 10, 11, 36, 58, 65

civil suits 28

class-action suits 33, 49, 50, 61

Clearinghouse on Women's Issues 180

Clinton, Bill 18, 65, 66, 67

Coalition of Labor Union Women 180

colleges and universities 21, 22, 32, 33

Colorado 185

come-ons 6

Commission on the Economic Status of Women 183

compensatory and punitive damages *see* damages

complaint 25–26

Conley, Frances K. 14, 60, 65

Connecticut 185

"conspiracy against rights" 38

Convention on the Elimination of All Forms of Discrimination Against Women (United Nations) 11, 59

Corne v. Bausch & Lomb (1975) 9, 26, 58

Cost Guard SPARS 57

Coughlin, Paula 17, 62, 65

court cases 40–55 *see also* specific case (e.g., *Meritor Savings Bank v. Vinson*); Supreme Court cases

Croaker v. Chicago and Northwestern Railway Company (1875) 8, 56

Cuomo, Mario 18, 65

D

Dalton, John H. 18, 62

damage awards 38, 46, 47

Davies, Carrie 7, 57, 65

Deep Throat (pornographic film) 13

Defense, Department of 9, 14, 58, 60, 62

Delaware 185

Denmark 28

"deprivation of rights under the color of law" 38

diaries 19, 63

discrimination *see* Title VII

District of Columbia *see* Washington, D.C.

Dreyer, Gwen Marie 14, 60

Dunleavy, Richard M. 17, 62

Durenberger, Dave 19, 62, 65

E

education *see* colleges and universities; schools

Education, Department of 9, 28, 37

Education Amendments of 1972 *see* Title IX

EEOC *see* Equal Employment Opportunity Commission

18 U.S.C. 241 (federal law) *see* Section 241

18 U.S.C. 242 (federal law) *see* Section 242

Eleanor Holmes Norton 59

electronic bulletin boards 34

Ellison v. Brady (1991) 15, 27, 55, 61

e-mail 34, 63

emotional distress 39

employer liability 53

employment practice liability 30

England *see* Great Britain

Equal Employment Opportunity Act (1972) 9, 36, 58

Equal Employment Opportunity Commission (EEOC) *see also* "Guidelines on Discrimination Because of Sex"

creation of 58

district, area, and local offices 193–196

enforcement of Title VII 9, 28, 58

response to complaints of harassment 37

statistics on complaints 26, 61

types of harassment 35

"Equal Opportunities
and Equal Treatment
for Men and Women
in Employment" (Inter-
national Labour Organ-
isation) 60
Equal Rights Advocates
180
European Community
12, 13, 14, 60
*Evans v. Sheraton Park
Hotel* (1979) 27
Eveleth Mines (Minne-
sota) *see Jenson v. Ev-
eleth Taconite Co.*
Executive Order 11246
(federal law) 28, 37
exhibitionism 6
extortion 39

F
"factory girls" 7, 8, 56
Factory Girls' Album (periodical) 8, 56
fair employment prac-
tices (FEP) offices 39,
184–193
Farley, Lin 10, 58, 65
Federal Contract Com-
pliance Commission 37
federal employment 36,
37, 59 *see also* Civil
Service Reform Act
Federally Employed
Women 180
Federation of Organiza-
tions for Professional
Women 180
feminism 3, 8, 57
FEP *see* fair employ-
ment practices
Florida 185
Forbes (magazine) 14
Forklift Systems (Nash-
ville, Tennessee) *see*

*Harris v. Forklift Sys-
tems, Inc.*
Fortune 500 companies
14, 29, 60
42 U.S.C. 1983 (federal
law) *see* Section 1983
Fourteenth Amendment
38
France 28
Frankfort, Bill 51
Franklin, Christine *see
Franklin v. Gwinnett
County Public Schools*
*Franklin v. Gwinnett
County Public Schools*
(1992) 18, 45–48, 61,
68, 204–216
Fund for the Feminist
Majority 180–181

G
GAO *see* General Ac-
counting Office
*Garber v. Saxon Business
Products Inc.* (1979) 27
Garrett III, H. Lawrence
17, 62, 65, 66
gender roles 4
General Accounting Of-
fice (GAO) 22, 63
Georgia 28, 38, 186 *see
also Franklin v. Gwin-
nett County Public Schools*
Great Britain 13, 28
Greenstein, Martin 20,
21, 68
"Guidelines on Discrimi-
nation Because of Sex"
(EEOC) 11, 27, 36, 40,
59, 60, 199–200
Gutek, Barbara 13
Gwinnett County, Geor-
gia *see Franklin v.
Gwinnett County Public
Schools*

H
Hardy, Charles 19, 54
Harris, Teresa *see Harris
v. Forklift Systems, Inc.*
*Harris v. Forklift Systems,
Inc.* (1993) 19, 27,
54–55, 63, 66, 67,
217–222
Harvard Business Review
12
Harvard Law Review 23
Harvard University
(Cambridge, Massachu-
setts) 13
Hawaii 186
*Heelan v. Johns-Manville
Corp.* 27
Henson v. City of Dundee
(1982) 12, 27, 40, 44,
49, 59
Hentz, Cheltzie 21
Hill, Andrew 45–46, 66
Hill, Anita F. *see* Hill-
Thomas hearings
Hill-Thomas hearings
(1991) 15, 16, 20, 61,
64, 66, 68
Hilton Hotel (Las
Vegas) 17
"Hostile Hallways" poll
21
hostile work environ-
ment harassment
cases involving
*Brown v. City of
Guthrie* 59
Bundy v. Jackson 59
*Harris v. Forklift Sys-
tems, Inc.* 55, 66
*Henson v. City of Dun-
dee* 59
*Jenson v. Eveleth Taco-
nite Co.* 66
Katz v. Dole 59
*Lehmann v. Toys R'
Us, Inc.* 53, 54

Index

*Meritor Savings Bank
v. Vinson* 60
*Rabidue v. Osceola Re-
fining Company* 60
*Robinson v. Jacksonville
Shipyards* 61
definition of 35, 36,
40, 41
House Armed Services
Committee 22
"housing harassment" 23
"How I Went Out to
Service" (Louisa May
Alcott story) 7, 56, 64
*Huebschen v. Department
of Health and Social Serv-
ices* 12
Human Goals Charter
(Department of De-
fense) 9, 58

I

Idaho 186
Illinois 11, 59, 186
Indiana 186
Industrial Revolution 7,
56
Inouye, Daniel K. 19, 62,
66
Institute for Women and
Work 181
intentional harm 39
International Labour Or-
ganisation 13, 60
Internet 34
Iowa 186
Ireland 28

J

Jackson, Lewis,
Schnitzler & Krupman
(law firm) 29
Japan 28
Jenson, Lois 66 *see Jen-
son v. Eveleth Taconite Co.*

*Jenson v. Eveleth Taconite
Co.* (1993) 16, 48–50,
61, 66, 223–232
Johnson, Lyndon B. 9,
36, 57, 66
Jonas, Eric 51, 52
Jones, Paula Corbin 65,
66, 67
jury trials 38

K

Kansas 186
Katz v. Dole (1983) 12,
27, 59
Kentucky 186–187
Klein, Freada 21
Kosmach, Patricia 48, 49
*Kyriazi v. Western Electric
Co.* (1979) 27

L

Labor, Department of
13, 57
Labor Statistics, Bureau
of 57
laws 35–55
Executive Order
11246 28, 37
Section 241 (18 U.S.C.
241) 38, 203
Section 242 (18 U.S.C.
242) 38, 203
Section 1983 (42
U.S.C. 1983) 12, 37,
59, 68, 202
tort law 28, 39
Lehmann, Theresa *see
Lehmann v. Toys R' Us,
Inc.* (1993)
*Lehmann v. Toys R' Us,
Inc.* (1993) 18–19, 27,
50–54, 63, 233–259
Lou Harris and Associ-
ates 21
Louisiana 28, 38

M

MacKinnon, Catherine
A. 11, 13, 41, 59, 67
Maine 187
Marine Corps 62
Marshall, Thurgood 14,
44, 67
Maryland 187
Massachusetts 187
Mead, Margaret 10, 58,
67
*Meek v. Michigan Bell
Telephone* (1992) 18
*Meritor Savings Bank v.
Vinson* (1986) 13–14,
27, 41–45, 55, 60,
260–273
Merit Systems Protection
Board 11, 13, 59
Michigan 187
Michigan, University of
34, 63
military *see* armed forces
military academies 22, 63
Military Academy, U.S.
(West Point, New
York) 22
Miller v. Bank of America
(1975) 9, 10, 26, 58, 59
Minnesota 28, 39, 188
Mississippi 28, 38
Missouri 188
Montana 188
Moore, Howard 51, 52

N

*Nairobi Forward-Looking
Strategies for the Ad-
vancement of Women*
(United Nations) 13, 60
Nashua Gazette (New
Hampshire newspaper)
8, 56
National Advisory Coun-
cil on Women's Educa-
tional Programs 3

National Affairs, Bureau of 12, 59

National Association for Women in Education 181

National Association of Commissions for Women 183

National Association of Working Women 24

National Council for Research on Women 181

National Employment Law Project 181

National Employment Lawyers Association 181

National Federation of Business and Professional Women's Clubs 57, 181

National Law Journal 14

National Lawyers Guild Anti-Sexism Committee 181

National Women's Law Center 181

National Women's Political Caucus 181

Naval Academy, U.S. (Annapolis, Maryland) 14, 60

Naval Investigative Service (NIS) 16, 62

Navy, U.S. 14, 16, 32, 60 *see also* Tailhook scandal

Navy WAVES 57

Nebraska 188

Netherlands 12

Nevada 188

New England Patriots (football team) 8, 15, 61, 67

New Hampshire 188

New Jersey 18–19, 188–189 *see also Lehmann v. Toys R' Us, Inc.* (1993)

New Mexico 189

New Republic (magazine) 34

New York State 18, 65, 189

New York Times (newspaper) 16

New Zealand 28

9 to 5, the National Association of Working Women 181–182

Nineteenth Amendment 57

NIS *see* Naval Investigative Service

Nixon, Richard M. 9, 37, 58, 67

"no-fault settlement" 37

North Carolina 28, 38, 189–190

North Dakota 28, 38, 190

North Gwinnett High School (Gwinnett County, Georgia) *see Franklin v. Gwinnett County Public Schools*

Northwestern University/Medill School of Journalism 24

Norton, Eleanor Holmes 11, 40, 67

Norway 13

NOW Legal Defense and Education Fund 182

O

Occupational Safety and Health Administration (OSHA) 28, 38

O'Connor, Sandra Day 20, 55, 67

Ohio 190

O'Keefe, Sean C. 17, 18, 62, 67

Oklahoma 190

Olson, Lisa 15, 61, 67

ombudsmen 31

on-line services 34

oppression 3

Oregon 190

organizations and agencies 179–196

OSHA *see* Occupational Safety and Health Administration

P

Packwood, Bob 19, 62, 63, 67, 68

pain and suffering 38

Pennsylvania 190–191

polls and surveys

Capitol Hill employees 20

colleges and universities 13, 21, 22

corporate executives 12, 30

Department of Defense employees 14, 60

federal employees 11

foreign countries 13

Fortune 500 companies 14

Hill-Thomas hearings 16

Illinois state employees 11

lawyers 14

military academies 22

Navy 14, 60

New York City-area executives 29

The New York Times
  readers 16
  professional women 14
  Redbook readers 10, 11,
    58, 59
  schoolgirls 21
  United Nations em-
    ployees 10
  victims' characteristics
    24
  Working Woman read-
    ers 20
  working women 13
pornography 5, 48
power relations 2, 3, 24
productivity loss 30
Project of the Center for
  the Study of Communi-
  cation 182
"Proposal: We Need Ta-
  boos on Sex at Work"
  (Margaret Mead article)
  10, 58, 67
public schools *see* schools
Puerto Rico 191
put-downs 5

Q

quid pro quo harassment
  35, 36, 40–41, 58, 59

R

*Rabidue v. Osceola Refining
  Company* (1986) 13, 55,
  60
Radtke v. Everett (1991)
  27, 51
rape 6, 39
Reagan, Ronald 37, 68
reasonable woman stand-
  ard
  accepted as new stand-
    ard 33, 35
  cases involving
    Ellison v. Brady 27,
      50–51, 61

*Jenson v. Eveleth Taco-
  nite Co.* 50
*Lehmann v. Toys R'
  Us, Inc.* 19, 27, 51,
  53, 63, 67
  Radtke v. Everett 27,
    51
Redbook (magazine) 10,
  11, 58, 59, 67
Rehnquist, William 44,
  68
retail sales 8, 56
Rhode Island 191
"right to sue" letter 37
*Robinson v. Jacksonville
  Shipyards* (1991) 15, 27,
  61

S

Scalia, Antonin 47
schools 21, 25, 28, 32,
  33, 39 *see also Franklin
  v. Gwinnett County Pub-
  lic Schools*
Schroeder, Patricia 23,
  63, 68
Section 241 (18 U.S.C.
  241) (federal law) 38,
  203
Section 242 (18 U.S.C.
  242) (federal law) 38,
  203
Section 1983 (42 U.S.C.
  1983) (federal law) 12,
  37, 59, 68, 202
Senate Ethics Committee
  19, 62, 63
Senate Judiciary Commit-
  tee 15–16, 61, 64, 66, 68
Seventeen (magazine) 21
sex discrimination, harassment as a form of 26–27
sexual assault 6
*Sexual Harassment of
  Working Women: A Case
  of Discrimination* (Cath-

erine A. MacKinnon)
  11, 41, 59, 67
sexuality, myths about 3
sexual revolution 8, 57
*Sexual Shakedown: The
  Sexual Harassment of
  Women at Work* (Lin
  Farley) 10, 58, 65
Shellhammer v. Lewallen
  (1983) 12, 59
slavery 7
Snyder Jr., John W. 17
Society for Human Re-
  source Management
  182
South Carolina 191
South Dakota 191
Spain 12, 28
Stanford University (Palo
  Alto, California) 14, 60,
  65
states 12, 38–39, 59,
  184–193
"street harassment" 23
stress 38
"strictly liable" 29
Stroh Brewery (Minne-
  sota) 18, 61
students *see* colleges and
  universities; schools
Supreme Court cases
  *Franklin v. Gwinnett
    County Public Schools*
    18, 45–48, 61, 68,
    204–216
  *Harris v. Forklift Sys-
    tems, Inc.* 19, 27,
    54–55, 63, 66, 67,
    217–222
  *Meritor Savings Bank v.
    Vinson* 13–14, 27,
    41–45, 55, 60,
    260–273
surveys *see* polls and surveys
Sweden 13, 28

Switzerland 28

T

Tailhook scandal (1991) 17–18, 62, 65, 66, 67, 68
Taylor, Sidney 41, 42, 43
Tennessee 28, 38, 191
Texas 28, 38, 191
textile mills 8, 56
Thomas, Clarence *see* Hill-Thomas hearings
Title IX (Education Amendments of 1972) 9, 10, 28, 35, 37, 58, 201
Title VII (Civil Rights Act, 1964) 9, 26–28, 35, 36, 40, 57, 198
Tomkins v. Public Service Electric & Gas Co. (1977) 9, 26, 58
tort law 28, 39
Toscano v. Nimmo (1983) 12, 59
Toys R' Us, Inc. *see Lehmann v. Toys R' Us, Inc.* (1993)
Tradeswomen, Inc. 182
Trans World Airlines (TWA) 57
Treasury Magazine 30
TWA *see* Trans World Airlines
typesetters 56

U

unions 32
United Nations 10, 11, 13, 59, 60
United States Student Association 182
Utah 191–192

V

Vermont 192

Veteran Affairs, Department of 32
victims 24–25
Vinson, Mechelle *see Meritor Savings Bank v. Vinson*
Vinson v. Taylor (1980) 14
Virginia 28, 39, 192
Virgin Islands 192
Voice of Industry (periodical) 8, 56, 64

W

Wall Street Journal 16
Washington, D.C. 39, 185
Washington Post (newspaper) 20
Washington State 192
Weeks, Rena 20, 21, 63, 68
West Point *see* Military Academy, U.S.
West Virginia 192
whistle-blowers 33–34
White, Byron 47, 68
White House Office of Personnel 10, 59
Wider Opportunities for Women (organization) 182
Williams, Diane 10
Williams v. Saxbe (1976) 10, 26, 40, 58
Wisconsin 192–193
Wisconsin Law Review 23
Women Employed Institute 182
Women for Racial and Economic Equality 182
Women Marines 57
Women Organized Against Sexual Harassment 183

Women's Action for Good Employment Standards 182
Women's Alliance for Job Equity 182–183
Women's Army Air Corps 57
Women's Army Corps 57
Women's Bureau (Department of Labor) 183
Women's Law Project 183
Women's Legal Defense Fund 183
women's movement 9
Women's Rights Litigation Clinic 183
Women Students' Sexual Harassment Caucus 183
Workers' Compensation Act 28, 38
Working Smart (newsletter) 14
Working Woman 14, 20, 30, 60
Work (Louisa May Alcott) 7, 56, 64
workplace practices and policies 29–33
World War I 57
World War II 57
W.R.A.T.H. (Women Refusing to Accept Tenant Harassment) 183
Wyoming 193

Y

Yale University (New Haven, Connecticut) *see Alexander v. Yale University*